Sicilian folklore:
a painted carretto and its proud owner

BAEDEKER'S BEST TIPS

Of all the Baedeker tips in this book, the most interesting ones are listed here! Experience and enjoy Sicily from its best side.

Capers
Their flowers are as beautiful as orchids; the best ones can be found on the Lipari Islands.

Via del Sale
Salt has been mined between Trapani and Marsala for centuries

The Greeks brought olive
trees to Sicily
► page 16

BACKGROUND

Price Categories

Hotels
Luxury: from 190 €
Mid-range: 80 – 190 €
Budget: up to 80 €
For a double room without
breakfast

Restaurants
Expensive: over 35 €
Moderate: 20 – 35 €
Budget: under 20 €
For a 3-course meal without
drinks

PRACTICALITIES

Discover Sicily on foot: six
particularly scenic hikes
► page 134

TOURS

SIGHTS FROM
A to Z

Climb down 242 steps to Ragusa Ibla, Ragusa's old town
► **page 371**

The Temple of Hera Lakinia can be found at the upper end of the row of temples in Agrigento
► **page 157**

Background

INTERESTING FACTS ABOUT SICILY, THE ISLAND
AND ITS PEOPLE, ITS POLITICS,
ECONOMY AND HISTORY, BUT
ALSO ABOUT EVERYDAY LIFE, SUCH
AS IN THE FISHING TOWN OF CEFALÙ
AND ABOUT ARTS AND CULTURE

BETWEEN TWO CONTINENTS

»Italy without Sicily makes no impact on the soul: it is only here that you find the key to it all,« enthused Goethe on 13 April 1787 in »Italian Journey« about the largest of the Mediterranean islands. It is located on the border between Europe and Africa, separated from the tip of Italy's boot only by a 3km/2mi strait.

According to an ancient legend, the island rests on three pillars, anchored deep in the sea, which reflect its roots, namely its Greek, Roman-European and Arab influences. A trip to Sicily that is intended to include more than just an exploration of city life can be a journey from one highlight to the next. Whether landscape or the remains of history and culture: Sicily is rich in all of these things. The hills and valleys in the island's interior, where almost every inch is put to agricultural use in a fertile garden of fruit and vegetable cultivation, stand in contrast to Mount Etna, the »mountain of mountains«, as the Sicilians call it, which has spewed steam and red-hot lava since time immemorial, and to the coastal landscape and the many offshore islands. The author **Giuseppe Tomasi di Lampedusa** describes »his« Sicily in his novel *The Leopard*: »Sicily, the atmosphere, the climate, the landscape of Sicily. Those are the forces which have formed our minds together with and perhaps more than foreign domination and all-assorted rapes; this landscape which knows no mean between sensuous slackness and hellish drought; which is never petty, never ordinary, never relaxed, as a country made for rational beings to live in should be; this country of ours in which the inferno around Randazzo is a few miles from the loveliness of Taormina Bay…«

Sun, sea, scenery
The coast in Zingaro Nature Park on the Gulf of Castellammare

Monuments of the Past

In addition to the island's natural beauty spots, many cultural monuments of the Sicels, Greeks, Romans, Arabs, Normans and Spaniards remain extant. Giuseppe Tomasi di Lampedusa wrote of: »… these monuments … of the past, magnificent yet incomprehensible because not built by us and yet standing around like lovely mute

← Cefalù

On Vulcano
*A bath in the lukewarm sulphurous mud
is a special pleasure and relaxation*

Captivated by Mount Etna
Hiking on Europe's largest and most active volcano

In the Monti Erei
*The Greeks settled in Morgantina, an ancient Sicel town,
in the 6th century BC*

La Zisa in Palermo
*Mosaics in the former summer residence of
the Norman kings*

Craftsmanship
*The artistically painted carretti have a long-standing
tradition; their miniature versions are popular souvenirs*

Castel di Tusa
*Concrete sculpture by Pietro Consagra
in the Fiumara d'Arte open-air museum*

ghosts.« These monuments include the Greek temples – in Magna Graecia (= Great Greece), as the Romans called southern Italy, there are more well-preserved temples than Greece itself – in Agrigento, Segesta, Selinunte and Syracuse, the Greek and Roman theatres in Catania, Segesta and Syracuse, the theatre of Taormina in its unparalleled location, and finally the mosaic floors in Villa Casale near Piazza Armerina. Significant cultural heritage dates back to the 11th and 12th centuries: Norman castles in Adrano, Aci Castello, Caronía and Paternò; Norman churches and monasteries in Catania, Cefalù, Messina, Monreale and Palermo; and royal architecture in Palermo. Great changes also took place during the 17th and 18th centuries, when, after the major earthquake in the southeast of the island, entire cities were rebuilt in the Baroque style. Good examples are Ávola, Grammichele, Noto and Pachino.

Stark Contrasts

Sicily is no paradise. A few »scars« cannot be overlooked: the ruthlessly logged hills and mountains, the large amount of concrete construction covering entire areas and coastlines, and the paper and plastic rubbish everywhere. Another problem is the stark social disparity: slums are often cheek by jowl with magnificent avenues. The external signs are façades in danger of collapse, and crime. Regarding this latter issue there is no need to panic, but it is best to be aware. Sicily's cities are all beautiful and ugly at the same time, as well as full of a will to live with artistic and cultural treasures from every

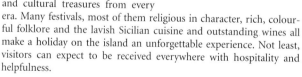

era. Many festivals, most of them religious in character, rich, colourful folklore and the lavish Sicilian cuisine and outstanding wines all make a holiday on the island an unforgettable experience. Not least, visitors can expect to be received everywhere with hospitality and helpfulness.

Temple of Castor and Pollux
The fragment is a landmark of Agrigento

Facts

Sicily is the largest island in the Mediterranean, boasting long beaches and in the interior unspoilt hills and mountains, among them Europe's largest volcano, Mount Etna. It is a mecca for sun worshippers, water lovers and nature enthusiasts. Unique evidence of the past is an inexhaustible source of pleasure for the artistically and culturally inclined.

Nature and Environment

Sicily is all that remains of a land bridge that once connected Europe with Africa. The island is situated exactly in the middle of the Mediterranean. At its closest point, Sicily is only separated from the Italian mainland by the 3.2km/2mi Strait of Messina. The island's distance from North Africa is 140km/85mi. Surrounded by three seas, the Tyrrhenian Sea, the Ionian Sea and the Libyan Sea, Sicily forms the border between the western and eastern Mediterranean basin, a crucial location for the island's history. The landscape is mainly characterized by hills and mountains (61 % hills – in Italy as a whole 42 %; 25 % mountains – Italy 35 %; 14 % plains – Italy 23 %). However, the mountain range that runs north-south on the Italian mainland turns in an east-west direction on the island, and runs along Sicily's northern coast.

»Stepping stone in the sea«

? DID YOU KNOW …?

■ According to ancient sources, the island used to be called Trinacria (the three promontories). The corresponding symbol consists of a woman's head, framed by snakes and small wings, in the middle of three bent legs running around the head (fig. p. 1). Trinacria was later named Sikania after the Sicani and finally Sikelía/Sicilia after the Sicels.

The Peloritani mountain range is, geologically speaking, the continuation of the Calabrian Aspromonte. It runs southwest from Messina and, up to the Taormina region, consists of the same gneiss and mica rocks that can be found on the mainland. The surface is very weathered and pervaded by gushing mountain streams (fiumare), particularly after rainfall. The highest peak, the Montagna Grande, has an altitude of 1374m/4508ft.

Peloritani

The sandstone and clay of the Monti Nébrodi, also known as Caroníe , run parallel to the north coast. These mountains largely consist of flysch (soft clay and sandstones), which results in a gently curving, rounded appearance. With altitudes ranging from 1000m/3300ft to almost 2000m/6100ft (Monte Soro, 1847m/6060ft), they are the island's backbone, the »Sicilian Apennines«.

Nébrodi

The mountains of the Madoníe roughly extend between the two towns of Gangi and Mistretta (easternmost point) to the 1326m/4350ft Monte San Calògero near Termini Imerese (westernmost point). The highest mountain is Pizzo Carbonara in the hinterland of Cefalù (at 1979m/6493ft Sicily's second-highest peak after Mount Etna). A further line of low mountain ranges (hardly higher than 1000m/3300ft) crosses the island diagonally and can be divided into

Madonie

← *Near Selinunte: an agricultural crop with archaic roots.*
The Greeks brought not just grapes, but also olives to Sicily.

Capo Graziano on the Lipari Island of Filicudi

the **Erean Mountains** (island interior and southwest) and the **Iblean Mountains** (island interior and southeast to Ragusa). These two mountain ranges run towards each other until they finally merge with the mountains that make up the western part of the island. These latter mountains do not form a chain, but stand in individual groups, separated by long, wide valleys.

The **Monti Sicani** branch off to the south of Palermo and run all the way to the south coast.

Island interior The island's interior is characterized by hills that reach an altitude of 1000m/3300ft and are transected by many valleys. These hills drop down in steps towards the south coast. The larger section consists primarily of upper tertiary clays and marlstones, from which every now and then rugged rocks – made of gypsum (Monte Paolino near Sutera), marly calcareous sandstone and conglomerate (local elevations of Enna and Calascibetta) – rise up like fortifications. For the rest, this area is a largely tree-less, and was known in Antiquity as »Italy's bread basket«.

Eastern Sicily Sicily's eastern side is highly volcanic. This zone starts with the Aeolian Islands to the north, then run southwards via Mount Etna to the Hyblaean Mountains, which continue on Malta. **Mount Etna**, Sicily's landmark, which the locals still call by its half-Italian, half-Arabic name »Mongibello« (»mons« and »gibel« both mean »mountain«), covers an area of approximately 1400 sq km/540 sq mi. Depending on the quantity of magma deposits, it is, at around 3350m/10,990ft, Italy's highest peak outside the Alps and Europe's highest volcano. In addition to Mount Etna, the Aeolian Islands, with the ever-active **Stròmboli** as well as the islands of Ùstica and Pantellerìa to the north and south of the main island, are also of volcanic origin.

Corresponding to this structure, the north coast drops steeply to the sea in many places. This is also true of the northern section of the east coast, while the remaining coastline tends to be quite flat. **Coasts**

A total of 37 smaller islands belong to Sicily. Around 15 years ago this number rose to 38 for a short while, when the small Isola Ferdinandea poked its head out of the sea between Malta and Pantellerìa. However, it disappeared again before keen European powers were able to claim it as their own. **Islands**
All of the inhabitable islands are popular holiday destinations: the Aeolian Islands or Lipari Islands (Lìpari, Salina, Filicudi, Alicudi, Panarea, Vulcano and Stròmboli), which, for administrative purposes, are part of the province of Messina; the island of Ùstica, situated around 60km/35mi off the coast of Palermo, the three islands of Favignana, Lévanzo and Maréttimo to the west of Tràpani, the island of Pantellerìa, which is closer to Africa than Sicily (these last four are part of Tràpani province), and the Pelagie Islands of Lampedusa, Linosa and Lampione (province of Agrigento), which are the furthest away from Sicily.

Sicily is naturally well-watered. Streams and rivulets have their sources in the mountain regions. Snow-covered Mount Etna is a veritable reservoir. However, as a result of centuries of logging, the ground has become dry and not very permeable. As a result water is not retained in the soil and quickly flows into the streams, which then burst their banks and flood the land. During the summer months, however, the fields wither from a lack of water. The problem lies in trying to hold on to the water obtained from the autumn and winter rains and snows in order to use it during the dry periods. **Rivers**
Among the island's rivers, the **Salso** is the longest, measuring 144km/89mi; it is dammed northeast of Enna, thereby forming Lago di Pozzillo. Another dammed river is the Belice in western Sicily; it is used to generate electricity. One river that is important to agriculture is the **Simeto** with its tributaries the Dittaino and the Gornalunga. Added to these natural watercourses and modern reservoirs, there are irrigation facilities, some of which date back to the time of the Saracens; it is to them that the Bay of Palermo, the Conca d'Oro, owes its fertility. Attempts are being made to reforest certain areas to lessen the problem in the long-term.

In the rural hinterland of Agrigento near Sant'Angelo Muxaro

Flora and Fauna

Flora   Sicily was originally covered largely by forest, which has been almost completely cut down to provide timber for ships and to create space for agriculture. The area covered in maquis has also been greatly reduced, but this kind of scrubland still flourishes in several arid regions along the western and southern coasts. Very recently attempts have been made to plant fast-growing species (eucalyptus) in order to counteract the effects of logging and its impact on the island's climate and water situation. The area covered by the original flora is now largely devoted to crops imported by the various occupiers: grape vines and olive trees were brought by the Greeks, lemons, cotton and sugar-cane by the Arabs, oranges, prickly pears and tobacco by the Spanish. Other noteworthy crops are banana trees (at the foot of Mount Etna and near Scicli and Ribera on the south coast), figs and almonds.

The richest vegetation and the highest-yielding agricultural regions are located in the irrigated areas in the north and east of the island, such as the Piana di Catania, the plain created by the sediment of the Simeto River, which is overlooked by Mount Etna's huge cone. Fruit and vegetables grow extremely well here: apricots and peaches, apples and chestnuts, almonds and medlars, as well as aubergines, artichokes, melons, chilli peppers, tomatoes and especially citrus fruits (blood oranges). It is a very different situation in the arid regions of the island's interior. Although olive trees and carob trees grow here, the fields are bare, particularly in the karstified limestone regions. Durum wheat is grown extensively.

Fauna

Sicily cannot boast great biodiversity. Livestock has long since pushed out most wildlife, even though there are still a few wild cats, rabbits and foxes left. Donkeys and horses have become almost superfluous with mechanization. Sicily is an important stopover and overwintering area for many birds. It is nice to see that their habitats are being put under increasingly strict protection. The situation at sea is significantly better. Despite millennia of fishing, **fish stocks are still plentiful**, particularly in the Strait of Messina. Plants and land animals have an area of refuge in Parco dell'Etna. Mediterranean plants and animal species, long extinct in the wild, have an area of 60,000 ha/150,000 acres where they can flourish (▶Practicalities, natural parks and nature reserves).

? DID YOU KNOW ...?

- When it comes to food, the Sicilians differ from mainland Italians. They eat more pasta, bread and fish and less meat per head, and although a fifth of Italian wine comes from Sicily, they themselves only drink around half as much as the Italian average.

Conservation

Sicily and environmental protection have a somewhat troublesome relationship. The first to damage the environment were the Phoenicians, the Greeks and the Romans, who logged parts of the mountainous island interior. Large-scale clear-cutting only began in the second half of the 19th century, as a result of the railway expansion and sulphur production. The result, bare hills and mountains, can still be seen and felt today. The biggest environmental damage of the post-war era was generally the **illegal construction** of tens of thousands of houses in protected coastal areas and on mountainsides by the sea. Further problems, such as high emissions, are caused by the out-dated industrial conglomerates in Gela and Augusta, as well as the **pollution of the sea** in places: as in other Mediterranean states, most Sicilian coastal towns do not have working sewage-treatment plants. There is good news as well, however. The first nature reserve was set up in 1980 (Lo Zingaro), not as a state initiative, but as a result of a widespread protest by the people against the construction of a road through an intact section of coastline. One year later a regional law ensuring the better protection of Mediterranean plants and animals was passed. In 1987 the Parco dell'Etna, the Parco delle Madoníe and the Parco dei Nébrodi were set up. Today around 10 % of Sicily's territory is protected. Organic farming has also found its followers. There are now many organic farmers, most of whom are also involved in agritourism, offering rural getaways.

Population · Politics · Economy

Population

Rural depopulation Sicily has around 5.1 million inhabitants, of whom 30 % live in the larger towns and cities. Palermo alone has a population of 660,000. There is a clear tendency to move from rural regions to urban ones. Rome, Milan and New York are home to more people of Sicilian origin than the whole of Palermo.

Melting pot ► Sicily's population contains elements from very different historical eras: from the original island inhabitants, the Sicani, the Elymians and the Sicels, from the Phoenicians and Greeks since the 1st millennium BC, the Romans since the 3rd century BC, and later the Byzantines, the Arabs (since 827), the Normans (from 1061), the Hohenstaufen from Germany (from 1194) and finally the Spanish. To this day the Albanians remain a small group with their own language, at least for talking among themselves. Their ancestors left their old home because of the Turkish threat in 1488 and settled south of Palermo in Piana degli Albanesi and Santa Cristina Gela.

»Santa Famiglia« Family ties and family traditions are strong. The concept of honour plays a central role. The Sicilian character, which does not fit the cliché of the fiery southerner, was significantly influenced by two and a half thousand years of foreign rule, which, along with the battle against the forces of nature (particularly around Mount Etna), produced a mix of fatalism and toughness. Sicilian society is marked by paralysis due to entrenched structures, with a big gap between the few major landowners and the large number of peasants who owned only a little land, or even, in the case of the so-called braccianti, none at all. These day-labourers usually lived in large villages with an urban feel far away from the fields, and only found seasonal employment in agriculture. For the rest of the time they lived from a kind of unemployment support. Land reform, industrialization (albeit only partially successful), emigration and remigration, growing tourism and women's increasing participation in public life have, however, noticeably opened up better prospects for the island.

> ## ! *Baedeker* TIP
>
> **Best time to go**
> »La primavera siciliana«, Sicily's spring, is famous; the island is awash with flowers (further information about when to go p. 116).

Festivals One bright aspect in the lives of the Sicilians are their festivals, mostly of a religious nature, with processions in honour of local patron saint or for the main church celebrations, such as Holy Week in Tràpani, Marsala and particularly in Enna. Ancient piety has a very lively outlet here.

Facts and Figures Sicily

©*Baedeker*

©*Baedeker*

Palermo

Sicily

▶ Palermo is Sicily's largest city with 660,000 inhabitants

Location
- ▶ 37–38 degrees north 13–15 degrees east
- ▶ 3.2km/2mi from the Italian mainland; 140km/85mi from the African mainland

Area
- ▶ 25,426 sq km/9817 sq mi (Italy: 301,323 sq km/116,341 sq mi)
- ▶ More than 1500 km / 930 mi of coastline (including Sicily's smaller islands)
- ▶ Largest island in the Mediterranean; east-west: 250 km/155 mi, north-south: 50 km/30 mi in the west, 180 km/110 mi in the east
- ▶ Italy's largest region

Topography
- ▶ 14% plains, 61% hilly, 25% mountainous
- ▶ Highest mountain: Mount Etna (approx. 3350 m/10,990 ft)
- ▶ Longest river: Salso (144 km/89 mi)

Population
- ▶ 5.1 million inhabitants
- ▶ 198 people per sq km/513 per sq mi

Administration
- ▶ 9 provinces with capitals of the same name: Agrigento, Caltanissetta, Catania, Enna, Messina, Palermo, Ragusa, Siracusa and Trapani
- ▶ Autonomous region with regional parliament and president
- ▶ Capital: Palermo

Wirtschaft
- ▶ Agriculture: wine, wheat, maize, olives, citrus fruits
- ▶ Tourism
- ▶ Fishing
- ▶ Oil and gas
- ▶ Unemployment: 16% (Italy: 10%)

Transport
- ▶ Ferries to the mainland; a bridge across the Strait of Messina is planned
- ▶ International airports in Palermo and Catania

Tourism
- ▶ In 2009 approx. 4.1 million visitors came to the island, 1.5 million of them from outside Italy
- ▶ Average length of stay: 3.5 days
- ▶ More than 900 hotels

Language Italian is the direct continuation of Latin. From the middle of the 3rd century BC Roman legionaries and farmers brought a kind of Latin to the island. This vulgar Latin could not be eradicated by subsequent conquerors. It lived and developed under the official Greek, Latin, Arabic and Spanish languages. In this Sicilian dialect the first Italian literature was produced in the 13th century at the Hohenstaufen court. In the development of the Italian language, the Tuscan dialect ultimately managed to assert itself over Venetian and Sicilian.

The **Sicilian dialect**, enriched with many words borrowed from Greek, Arabic and Spanish, is spoken particularly in rural areas these days. As a rule of thumb, »u« stands for the Italian »il« (the, article); and everything that ends in »o« in Italian tends to also end in »u«. The sentence structure and intonation differ in Sicilian, and certain consonants have changed: »beddu« stands for »bello« (beautiful), »vasa« for »bacio« (kiss).

Sicilian is rich in songs and proverbs. Folklore researchers have collected more than 5000 well-known folk songs and several thousand sayings. Sicilian is being given new literary outlets in the successful crime novels of Andrea Camilleri (▶Famous People).

Mafia Exploiting fear for money happens all around the world, and the Sicilian Mafia is just one possible form of organized crime (▶Baedeker Special p. 26). There are various theories about how it developed. They all have the idea in common that during Sicily's long, dependent history an ambiguous intermediate class formed between the ruler and the upper class, and between the upper class and the underclass, which fed off mutual distrust. This intermediate class organized itself in a secret alliance and called itself the **»L'Onorata Società«**, the »Honourable Society«; instead of attacking the central power that lay far away from the island, it started interfering in confrontations between the rulers and the ruled. Its ability to survive is based not least on the fact that admiration for it is often even greater than the disgust that is felt. It was not just Leonardo Sciascia (▶Famous People) who, in his literary works, addressed the Mafia and its involvements in detail.

Politics

Administrative structure Sicily has possessed a »statuto speciale« since 1946; like Sardinia, the Val d'Aosta, South Tyrol (Bolzano – Alto Adige) and Friuli it is an autonomous region, divided into nine provinces. This partial autonomy, guaranteed by the constitution, means Sicily has its own

The nets also need looking after: a fisherman at work

parliament, its own president and a certain amount of independence with regard to conservation, taxes and the like.

Economy

Of the approximately 5.1 million inhabitants, a little over 1.2 million are registered as being in regular employment. Of those officially employed, around two-thirds work in the service and tourism sector, and the other third (in approximately equal parts) in agriculture (including fishing), construction and industry.

Employment situation

The official unemployment rate fluctuates around 16 % (Italy: 10 %). The estimated actual number is much higher: various governments have tried to improve the disastrous employment situation in recent decades by making publicly owned companies invest in Sicily. These attempts, influenced by cronyism from the start, were unsuccessful.

Unemployment

A memorable day in the fight against the Mafia: Giovanni Brusca, one of the most wanted Mafia bosses, is caught by the police

COSA NOSTRA ETC

The Mafia is the most widespread criminal organization in the world. Extorting protection money, abductions, trading in drugs and arms, and dirty deals with rubbish are just a selection of the activities that come to mind when thinking about the Mafia. And murder of course.

»Lupara bianca« is the term applied when a person is abducted and vanishes without trace, being encased in concrete, burned, buried, sunk in the sea or dissolved in a vat of acid. In the past the Mafia's main modus operandi for murders was to shoot its victims with a sawn-shotgun and then encase the dead bodies in the concrete of new construction projects. Since lime was also used for this, this ritual was called »lupara bianca«, »white shotgun«. However, the Mafia also did not shy away from murdering in front of witnesses. Everyone has seen pictures in the media of victims pierced by bullets or torn apart by bombs.

Creation

The term »Mafia« appeared for the first time in 1862 in the play *I Mafiusi di la Vicaria di Palermo*, which was about the ringleaders of the inmates of Vicaria prison in Palermo. In 1865 the Mafia was mentioned as a »criminal gang« in a report to the interior ministry in Rome. The report stated that this gang forced destitute Sicilian farmers to pay interest on their leases to the feudal landowners. According to experts, the Mafia formed in rural Sicily in the 19th century. The »boss« probably hearkens back to the land tenant who had received far-reaching rights from the nobility that had moved to the cities. As the mediator between the »government« and the governed, these leaseholders over time became the true lords. On the one hand they forced farmers to pay interest on their leases, while on the other hand they claimed to protect those same farmers against feudal mismanagement and land theft. In order to obtain this protection, the farmers had to acquiesce to a code of silence, an **»omerta«**. This code of silence is still the reason why courageous anti-Mafia investigators do not get anywhere with their work today: the people say nothing in order to stay part of the »onorata societa«, the »honourable society« and to avoid revenge. The new masters in the countryside did not extend their power into the towns until the 20th century. The Mafia has a code of

honour that has been mythologized in countless films: they talk about oaths of blood made over an image of the Virgin Mary and other secret rituals. **Fascism** was the first force that seriously tried to tackle the Mafia. But towards the end of the Second World War organized crime managed a comeback – with the help of the Americans, of all people.

The Mafia and the United States

In order to prepare the arrival of the Allies in Sicily, the Americans co-operated with the Cosa Nostra, the Sicilian Mafia. The middleman was the Mafia boss Lucky Luciano, who was incarcerated in the United States. The deal was successful. As a result Luciano and other »helpful« Mafiosi were not just released from prison, but at the behest of the United States were even given important positions in Sicily's post-war politics and business. This »marriage of convenience« was also popular with the Democrazia Cristiana party that held power in Italy after the Second World War. For decades the region, and Italy generally, experienced a disastrous mixture of political and Mafia interests.

In the 1960s the agricultural Mafia became an **urban Mafia**. Organized crime and politics shared the deals, particularly those in the lucrative **construction sector**. In the 1970s the Mafia got involved in **dealing drugs and arms**. Along with extorting protection money (pizzo), waste disposal remains a highly lucrative pursuit. Estimates by the parliamentary anti-Mafia commission state that 70% of all southern Italian landfills are in Mafia hands.

Fight against the Mafia

When the Mafia restructured, the level of violence also increased and finally the state reacted. The fight against the Cosa Nostra claimed many victims, such as the Carabinieri general Carlo Alberto Dalla Chiesa, who was shot in 1982. The assassination of the two popular anti-Mafia investigators Giovanni Falcone and Paolo Borselino in 1992 created even more of a furore, and for the first time the public stirred in resistance: thousands of people took to the streets and demonstrated against the Mafia. Even Pope John Paul II went to Agrigento and demanded that all believers rebel against the bosses. Since the mid-

Ever since the Italian government began confiscating land from members of the Mafia and making it available for civilian purposes several cooperatives have been started on Sicily. Not only Mafia-free organic products grow here, some under the label »I Sapori della Legalità«, but also signs of social change. More information at: www.liberaterra.it, www.libera.it

1990s the police have managed to catch several important mafiosi, including Toto Riina in 1993 and, in 1996, his successor, Giovanni Brusca, who is accused of the assassination of Falcone. In 2006 Bernardo Provenzano was caught by the police in Corleone. He was the mafioso who had been wanted by the police for longest (43 years!). In 2007 Salvatore Lo Piccolo was caught after 24 years. The **anti-Mafia association Libera** managed to pass a law via a referendum in 1996 that allows the judiciary to seize Mafia assets and donate them to charitable organizations. According to Libera, more than 4000 mansions, flats and properties have been seized and put to social uses. Co-operatives are now flourishing on former Mafia land, whose produce is guaranteed to be »Mafia-free«, while elsewhere police barracks and schools are built. Around 600 million euros were seized in the province of Palermo between January and November 2008 alone (by comparison: the business association Confesercenti estimates that the Italian Mafia generates a turnover of 130 billion euros per year).

»**Addio pizzo**« (»goodbye protection money«) is the name of a courageous movement by entrepreneurs, retailers and consumers and a declaration of war on the Mafia: pizzo is not just a source of income, it is also a symbol of power. Those who pay pizzo obey the Cosa Nostra. In Palermo alone more than 390 shops have the Addio Pizzo symbol on the door, including the »Supermarket of Legality« (Punto Pizzo-free, Via Vittorio Emanuele 172; Information: www.addiopizzo.org).

No danger to visitors

Although the Mafia will not be defeated that quickly, tourists do not need to fear it. Tourism is far too lucrative for that. Tourism generates millions for hotels and restaurants, by property speculation and new hotel construction projects, and it is also a clever way of laundering dirty money. Visitors are better off watching out for petty crime such as pickpocketing and having their cars broken into. Although the Mafia is not involved in this »line of business«, it observes the goings-on. Maybe a small-time crook could be used as a pizzo collector or killer.

Global »branches«

The term »Mafia« no longer just refers to the **Cosa Nostra** (»our business«) on Sicily. The »**Camorra**« group in Naples is an offshoot, as is the Calabrian »**Ndrangheta**« (Greek »andreia kai agathiau« means »manfulness«, »respectability«) and the Apulian »**Sacra Corona Unita**« (»United Sacred Crown«).

Although the proportion of Sicilians employed in agriculture has dropped from a good 50 % in 1950 to 11 % at present, a quarter of the island's area is still used for agriculture. The situation is characterized by two factors: first, the soil quality, which varies a great deal from the arid interior to the irrigated coastal regions; and secondly the very uneven land distribution and the resulting difference in efficiency. Land reform laws of 1948 and 1950 limited the »latifondi« established in Antiquity, with the result that new estates with a total of 300,000 ha/740,000 acres were formed. Nevertheless 90 % of the agricultural operations worked on just 25 % of the agricultural land, meaning that on average each had less than 10 ha/25 acres of land, while 2 % of the farms were latifundia and possessed more than 50 % of the agricultural land; the methods of small farms are non-intensive, so that they only produce 10 % of the wheat on 30 % of the land used for it. The cultivation of citrus fruits, on the other hand, is intensive: 60 % of Italian oranges and mandarins come from Sicily, as well as 90 % of all lemons (more than 50 % from the Etna region alone). Grapes are cultivated on around 20,000 ha/50,000 acres. In addition to dessert grapes they yield around 9 million hectolitres (2 million gallons) of wine, or 14 % of the country's total production.

Agriculture

Around 25,000 fishermen catch 20 % of Italy's total fish in the waters around Sicily. The main species are tuna off the northwest coast, sardines on the north and south coasts, as well as swordfish on the east coast.

Fishing

Sicily is not rich in resources. There are oil and natural gas, which has been economically beneficial for the Ragusa region. In addition the island produces salt, whereas the sulphur industry, once the global leader, has declined in the face of American competition.

Resources

Industry has developed particularly well around Palermo, Catania, Milazzo, Syracuse and Gela. The main sectors are engineering, shipbuilding and petrochemicals. Only part of the labour no longer needed in agriculture can find employment in industry, which therefore only makes a small contribution to preventing emigration to northern Italy.

Industry

One area with a future is tourism. A trip to Sicily is no longer just »Taormina and ancient ruins«. Intense encounters with the country and its people have allowed the development of *agriturismi* in rural areas as well as charming guesthouses and B&B's in historic towns. Thanks to the extension of nature parks and hiking trails, Sicily is not just a destination for those with an interest in cultural attractions; it is becoming increasingly appealing to those with a love of the outdoors and more active pursuits. Both Italian and foreign guests love discovering the wine island's rich culinary offerings.

Tourism

History

Over the course of its history, Sicily has undergone almost two dozen invasions. All of the foreign peoples who came left their mark. The following section presents the most important events of the island's eventful past.

Early History

6000 BC	Oldest traces of human settlement
2000 BC	Elymians and Sicels migrate to Sicily.
1000 BC	Phoenicians settle in Sicily.

The earliest traces of human habitation on Sicily were found in the Grotta dell'Addaura on Monte Pellegrino near Palermo and in the Grotta del Genovese on the island of Lévanzo; they are from a Neolithic culture dating back to the 6th millennium BC. After that came the Bronze Age Castelluccio and Thapsos cultures on the mainland as well as the Capo-Graziano and the Capo-Milazzese cultures on the Aeolian Islands and finally the Pantàlica culture. All this took place between 6000 and 1200 BC.

The first Sicilians

The oldest settlers were the **Sicani**, who farmed the land and lived in villages. Their capital was Kamikos, modern-day Sant'Angelo Muxaro near Agrigento. Their language is unknown. Towards the end of the 2nd millennium BC the **Elymians** arrived in the west of the island and founded Eryx, Segesta and Entella. According to ancient sources they were the descendants of Trojans who had fled Troy; after their Hellenization in the 5th century BC they were no longer mentioned as a people. Also at the end of the 2nd millennium BC the presumably Indo-European **Sicels** arrived from Italy. they lived in fortified hilltop towns and created vast necropolises; they forced out the Sicani from the east of the island. In around 450 BC they unsuccessfully tried to assert themselves over the Greeks, with whose culture they merged.

In around 1000 BC the **Phoenicians** arrived in Sicily from what is now Lebanon as part of a mercantile expansion that encompassed the entire Mediterranean region. They set up numerous trading posts on the island. When the Greeks came on the scene, they withdrew to Motya (Mózia), Solus and Panormos (Palermo) in western Sicily.

Greeks

800/700 BC	Start of Greek immigration
575 BC	End of Greek colonization process
409–405 BC	Carthaginians destroy Greek towns – Syracuse becomes the largest city of the Greek world.

← *The Addaura Grotto on Monte Pellegrino near Palermo has seen human use since the earliest prehistoric times*

Participation in Antiquity: up to 3000 Greeks gathered in the ekklesiasterion in Agrigento for citizens' assemblies and voting

Magna Graecia   Greek immigration, which had a lasting impact on Sicily's political and cultural history, took place in the 8th and 7th centuries BC. The first colonists were **Ionian Greeks** from Chalcis on Euboea and from Naxos. They founded the town of Naxos (near Taormina) in 735 BC, near which they built the Temple of Apollo Archegetes as the religious centre of the »Siceliotes«, as the Sicilian Greeks called themselves. Thucles of Naxos then founded the Ionian colonies of Leontinoi (729 BC, modern-day Lentini) and Katana (Catania).

Also in the 8th century BC, in around 730 BC, more settlers came to Sicily from Chalcis, after first stopping in Cumae (on the Bay of Naples), the oldest Greek colony on Italian soil. On Sicily they then founded the colony of Zankle. When later, in 410 BC, lots of refugees came to Sicily looking for a new home after being forced out of Messene (Peloponnese region) by the Spartans, the town was called Messana/Messene. One fact of significance for the Greek colonization of

Sicily was that Himera was founded by settlers in Zankle/Messana in 649 BC; it was quite far to the west, and for a long time the only Greek city on Sicily's north coast. The number of **Doric Greeks** was also significant. In 734–733 BC, i.e. shortly after Naxos was founded, colonists from Corinth, led by Archias, reached Sicily's east coast and founded Syracuse on the island of Ortygia and the mainland; Syracuse was to become the largest and most powerful Greek city on Sicily. Syracuse is just a few years old when, under Lamis, colonists arrived from Megara (near Athens, 729–726 BC). After two stops on the way, they found their new home in Megara Hybaea on the east coast. Around a century later, in 628 BC, they founded the town of Selinus as the westernmost Greek outpost. This town's vast collection of temples has ensured its fame to this day. This leaves Gela on the south coast. It was founded in 690 (or 710) BC by colonists from the town of Lindos on Rhodes; it was originally named Lindioi. Finally, in 599 BC, towards the end of the Greek wave of colonization, colonists from Gela founded the town of Akragas (Agrigento).

At the end of the Greek colonization process came the group led by Pentathlos from Knidos in 575 BC. Pentathlos came with settlers from his home town and from Rhodes. They wanted to settle in the Phoenician west of Sicily, but were beaten in their battles with the Elymians and Phoenicians. The group subsequently sailed to the Aeolian Islands, where they founded Lipara (Lìpari).

Ernst Langlotz (1895–1978) said about the Greek colonists in southern Italy and Sicily: »As a result of their geographical proximity to their mother country, the same climatic conditions and much better living conditions, a new Greek world was able to develop here in the 6th and 5th centuries BC, which, although constantly threatened by the native population in the hinterland, was able to develop its own highly significant and, intellectually, very influential culture. Their poetry (Stesichorus, Ibycus, Epicharmus), philosophy (Xenophanes, Parmenides, the Eleatics), their religious sects (Orpheus, Zaleucus, Pythagoras), natural sciences, but especially their mathematics (Pythagoras, Archimedes) and medicine (Alcmaeon, school of Croton) had a significance for the intellectual history of the entire Greco-Roman period that cannot be exaggerated.« In addition there was their contact with the native population. »As a result of the mixing of blood that was inevitable in some towns ... a population bedrock was gradually formed that had a crucial impact on a colony's politics, arts and culture. ... It was especially because of this fusion and assimilation with the aboriginal population that the

A »new« Greek world

The small bronze horse dates back to the 8th century BC (museum in Agrigento)

Sicily in Antiquity Map

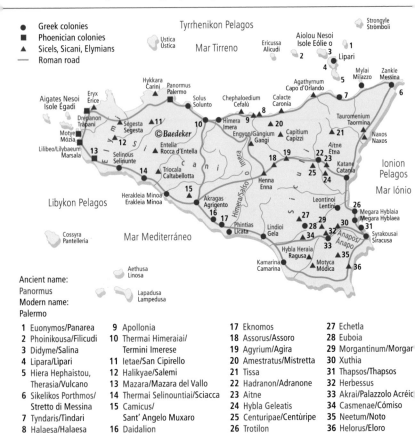

- ● Greek colonies
- ■ Phoenician colonies
- ▲ Sicels, Sicani, Elymians
- — Roman road

Ancient name:
Panormus
Modern name:
Palermo

1 Euonymos/Panarea	9 Apollonia	17 Eknomos	27 Echetla
2 Phoinikousa/Filicudi	10 Thermai Himeraiai/	18 Assorus/Assoro	28 Euboia
3 Didyme/Salina	Termini Imerese	19 Agyrium/Agira	29 Morgantinum/Morgar
4 Lipara/Lìpari	11 Ietae/San Cipirello	20 Amestratus/Mistretta	30 Xuthia
5 Hiera Hephaistou,	12 Halikyae/Salemi	21 Tissa	31 Thapsos/Thapsos
Therasia/Vulcano	13 Mazara/Mazara del Vallo	22 Hadranon/Adranone	32 Herbessus
6 Sikelikos Porthmos/	14 Thermai Selinountiai/Sciacca	23 Aitne	33 Akrai/Palazzolo Acréid
Stretto di Messina	15 Camicus/	24 Hybla Geleatis	34 Casmenae/Cómiso
7 Tyndaris/Tindari	Sant' Angelo Muxaro	25 Centuripae/Centùripe	35 Neetum/Noto
8 Halaesa/Halaesa	16 Daidalion	26 Trotilon	36 Helorus/Eloro

intellectual seed of the Greeks became particularly fertile around their cities, giving rise to new cultures.«

The Greeks mainly settled along the coast and in areas close to the coast, while the previous settlers lived in the interior. The cult of the goddesses Demeter and Persephone/Kore, who were worshipped as the rulers of the island, goes back to the older population and was adopted by the Greeks.

Tyrants The individual Greek states were ruled by tyrants from time to time, including Phalaris of Akragas (570–554 BC). Gelo became the ruler of Syracuse in the early 5th century (485–478). He strengthened the city's power so that he, together with Theron of Akragas, was able to ward off the attack of the Carthaginians led by Hamilcar that took place in Himera in 480 BC; it was in that same year that the Athenians defeated the Persians, who were allied to Carthage, at the Battle of Salamis, as a result of which the attempt to surround Greece was doomed to failure. After Gelo's death, his brother Hieron I took over (478–466 BC). He was able to extend his power to the mainland. He called Aeschylus and Pindar to his court, which he turned into a cultural centre of the Greek world.

The Doric and Ionian cities were often in conflict with each other. **Tensions** Tensions also existed with the Sicels, who rebelled in 452 BC under their leader Ducetius. Further unrest arose when Athens responded to a plea for help from the Elymian town of Segesta in 414 BC, during the Peloponnesian War, by sending a naval expedition to Syracuse, which was politically close to Athens's enemy Sparta. The war ended disastrously for Athens (414 at sea, 413 BC on land near Noto). Soon afterwards the old enemy Carthage came back on to the scene and launched a large-scale attack. Under Hannibal (grandson of Hamilcar, who lost the battle of 480 BC), and after his death in 406 BC, under his nephew Himilco, Carthage conquered and destroyed one Greek town after another between 409 and 405 BC. Only Syracuse held firm. The tyrant Dionysius I ruled here (approx. 405–367 BC; ▶Famous People). He expanded Syracuse's power-base all the way to the Italian mainland and brought Plato to his court. Syracuse grew to become the largest city of the Greek world. His son, Dionysius II, was forced out in 357 BC by Dion. Timoleon of Corinth put an end to tyranny in Syracuse in 344 BC. However, at the end of the 4th century BC Agathocles (361–289 BC) established himself as a tyrant. After a military campaign by Pyrrhus of Epirus, Hieron II (275–215 BC) became tyrant of Syracuse and, like the rulers of all the other Hellenistic territories, called himself king.

Romans and Byzantines

264–241 BC	First Punic War
218–201 BC	Second Punic War – Sicily becomes a Roman province.
AD 440	Vandals invade.
535–827	Sicily falls to Byzantium.

When the Phoenicians asserted themselves on Sicily again, the First **Rome's bread** Punic War (264–241 BC) broke out, during which Hieron II of Syr- **basket** acuse took Rome's side. Western Sicily emerged as Rome's first prov-

The famous Greco-Roman theatre in Taormina

ince outside mainland Italy, while eastern Sicily, under Hieron, remained autonomous for the time being. Since his successor and grandson Hieronymus allied himself with the Carthaginians, Rome conquered Syracuse and Akragas (212–210 BC) in the Second Punic War (218–201 BC), meaning Rome now controlled the whole of Sicily. Between 210 BC and AD 440 Sicily was a Roman province. It was ruled by governors and exploited as Rome's bread basket.

Remarkable events Among noteworthy events were the **slave wars** (135–132 and 104–100 BC), that targeted the latifundia, as well as the civil war between Pompey and Octavian (43–36 BC), after Sicily had become a senatorial province, governed by a praetor. The misrule of the **notorious governor Verres** (73–71 BC) is known from Cicero's speeches. Verres did not just ruin Sicily's agriculture and embezzle money, he also turned out to be an art thief. Under Emperor Gallienus (AD 260–268) there was a further slave revolt. On the other hand the lifestyle led by the inhabitants of Sicily's villas was lavish; one example of this is the villa on Piazza Armerina, which features beautiful mosaics.

Invasions and conquests After the Roman Empire was divided, the later Western Empire's waning power saw Germanic invasions and conquests: in AD 440 by the Vandals, AD 493 by the Ostrogoths. Emperor Justinian's general

Belisarius put an end to their rule by winning Sicily back for Byzantium, the Eastern Roman Empire, in AD 535. It remained Byzantine for 300 years. For the ruler in Constantinople this part of the empire was so important that Emperor Constans II (AD 663–668) temporarily moved his residence to Sicily when his capital was under threat from the Arabs. In 751 Sicily was removed from the pope's jurisdiction and handed over to the patriarch of Constantinople, a situation which Rome rectified, from its point of view, after the fall of Constantinople.

Arabs

827–902	Arab conquest
925	Palermo becomes the capital.

Byzantine rule came to an end when Admiral Euphemius, governor of Syracuse, rebelled against the emperor and called on Arabs to come to his support in Sicily. The Emir of Kairouan arrived near Mazara on 17 June 827. That was the start of the **Arab conquests**, which only ended after almost 100 years with the taking of Taormina in 902 and Rometta to the west of Messina in 925. Sicily was divided into three administrative districts: Val di Mazara (west), Val di Noto (southeast) and Val Démone (northeast). The word »Val« probably did not come from the Italian word Valle (valley); it is more likely that it came from the Arab word Wilayah (administrative district). Palermo replaced Syracuse as the main city on Sicily. An Arab chronicler registered more than 300 mosques here in 972. The city is likely to have had more than 100,000 inhabitants, making it one of the largest of those times after Constantinople and Cairo (both approx. 500,000), Córdoba and Kairouan (both around 200,000) – far larger than Rome (35,000) and Naples (25,000).

Under the banner of the prophet

Emirs resided here and their reign was characterized by fair taxes and religious tolerance. There was gradual Islamization, so that the number of Muslims was greater than that of Orthodox Christians by the 11th century; however, Christians remained in the majority in the northeast of the island: in Val Démone (with a view of Calabria, which was still under Byzantine rule), where resistance against the Arab conquest had been most stubborn. Religious tolerance made the **peaceful co-existence** of Muslims, Christians and Jews possible. Trade and crafts flourished. The new rulers brought new growing

? DID YOU KNOW …?

■ Muslims brought not only many unknown varieties of fruits, vegetables and legumes, but also paper, hydraulics and algebra to Sicily.

methods and plants to the island, including citrus fruits, aubergines, melons, pistachios, sugar cane and date palms. Silk-worm farming also began with the introduction of the mulberry tree. When the Saracens arrived, pasta, pizza and ice cream came with them. Sicily's mineral resources were used and salt evaporation ponds were created to mine salt. The natural sciences were supported. As a result this period gave the island incredible wealth and a flourishing cultural life. Although the faded red cupolas of San Giovanni degli Eremiti in Palermo are unmistakably Arab, there are almost no other extant buildings from this era. They must have been systematically destroyed at a later date, after the end of the Hohenstaufen period.

Normans and the House of Hohenstaufen

1061–1091	Norman conquest
1130	Sicily becomes a kingdom under Roger II.
1194–1250	Henry VI and Frederick II from the House of Hohenstaufen rule Sicily.

Normans in the south Arab rule came to an end just as it had begun: discord among the emirs caused them to ask for help from the Normans. Counts Robert Guiscard and Roger, sons of Tancred from the northern French

Roger II is crowned, La Martorana

house of Hauteville, were on an expedition to seek loot and adventure when they arrived in Sicily on 18 May 1061. They conquered the island within three decades; when Noto fell in 1091, the Normans ruled the entire island, which they continued to do until 1194. These conquerors, who had previously been occupied with waging wars and looting, developed into great statesmen. They were supported by the powerful monastic orders and the native aristocracy. Latin and Greek monks provided the architects, sculptors and decorators; the patricians, shaped by Byzantium, became administrative experts, jurists and notaries. »The high officers of the kingdom, who represented the Byzantine culture, were mainly the admirals (Christodulus, George of Antioch, Eugene, Margaritus of Brindisi), the chancellors (Nicola, John of Calabria, Nicola of Mesa, Maio of Bari, Henry Aristippus, while Latin culture got the upper hand under Matteo of Aello) and the educated monks (Neilos Doxapatros, Scolario Sabas, Philagathus of Cerami). ... This resulted in a very heterogeneous amalgam in which the Norman element represented the military side, while the innovative spirit in architecture came from the monks and the governmental reforms were of Byzantine origin.« (Cassata/Costantino/Santoro).

The Normans practised religious and linguistic tolerance in this new state. In addition to Latin and Greek, Hebrew and Arabic were officially recognized languages; they allowed agriculture, commerce and trade to flourish, they possessed a good administrative system and beautified the island with a wealth of buildings that survive to this day as testimony to a mixed Norman-Arab-Byzantine culture.

◀ Tolerance in the Middle Ages

Roger I unified state and church power within himself as Great Count (Gran Conte) and Apostolic Legate (Legatus Apostolicus). This was an important factor in Norman rule. When he died in 1101, he had a significant successor in his son **Roger II** (1095–1154), whose mother Adelaide del Vasto acted as regent until 1112; in the 42 years that followed he led his kingdom to a political, economic and cultural golden age. Through the Assizes of Ariano he gave his tightly organized state a legal system in 1140. His reign extended to southern Italy (Apulia, Calabria) and parts of modern-day Tunisia; in 1130 he took these territories as a fief from the pope. As a result he was crowned **Rex Siciliae et Italiae**, an event that took place in Palermo on 25 December 1130. By choosing this date, Roger II equated himself with Charlemagne, the first emperor of the revived Western Empire, who was crowned on Christmas Day (Rome, AD 800). The fact that he wanted his kingdom to be perceived not just as the continuation of a historical tradition, but also as a political programme and especially as a holy institution, is demonstrated in a mosaic in the Martorana church in Palermo (photo p. 38): it de-

Sicily becomes a kingdom

William II is crowned, Monreale

picts Roger being crowned by Christ, a motif that had hitherto been reserved exclusively for the emperor in Constantinople, and as such must have been unpopular with both the emperor and the pope!

Roger's successor was less significant. Under William I (»the Wicked«, 1154–66), the barons became stronger and there were attacks on the Muslims. **William II** (»the Good«, 1166–89), also had problems with the Norman barons, but vehemently proclaimed the sacred nature of his kingship in the Cathedral of Monreale. William II died when he was just 35, without an heir apparent. As a result the throne went to his aunt Constance (1154–1198), a daughter of Roger II, who had been married to Emperor Henry VI, eleven years her junior, since 1186. Thus the German House of Hohenstaufen inherited Sicily from the Normans. The Sicilian barons meanwhile elected Count Tancred of Lecce, one of Roger II's grandsons, to succeed William II. Tancred died soon afterwards in 1194, whereupon the throne went to his son William III, a minor at the time.

Sicily in the hands of the Hohenstaufen

Henry VI, Holy Roman Emperor since 1191, brutally put down the »rebellion« of the Sicilian barons and had himself crowned king of the Monarchia Sicula in Palermo at Christmas 1194. Hohenstaufen rule in Sicily lasted until 1268.

Frederick II, a friend of the Arabs on the imperial throne ▶

Henry VI died in Messina in 1197. His widow, Constance, had her three-year-old son **Frederick II** (1194–1250, ▶ Famous People) crowned king of Sicily in May 1198, six months before her death, making Pope Innocent III his guardian. The young orphan grew up in Palermo. When he was 17 he set off across Italy to Germany, where he was crowned King of Germany in Mainz in 1212 and again in Aachen in 1215. His imperial coronation in Rome took place on 22 November 1220.

Frederick subsequently returned to his Sicilian kingdom, where unrest had developed. He came down hard on the dissenters, particularly on the Islamic mountain farmers. 12,500 Arabs were moved to Lucera (Apulia), but Frederick treated them in such a way that this group of enemies became loyal to him. He moved his residence from Palermo to Foggia, in Apulia. In his hereditary Sicilian kingdom, where, in contrast to his German territories, his hands were not tied by having to be considerate towards rulers of principalities, he created a modern, autocratic state, whose higher officers received their training at the University of Naples, which Frederick founded in 1224.

When Frederick II died in Castel Fiorentino in Apulia on 13 December 1250, his Saracen guard carried his body to Palermo. He was buried in the city's cathedral in a porphyry sarcophagus. The pope celebrated the »death of the Antichrist«, but the world praised Frederick as »stupor mundi« – the wonder of the world – as he was considered to have been extraordinarily educated. He was a brilliant astrologer, poet and scientist, his books on falconry are still heeded today, he was fluent in Italian, French, Latin and Greek; and while he had little German, he certainly spoke Arabic.

He was succeeded by his bastard son Manfred, who fell at the Battle of Benevento in 1266 at the hands of Charles, Count of Anjou, the candidate favoured by the pope. Charles had the young prince Conradin, one of Frederick II's grandsons, beheaded on the market square in Naples in 1268. Manfred's three sons were imprisoned in Castel del Monte in cruel conditions, as they were to »live as if they had never been born«. Thus, after the fall of the House of Hohenstaufen, Manfred's only surviving issue was his daughter Constance. She was married to Peter of Aragon. This was to become significant in 1282, after the »Sicilian Vespers«.

Anjou and Aragon

1266–1302	Reign of the House of Anjou-Sicily
1302–1713	French rulers succeeded by the House of Aragon
1669	Etna eruption destroys Catania.
1693	Earthquake in eastern Sicily claims 100,000 lives.

The pope, whose relationship to the House of Hohenstaufen had always been tense, had banked on the French. He gave **Charles of Anjou**, the brother of the French king Louis IX, the kingdom of Naples and Sicily as a fief. Naples was now the capital and Sicily became secondary, a position it held ever after. The brutality, extravagance and corruption of the new regime aroused the resistance of the Sicilian barons and the people. It was not long before this anger found a voice before evening prayers in Palermo on 30 March 1282: the »Sicilian Vespers« that forced the French rulers out of the country (►Baedeker Special p. 42).

Loyal to the pope

Sicily's aristocracy, especially the Chiaramonte family, picked up the Hohenstaufen tradition and called on **Peter of Aragon**, the husband of Constance, as the »last of the House of Hohenstaufen«. Don Pedro took the office of Rex Siciliae. After his death in 1295, the parliament of barons, which was set up under Roger I, elected his son Frederick III as king. In 1412 the traditional rights of this parliament were revoked when Ferdinand of Aragon, assuming absolute power, appointed a viceroy for the first time. One of his successors, Alfonso I (1416–58), the founder of the University of Catania, also took the Angevins' Neapolitan throne in 1442, so that Naples and Sicily were reunited again, except for an episode between 1713 and 1720. During the 16th and 17th centuries Spanish rule became oppressive, although the barons adapted to the Spanish way of life. In 1516 and 1647 there were rebellions in Palermo, and an uprising in Messina,

Under Spanish rule

On 30 March 1282 the great massacre began. The anger of the people, which had been suppressed for a long time, blew up in the Sicilian Vespers; in addition a cleverly planned intrigue was successful (colour lithograph based on a painting by Nicolo Barabino, 1832–91)

SICILIAN VESPERS

After the execution of the king of Sicily, Conradin from the House of Hohenstaufen, on the marketplace in Naples on 29 October 1268, southern Italy and Sicily were ruled by Charles of Anjou, the brother of the king of France. On 30 March 1282 a group of French people joined those waiting outside the church of Santo Spirito in Palermo for the start of the service. A French man molested a young married woman, and her husband struck him down.

In next to no time Sicilian hatred, which had been building up for a long time, was unloaded. All of Palermo was gripped by bloodlust. Armed men killed every French person they could get their hands on, as well as Sicilian women who had got involved with French men and French monks in Palermo's monasteries. That night around 2000 people died in Palermo alone.

The rebellions spread

Rebels tore down the flag of Anjou and hoisted in its stead the imperial eagle, which had been the city's coat of arms since Frederick II (House of Hohenstaufen). Bloody uprisings followed in the whole of Sicily. On 28 April the royal fleet in the harbour of Messina was set on fire. The city proclaimed itself a commune, elected representatives and asked the pope for protection. After he refused, a different idea established itself: the last ruler of Sicily from the House of Hohenstaufen (prior to Conradin) had been Manfred, son of Frederick II, who had fallen in battle near Benevento in 1266. His daughter and heiress Constance was married to Peter III of Aragon. Sicilian delegates now offered this couple the crown of Sicily.

Change of power

Peter III of Aragon agreed. On 30 August 1282 the fleet carrying the royal couple arrived in Trapani. Thus began Aragonese or Spanish rule over Sicily, which lasted until the early 18th century.

A **key figure** in the complicated, eventful history is Charles of Anjou, who defeated Manfred of Hohenstaufen near Benevento in 1266, thereby becoming ruler of southern Italy and Sicily. He was a man with great governing talents and was also very ambitious. He implemented his policies

with extreme relentlessness. In addition to domestic political troubles, Charles was involved in international politics. **Constantinople** is one example. The largest and richest city in Europe had been captured and plundered by crusaders in 1203–04. In place of the Byzantine Empire, the Latin Empire of Constantinople was set up with »Frankish« monarchs and a Catholic hierarchy, which suppressed the Orthodox church. In 1261 the Latin Empire collapsed: the Byzantine people reconquered Constantinople and reestablished the Byzantine Empire under Emperor Michael VIII. As a result Constantinople was once again on the radar of European powers. Charles of Anjou also dreamed of annexing Byzantium. The time for an attack seemed to have arrived in 1282, but then the rebels destroyed his fleet in Messina harbour.

Thwarted plans

This was certainly not an accident. Michael VIII had watched Charles of Anjou's preparations for attack for years. Although he had hardly any allies and his troops were tied down elsewhere, Byzantium still had one effective weapon: gold. Michael sent much of it to Sicily in order to **fan the rebellion against Charles of Anjou.**

This was a very successful move, even with regard to the timing of the outbreak of the Sicilian Vespers shortly before the scheduled departure of the fleet. Byzantium was saved, and Charles of Anjou's ambitious endeavour had failed. At this point **another key figure** needs to be introduced: John of Procida, a doctor from Salerno who had treated Frederick II during his final illness. He later became an advisor to Manfred's daughter Constance and from 1276 was the chancellor of the king of Aragon. Convinced that Queen Constance had to avenge the fate her Hohenstaufen ancestors had suffered at the hands of Charles of Anjou, Procida got busy and his actions were later romanticized by legend. What is certain is that he had **far-reaching connexions** to the Byzantine court and to its ally Genoa, as well as to the Hohenstaufen party in Sicily and the many Greeks that were still living here. In the background he prepared the rebellion, which was based on weapons, gold and emotions. The organization of the conspiracy and the allegiances that helped it to success are attributed to John of Procida, but the funding and timing were the work of the emperor in Constantinople.

fuelled by France, lasted for six years (1672–78). The period was characterized by rivalries between the prominent aristocratic Sicilian families and their attempts to undermine the power of the viceroys. This, and also under the Barbary incursions from north Africa, caused suffering to the population. In addition Mount Etna erupted in 1669, destroying Catania, and the terrible earthquake of 1693 in southeastern Sicily ruined dozens of towns and killed more than 100,000 people.

From the 18th century to the Present Day

1713 – 1860	Sicily passes to the House of Savoy, then to the Habsburgs and in 1735 to the Spanish Bourbons.
1860	Garibaldi arrives in Sicily – Sicily becomes part of the Kingdom of Italy
1946	Sicily gains autonomy.
2008	The government once again agrees to a bridge between Messina and the Italian mainland.

Changing rulers In the 18th century the island changed rulers in quick succession. The dukes of Savoy-Piedmont (1713 – 1720) and the Habsburgs (1720 – 1734) were followed by the Spanish Bourbons under Charles III of Naples, an enlightened monarch who was not, however, able to assert himself against the Sicilian parliament of barons. His successor, Ferdinand IV (1759 – 1814), and his viceroy Domenico Caràcciolo (▶ Famous People) suffered a similar fate; the economist Paolo Balsamo tried to assist in efforts to eliminate the people's economic and social misery. King Ferdinand withdrew to Palermo when the Parthenopean Republic was proclaimed in Naples (on the initiative of the revolutionary regime in Paris) and then Joseph Bonaparte and Joachim Murat ruled Sicily as kings, a right given to them by Napoleon. After the fall of Napoleon, Ferdinand returned to Naples. In 1816 he united, as Ferdinand I, Naples and Sicily and called it the »Kingdom of Two Sicilies«. There were once again great social tensions in Sicily, which resulted in a rebellion in 1820–21 and a revolution in 1848.

Usurper Garibaldi ▶ The ancien régime of the Bourbons collapsed when **Garibaldi** landed in Marsala on 11 May 1860 and took Sicily with his »Expedition of a Thousand«. On 22 October 1860 a plebiscite decided that Sicily should join the newly founded Kingdom of Italy.

Sicily in the 20th and 21st centuries The young Italian national state was not able to solve the island's old social problems. As a result, hundreds of thousands of Sicilians emi-

Art History

Prehistory

Sicily exhibits traces of human culture dating back to the 6th millennium BC. In those Stone Age days the cave drawings in the Grotta del Genovese on Lévanzo and the human figures by the Sicanion the walls of the Addaura grotto near Palermo (photo p. 30) were made.

Sicels

The necropolis of Pantàlica was created in the 2nd millennium BC. The Sicels, who had come to Sicily from Italy, built their capital on a plateau above the Anapo Valley in the 13th century BC. A megaron-like building was uncovered in this complex (11th century BC). The necropolis below the town, which features more than 5000 rock tombs (13th–8th centuries BC) is even more significant. During the time of the Saracens, Christian refugees transformed some of the tombs into chapels.

Short glossary

- There is a short guide to art and historical terminology at the end of this book (p. 446).

Phoenicians

The Phoenicians, who arrived on the island in around 1000 BC, withdrew in the face of the Greek colonists to three fortified locations: Motya, Solus and Panormos. Motya (Mózia) was situated on a round island 8km/5mi north of Marsala. The town walls with 20 towers and bastions as well as a temple and two necropolises survive. Solus (Soluntum), on Sicily's north coast, was destroyed in 254 BC by the Romans, who then replaced it by a new town. It is only from this Roman town that significant remains survive.
The third fortified site, whose Phoenician name is not known, is modern-day Palermo. Excavations on both sides of Corso Calatafimi in 1953–54 revealed a large necropolis, which was used from Phoenician to Roman times.

Greeks

A crucial change in the ethnic composition and history of Sicilian towns occurred with the arrival of Greek colonists. In the 6th and 5th centuries BC the temples of Syracuse, Akragas and Segesta were built, as were secular buildings such as the theatre of Syracuse (from 470 BC, one of the oldest of the Greek world), as well as the theatres in Gela and Tyndaris. Also of note is the great fortification of Euryalus in Syracuse. Apart from the metopes and other **architectural decoration** from Selinunte, Sicily's museums house masterpieces such as the Agrigento Ephebe (490 BC, Greek marble, museum in Agrigento), the Selinunte Ephebe (460 BC, bronze, Castelvetrano) and the »Venus Landolina« (Hellenic, marble, Syracuse).

← *In the choir of Monreale Cathedral: Christ Pantocrator has his place above his mother Mary.*

Terracotta relief: lion defeating a bull, end of the 6th century BC; now in the museum of Syracuse

The **coins** of this period, particularly those from Syracuse, are great significance. Famous coin makers were Eumenes, Euainetos, Kimon and Eucleides. Coins from Syracuse referred to the myth of the nymph Arethusa, who had come to Sicily through the sea when she was escaping from the Greek river deity Alpheus, reappearing in Syracuse as the Arethusa spring: they depict her head between dolphins. Naxos coins are reminiscent of those of the eponymous Greek island and depict the head of the god Dionysus.

Several coins contain punning references to the names of their respective towns, namely those of Himera (a cockerel, announcing the day – Greek: himera), Leontinoi (the head of a lion – Greek: leon) and Selinus/Selinunte (a leaf of wild celery). Messina was originally called Zankle (sickle) and »alludes to the special shape of its harbour with the sickle-shaped line into which a dolphin swims « (M. Sipsie-Eschbach). Akragas, situated between a river and the sea, chose crabs for its coins, the town of Gela adopted the river god Gelas, depicted as a bull with a human head. The head of Apollo can be seen on coins from Katane, the head of Heracles on those from Kamarina.

History of ideas The intellectual contribution made by the Siceliotes is outstanding. The first person to mention here is the poet Stesichorus from Himera (6th century BC). He was a lyric poet and »addressed material from heroic sagas and from the tradition of his home in a ballad style, which has its place between epic and tragedy« (W. Buchwald). In Antiquity 26 books with works by him were known. Epicharmus from Megara Hyblaea (around 550–460 BC) was the best-known representative of Doric comedy, which, with its slapstick nature, was closely related to Phlyax plays; a total of 36 titles of his works are known.

The natural philosopher and doctor Empedocles (around 483–423 BC) from Akragas, who wrote the cosmological work *On Nature*, was a man shrouded in legend. Hölderlin devoted a tragedy to him. Gorgias from Ionian Leontinoi (483–376 BC) had a longer life. He performed as an itinerant orator in Delphi, Athens and Olympia, and was the most significant rhetorician and defender of Sophism.

Famous historians include Timaeus from Tauromenion (approx. 350–250 BC), who spent at least 50 years in Athens, as he was banished for his opposition to tyranny. Then there is his contemporary Philistus, a statesman and historian from Syracuse. In the 3rd century BC the mathematician, physicist and mechanical engineer Archimedes (287–212 BC; ► Famous People) lived and worked in Syracuse. His contemporary was Theocritus (first half of the 3rd century BC) from Syracuse, who lived in his home town, in Kos and Alexandria and was the founder and most renowned exponent of Greek bucolic poetry. The influence of his pastoral works can be found in Virgil. Last but not least there is the historian Diodorus Siculus (1st century BC), who was born in Agyrion (modern-day Agira). He wrote a Greek history of the world from mythical times to the invasion of Britannia by Caesar in 54 BC. However, the greatest contributions of the Sicilian Greeks were their temples, which is why the following digression is dedicated to them.

Head from Temple E in Selinunte, c. 460 BC

Digression: Greek Temples in Sicily

Greek temples are among the most significant cultural achievements left behind by the eventful history of the island. Earlier travellers were already awestruck when they saw these ancient structures. When the Greek motherland was still ruled by the Turks and therefore not generally accessible, the obvious answer was to visit Sicilian temples to see examples of ancient sacred architecture. This has changed. Everyone can now go to Greece and its monuments have been thoroughly researched. As a result it is now possible to make comparisons between the structures in Greece itself and those in its western colonies. It is now known to what extent the Sicilian temples are the same as those in Hellas and how far they differ. To see both and explore the intellectual and religious attitude behind them is an informative undertaking that aids understanding of them.

Doric order

Since most of the Greek colonists came from Doric cities, it comes as no surprise that their temples in Sicily were also built according to the Doric order. This order was perfected in the 6th century BC. One of its classic examples is the Temple of Zeus in Olympia, built by Libon of Elis between 470 and 456 BC. The Greek temple, alongside the theatre one of the great achievements of ancient architecture, is a house of god in the strictest sense of the term, i.e. not a place for the followers, but for the deity himself or herself, where the cult image was located. The followers gathered in front of the temple, where sacrifices were made at the altar outside the entrance, generally on the temple's eastern side.

Temple structure

The temple structure was based on the megaron of residential buildings, such as existed in the throne rooms of Mycenaean castles. The classical form is the peripteros, where the cella is surrounded on all four sides by an arcade (peristasis). In the 6th century elongated floor plans were preferred, with a column ratio of 6 to 16 (Temple of Hera at Olympia) or 6 to 15 (Temple of Apollo at Delphi). In the 5th century architects arrived at the classical proportions, in which the long sides had twice the number of columns as the short sides, plus one, i.e. 6 to 13 (Temple of Zeus in Olympia) or 8 to 17 (Parthenon in Athens). A striking and characteristic feature is that all of the exteriors were treated the same, and thanks to this homogeneity no façade was clearly defined as the front.

The cella, the room for the cult image, has a pronaos at its entrance side, while the corresponding feature at the other side is the opisthodomos. The cella's interior was often divided by two colonnades. It had no windows. The only source of light was from the open temple doors.

Sicilian characteristics

Doric temples possess »an intellectually clear relationship to the gods«, which had been victorious »over the old faith dominated by fear of demons«. In the west of the Greek world, on the other hand, in Sicily, »the chthonic cults dedicated to the underworld maintained the upper hand« (G. Gruben) – all over Sicily **Demeter and her daughter Persephone**, who spent half the year of every year in the underworld, were worshipped as great goddesses. The cult therefore largely had the character of a mystery religion. The obligatory structuring of the cella that we find in Greece is rarely found in Sicilian temples. Usually the room behind the cella, the opisthodomos, is missing. Instead, there is a separate dark room at the back of the cella, the adyton. It contained the cult image, which was no longer at

Basic types of Greek temples

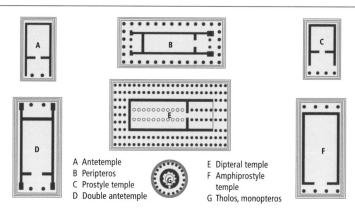

A Antetemple
B Peripteros
C Prostyle temple
D Double antetemple

E Dipteral temple
F Amphiprostyle temple
G Tholos, monopteros

Components of the Greek temple

(Hexastyle = peripteros with six columns at the narrow ends)

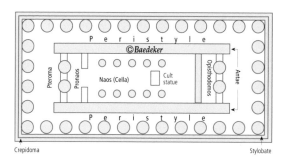

the centre of the complex, but rather its mysterious, innermost destination. In line with this is the emphasis placed on the temples' entrance sides, in the spirit of a polar tension between the followers
and the concealed cult image: with steps, rows of double columns
and an enlarged portico.

A second characteristic is an altered relationship to space. The Sicilian architects preferred **wide, hall-like rooms** and airy colonnades.
They developed beam constructions consisting of braced triangles,
which made it possible to cover incredible breadths, up to 9.68m/
32ft (Treasury of Gela in Olympia), or even 13m/43ft (Olympieion
in Akragas)! This meant that the buildings did not need internal support from columns; therefore the cella could be designed as an undi-
vided room. The aisles between the cella and the columns matched
these large interiors; the Greek canon stated the width should be one

Impressive remains of the Doric Temple of Heracles in Agrigento

jugerum, while in Sicily two jugera were preferred, thereby creating »autonomous flights of rooms « (Gruben).

Thirdly it can be observed that in some cases, such as the Olympieion in Agrigento, Temple F in Selinunte and the Temple in Himera, the gaps between the columns were closed by half-height or full-height walls. This produced an effect that was otherwise peculiar to the Eleusian Mysteries, i.e. that the cult following was sealed off from the outside world and their processions around the walkways could not be spied on – a clue to the **mystery character** of the Sicilian cults.

The fourth characteristic of Sicilian temples has its roots not in religious, but in political and economic aspects. The colonists found unexpected opportunities for economic prosperity in Sicily compared with Greece – Sicily was something like the »America of the Greeks«, a land of boundless opportunities. Associated with this was the urge of the Sicilian tyrants to cultivate their image, which led to temples such as Temple G in Selinunte and the Olympieion in Akragas being built on such a megalomaniac scale that puts the monumental aspect of Doric buildings in the shade but at the same time appears coarse and excessive.

All of these trends that were developed in the 6th century BC became less significant after 480 BC: the classical style of the mother country reached Sicily. In a short period of time no fewer than eight temples were built that followed the new ideas, including – under the influence of the Temple of Zeus in Olympia – the Temple of Hera E in Selinunte.

Classical Greek architecture

However, this development had no innovations of its own. The elements adopted from the mother country were maintained. Early classical capitals, for example, were used for almost half a century without change. Instead of lively development, there was no creativity. The end came with the destruction of the Greek cities in Sicily by the Carthaginians at the end of the 5th century BC. Only Syracuse continued to exist, but here too, despite the enormous increase in wealth and power, there were no further temples of the same quality. During the classical period the Doric temple had an effect even beyond the Greek sphere. A famous example is the peripteros, which Athenians started building in Elymian Segesta in around 430 BC. This temple, which was never completed, owes its state of preservation to its isolated location.

Other ancient temples fell victim to earthquakes (Selinunte) or were destroyed by human hand. Two buildings escaped this fate because they were **transformed into churches during the Christian period**: the Temple of Athene in Syracuse, whose Doric columns can still be seen in the cathedral's wall, and the Temple of Condordia in Agrigento, which was turned into a Christian basilica by Pope Gregory

A Roman work of art: Phaedra sarcophagus in the church of San Nicola in Agrigento; Hippolytus and his friends; 2nd century AD

the Great in around 600, but which was restored to its ancient form again in 1748. The best-preserved Doric temple in Italy!

Romans Sicily's Roman period began with the island's conquest in the Second Punic War (218–201 BC). The characteristic Roman buildings were baths (Catania) and amphitheatres (Catania, Syracuse, Termini Imerese). The Villa Casale near Piazza Armerina (3rd–4th century AD) became famous because of its large mosaic floors. Two further very large villas were discovered in the 1970s, finds with a similarly sensational impact. One is part of a complex that measures 20,000 sq m/24,000 sq yd, northwest of Patti, while the other is the Villa del Tellaro, named after the river to the south of Noto.

Early Christian, Arab and Norman periods The early Christian and Byzantine period has, just like the following Arab period, left few traces. The monuments of the Norman period are all the more impressive (1061–1194). Quite a few of them survive, such as the Cuba and the Zisa palaces in Palermo, but particularly the churches in Palermo, Monreale and Cefalù. The characteristic features of these buildings are that they pick up Byzantine and Arab elements and merge them with Western traditions. The **Cappella Palatina** in the Norman palace of Palermo has not just the Western floor plan of a columned basilica with a nave and two aisles, it also has the throne and the choir opposite each other: a polarity of westwork and altar that is familiar from early Romanesque churches.

The dome and the mosaic ornamentation on the other hand were inspired by Byzantium. When it came to inscribing the mosaics however, the Sicilian Normans once again revealed their dual orientation towards the Latin West and the Greek East: they used both languages. The cupola's squinch construction and the stalactite ceiling were made by Arab artists following typical Islamic architecture. »Next to the Doric columned building was the Christian cathedral, next to the serious stone magnificence of the Temple of Juno in Agrigento the gleaming, golden church of the Virgin Mary in Monreale, monuments of two memorable phases in human history« (F. Gregorovius).

Digression: Mosaics

The late Roman mosaics of Piazza Amerina (3rd–4th century) and the mosaics from the Norman period in Palermo and Cefalù (12th century) follow a tradition that can be traced back in Greece to the 5th century BC. In Antiquity the initial purpose was to adorn floors with ornamental or figurative depictions made from small stones at first, later also from pieces of glass. The earliest form are pebble mosaics. Well-known examples exist in Pella, the capital of Macedon (4th century BC), where Gnosis is the first mosaicist to be known by name as he signed his works, and Motya. In the 3rd century BC the use of colourful stones called tesserae because of their almost square shape (Greek: tessares = four) became fashionable. This method flourished in the Hellenistic period (discoveries in Pergamon, Delos and Alexandreia).

Mosaic floors had been known in Italy since the 2nd century BC. The works in Pompeii (»Alexander mosaic«) are well known. Mosaics became very widespread during the Roman imperial period, throughout the empire (Hadrian's Villa in Tibur/Tivoli, 2nd century, and in the port of Ostia). The large figurative mosaics in **Villa del Casale** in Piazza Armerina were made in the late 3rd and in the 4th century. 3500 sq m/4200 sq yd have been uncovered. At this time mosaics were no longer used just to decorate floors, but were also put on walls and in vaulted ceilings, such as in public baths and palaces.

The »bikini girls« in Villa del Casale

This trend up into vaulted areas continued in the early Christian period, when mosaics were used as the most exclusive decoration of sacred spaces, but also because they made a theological statement. Among the highlights of this art are the wall and ceiling mosaics in the churches of Ravenna. In the Byzantine Empire (Constantinople, Thessaloniki) this art of making mosaics was developed further. From the 9th century it was used to adorn churches with a system of theologically motivated picture cycles, for which, as for the corresponding fresco painting, one can talk of the »liturgy of the picture«.

There had long been a move away from the ancient »opus vermiculatum«, which used very small stones, to larger tesserae, whose colourful nature stood out more. Stone was no longer the only material – it had been necessary for floor mosaics because of its durability. More delicate materials also become options: vitreous enamel, on a colourful or on a gold or silver-leaf base, terracotta, mother-of-pearl and porphyry. The mosaicists had also recognized the expressive possibilities that arise when the tesserae are not laid parallel to the base, but at an angle to the grouted surface. If there were a gold ground, this would give the mosaic a mystical sheen.

The effect of this religious art was so strong that it came back all the way from Byzantium to the West, and to Sicily in particular, where some examples exist from the time of the Norman kings. The works were produced by immigrant or abducted Byzantine artist groups or by local mosaic schools practising the Byzantine style. In 1143 work began on decorating the Cappella Palatina in the royal palace in Palermo, where the images of the Sala di Ruggiero date from 1170. The Martorana was also given mosaics in 1143. The mosaics in Cefalù Cathedral date back to 1148, and in 1179–82 the genre, which used elaborate materials to achieve qualities of subtle spirituality, reached a final climax in the cathedral of Monreale (6340 sq m/7585 sq yd of wall surface).

Gothic   In 1174 the Norman king William II had given Monreale a large Benedictine abbey, but in the following Hohenstaufen era the reformed order of the Cistercians with its Gothic architecture became more prominent (Santa Maria degli Alemanni in Messina, chapel of the hospice of the Teutonic Knights; 12th–13th century, restored as a ruin). The Hohenstaufens are distinguished not by their church building, however; instead they built castles (Catania, Augusta, Syracuse), whose best-known and most consummate example, Castel del Monte, is not in Sicily, but in Apulia.

When the Hohenstaufen era, the »epoca sueva« and the Anjevin era were over and Sicily was ruled by the House of Aragon, the aristocracy gained much more influence over the central power. »Thus the 14th century became a period of great feudal lords. ... The most prominent name is that of the Chiaramonte family (›età chiaramontana‹, ›stile chiaramontano‹ 14th century)« (W. Krönig). The strengthening of feudalism was expressed in the many palaces (such as Chiaramonte in Favara and Palermo, Sclàfani in Palermo), as well as in the cathedrals and newly founded towns.

Renaissance   Between 1415 and 1712 Sicily was governed by Spanish viceroys. As a result the island only gradually opened up to the forms of the Italian Renaissance. Sicily experienced a late **»Catalan Gothic«** style that was dominant until the 16th century. An example of this style is the large portico of Palermo Cathedral (around 1465). A typically Sicilian mix of Gothic and Renaissance elements can be found in churches such as Santa Maria della Catena in Palermo (around 1500). The most influential sculptors were Francesco Laurana (1420–1503) as well as the Gagini family with its artistic members Domenico

Catalan Gothic in Sicily: the portico of Palermo Cathedral

(1420–92) his significant son Antonello (1478–1536) and Gian Domenico (approx. 1503 – approx. 1567) as well as Vincenzo (1528–95) and Antonino (1541–75). A characteristic feature of this period was the endeavour to adorn the entire church interior with sculptural ornamentation; this was possible thanks to the new technique of making stucco figures. Masters of this art were the members of the Serpotta family: Giuseppe (1653–1719), Giacomo (1656–1732) and Procopio (1679–1755).

Sicily attracted many painters, but before Renato Guttuso it only produced one of international standing: Antonello da Messina. He is credited with having taught the Venetian painters the old Netherlandish form of oil painting with resin. In addition to this teaching activity, his own works still speak to us today. In Sicily, there are works by him in Messina (Museo Regionale), Syracuse (Museo Bellomo), Cefalù (Museo Mandralisca) and Palermo (Palazzo Abatellis). Antonello was born in Messina in around 1430. He was the son of a stonemason. His teacher was presumably the Neapolitan painter Colantonio, who had adopted the refined oil technique of artists from the Netherlands. Their influence can be explained by the political situation: Alfonso of Aragon, who had conquered Naples in 1442, brought Spanish and Catalan artists to his court, and they were under Flemish influence at the time. It is not known when Antonello was trained in Naples. He was back in Sicily in 1455. In 1475 he went to Venice, where his mastery of the oil technique had a lasting impact: he painted a picture for the Venetian church of San Cassiano,

Antonello da Messina

thereby creating »the standard Venetian altarpiece, as we know it from works by Giovanni Bellini and his contemporaries; it remained binding in this form for Venetian painting for almost half a century« (Jan Lauts). One of his main works, *St Sebastian* (now in Dresden), also dates back to this time. In 1476 Antonello was back in his home town of Messina and in 1479, still aged less than 50, he died. One of Antonello's major motifs was the **Annunciation**. It is a common subject in Sicilian museums. A polyptych in Messina (1473) depicts the Madonna and Child in the lower section and the Annunciation above it. The picture was damaged in the earthquake of 1908, but has not lost the splendour of its colours. The Madonna on the Annunciation picture in Syracuse was painted in 1474. Although this picture is severely damaged, at least the angel's hand, wings and face survive and Mary survives almost completely. The same model can be seen on the Annunziata in Munich and especially on those in Palermo. It is not known when exactly this late work, fortunately preserved in its entirety, was made. In addition to its colour quality, it has a veritable three-dimensional physicality. The austere beauty of the face is fascinating. It is surrounded by the calm blue of the cloak. The half-defensive, half-surrendering reaction of the girl to the message of the angel (not within the picture) is clearly visible in the position of the two hands that emerge in a very lively manner from the blue cloak.

From Baroque to the 18th century

The character of Sicilian towns is greatly influenced by their buildings constructed in the **Baroque** style. The desire for renewal, supported by substantial prosperity, led to towns such as Vittória (1607) and Palma di Montechiaro (1637) being re-founded. A major impetus came from the damage caused by the 1669 earthquake, which led to much new construction in southeastern Sicily, including in Belpasso, Catania and Vizzini. At the end of the 17th century there was even more building going on in the towns that had been destroyed by the 1693 earthquake. The geometrically planned towns of Ávola and Grammichele (hexagonal plan), Noto and Pachino (square plan) were built at this time. The towns of Caltagirone, Cómiso, Íspica, Módica, Ragusa and Scicli were also renovated or newly founded. In addition, many buildings were restored, modernized or newly built in the Baroque style. The Sicilian preference for exuberant ornamentation, borrowed from Lecce Mannerism, played an important role; secular buildings were given imaginatively designed balcony corbels, while interiors had elaborate staircases. Giovanni Battista Vaccarini (1702–68) mainly built in Catania. Rosario Gagliari and Vincenzo Sinatra (Noto), Giulio Lasso (Quattro Canti in Palermo), Giovanni Vermexio (bishop's palace and senatorial palace in Syracuse) and Andrea Palma (cathedral façade in Syracuse) also deserve mention.

A strong impulse emanated from the Roman »Ecclesia triumphans« of the Counter-Reformation, whose elements can be seen in Jesuit churches such as Casa Professa in Palermo. Dating from the

17th–18th centuries, promoted by Francesco Borromini (1599–1667), it features concave and convex church facades.

When Charles III commissioned the Albergo dei Poveri in Palermo in 1746, Baroque traditions continued to have an effect on neo-Classical design. The poor-house is a huge, ambitious structure, inspired by monasteries and palaces. One example of neo-Classicism, a style that was also prepared by artists such as Giacomo Serpotta (1656–

Balcony corbels on Palazzo Villadorato in Noto

1732) and Ignazio Marabitti and shaped by the architect Venanzio Marvuglia, is the monumental gate of the Botanical Garden (1785) in Palermo.

The 19th century brought revivalism to Sicily too. Examples of this include G. B. Basile's Teatro Massimo in Palermo (1875–97). It is not just in Palermo that the subsequent architectural development known variously as Art Nouveau or Stile Liberty found an outlet.

19th century

Literature

Sicily has produced world-class writers since Antiquity. They include Giovanni Verga (1840–1922); he wrote the words to Pietro Mascagni's opera *Cavalleria rusticana* as well as the novel *Mastro Don Gesualdo*. Then there are Federico De Roberto (1866–1927, *I Vicere*), **Luigi Pirandello** (1867–1936, Nobel Prize in 1934, *Six Characters in Search of an Author*), **Giuseppe Tomasi di Lampedusa** (1896–1957, *The Leopard*), the lyricist **Salvatore Quasimodo** (1901–68, Nobel Prize in 1959) as well as **Leonardo Sciascia** (1921–89, known for his crime fiction novels). In 1988 Gesualdo Bufalino (1920–96) was awarded the Strega literary prize for his novel *Night's Lies*. The most recent author to receive widespread attention is **Lara Cardella** (b. 1969), with her authentic novel *Volevo i pantaloni* (*Good Girls Don't Wear Trousers*, 1990). The crime fiction novels by Andrea Camilleri as well as those by Santo Piazzese (set in Palermo) and the nostalgic saga *Il Bastardo di Mautana* by Silvana Grasso have been translated into other languages.

Famous People

What connects the mathematical genius Archimedes with the resourceful Commissario Montalbano, or the Mafia stooge Salvatore Giuliano with Holy Roman Emperor Frederick II? Small tributes to well-known or less well-known individuals who shaped Sicily's reputation or who are associated with the island.

Archimedes (around 287–212 BC)

The mathematician and mechanical engineer Archimedes from Syracuse was friendly with Hieron II and his son Gelon, but also with the mathematician Dositheus, whom he met in Alexandria. He taught how to extract square roots, how to solve cubic functions and how to calculate the areas and circumferences of circles; he discovered how to calculate the centre of gravity and the law of the lever, the inclined plane and specific gravity. As a significant engineer, he built hydraulic machines (Archimedean screw) and catapults, which were successfully deployed in Syracuse's defence against the Romans. When Syracuse fell anyway in 212 BC, Archimedes was killed by a Roman soldier.

Mathematical genius

Vincenzo Bellini (1801–35)

Catania's most famous resident, Vincenzo Bellini, was born in this town in 1801. His father and grandfather, both directors of music in the cathedral, educated him. He studied at the conservatory in Naples and quickly received recognition for operas he composed for the Neapolitan theatre and La Scala in Milan (e.g. *Bianca e Fernando*, 1826). He moved to Paris in 1833. His lyrical, dramatic style influenced even Verdi and Wagner (*La Somnambula*, *Norma*, both 1831). He fell ill at the age of 34. It was believed to be cholera, and he died lonely and abandoned. Initially laid to rest in Paris, his coffin was moved to Catania Cathedral 40 years later.

Andrea Camilleri (b. 1925)

The director and screenwriter, who has lived in Rome for a long time now, has topped the international bestseller charts for years with his entertaining crime fiction novels set in Sicily. His main character, Commissario Montalbano, investigates in Vigàta and Montelusa, the fictitious and yet very typical locations on the island, where »sicilianità« comes alive on the page. Those so inclined can discern in these places modern-day Porto Empédocle, the author's birthplace, and the neighbouring provincial capital Agrigento. Here is a short selection of his global successes, all of which feature a culinary aspect: *The Terracotta Dog*, *The Shape of Water*, *The Snack Thief*, *The Voice of the Violin* and *The Patience of the Spider*. His Italian, spiced up with Sicilian, frequently gives translators some tricky challenges. Only southern Italians well-versed in his dialect are able to fully appreciate his linguistic gymnastics.

Director, screenwriter and crime fiction author

◀ Camilleri fan club: www.vigata.org

← *Maria Grazia Cucinotta as a young widow in the Academy Award-winning film »Il Postino«*

Domenico Caràcciolo (1711–89)

Freethinker and politician Domenico Caràcciolo, from an aristocratic Neapolitan family of Greek origin, was an enlightened freethinker, who was in Paris as an emissary of the Kingdom of Naples and in 1781 assumed the office of viceroy in Sicily, which he held until his death. Together with the economist Paolo Balsamo he tried to reduce the privileges of the Sicilian barons and to put through an agricultural reform. He failed, just as Vittorio Amadeo of Savoy (1700–20) and Charles III of Naples had; his ideas of enlightened despotism could not be asserted against the aristocracy.

Maria Grazia Cucinotta (b. 1969)

Actress Her enchanting character role as a voluptuous young landlady at the side of the unforgotten Massimo Troisi in the nostalgic, Oscar-winning southern Italian film *Il Postino* (*The Postman*) made the black-haired beauty from Messina the »new« Sophia Loren over night. This image of Mediterranean seductress was emphasized by her lead role in the post-war epic *Malena*, by Sicilian director Giuseppe Tornatore. The fact that she is a happily married mother does not stop Italy's men dreaming of spending their wedding night with her, according to opinion polls. Her step from successful, but silent model in Milan to actress was a brave one, because she first had to take elocution courses to get rid of her accent. Hollywood has also long since discovered her, as the opponent of James Bond in *The World is Not Enough* and as Mary Magdalen in Mel Gibson's *The Passion of the Christ*. She does not feel above Italian comedies such as *Miracolo a Palermo* either.

Dionysius I of Syracuse (around 430–367 BC)

Brilliant commander Dionysius I founded the longest and most powerful tyranny of Antiquity. He seized sole rule of Syracuse, initially by legal means, by having himself elected the sole commander in 405 BC and subsequently installing a bodyguard in response to a sham assassination attempt. In order to protect himself from domestic enemies, Dionysius developed the island of Ortygia into a fort. He increased his following by dispossessing the oligarchs and by distributing land to his mercenaries. He defeated the democrats who besieged him in his fort, and in 403 BC he defeated the Ionian cities of eastern Sicily and moved their populations to Syracuse. He turned Syracuse into Sicily's strongest fortress by extending Euryalus Castle. It was during his reign that the catapult was constructed in Syracuse. In 398 BC he attacked the unprepared Carthaginians and advanced to Sicily's western tip. Dionysius further extended the power of Syracuse by his policies regarding Italy (conquest of Rhegium in 386, colonies on Dalmatian islands and at the mouth of the River Po in 385–384). In 368

Athens declared him an honorary citizen and in 367 agreed a defensive allegiance with him. After having ruled on his own for 38 years, he died in battle with Carthage.

Frederick II of Hohenstaufen (1194–1250)

Emperor

Frederick II, son of Emperor Henry VI and Constance, the heiress to the Norman throne, was elected King of the Romans (designating him the imperial heir) in 1196, and in 1198, after his father's death, he became King of Sicily. His mother put him under the guardianship of Pope Innocent III, who supported Frederick's claim to be King of Germany in 1211. Frederick undertook an adventurous trip from Sicily to Germany, where he was crowned king in Mainz (1212) and again in Aachen (1215). In 1220 he was crowned emperor in Rome. Later Frederick returned to Germany only once, in 1235–36. In Sicily he created an efficient bureaucracy. Tensions arose with the pope because of the Fifth Crusade, which the pontiff had agreed to but had repeatedly delayed, and which Frederick then undertook in 1228–29 despite having been excommunicated. He managed to achieve, without bloodshed, the restitution of the holy sites in Jerusalem and crowned himself King of Jerusalem there. His quarrel with the pope continued in the period that followed. However, even the deposition announced by Pope Innocent IV in Lyon in 1245, and the naming of rival kings, were not able to shatter

Frederick's sense of mission. He mostly resided in Apulia, which he preferred to Sicily. He built a number of castles here, the most famous being Castel del Monte.

Frederick II was labelled »stupor mundi«, the »wonder of the world«, during his lifetime. Having grown up in Palermo, he had acquired an extensive education, particularly by consorting with Arab scholars. He promoted philosophical, mathematical and scientific studies, created a Sicilian school of poetry and wrote a much-heeded book about falconry. After his death legend placed him in Mount Etna, from which he will emerge again at the end of time.

Salvatore Giuliano (1922–50)

People's hero or mafioso?

Salvatore Giuliano, for some a people's hero, for others a criminal and Mafia stooge, died on the morning of 5 July 1950, pierced by the bullets of a submachine gun.

His career, impressively portrayed by the Italian director Francesco Rosi (*Salvatore Giuliano*, 1961) and Michael Cimino (*The Sicilian*, 1988), began on 2 September 1943 on a small street near Montelepre, the town of his birth, when he was caught smuggling by carabinieri. During the exchange of fire that followed he killed a police officer and fled to the mountains. He and his gang were always able to count on the support of the people, in return for which he showed his gratitude with money. He also had friends among the separatists who sought Sicilian independence from Italy. They placed one of their main fighting platoons under Giuliano's command. In

that way he was even able to continue his mischief in the name of Sicilian independence. The vain bandit liked giving interviews, wrote letters to ministers and governments and even offered Sicily to the President Harry S. Truman as a US state (the White House never responded to him). The government in Rome sent out around 2000 carabinieri in order to capture him, but they would never have succeeded on their own. In 1947 he began working for the Mafia and, at their behest, had bullets fired into a crowd on a communist-organized May Day event that the »Honourable Society« believed to be a threat to the upcoming elections. Among the eleven dead and 50 seriously wounded individuals were women and children. His reputation as a friend of the people was thus lost, but he still enjoyed Mafia protection. However, then the unbelievable happened: he killed five members of the Mafia. As a result there were allegedly negotiations between the government and the »Honourable Society« to put an end to his activities once and for all. Immediately a traitor from Giuliano's own ranks was available to reveal his hiding place to the carabinieri in Castelvetrano.

Renato Guttuso (1912 – 1987)

Painter   Renato Guttuso is one of the best-known Italian painters of the 20th century. He was born in Bagheria in 1912, the son of a surveyor. He learned how to work with brushes and paint in the shop of a cart painter in 1923. After dropping out of legal studies, he decided to become a painter. Just three years later, and purely self-taught, he had his first important exhibition in Milan. Guttuso was a politically committed artist. His paintings in strong, warm colours are representational, committed to critical realism. One of his greatest role models was his friend Picasso.

Leoluca Orlando (b. 1947)

Almost more popular abroad than in his Sicilian home, the charismatic politician and two-time mayor of Palermo was long considered the figurehead of the civil anti-Mafia alliance. Despite the catchy slogan »Sindaco di Sicilia« (mayor of Sicily) he lost the election to become president of Sicily in a landslide defeat by the candidate of the Berlusconi movement »Casa della Libertà«. Orlando has made a name for himself as an author of autobiographical books and as an internationally sought-after specialist in the battle against organized crime.

Politician

Luigi Pirandello (1867–1936)

The author Luigi Pirandello came from Agrigento. He studied literature and history in Palermo, Rome and Bonn. He founded the Teatro d'Arte in Rome in 1925 and became its manager and director. Pirandello was among the most innovative Italian storytellers and playwrights of the 20th century. Committed to the Italian novella tradition, he preferred subjects such as the boundary between illusion and reality in narrative literature and dramatic art. Psychological analysis takes centre stage in all of his works: every character wears a mask, which also changes all the time, depending on the situation the character is in and on the other people who are around, watching. He became known around the world through his drama *Six Characters in Search of an Author* (1921). He was awarded the Nobel Prize for Literature in 1934. The brothers Paolo and Vittorio Taviani turned Pirandello's stories into films under the titles *Kaos* and *E tu ridi*, in 1984 and 1998 respectively.

Author

Salvatore Quasimodo (1901–68)

Salvatore Quasimodo from Módica was one of the most renowned modern Italian lyricists. The Sicilian landscape and Antiquity were subjects he addressed a lot in his early »hermetic« poems. A second phase dealt with the subjects of his time: war, resistance, suffering, loneliness and love. He was awarded the Nobel Prize for Literature in 1959.

Lyricist

Roger II (1095–1154)

Norman king Roger II from the Norman House of Hauteville, became the count of Sicily on the death of his father, Roger I. He extended his domain to Calabria, Apulia and to what is now the Tunisian coast in northern Africa, territories which were granted to him as a kingdom by the pope in 1130. That same year he had himself crowned king in Palermo. By choosing Christmas as the date for his coronation, he followed in the footsteps of the imperial coronation of Charlemagne, while the pictorial representations (mosaic in the Martorana) were in line with the sacred traditions of the Byzantine Empire. He founded a modern bureaucracy and emerged as a builder of Norman-Sicilian churches (Cefalù, Cappella Palatina in Palermo) and palaces.

Leonardo Sciascia (1921–89)

Crime fiction author and writer Leonardo Sciascia, for a long time Italy's most famous crime-fiction author, was born in Racalmuto near Agrigento, the son of a miner. After working as a teacher in the town of his birth until 1957, he became an author. His poems, stories and crime fiction examined the historical roots of an unjust society dominated by violence. He stubbornly denounced the influence of the Mafia on public institutions. As a member of the committee inquiring into the Moro affair, he shocked the public with a theory first voiced by him, namely that Aldo Moro had been deliberately sacrificed by the politicians.

In his books he combines fiction with historical facts, such as in *The Day of the Owl*, *Sicilian Uncles*, *To Each His Own*; *The Mystery of Majorana*; *The Moro Affair*. His heroes detect the machinations of the powerful, but ultimately fail in the face of corruption.

Elvira Giorganni Sellerio (1936–2010)

Author and publisher The bibliophilic books by Sellerio editore Palermo (collana blu) with their blue covers are an unmistakable sight on Italy's bookshelves. Supported by Leonardo Sciascia (► above) and the anthropologist Antonino Butitta, Elvira Giorganni Sellerio, who studied law and was a committed human rights activist, and her husband, photographer Enzo Sellerio, took the brave step of going into publishing in 1969. From 1979 until her death in 2010 Elvira Sellerio ran her publishing company on her own. She first published the successful Sicilian authors Giuseppe Bufalino, Andrea Camilleri (► above) and Anto Piazzese. The list of titles published by her has grown to more than 2000 (information: www.sellerio.it).

Giuseppe Tomasi di Lampedusa (1896–1957)

Author Giuseppe Tomasi, Duke of Palma and Prince of Lampedusa, came from an old Palermitani family. Until 1925 he was an officer. While

Mussolini was in power he spent a lot of time outside the country, and in 1954 wrote his only novel, *The Leopard* (published posthumously in 1958). The subject is the decline of a Sicilian aristocratic family from the time of Garibaldi to the eve of the First World War. The novel's depiction of an historical era reveals much about the character of Sicily and its people and is at the same time a subtle and colourful cross-section through the mind of a man on the verge of modern times.

Giovanni Verga (1840–1922)

Giovanni Verga was born near Catania in 1840. Inspired to write by a teacher, he initially wrote political historical novels. His first success came with *Carbonari of the Mountain* (1861), in which he addressed the rebellion in Calabria against the French under Murat.

Author

In his later works he began writing, from personal memory, about the lives, customs and habits of Sicilian farmers and fishermen. His talent for observation and objectivity made him one of the most significant representatives of Verismo, a literary movement that arose in Italy in around 1870, in which the truth was to take the place of the beautiful, and the terrible and ugly side of life was to be shown too, a movement clearly influenced by French naturalism. Following the example of Zola's novel cycle *Rougon-Macquart*, Verga started a cycle of five volumes entitled *I Vinti*, about the social climb and fall of a fishing family after 1860. Two volumes were published: *I Malavoglia* and *Mastro Don Gesualdo* (1881 and 1889); they are set in the area around Acireale. His novella *Cavalleria rusticana*, set to music by Mascagni in 1889, is also world famous.

Practicalities

HOW TO GET TO SICILY –
BY PLANE OR BY CAR AND
BOAT? GET ANSWERS
TO THESE AND FURTHER
QUESTIONS, AS WELL AS
TIPS AND ADDRESSES HERE –
BEST BEFORE YOU GO!

Accommodation

Big choice   The accommodation spectrum ranges from luxurious to basic, from city and rural hotels to agriturismi, holiday lets and private accommodation. The accommodation directory »Where to sleep in Italy: Sicily« (available through ENIT, ► Information) provides an overview. Price-conscious travellers will find recommended addresses at www.sicilyhotelsnet.it (English version available); the 3-star hotels listed here stand out as good value for money, but do not expect a particularly special or romantic ambience. For travellers with somewhat deeper pockets, who care about a stylish to classy ambience, the website »Le Soste di Ulisse« (»The Stations of Ulysses«; www.lesostediulisse.it, in Italian) is an excellent source. It lists outstanding restaurants, special hotels as well as selected vineyards on Sicily.

Price Categories

- The hotels recommended in this travel guide are divided into the following price categories (double room per night without breakfast):
Luxury: from EUR 190
Mid-range: EUR 80 – 190
Budget: up to EUR 80

Agriturismo   Agriturismo means »holidaying in the countryside«. The range of accommodation is wide, encompassing campsites, rooms on farms, comfortably furnished apartments and holiday lets.

Bed & breakfast   The market leader in brokering private accommodation is »Bed & Breakfast Italia«. The choices range from rooms (not en-suite, 2 stars) to accommodation in renowned historic buildings (en-suite, 4 stars). The local tourist information offices will also help with finding accommodation.

Camping and Caravanning
Wild camping ►   There are around 100 campsites on Sicily and the surrounding islands. During the peak season (mid-July – mid-Sept) it is advisable to book in advance. Camping is not allowed except on authorized sites. Those travelling with motor homes and caravans can spend a night on a car park or in a rest stop, as long as this is not expressly forbidden. Campsite directories are published by ENIT (► Information) and by the Italian camping club.

Hotels   Hotels are divided into five categories in Italy, from luxury hotels with five stars down to basic accommodation with one star. In addition to these options, there are other facilities which are not part of this classification. The number of stars provides only limited information about the actual comfort levels and prices, which can vary significantly depending on the season and region. During the summer months a double room on the coast can cost three times what the same room would cost inland.

USEFUL ADDRESSES

AGRITURISMO

▶ **Agriturist Sicilia**
Via A. d. Giovanni 14
90144 Palermo
Tel. 0 91 34 60 46
www.agriturist.it

▶ **Turismo Verde Sicilia**
Via Remo Sandron 65
90143 Palermo
Tel. 0 91 30 81 51 and 0 91 34 58 78
www.turismoverde.it

▶ **Further information**
www.terranostra.it
www.enexa.com/agriturismo

BED & BREAKFAST

▶ **B & B Italia**
Corso Vittorio Emanuele II 282
00186 Roma
Tel. 0 66 87 86 18
www.bbitalia.it, www.bbsicilia.
com, www.italiabb.com

CAMPING/CARAVANNING

▶ **Federazione Italiana del Campeggio e del Caravaning**
Via Vittorio Emanuele 11
50041 Calenzano (Firenze)
Tel. 0 55 88 23 91
www.federcampeggio.it
wwww.camping.it

YOUTH HOSTELS

▶ **Youth Hostels Association**
Trevelyan House, Dimple Road
Matlock DE34 3 YH
Tel. 0 16 29 / 59 26 00
www.yha.org.uk

▶ **Associazione Italiana Alberghi per la Gioventù**
Via Cavour 44
00184 Roma
Tel. 0 64 87 11 52
www.aighostels.com

In hotels and restaurants the service fee is included in the price, however 5 – 10 % of the bill is expected as a tip (mancia). In bars and cafés the service fee is not included, so give 12 – 15 %.

Tips

Italian youth hostels (alberghi per la gioventù) are part of Hostelling International. An HI membership card is necessary to stay at one, available for example through the YHA. Sicily has youth hostels in Catania, Palermo, Piazza Armerina and Noto (also see www.aighostels.com), where advance booking is advisable.

Youth hostels

Arrival · Before the Journey

The long journey by car is time-consuming (allow two days to Sicily from the Swiss or French border) and expensive (motorway tolls). The car ferries crossing the Strait of Messina (Villa San Giovanni –

By car

ARRIVAL

BY AIR

▶ **Air One**
www.flyairone.it (London Gatwick to Milan with further connections to Catania and Palermo)

▶ **Alitalia**
www.alitalia.com (many Italian domestic flights)

▶ **easyjet**
www.easyjet.com (London Gatwick to Catania and Palermo)

▶ **Ryanair**
www.ryanair.com (London Stansted to Palermo)

AIRPORTS ON SICILY

▶ **Catania Fontanarossa**
Fontanarossa, 7km/4mi south of Catania
Shuttle bus to Piazza Repubblica and the main station
Tel. 09 57 23 91 11
www.aeroporto.catania.it

▶ **Palermo Falcone-Borsellino**
Punta Raisi, 32km/20mi west of Palermo
shuttle bus and Trinacría-Express to the central station
Tel. 0800 541 880, www.gesap.it

▶ **Reggio di Calabria Aeroporto dello Stretto Tito**
Minniti, 4km/2.5mi outside town
Bus connections to the main station, to the harbour of Reggio (from here hydrofoils to Messina) and to Messina
Tel. 09 65 64 05 17, www.sogas.it

▶ **Tràpani Sen. Vincenzo Florio**
Birgi, 15km/9mi south of Tràpani

Shuttle bus to Corso Italia 52; the Bus Navetta runs between the airport and Stazione Marittima (ferry terminal for the Aegadian Islands).
Tel. 09 23 84 25 02
www.trapaniairport.it

▶ **Comiso V. Magliocco**
20km/12mi northwest of Ragusa (7km/4mi north of Comiso) airport opened in 2011 for charter flights.
Tel. 09 32 96 14 67
www.soaco.it

BY BOAT

▶ **Shipping Companies**
Grandi Navi Veloci, www.gnv.it
Tirrenia / Siremar
www.tirrenia.com, www.siremar.it
Ùstica Lines, www.usticalines.it
Snav, www.snav.it
TTT Lines, www.tttlines.it
Trenitalia/Bluvia
www.trenitalia.de, www.rfi.it

▶ **Agencies**
Traghettionline
Tel. 89 21 12
www.traghettionline.net

Direct Ferries Europe
www.directferries.de

Armando Farina
Tel. 0 93 71/ 6 69 37 36
www.armandofarina.de

Neptunia
Tel. 700 63 78 86 42
www.neptunia.de

BY BUS

▶ **Eurolines**
www.eurolines.com

BY RAIL

▶ **Eurostar**
Tel. 08 705 / 186 186
www.eurostar.com

OTHER WEBSITES
www.seat61.com

www.nationalrail.co.uk – click on
Travel Abroad
www.thomascookpublishing.com
– buy complete European train
and ferry timetables here
www.trenitalia.com – Information
and reservations

Messina; approx. 30 mins) leave around the clock. During the summer months expect to have to wait a while. A pleasant alternative is to travel to Sicily by ship from Genoa or another port (▶p. 76).

◄ By boat

Motorways in Italy (to Salerno) are toll roads. The motorway tolls can either be paid in cash, by credit card or by Viacard, which is available from automobile clubs, at important toll points (»Punto Blu«), at filling stations and at motorway service areas.

Motorway tolls
◄ www.auto strade.it

For travellers starting in London, the simplest route is to take Eurostar to Paris and a high-speed TGV train to Milan or Turin, from where there are high-speed connections south to Rome. Alternative routes go from Paris to Zurich or, for those travelling to Italy from points further east, via Munich. From Munich, changing trains in Milan or Rome, the journey to Sicily takes around 20 hours. Information about schedules, prices and discounts, reservations and additional fees for sleeper carriages and fast trains is obtainable from travel agencies or from various websites. International tickets are valid for two months from the date of issue. The journey can be interrupted as many times as desired. Tickets bought in Italy are valid for 6 hours for distances of up to 200km/125mi and between 24 and 28 hours for distances over 200km/125mi. Tickets have to be stamped at the departure station in the orange machines.

By rail

Eurolines offers inexpensive coach trips to Sicily from other European countries, with a change in Italy – there are no direct coach connections from Britain. The travel time to Sicily from Italy's neighbouring countries is 26 – 40 hours.

By bus / coach

Sicily's two most important international airports are Catania and Palermo. Comiso Airport (Ragusa Province), which was opened in 2011, is meant to service international passenger charter flights. Birgi near Tràpani only runs domestic flights. Messina can also be reached via the airport near Reggio di Calabria (mainland). Direct connections from Britain are operated by easyjet and Ryanair. Air One, Alitalia and others fly from the Italian mainland to Sicily. There are **direct buses** to Messina, Taormina, Ragusa, Enna, Cefalù, Agrigento and Syracuse from Catania Airport, and to Tràpani from Palermo

By air

The longest suspension bridge in the world and a masterpiece of engineering: here as a computer simulation, the plan is to build a 3.3km/2mi bridge to span the strait between Messina and Reggio di Calabria on the Italian mainland

AN UMBILICAL CORD OF STEEL

Only two miles separate Messina from the Italian mainland. The dream of a fixed link is thousands of years old. The Romans wanted to build a bridge of boats during the Punic Wars. Charlemagne dreamed of a solid bridge. At the end of the 19th century there were plans to build a tunnel under the strait. Concrete plans have been in existence for 30 years now. Prime Minister Silvio Berlusconi wanted to see a »Mega Ponte« between Messina and Calabria, while Romano Prodi's government temporarily shelved the plans.

It would be the »largest bridge in the world« with a span of 3300m/3600yd, beating the current record-holder, the Akashi Kaikyo Bridge in Kobe by 1309m/1432yd. The two pillars, both 383m/1257ft high (Akashi Kaikyo Bridge: 298m/978ft, Empire State Building: 394m/1293ft, Eiffel Tower: 324m/1063ft) will rest on foundations 60m/200ft deep. Four steel ropes, 1.24m/4ft thick and 5.3km/3.3mi long, would support the whole construction. Every one of these steel ropes would consist of 44,352 wires, made into 504 bundles of 88 wires each. The steel ropes, weighing 166,800 tons, would be anchored in the ground on both sides of the strait with gigantic blocks made of reinfor-

ced concrete (238,000 cu m/8,400,000 cu ft and 328,000 cu m/11,600,000 cubic ft). The roadway would measure 3666m/4009yd in length, would be 60.4m/66yd wide and, at 66,500 tons, would also be comparatively light. There would be ten lanes, eight for cars and lorries and two for trains, running 60m/200ft above the sea. Up to 9000 vehicles and ten trains could cross the bridge every hour. The plans – estimated construction costs: six billion euros – would »bring Europe to the heart of the Mediterranean« and turn the combined city of Messina-Reggio di Calabria into the »capital of the Mediterranean and northern Africa«, according to enthusiastic politicians and investors.

Opposition to the project

Critics object that, in the light of its antiquated single-track train lines, Sicily needed »real infrastructure and not cathedrals in the desert«. They object that corrupt politicians and the Mafia in particular sense the »deal of the century« here: up until the start of 2003 the semi-governmental operating company »Stretto di Messina« spent more than 100 million euros in planning costs alone. They object that the funding plans, 50% state-funded, 50% from private investors, to be recouped by levying a toll, are not realistic because of inadequate traffic volumes (drivers currently cross the strait in half an hour on a ferry; however, during peak travel times this trip can take considerably longer). Environmentalists raise the concern that around 140 fish species in the strait would be decimated as a result of the enormous structure and that migratory birds would not recognize their nesting sites anymore.

Finally, there are two »natural« enemies to the project: winds reaching up to 150kph/90mph, and the earth itself. The region is one of the seismically most dangerous in the world, as this is where the African and Eurasian plates collide. Every decade the Calabrian mainland moves by around 1.5cm/0.6in and the landmass on the Sicilian side by 0.4cm/0.16in. The elastically constructed bridge could cope with this movement, but it also has to withstand quakes through which the plates unload their tension. The last major earthquake in 1908 (experts estimate it must have reached 7.1–7.24 on the Richter scale) destroyed Messina and claimed more than 80,000 lives in Calabria and Sicily. According to the plans, the bridge could withstand an earthquake of up to 7.1 on the Richter scale and winds of up to 270kph/170mph.

However, regardless of whether the »Mega Ponte« across the Strait of Messina is really built or not, bridge builders have already set their sights on bigger endeavours, such as a crossing of the Strait of Gibraltar (14km/8.5mi) or a connection between Russia and Alaska across the Bering Strait (85km/53mi at the narrowest point).

From Reggio di Calabria to Sicily by ferry

Airport. There are daily **flights** to the islands of Lampedusa (from Palermo) and Pantellería (from Palermo and Tràpani). Information is available from ENIT (▶ Information), travel agencies and airline companies.

To Sicily by boat There are regular passenger and car ferries (duration: approx. 25 mins) between Villa San Giovanni and Reggio di Calabria on the mainland and Messina on Sicily. Trains also board ferries in Villa San Giovanni.

There are also ferry connections between Sicily and Genoa (20 hrs to Palermo), Livorno (Palermo 17 hrs), from Rome (Civitavecchia Palermo Harbour 15 hrs), Naples (Catania 10.5 hrs; Palermo 11 hrs; Tràpani 6.5 hrs), Salerno, Cagliari, Malta, Valencia (Spain) and Tunisia (Tràpani 11 hrs).

To the islands ▶ Aegadian Islands: ferries from Tràpani

Lipari (Aeolian) Islands: ferries and hydrofoils form Milazzo and Naples, in summer also from Palermo and Cefalù

Pantellerìa from Tràpani and Mazara del Vallo

Lampedusa from Porto Empédocle (Agrigento)

Ùstica from Palermo and Naples

The vessels in use are traghetti (ferries) and the faster aliscafi (hydrofoils) or catamarani (catamarans). Book via travel agencies, through shipping companies and through agencies. Price lists, schedules and information about the permitted vehicle measurements on the vessels are available from the same sources.

Ferries tend to get booked out during the Italian summer holidays, so it is necessary to book several weeks in advance through shipping companies, in travel agencies or other agencies.

◀ Book in good time

Travel Documents

A valid identity card or passport suffices for citizens of EU countries and Switzerland. The same applies to citizens of Canada, Australia, New Zealand, the United States and certain other countries (enquire) for visits to Italy of up to 90 days.

Identity card

In the event of stolen documents, consulates will provide assistance, but the first port of call should be the police, because a copy of the police report is vital. The relevant embassy or consulate address is available from the your country's foreign ministry website (▶ p. 91). Replacements are far easier to come by if you have paper or electronic copies of the relevant documents.

◀ Loss

Anyone wishing to drive in Sicily must have a valid licence and vehicle registration. Vehicles must be marked with the oval country ID if they do not have a European number plate.

Vehicle papers

Anyone wishing to travel to Italy with pets (dogs, cats) will require an EU pet passport, which confirms that the animals are up to date with their rabies vaccinations. In addition it is necessary to either tattoo the animals or have a microchip implanted to allow its identification. A muzzle and leash must also be brought.

Pets

Customs Regulations

Within the EU the movement of goods for private purposes is largely duty-free: the following maximum quantities are in place to demarcate the line between private and commercial use: 800 cigarettes, 400 small cigars, 200 cigars, 1 kg tobacco, 10 litres of spirits, 20 litres of intermediate goods, 90 litres of wine (of which a maximum of 60 litres of may be sparkling wine) and 110 litres of beer. In the event of an inspection, make it clear that the goods really are just for private consumption.

EU
◀ Information: www.hmrc.gov.uk/customs

For travellers from non-EU countries the duty-free limits for people over the age of 17 are 200 cigarettes or 100 small cigars or 50 cigarettes of 250 g of tobacco, 2 litres of wine and 2 litres of sparkling wine or 1 litres of spirits of more than 22 % or 2 litres of spirits of less than 22 %, 500 g coffee or 200 g coffee extracts, 100 g tea or 400 g tea extract, 50 g perfume or 25 ml of eau de toilette. Gifts up to a value of EUR 430 also fall under the duty-free bracket.

Entry from non-EU countries

Beaches

In addition to cultural attractions, this **sunny island**, which has more than 1000km/600mi of coastline (1500km/900mi when including the smaller islands), is increasingly scoring as a destination for beach tourism among non-Italians. However, unlike on the mainland, beach tourism with »ombrelli e lettini« (»sunshades and sun loungers«) is limited to just a few beaches. Large tracts of coastline are, if they have not fallen victim to illegal construction, freely accessible. It is not until mid-May that the sea reaches temperatures of more than 20°C/70°F, which it then maintains until late autumn. Nevertheless, the Italians do not tend to get into the water before mid-July or after the end of August. A few beaches have managed to obtain the sought-after blue flag (www.blueflag.org) to prove their high water quality. The independent Italian environmental association Legambiente also tests the beaches for their water quality and other criteria and publishes the results on the website www.legambiente.it (click on Turismo, Guide Blu).

Overview
East coast ► | **Taormina** attracts the greatest number of bathers to Sicily. That was not always the case. The charming mountain town with its steep

Sun, sand and sea: enjoy them in Mondello, Palermo's popular beach resort

cliffs and tiny pebble bays was originally a place for the upper crust to enjoy the winter season. Today most sun worshippers can be found along the many miles of pebble beaches around **Letojanni** and in the Bay of **Naxon**. The sometimes rocky Ionian beaches along the Riviera dei Ciclopi, between Taormina and Catania, are of more interest to the locals, because the high population density along the coast is not conducive to good water quality. The water of the coastline north of Syracuse, which is used for industrial purposes, also suffers. There are, however, some nice sandy and gently sloping **natural beaches** between Syracuse and **Capo Passero** as well as to the west of it. That is also where Club Méditerranée has its huts near Camerina. Apart from the industrial juggernaut Gela and the city of Agrigento, the choice of clean sandy beaches with dunes along the southern coast is huge. Along the short western coast, lagoons and salt pans do not leave much room for beach life.

◀ Southern coast

◀ Western coast

◀ Northern coast

San Vito lo Capo on the north coast is a family-friendly seaside town with excellent sandy beaches. Adjoining it to the south is Zingaro Natural Park, whose magical bays can only be reached on foot. Those who really want to go for a dip in Palermo should hire a sun lounger in the swanky sandy bay of **Mondello**. Unadulterated seaside fun further east can only be had in **Cefalù** again. The beaches towards Milazzo and Capo d'Orlando have been opened up less to tourism. The lagoons around **Capo Tíndari** have their very own appeal.

The **islands around Sicily** have absolutely wonderful beaches. Those of the Pelagie Islands south of Agrigento are sandy with crystal-clear water, and sea turtles lay there eggs there. During mid-summer Linosa, Lampione and Lampedusa are firmly in the hands of the northern Italian in-crowds. There are no sandy beaches on the black volcanic island of Pantellerìa, but it boasts coastal lakes fed by thermal springs that are even warm enough for bathing in the winter. The marine park around the Aegadian Islands in the west of Tràpani guarantees the highest water quality. Sandy and bizarre rocky beaches can be found on Favignanna, hidden pebble bays on Lévanzo and Maréttimo. The crystal-clear sea and the rich fish stocks around volcanic Ùstica holds a particular appeal for divers and snorkellers. Despite their common volcanic origin, the seven Aeolian or Lipari Islands are very different. While Lìpari, Vulcano and Stròmboli also feature black lava beaches, they are otherwise dominated by steep cliffs and crystal-clear pebble bays. One special attraction is to swim between hot steam vents on Vulcano and between drifting pumice stones on Lìpari.

True beach heaven

There are no official nude beaches on Sicily, because nude bathing is generally not allowed and goes against Italian morals. There are, however, holiday villages on the islands of Filicudi and Lampedusa that have nude beaches, and also some remote places on Vulcano where people go skinny-dipping.

Naturism

Highlights The best beaches

Taormina – Isola Bella
The most popular beach with the most expensive sun loungers and the greatest flirt factor is situated right below the steep cliffs. Row to the Blue Grotto!
▸ page 414

Pozzallo
Child-friendly beaches and dunes with their positive environmental rating characterize this plain little coastal town south of Módica.
▸ page 267

Marina di Ragusa
Not remote, but the long sandy beaches to the west of the estuary of the Irminio River are very well cared for in summer.
▸ page 363

Eraclea Minoa
Chalk cliffs, like the white cliffs of Dover, with a pine forest below as well as an endless sandy beach that crosses over into dunes. Rarely overcrowded, even in mid-summer
▸ page 199

Marinella di Selinunte
Pleasant family beach with lots of beach bars at the foot of the ancient acropolis. The wide sandy beach a few miles east, in the estuary of the Belice River, has been spared illegal development, save for one hotel.
▸ page 375

Favignana – Cala Rossa
The appeal of the Aegadian Islands is the turquoise water in the bizarre bay, where the white tuff was already quarried during the days of the Carthaginians.
▸ page 189

Mondello
The local beach of the island capital of Palermo since the Belle Époque. Art Nouveau villas, stripy sun loungers and beach huts as well as cheeky beach boys at the wide, well-tended Spiaggia of the fishing town with the Saracen tower. This is where Palermo's jeunesse dorée come to sun themselves.
▸ page 337

San Vito lo Capo and Riserva dello Zingaro
Sandy family beaches in San Vito, crystal-clear water and lonely pebble bays in the pretty nature park
▸ page 429 and 164

Cefalù
Wide, well-tended sandy beach right next to a picture-book fishing town. Swim out a little way to see the cathedral looking like a mirage from the sea.
▸ page 183

Capo d'Orlando
The hang-out of Sicilian provincial gigolos: the extensive pebble beaches in the youthful seaside resort with charming cliffs on the north coast are firmly in the hands of the locals; beach life and surfing during the summer months.
▸ page 160

Oliveri – Capo Tìndari
Sicily's boldest surfers race past huge sandbanks with shallow laghetti.
▸ page 424

Salina – Pollara
Aeolian natural beach set in a magnificent crater landscape: this is where the movie *The Postman* was filmed.
▸ page 234

Children

Italians have a special relationship to children, regardless of whether it is their own or other people's »bambini«. Children are a major factor in determining the course of the day. However, there are no special facilities for children on Sicily, bar a few exceptions. Apart from the customary hits such as beaches (►beaches) and ice cream parlours there are a Museo delle Marionette and a puppet theatre in Palermo (only in Italian; ►Baedeker Special p. 342), as well as the **Città dei Ragazzi**, children's city. There is a fun **labyrinth** in the palace grounds (►Ragusa) and a little outside Catania is »**Etnaland**« with a safari park, a dinosaur world and a water park (mid-March – mid-Sept, daily 9am–4pm, zoo closed on Wed; motorway towards Palermo, exit Gerbini, www.etnaland.eu). **Water adventure parks** can be found in Monreale (www.acquaparkmonreale.it) and Marina di Ragusa. Old crafts and workshops can be experienced in Buscemi, a museum village in the southeast of Sicily (p. 308). The widest selection of activities will definitely be offered by a club holiday, where children are generally looked after and entertained well.

Electricity

Sicily's electricity grid supports an alternating current of 220 Volts. The sockets will only take standard continental European plugs, so for travellers from Britain and North America adapters are necessary (spina di adattamento).

Emergency

► **Free emergency numbers**
From mobile phones and landlines (Carabinieri, Soccorso pubblico):
Tel. 112

► **Fire brigade**
(Vigili fuoco)
Tel. 115

► **Cega Air Ambulance (world-wide service)**
Tel. +44(0)1243 621097
Fax +44(0)1243 773169
www.cega-aviation.co.uk

► **US Air Ambulance**
Tel. 800/948-1214 (US; toll-free)
Tel. 001-941-926-2490
(international; collect)
www.usairambulance.net

Etiquette and Customs

What goes down
well in Italy?
What doesn't?

Bella figura, an attractive external appearance, is an inner need for most Italian men and women. Even when they are just going to the post office or shopping at the market, when leaving the house, Italians like to dress up in public, following Coco Chanel's motto that a woman should always dress as if she could run into the man of her life. When in doubt, money should be spent on fashion (and good food) rather than on furniture or having the house façade painted. The Italians are therefore uncomprehending or amused by ill-mannered tourists who enter churches in flip-flops, visit galleries in shorts or sit in restaurants in sandals, or who even walk through the old town bare-chested. That would hardly even occur to the tifosi, the football fans of Juventus Turin, Lazio Roma or Sampdoria Genoa.

Baristas

The true leading performers in the thousand bars from Bolzano to Palermo also present a bella figura every morning: the baristas who provide steaming espressos usually wear proper serving jackets and dapper caps, serving foaming cappuccinos, freshly baked cornetti and glasses of fresh water to their customers calmly and with inimitable elegance. A seated breakfast is boring by comparison! Break free from the hotel routine and treat yourself to a colazione all'italiana. Give the men behind the counters a small tip. Service jobs are often poorly paid.

Taking photographs

A bella figura is also helpful for photographers. Most Italians are happy to be photographed. Use the opportunity to have a chat, which can quickly develop into a talent show. Often the neighbour also wants to get into the picture and the children beckon their entire class to come over, while the padrone insists that the waiters and waitresses are also included. A photograph is always a public event, a moment of being chosen and of joie de vivre.

Traffic

Italians are also spontaneous behind the wheel. Even though Berlusconi's government decided in 2004 that it would institute a central index for traffic offences on the pattern of other countries, southern Italians are particularly adept at overtaking others in their Fiats on the hard shoulder or at triple parking, all while remaining entirely unconcerned. It is nice when the traffic chaos sorts itself out after all and as many people as possible participate in that process with as many gestures as possible. At moments like that the streets turn into

In San Vito lo Capo

lively piazzas and the mechanized routine of everyday life is interrupted. The fact that this is about communication and almost never about proving who is in the right is demonstrated by a polite respect for pedestrians, which stands out positively, unlike in other Mediterranean countries.

If you who approach individual Italians and show them with a smile   Arrangiarsi
or a gesture that they are happy to be dealing with such a competent
and winning person, you will have a good time in Italy. Definitely
ask for the waiter or waitress's first name; it is better to call out a
»bravo«, »grande« or »bello« too many than too few. If something
does not work out, then be Machiavellian and practise the ancient
Italian art of »arrangiarsi«: when dealing with people from Tuscany,
Rome, Milan, Naples and Sicily, an understanding compliment will
produce the desired effect more quickly than threats, which, as you
may have suspected, damage the bella figura.

Festivals · Holidays · Events

The most important religious event of the year is Settimana Santa,
Holy Week. Further highlights include the Assumption of the Virgin,
various Marian pilgrimages, and Carnevale, which is celebrated almost
everywhere. During the summer many places host open-air
performances. Further information about the festivals in individual
locations can be found under the relevant headings in the chapter
»Sights from A to Z«.

▶ HOLIDAY CALENDAR

HOLIDAYS

1 January: New Year's Day; Capodanno

6 January: Epiphany; Epifania

Easter Monday: Lunedì dell'Angelo or Pasquetta

25 April: Liberation Day 1945; La Resistenza

1 May: Labour Day; Festa del Lavoro

2 June: Day of the Republic; Festa della Repubblica

15 August: Feast of the Assumption; Ferragosto; peak time for Italians to go on holiday

1 November: All Saints; Ognissanti

8 December: Feast of the Immaculate Conception; Immacolata Concezione

25 and 26 December: Christmas; Natale and Santo Stefano

EVENTS

▶ January

Epiphany: 6 January (Epifania), particularly impressive in Piana degli Albanesi

▶ February

Sagra del mandorlo in fiori: Beginning of February, almond blossom festival in Agrigento, in the Valle dei Templi

Sant'Àgata: 3 – 5 February, festival in honour of Saint Agatha in Catania (procession of the cannalori)

At Palio dei Normanni in Piazza Armerina the whole town gets involved

▶ February – March

Carnevale: Carnival (Shrove Tuesday) with processions, music and dance, in places such as Acireale, Sciacca – a carnival stronghold – and in Termini Imerese, Castelvetrano and Taormina; children's mask festival in Tràpani

▶ March – April

Vampa: 19 March, Feast of Saint Joseph (San Giuseppe) in Niscemi, Ribera and Salemi
Settimana Santa, Holy Week: Maundy Thursday and Good Friday processions and mystery plays in many places, such as in Caltanissetta, Marsala and Érice, Tràpani, Acireale, Enna, Isnello, Piana degli Albanesi, Gela
Easter: celebrating the Resurrection in Castelvetrano; celebration of La Diavolata in Adrano
Ballo dei Diavoli, devil's dance in Prizzi processions and dances performed by Albanians in magnificent costumes in Piana degli Albanesi

▶ April

Saint George's Day (San Giorgio): 23 April, all over Sicily, such as in Castelmola
Processions with Sicilian carts (carretti): End of April in Palermo and Taormina

▶ May

Classical plays in the Greek theatre in Syracuse (until June)
Saints' days: 1st Sunday in May, celebration in honour of Santa Lucìa in Syracuse and day of San Michele in Caltanissetta; 9 and 10 May, Day of San Alfio in Trecastagni
3 Sunday in May: Saluto alla Primavera, Primavera Barocca in Noto

Sagra del Tataratà: big local festival in honour of the Holy Cross, celebrated for more than 300 years on the last weekend in May in Casteltèrmini; in historical costumes

▶ June

Feast of Saint Peter: 29 June, the patron saint of fishermen is celebrated in every fishing village.

▶ July

International underwater show in Ùstica
U Fistinu in Palermo: 11 – 15 July, in honour of St Rosalia
La Luminaria: 24 / 25 July, feast in honour of San Giacomo (St James) in Caltagirone
Opera season in Castello Lombardo in Enna

▶ July – August

Taormina Arte: Festival with films, art exhibitions, plays and opera evenings in the ancient theatre in Taormina
Estate Ericina: Summer festival with classical music and plays in Érice
Orestiadi: Classical plays performed in the ruins of Gibellina (Information: ▶p. 180)
Classical plays in the Greek theatre in Segesta

▶ August

Palio dei Normanni: 13 August, equestrian competition in historical costumes in Piazza Armerina
Passeggiata dei Giganti: 14 and 15 August, commemoration of the legendary city founders Mata and Grifone in Messina with larger-than-life figures.
San Vito Jazz Festival: Jazz festival in San Vito lo Capo

▶ **September**
Harvest festival in many towns
Saints' festivals: 3–4 September,
pilgrimage to the Grotto of Rosalia
on Monte Pellegrino near Palermo
8/9 September, festival of the Black
Madonna in Tìndari and
festival of the Madonna of Gibilmanna

▶ **November**
Start of the opera season in
Catania, Messina and Palermo (it
ends in May)

*International week of
ecclesiastical music* in Monreale

▶ **December**
*Award of the »Brancati« literature
prize* in Zafferana Etnea
Feast of St Lucia: 13 December in
Syracuse
Christmas: Advent and nativity
plays in many towns, such as
Custonaci

Food and Drink

Eating habits
The Italian breakfast (colazione) is often limited to just a cappuccino or a caffè (espresso) with a pastry, such as a fresh croissant (cornetto). The hotels tend to cater to the habits of their foreign guests, however, and offer a more or less comprehensive breakfast buffet. It is still a good idea to have breakfast in a normal bar: at the counter with a tramezzino, a focaccia or something similar with ham, salami, cheese, tuna etc. Anyone still wanting something sweet after that can choose from various dolci. Lunch (pranzo) usually consists of an antipasto (starter), primo (pasta, risotto or soup), secondo (fish or meat) with vegetables (contorno) or salad (insalata). After that, choose between formaggio (cheese), dolce (dessert), gelato (ice cream) or frutta (fruit). An espresso completes the meal (only foreigners drink cappuccino). Some order it »corretto« (»corrected« with grappa, cognac, amaro or sambuca). Dinner (cena), during which the sequence of dishes is the same as at lunch, is rarely served before 7pm.

i **Price Categories**

■ The restaurants recommended in the chapter
»Sights from A to Z« of this travel guide are
divided into the following price categories
(3-course meal without wine):
Expensive: more than 35 €
Moderate: 20 – 35 €
Inexpensive: under 20 €

Restaurants
It is not customary for diners to choose their own table in Italian restaurants. Instead, guests wait to be seated. In addition to the normal prices for the food, some places add a service fee (servizio) and / or a cover charge (coperto). It is important to note that in August many places are closed, except in holiday resorts.

Italian temptations begin with the antipasti, the starters

In hotels and restaurants the service fee is included in the price. ◄ Tips
However, an additional tip (mancia) of 5 – 10 % of the bill is expected. In bars and cafés the service fee is often not included; in this
case it is customary to give 12 – 15 % as a tip.

Every restaurant must issue guests with a receipt (ricevuta fiscale)
that must be shown to tax-fraud investigators in the vicinity of the
restaurant upon request (failure to do so could result in a fine).

The Stars of the South

Sicily's cuisine is excellent. Firstly the island's chefs can tap into a
great culinary heritage, and secondly the products are top quality. Sicilian markets are among the most opulent and beautiful in the
world. There are plenty of fish, shellfish and crustaceans from the
sea, the meat from cattle, lamb, pigs and goats is exceptionally tasty,
fruit and vegetables flourish all year round and the forests provide
delicious fungi, while aromatic herbs, vegetables and leaf salads grow
in fields and meadows. Everything is served in a plentiful, colourful
and luxurious manner. The Arab influence is most noticeable in the
very sweet dolci and in the combination of savoury and sweet ingredients (such as raisins with meat). Muslims built the first pasta factory near Palermo in the early 10th century, and **pasta** remains the

queen of all the dishes. Everyone should try the famous »ncasciata« (pasta speciality from Ragusa) at least once in order to understand the Sicilian passion for pasta. Other good choices are »pasta con le sarde« (pasta with sardines), »pasta alla norma« (pasta with aubergines) and »cannelloni alla siciliana« (stuffed pasta). The Arab legacy, »cùscusu« (couscous) is equally popular. The Sicilian variant of this dish is enriched with fish and seafood and is available near Tràpani as well as on the nearby islands. As already mentioned, sweet dishes have a high standing; they are largely based on marzipan, almonds and candied fruits. They look colourful and imaginative, a little Baroque even. The following section introduces a small selection of regional specialities: tasty dishes for both Italians and holidaymakers from other countries:

Regional specialities

Arancini di riso: rice balls filled with meat and peas

Cannelloni alla catanese: pastry rectangles filled with cooked white meat, in a tomato sauce seasoned with sage leaves and covered in sheep's cheese

Cannoli di ricotta (a sweet dish): pastry rolls with curd

Caponata: cooked aubergines stuffed with capers, pumpkin, tomatoes and olives

Cassata siciliana: sweet dish with candied fruits, fresh curd, marzipan and sponge cake

Cobaita (sweet dish): sesame pastry with almonds and honey

Falso magro alla siciliana: veal, stuffed with a paste of chopped mortadella, cheese, eggs and mince meat, that is first fried and then stewed

Focacce: flat bread stuffed with vegetables

Girelli: veal croquettes, stuffed with parmesan and ham

Involtini: meat stuffed with cheese, onions, salami and eggs

Minestra di ceci: chickpea soup

Mpanata di pasqua: breaded lamb, particularly for Easter

Ncancarnancá: cheese soup

Pasta con le sarde: spaghetti with sardines, raisins, pine nuts, wild fennel and saffron

Pesce spada: swordfish; pesce spada a ghiotta: swordfish cut into thick slices, fried in olive oil and seasoned with a mix of tomato sauce, celery, capers, black olives and a little red wine vinegar; pesce spada a summarigghiu: swordfish in a sauce of oil, marjoram and red, roughly chopped chilli peppers; pesce spada ai ferri: grilled swordfish; pesce spada (involtini): as a roulade, seasoned with oriental spices

Pignolata (sweet dish): pastry in the shape of pine nuts, covered in syrup

Sarde a beccafico: sardines stuffed with breadcrumbs, bay and a little orange juice
Seppie ripiene: grilled squid, stuffed with grated pecorino and lots of parsley
Sfincioni: baked cheese with oil, pepper and tomatoes
Vope all'agrodolce: roasted sardines in an onion, vinegar and honey marinade
Spaghetti alla norma: spaghetti with fresh tomatoes and fried auber-gines (named after the opera by Vincenzo Bellini)

The standard drinks with every meal are wine (▶Wine) and mineral water (sparkling / still, con / senza gas). Beer (birra) is also available everywhere, both the light Italian type as well as German, Danish and Dutch brands.

Drinks

Health

In many places the Guardia Medica is available to provide medical care. Emergency services / first aid services (Pronto soccorso) are provided by hospitals (Ospedali) as well as by the White Cross (Cro-ce Bianca), the Green Cross (Croce Verde) and the Red Cross (Croce Rossa Italiana), whose addresses can be found in the first few pages of the telephone directory (Avantielenco). Dentists are listed in tele-phone books under »Medici dentisti«.

Medical care

UK residents have the right to be treated on the same terms as Ita-lians in Sicily if necessary. Travellers must obtain the **European Health Insurance Card** prior to departure (see https://www.ehic.org. uk/Internet/home.do) and present it to the doctor or in the hospital. If the card is not accepted, ask for the receipts and prescriptions. You may be able to apply for a refund. Non-EU residents must pay for their own treatments and medications (enquire about reimburse-ment from your health insurance).

Health insurance

Pharmacies (Farmacie) are generally open Mon – Fri 9am – 12.30pm and 4pm – 7.30pm. They close Wednesdays or Saturdays (but not all at once). A directory with the pharmacies that are open at night and on holidays (Farmacie di turno) can be found in the windows or on the doors of every pharmacy.

Pharmacies

Hot springs have been used in Sicily for therapeutic purposes since Antiquity. The major spa towns are Acireale, Castroreale, Sciacca, the island's largest and most modern spa centre, Termini Imerese and Alí Terme. Information: ENIT (▶ Information) and www.termeital iane.com.

Spas

Information

General information

The first port of call for information is the Italian National Tourist Office (**ENIT**, Agenzia Nazionale del Turismo). The region or the office of tourism (Assessorato Regionale al Turismo) are responsible for tourism policy on Sicily, as are the tourism offices of the nine provinces (addresses ► www.regione.sicilia.it/turismo). Information about local activities, addresses for accommodation etc. is available from the tourist information offices in the holiday resorts (Ufficio Informazioni, Pro Loco). These addresses can be found in the chapter »Sights from A to Z«.

● USEFUL ADDRESSES

INFORMATION AT HOME

► **Agenzia Nazionale del Turismo (ENIT)**
Office in UK
1 Princes St
London / W1B 2AY
Tel. 0 20 / 7408 1254 ,
fax 7399 3567
www.enit.it/en
Excellent website with general information, including addresses of offices in various countries.

IN USA

► **Italian State Tourist Board**
630 Fifth Avenue, Suite 1565
10111 New York
Tel. 212 245 48 22

ON SICILY

► **Assessorato Regionale al Turismo**
Via Emanuele Notarbartolo 9
90141 Palermo
Tel. 09 17 07 82 30

ONLINE

► **www.regione.sicilia.it/turismo**
Tourism website for Sicily in Italian and English

► **www.alice.it**
Italian web directory, yellow pages, atlas and search engine

► **www.sicilyweb.com**
A lot of information in Italian and English

► **www.itwg.com**
Hotel reservations in Italy

► **www.bestofsicily.com**
A treasure trove on (almost) all subjects to do with Sicily (in English)

► **www.emmeti.it**
Commercial tourism portal

► **www.museionline.it**
Lots of information in Italian about museums, cultural events and exhibitions

► **www.comuni-italiani.it**
The websites of many towns and communes, unfortunately only in Italian

► **www.parks.it**
Links to the three regional parks Parco dell'Etna, Parco delle Ma-

donie and Parco dei Nebrodi as well as to all the other protected areas on Sicily

► **www.pupisiciliani.it**
A website in Italian about the Sicilian puppet theatre (»Opera dei Pupi«)

► **www.sicilia.indettaglio.it**
Information on almost everything and almost every place. Also in English

► **www.movimento turismovino.it**
Wines and wine growers on Sicily

► **www.acena.it/sicilia.html**
Select Sicilian restaurants from different gourmet guides (in Italian)

► **www.stromboli.net**
Lots of information, photos, maps and more for those interested in volcanoes.

EMBASSIES IN ROME

► **Australian embassy in Rome**
Via Antonio Bosio 5
Tel. 06 85 27 21
www.italy.embassy.gov.au

► **British Embassy**
Via XX Settembre 80a
00187 Roma

Tel. 06 42 20 00 01
http://ukinitaly.fco.gov.uk/en/

► **Canadian embassy in Rome**
Via Zara 30
Tel. 06 85 44 41
www.canada.it

► **Embassy of the Republic of Ireland in Rome**
Piazza Campitelli 3
Tel. 06 69 79 121
www.ambasciata-irlanda.it

► **New Zealand embassy in Rome**
Via Clitunno 44
Tel. 06 853 75 01
www.nzembassy.com

► **Embassy of the United States**
Via Vittorio Veneto 121
00187 Roma
Tel. 06 46 741
http://italy.usembassy.gov/

CONSULATES IN SICILY

► **American Consulate**
Via Vaccarini 1
Palermo
Tel. 0 91 30 58 57
http://italy.usembassy.gov/

► **British Consulate**
Via Cavour 117
Palermo
Tel. 091 32 64 12
http://ukinitaly.fco.gov.uk/en/

Language

Italian developed from Latin and is closer to it than any of the other Romance languages. Lots of dialects developed, not least because of the country's earlier political disunity. During the 13th and 14th centuries Tuscan established its dominance and became the modern written language.

General information

Stress   In words with several syllables, it is usually the penultimate syllable that is stressed; if the stress is on the last syllable, this is marked by an accent (grave, e.g. città). If the stress is on the third syllable from last, an accent can be placed there too; this travel guide does so the first time a place name is given.

Basic phrasebook Italian

At a glance

Sì / No	yes / no
Per favore / Grazie	please / thank you
Scusi! / Scusa!	Excuse me!
Come dice?	Pardon?
Non La / ti capisco	I don't understand you (polite / familiar)
Parlo solo un po' di ...	I only speak a bit of ...
Mi può aiutare, per favore?	Could you help me please?
Vorrei ...	I would like ...
(Non) Mi piace	I (don't) like that
Ha ...?	Do you have ...?
Quanto costa?	How much is?
Che ore sono? / Che ora è?	What time is it?
Come sta? / Come stai?	How are you (polite / familiar)?
Bene, grazie. E Lei / tu?	Good, thanks. And you (polite / familiar)?

On the go

a sinistra / a destra / diritto	to the left / to the right / straight on
vicino / lontano	nearby / far away
Quanti chilometri sono?	How many kilometres is that?
Vorrei noleggiare ...	I would like to hire ...
... una macchina	... a car
... una bicicletta / una barca	... a bicycle / a boat
Scusi, dov'è ...?	Excuse me, where is ...?
la stazione centrale	the central station
la metro(politana)	the underground
l'aeroporto	the airport
all'albergo	the hotel
Ho un guasto	I've broken down
Mi potrebbe mandare ...	Could you send me a ...
... un carro-attrezzi?	... tow truck?
Scusi, c'è un'officina qui?	Is there a garage nearby?
Dov'è la prossima stazione di servizio?	Where is the nearest petrol station?
benzina normale	regular petrol
super / gasolio	Super / diesel
deviazione	diversion

senso unico	one-way street
sbarrato	closed
rallentare	drive slowly
tutti direzioni	all directions
tenere la destra	go right
zona di silenzio	no honking allowed
zona tutelata inizio	start of the no parking zone
Aiuto!	Help!
Attenzione!	Watch out!
Chiami subito ...	Quickly call ...
... un'autoambulanza	... an ambulance
... la polizia	... the police

Going out

Scusi, mi potrebbe indicare ...	Where can I find ...
... un buon ristorante?	... a good restaurant?
... un locale tipico?	... a typical restaurant?
C'è una gelateria qui vicino?	Is there an ice cream parlour here?
Può riservarci per stasera	For tonight, can I book
... un tavolo per quattro persone?	... a table for four?
Alla Sua salute!	Cheers!
Il conto, per favore	The bill, please
Andava bene?	Did it taste nice?
Il mangiare era eccellente	The food was excellent
Ha un programma delle manifestazioni?	Do you have an event calendar?

Shopping

Dov'è si può trovare ...	Where can I find ...
... una farmacia	... a pharmacy?
... un panificio	... a bakery?
... un negozio di articoli fotografici	... a photo shop?
... un grande magazzino	... a department store?
... un negozio di generi alimentari	... a grocery store?
... il mercato	... the market?
... il supermercato	... the supermarket?
... il tabaccaio	... the tobacconist?
... il giornalaio	... the newsagent?

Accommodation

Scusi, potrebbe consigliarmi ...?	Could you recommend ...?
... un albergo	... a hotel
... una pensione	... a guesthouse

A large selection of cheeses on the market in Syracuse

Ho prenotato una camera.	I have a room reservation.
È libera ...	Do you have ...
... una singola	... a single room?
... una doppia	... a double room?
... con doccia / bagno	... with a shower / bath?
... per una notte	... for one night?
... per una settimana	... for a week?
... con vista sul mare	... with sea views?
Quanto costa la camera ...	How much is the room ...
... con la prima colazione?	... with breakfast?
... a mezza pensione?	... half board?

Health

Mi può consigliare un buon medico?	Can you recommend a good doctor?
Mi può dare una medicina per ...	Could I have some medicine to treat ...
Soffro di diarrea	I have diarrhoea
Ho mal di pancia	I have a stomach ache
... mal di testa	... headache
... mal di gola	... a sore throat
... mal di denti	... toothache
... influenza	... flu
... tosse	... a cough
... la febbre	... a temperature

... scottatura solare ... sunburn
... costipazione ... constipation

Numbers

zero	0
uno	1
due	2
tre	3
quattro	4
cinque	5
sei	6
sette	7
otto	8
nove	9
dieci	10
undici	11
dodici	12
tredici	13
quattordici	14
quindici	15
sedici	16
diciassette	17
diciotto	18
diciannove	19
venti	20
ventuno	21
trenta	30
quaranta	40
cinquanta	50
sessanta	60
settanta	70
ottanta	80
novanta	90
cento	100
centouno	101
mille	1000
duemille	2000
diecimila	10,000
un quarto	1/4
un mezzo	1/2

Menu

prima colazione	breakfast
caffè, espresso	a small coffee without milk

caffè macchiato	a small coffee with a little milk
caffè latte	coffee with milk
cappuccino	coffee with frothy milk
tè al latte / al limone	tea with milk / lemon
cioccolata	chocolate
frittata	omelette / pancake
pane / panino / pane tostato	bread / roll / toast
burro	butter
salame	salami
prosciutto	ham
miele	honey
marmellata	jam
iogurt	yogurt

antipasti	starters
affettato misto	cold cuts
anguilla affumicata	smoked eel
melone e prosciutto	melon with ham
vitello tonnato	cold roast veal with tuna sauce

primi piatti	pasta and rice dishes, soups
pasta	pasta
fettuccine / tagliatelle	ribbon noodles
gnocchi	small potato dumplings
polenta (alla valdostana)	boiled cornmeal (with cheese)
vermicelli	long, round pasta
minestrone	thick vegetable soup
pastina in brodo	meat broth with thin pasta
zuppa di pesce	fish soup

carni e pesce	meat and fish
agnello	lamb
ai ferri / alla griglia	grilled
aragosta	crayfish
brasato	roast
coniglio	rabbit
cozze / vongole	mussels / clams
fegato	liver
fritto di pesce	fried fish
gambero, granchio	shrimp
maiale	pork
manzo / bue	beef / ox meat
pesce spada	swordfish
platessa	plaice
pollo	chicken

rognoni	kidneys
salmone	salmon
scampi fritti	fried scampi
sogliola	sole
tonno	tuna
trota	trout
vitello	veal

verdura	vegetables
asparagi	asparagus
carciofi	artichokes
carote	carrots
cavolfiore	cauliflower
cavolo	cabbage
cicoria belga	chicory
cipolle	onions
fagioli	white beans
fagiolini	green beans
finocchi	fennel
funghi	mushrooms
insalata mista / verde	mixed / green salad
lenticchie	lentils
melanzane	aubergines
patate	potatoes
peperoni	peppers
pomodori	tomatoes
spinaci	spinach
zucca	pumpkin

Formaggi	cheese
parmigiano	parmesan
pecorino	sheep's cheese
ricotta	ricotta
Dolci e frutta	desserts and fruit
cassata	ice cream with candied fruits
coppa assortita	mixed ice creams
coppa con panna	ice cream with whipping cream
tirami su	sponge biscuits with mascarpone cream
zabaione	custard-like dessert
zuppa inglese	ladyfingers doused in liqueur with vanilla cream

Bevande	beverages
acqua minerale	mineral water
aranciata	orangeade

bibita	soft drink
bicchiere	glass
birra scura / chiara	dark / light beer
birra alla spina	draught beer
birra senza alcool	non-alcoholic beer
con ghiaccio	with ice
digestivo	bitters
gassata / con gas	sparkling
liscia / senza gas	still
secco	dry
spumante	sparkling wine
succo	fruit juice
vino bianco / rosato / rosso	white wine / rosé / red wine
vino della casa	house wine

Learning Italian during the holidays? There are various institutions on Sicily offering Italian-language courses, both for beginners and those at a more advanced level, with accommodation or without, e. g. Solemar, Via F. Perez 85 a, 90010 Aspra / Palermo, tel. 33 87 37 28 33, www.solemar-sicilia.it. Information is also available from the Italian cultural institutes and ENIT (▶Information).

Literature

Sicilian society, travel writing

Roberto Alajmo: Palermo, The Armchair Traveller 2010. The author, a journalist, has succeeded in enticing even fearful readers to discover his home city.

Horatio Clare: Through Writers' Eyes: Sicily, Eland 2006 – An excellent anthology of writings about Sicily since ancient times, from Herodotus right up to modern authors such as Pirandello and D.H. Lawrence.

Giovanni Francesio, Enzo Russo: Sicily, DK Publishing, 2011 – Sicily's beauties in words and pictures

Brian Johnston: Sicilian Summer: A Story of Honour, Religion and the Perfect Cassata, Orion 2007 – A humorous take on Sicily today, with lots of village stories and eccentric locals.

Norman Lewis: The Honourable Society. The Sicilan Mafia Observed, Eland 2003 – By one of the most admired British travel writers of modern times, who fought in Italy in 1944, first published in 1963.

Peter Moore: Vroom by the Sea, Summersdale 2007 – Light-hearted story about zooming around Sicily on a Vespa scooter.

Peter Robb: Midnight in Sicily, Panther 1999 – A book of real distinction, combining meticulous research about the Mafia and the society of Mezzogiorno Italy with high literary quality.

Mary Taylor-Simeti: On Persephone's Island, Bantam Books 2011 – Written in the 1980s by an American who went to live on the island in 1962, this book offers profound insights into the Sicilian way of life, including its food.

Rick Atkinson: The Day of Battle – The War in Sicily and Italy, 1943–44, Little, Brown and Co. 2007 – Dramatic narrative of a bloody campaign, as the Allies fought their way across Sicily and up the Italian peninsula.   History

John Dickie: Cosa Nostra. A History of the Sicilian Mafia, Hodder, London, 2007 – Researches into organized crime

Moses I. Finley, Denis Mack Smith, Christopher Duggan: A History of Sicily, Viking, London, 1987

John Julius Norwich: The Normans in Sicily, Penguin Books 2004 – Highly readable portrait of an era that shaped the island.

Steven Runciman: The Sicilian Vespers. A History of the Mediterranean World in the late 13th Century, CUP 1992

Manuela Darling-Gansser: Spring in Sicily, Hardie Grant Books 2010 – Lots of recipes combined with background information on where they come from, and fine photographs.   Cuisine

Matthew Fort: Sweet Honey, Bitter Lemons, Thomas Dunne Books 2009 – One of the best contemporary British food writers journeyed around the island on a personal quest with a strong culinary bias and informs his readers about the ingredients and the dishes of Sicily.

Andrea Camilleri: crime fiction, published by Picador, set on Sicily. The main character is the good-natured, moody and clever Commissario Montalbano from Vigàta, a fictitious small town in Sicily (▶Famous People).   Fiction

Robert Harris: Imperium, Arrow 2009. Historical fiction: Cicero prosecutes Sicily's corrupt governor.

Giuseppe di Lampedusa: The Leopard, Vintage Classics 2007 –The decline of a Sicilian noble family during Garibaldi's time

Massimo Troisi, Philippe Noiret and Maria Grazia Cucinotta in the enchanting film »Il Postino« (1994)

SICILY IN FILM

No other Italian region has featured so much as a location and subject of films as Sicily. Of course the island and the smaller surrounding ones have plenty of visual appeal: rugged mountains, deep valleys and gorges, volcanic landscapes, craters, blue sea, ancient towns and villages with magnificent aristocratic palaces and grand churches that frame the piazzas in the town centres.

However, the thing that always interested filmmakers most about Sicily was its people and their lives, some of which are still shaped by feudal social structures and medieval conceptions of honour, characterized by a cycle of violence.

Flops

In 1947 the Italian director Luchino Visconti made the film *La terra trema* (*The Earth Trembles*). Based on the novel *I Malavoglia* by Giovanni Verga (1840–1922), Visconti told the story of the young fisherman Ntoni Valastro from the village of Aci Trezza and his rebellion against the dictatorship of the »padroni«, the exploitative fish wholesalers and boat owners. Without support from the other fishermen, who had lost all initiative and hope after centuries of slavery, he was ultimately defeated in his struggle against the wholesalers and had to submit to them again. But for the first time »the earth trembled«, and Ntoni

recognized the possibility of liberation in the future through his defeat. At the Venice Biennale in 1948, the film won an award, but it was a box-office flop.

Also set in a fishing village, this time on the volcanic island of Stromboli, Roberto Rossellini's film *Stromboli, terra di dio* (1949) tells the story of the Lithuanian woman Karin (Ingrid Bergman), who, married to a young fisherman from Stromboli, battles with the different habits and customs on the island. During the filming of this rural melodrama, which is only of interest for its documentary footage of a volcanic eruption, that the close professional and private liaison began between the director Rossellini and the Swedish Hollywood star Bergman. Pietro Germ made a name for himself as a critic of Sicilian customs. In his jolly and ironic film *Divorzio all'italiana* (*Divorce Italian Style*, 1961) he described how, for centuries, divorces were often handled in Italy. Baron

Ferdinando Cefalu (Marcello Mastroianni), a decadent scion of a Sicilian aristocratic family, wants to get rid of his wife in order to focus on his pretty cousin Angela. Since divorce is not possible, he firmly pushes his wife into the arms of a painter with the plan of catching them in flagrante and shooting her. After serving an 18-month sentence for his honour killing (for a long time treated by Italian law as a relatively mild offence), he was finally able to marry his beloved Angela. The film *Sedotta e abbandonata* (*Seduced and Abandoned*, 1963) is also about damaged honour. In this film Germi denounces the cruel laws of Sicilian society aimed at preserving the family honour, using the 16-year-old protagonist Agnese, robbed of her innocence, as an example.

The film *Kaos* (1984) by the Taviani brothers is set in rural Sicily. It is based on four stories by Luigi Pirandello, a recipient of the Nobel Prize for Literature, which address emigration, death, motherly love, the connexion to one's country, alienation, infatuation and transience. Even though some of the subjects seem a little over the top (a full moon arouses a farmer's desires and turns him into a wolf, for example), this work was a great piece of narrative cinema.

Hits

Luchino Visconti's film *Il gattopardo* (*The Leopard*, 1963) by is based on a different literary model, the novel of the same name by Giuseppe Tomasi di Lampedusa. It is about the fate of the Sicilian aristocracy at the time of Garibaldi's unification efforts in Italy in the mid-19th century: much to the surprise of his fellow aristocrats, Fabrizio, Prince of Salina (Burt Lancaster), takes the side of the new regime, but refuses to participate himself in the new Kingdom of Italy and laments Sicily's eternal colonial

In »Il Gattopardo« Giuseppe Tomasi di Lampedusa portrays Sicilian history at the time of Garibaldi's unification efforts. Here: Burt Lancaster stars as Prince Fabrizio Salina in Visconti's famous film of 1963.

fate. The film is mostly criticized for its length (depending on the version, up to nearly four hours; the standard version in the English-speaking world is 185 minutes).

Sicilian history, but of a very different kind, can be found in *Cinema Paradiso* (1988) by Giuseppe Tornatore, in which a former projectionist looks back at the arrival of films with sound in a small Sicilian town in a sentimental, humorous manner. The film is one of the most successful foreign films ever to have been shown in the United States. It was filmed in Palazzo Adriano.

Heroes and Mafiosi

Of course Salvatore Giuliano (▶ Famous People), for many still Sicily's greatest popular hero, was also portrayed in film. The most impressive film about this bandit was made by Francesco Rosi (*Salvatore Giuliano*, 1961). Rosi's achievement consists in absolutely avoiding turning Salvatore Giuliano into a tragic hero; the director only addressed facts that gradually came to light. Nevertheless Rosi managed to produce a film that was artistically, politically and socially significant.

The most popular subject of films associated with Sicily is the Mafia. The list of Mafia films is correspondingly long. The best-known trilogy is not

an Italian production, but an American one. *The Godfather* (1971) was based on the novel of the same name by Mario Puzo. The focus of the film is the Mafia system, represented in the story of a family clan whose leader, Don Corleone (Marlon Brando) was one of the top dogs of the American crime world. These films laid the groundwork for several other Mafia films, and the interest in such films seem unabated. The Italian state-owned broadcaster RAI, which has produced films in collaboration with other European television stations, including the series *The Octopus*, is once again producing a film about the still intact criminal organization, this time about the priests' battle against the Sicilian Mafia.

Romance

But films for the heart are also booming. *Il Postino* (*The Postman*), filmed by the British director Michael Radford in 1994, is a romantic film about the wonderful power of emotions. The book that the film was based on was written by the Chilean author Antonio Skarmete. *Burning Patience* is the story of a friendship between Pablo Neruda, the aging Chilean poet (who received a Nobel Prize in 1971 for his lyric poetry and spent some time in exile in Italy), and Mario, a young man who delivers his

mail. Radford moved the story to the Lipari island of Salina. Neruda (Philippe Noiret) teaches Mario (Massimo Troisi) the magic and beauty of words and metaphors. Mario learns that they can even be used to win over the heart of a woman (Maria Grazia Cucinotta). One of the most recent offerings is *L'Uomo delle Stelle* (*The Star Maker*), for which the Sicilian director Giuseppe Tornatore received the jury's special prize in Venice in 1995. The conman Morelli allegedly travels through Sicily in 1953, searching for talent for Roman film studios. »What a face!« he assured successful old people, men and women in their prime, young girls and adolescent lovers, who all hope to be discovered for the big screen. But before Morelli immortalizes them on celluloid, they first have to pay their 1500 lire for the test film. The wily con-man – the film in his spool has long become unusable – is finally tricked by even less scrupulous con-men. The special thing about this film are the people themselves, their faces and their stories: in addition to actors, Tornatore, who already combined his two favourite subjects, Sicily and cinema, in an excellent manner in *Cinema Paradiso* (see above), got around 100 amateurs in front of the camera.

A film that was made with a relatively small budget and won several awards shortly after its release in 2000 is *I cento Passi* (*One Hundred Steps*). Marco Tullio Giordana tells the true story of Giuseppe Impastato, known as Peppino. He came from the small town of Cinisi, a stone's throw from Palermo airport, and worked hard for a left-wing party in the 1970s. In a radio show he mocked the local Mafia boss Gaetano Badalamenti (Don Tano), whose house was just »one hundred steps« from his own. Peppino's father, a Mafia member himself, subsequently threw his son out. On the night of 8 May 1978 Peppino's body was found, torn apart by a bomb. The investigation report determined »death by suicide«. Peppino's friends spent more than 20 years trying to get the case heard in court. Badalamenti, who was in prison in the United States for other offences, was given a life sentence as the man who ordered Peppino's murder.

Dacia Maraini: The Silent Duchess, Arcadia Books 2010 – Historical novel by a feminist novelist, telling the tale of three generations of a noble family in the mid-18th century.

Leonardo Sciascia: various books with a Sicilian theme. A Simple Story, Hesperus, London, 2010. Young Sicilian policeman finds dead diplomat.
Sicilian Uncles, Granta, London, 2001. Judges get murdered, in Sicily, where else?
The Day of the Owl, New York Review of Books Classic, New York, 2003. An attempt to break the wall of Mafia silence

Giovanni Verga: Mastro Don Gesualdo, novel, translated by D.H. Lawrence, Daedalus, London, 1999; Little Novels of Sicily, also translated by D. H. Lawrence, Steerforth. London, 2000

Media

British newspapers and magazines are available in Palermo, Taormina, Catania and in Lìpari (usually a day late).
Sicilians read the liberal *Giornale di Sicilia* or the more conservative paper *La Sicilia*. In Messina there is also the *Gazzetta del Sud*. The two monthly magazines *Ciao Sicilia* (in English and Italian) and *Un mese a Palermo* are also of interest to visitors, since they contain a lot of information about the island and the most important events.

Money

Euros
Since 1 January 2002 the euro has been the official currency of Italy and a number of other countries in the European Union.
1 GB £ = 1.20 EUR, 1 EUR = 0.83 GB £
1 US-$ = 0.77 EUR, 1 EUR = US-$ 1.30

Foreign currency regulations
EU residents are allowed to import and export unlimited amounts of euros or other EU currencies.

Banks
With minor deviations, banks are open Mon–Fri 8.30am–1pm; the opening hours vary in the afternoon (approx. 2.30pm/3pm–4.30pm). On days before holidays (prefestivi) the banks close at 11.20am.

ATMs, bank cards, credit cards
There is no problem taking out money around the clock from ATMs using credit and debit cards that have PIN numbers. A maximum of EUR 500 is available per day and account with a debit card. Credit cards have higher limits.

CONTACT DETAILS FOR CREDIT CARDS

In the event of lost bank or credit cards you can contact the following numbers in UK and USA (phone numbers when dialling from abroad):

▶ **Eurocard/MasterCard**
Tel. 001 / 636 7227 111

▶ **Visa**
Tel. 0800 / 811 84 40

▶ **American Express UK**
Tel. 0044 / 1273 696 933

▶ **American Express USA**
Tel. 001 / 800 528 4800

▶ **Diners Club UK**
Tel. 0044 / 1252 513 500

▶ **Diners Club USA**
Tel. 001 / 702 797 5532

Have the bank sort code, account number and card number as well as the expiry date ready.

The following numbers of UK banks can be used to report and cancel lost or stolen bank and credit cards issued by those banks:

▶ **HSBC**
Tel. 0044 / 1442 422 929

▶ **Barclaycard**
Tel. 0044 / 1604 230 230

▶ **NatWest**
Tel. 0044 / 142 370 0545

▶ **Lloyds TSB**
Tel. 0044 / 1702 278 270

Banks, hotels, restaurants, car rental offices and shops generally accept international credit cards.

In the event that a credit card or debit card is lost, it is possible to call an **emergency number to block the cards**. This should be ascertained and noted before arrival. — *Loss*

In Italy, customers are always required to demand and keep receipts (Ricevuta fiscale or scontrino). It can happen that an officer of the fiscal police will ask to see a receipt when you leave a shop in order to make tax fraud more difficult. — *Receipts*

Nature Parks · Nature Reserves

There are three regional parks and many protected areas in Sicily; almost 10% of the island is protected. Information about the individual protected areas is available from ENIT, the local tourist information offices and under www.parks.it/regione.sicilia/index.php (in Italian and in English in places).

The **Parco dell'Etna**, the area around Mount Etna and Sicily's east coast, is one of Italy's largest regional parks.

The **Riserva Naturale dello Zingaro**, named after the town of Zingaro, is located in northwestern Sicily, between Palermo and Tràpani.

Bosco della Ficuzza, an extensive area of forests and fields between Palermo and Agrigento, dominated by the limestone wall of the Rocca Busambra, used to be the royal hunting grounds.

Riserva Naturale Orientata Vendicari, the wetlands in the south of the island, is an important sanctuary for birds.

Parco delle Madonie and **Parco dei Nébrodi** in the hinterland of the north coast are popular destinations with accommodation (refuges, agriturismi and basic hotels).

The sea around Ùstica island is a paradise for snorkellers and divers, being a designated marine reserve, namely the **Riserva Naturale Marina Isola di Ùstica**. The **Isole Eolie** are also protected and are UNESCO World Heritage sites.

Opening Hours

Churches
Many churches are closed between noon and 4pm / 5pm (apart from Palermo Cathedral).

Museums
Opening hours of museums, especially the smaller ones, depend on the season and change frequently. Detailed information about the major ones can be found in the chapter »Sights from A to Z«. Those who want to make sure should enquire in the local tourist information. Generally speaking, museums are open between 9am and 1pm, except for Mondays, and some open again after a lunch break from 3pm / 4pm until 7pm. Last admissions are often half an hour before closing.

Excavations
Archaeological sites are usually open Tue–Sun from 9am until an hour before sunset.

Post · Telecommunications

Post offices
It is not possible to make telephone calls from Italian post offices; they only deal with letters and parcels. Open Mon–Fri 8.30am–1.30pm, Sat 8.30am–noon.

Stamps
Stamps (francobolli) are available in post offices and tobacconists (they can be recognized by their »T« sign). Letters weighing up to 20g and postcards to European countries cost EUR 0.75.

DIALLING CODES

► **from Italy ...**
    ... to the UK 00 44
    ... to North America 00 1
    ... to Australia 00 61
    ... to Ireland 00 353
    (after that the local dialling code, omitting the »0«)

► **To Italy**
00 39 (then the local dialling code together with the »0«)

► **Directory enquiries**
Domestic: tel. 412
Foreign: tel. 176

Almost all public telephones now take nothing but telephone cards (Scheda or Carta telefonica), which are available in bars, from tobacconists and news agents. **The local dialling codes including the zero are part of the Italian telephone numbers**. As a result they have to be included in the number; even when making local calls, and when calling from other countries, the zero must not be omitted. This does not apply to emergency calls, service numbers and mobile phone numbers (they do not start with a zero). Service numbers starting with 800 are free.

Telephone calls

It is possible to use mobile phones (telefonini, cellulari) everywhere. Since the fees for using them within the EU are capped, the costs are almost identical in all the roaming networks.

Mobile phone calls

Prices and Discounts

Visitors from the EU who are under 18 and pensioners get free admission to many attractions. 18 to 25-year-olds will often benefit from asking about young persons' discounts.

Admissions

►Food and Drink and ►Accommodation

Tips

▶ WHAT DOES IT COST?

Basic double room
from € 60.00

Hire car
from € 280 per week

Petrol
about € 1.60 per litre

Simple meal
€ 8.00

3-course menu
from € 25

Cup of coffee
about € 1.50

Shopping

The typical shop opening hours are 8.30am/9am – 1pm and from 4pm/4.30pm – 7.30pm (winter). The hours tend to move back by about an hour during the summer months (5pm – 8.30pm). Many shops stay closed on Monday morning.

Despite the more or less industrial manner in which souvenirs are manufactured, in some cases even outside Europe, traditional handicrafts are also available in Sicily. Pottery, hand-woven fabrics and rugs, leather bags, wrought-iron goods and a lot more is largely made for tourists, but often based on traditional examples, in good quality and affordable. In addition there is a large selection of culinary souvenirs, such as wine (► wine), capers, olive oil, almond biscuits and other sweets. Visiting the markets or speciality shops will provide sufficient ideas.

Typical souvenir from Sicily: colourful ceramics

The main souvenirs in Santo Stéfano di Camastra, Burgio, Sciacca and Caltagirone are **ceramic goods**. The province of Ragusa is known for its vases. Around Monreale the Cannestrari weave baskets and chairs. **Rugs and fabrics** are mainly manufactured around Palermo. Enna is the centre of **lace production**. All kinds of **puppets** and the famous painted **wooden carts**, carretti, or their miniature versions, the carrettini, are available in every souvenir shop, the latter particularly in Bagheria, Vittória and Tràpani. Giarre is known for its utility objects and ornaments made of **wrought iron**. Almost everything, from candlesticks to terrace lamps and bedsteads can be found here. Goods made of coral, an industry for which Tràpani was once famous, have all but disappeared since the depletion of the corals off Sicily's western coast.

Every time you make a purchase, keep the receipt (scontrino or ricevuta) for a while (in order to make tax fraud more difficult). Italians too will also purchase fake and unbeatably cheap branded goods, which are on offer everywhere. Although the police often turn a blind eye, this is not always the case! If they don't, the almost real Prada glasses or the Dolce e Gabbana shirt could become very expensive very quickly.

Sport and Outdoors

There is a choice of several different water sports on Sicily and the surrounding islands. The trail and biking network has also been expanded in recent years. Information is available from ENIT, the local tourist information offices and specialist tour operators.

No permission is needed to fish in the sea, but permits are needed for rivers and lakes, which are available for a fee from the relevant organizations (refer to the tourist information offices) as well as from the Federazione Italiana Pesca Sportiva (www.fipsas.it). All divers aged 16 and up are allowed to engage in spear-fishing (pesca subacquea). The use of diving cylinders is not permitted, however.

Fishing

There are sailing, surfing and diving schools along the coast. Windsurfing world championships are held every year in Mondello (near Palermo). To hire a boat, a sailing or motorboat licence is necessary. For boats with engines of more than 3 horsepower, third-party insurance is also necessary.
Ùstica and also the other, smaller islands around Sicily are veritable snorkelling and diving paradises; information is available from the tourist information offices.

Sailing, surfing, diving

Sicily is beautiful under water too, as in Ustica

Skiing Conditions are guaranteed to be suitable for winter sports on Mount Etna above 2500m/8200ft between December and April. There are lifts and refuges on the north side. The south side is suitable for those experienced in skiing in powdery snow. Higher up in the Madoníe and the Monti Nébrodi there are also ski slopes (with lifts) and cross-country ski runs.

Golf An 18-hole golf course is attractively situated at the foot of Mount Etna. Adjoining it are a small hotel and a restaurant (Il Picciolo Golf Club, 95012 Castiglione di Sicilia, Contrada Rovittello, tel. and fax 0 95 98 62 52, www.ilpicciologolf.com).

Walking ►Walking

Time

CET Italy follows Central European Time (CET). From the last weekend
CEST in March to the last weekend in October all of Europe adheres to Summer Time (CEST = CET + 1 hr = GMT + 2 hr; CET = GMT + 1 hr).

Transport

Motorways Almost all motorways (autostrada) in Italy are toll roads (pedaggio), including the one between Messina and Palermo and the one between Messina and Catania. The toll can either be paid in cash, with a credit card or with a Viacard (available from automobile clubs, ACI offices at the border crossings, at motorway junctions, in tobacconists and at petrol stations).

Petrol stations The import and transport of petrol in canisters is not allowed. Petrol stations stock regular unleaded petrol (95 octane, benzina senza piombo or benzina verde), premium (97 octane) and diesel (gasolio). Petrol stations are generally open daily 7am– noon and 2pm– 8pm. Motorways usually have 24-hour service stations. At weekends, and increasingly also during lunch breaks and at night, many petrol stations only have self-service pumps available.

Traffic The legal alcohol limit in Italy is 50 milligrams per 100 millilitres.
regulations Outside towns dipped headlights have to be switched on even during the day; the speed limit on motorways in the rain is 110 kmh/70 mph instead of 130 kmh/80 mph! In all other cases the following speed limits apply: cars, motorbikes and caravans up to 3.5t 50 kmh/ 30 mph in towns, 90 kmh/55 mph outside towns, on fast roads (dual

USEFUL ADDRESSES

CAR RENTALS

▶ **Avis**
Tel. 06 452 10 83 91
www.avisautonoleggio.it

▶ **Europcar**
Tel. 199 30 70 30
www.europcar.it

▶ **Hertz**
Tel. 02 694 30 019
www.hertz.it

▶ **Sixt**
Tel. 06 65 21 11
www.sixt.it

BREAKDOWN SERVICES

see emergency services p. 81

carriageways) 110 kmh/70 mph and 130 kmh/80 mph on motorways (autostrada); cars and caravans weighing more than 3.5t 80 kmh/50 mph outside towns, 80 kmh/50 mph on fast roads and 100 kmh/60 mph on motorways. Those who drive too fast and are caught face heavy fines. Important: it is compulsory to carry **high-visibility jackets** in your car in Italy!

Private towing is not allowed on motorways. In the event of a breakdown, foreign cars and motorbikes are towed to the nearest garage by the breakdown service of the Italian automobile club. Motorcyclists riding bikes of more than 50 cc must wear a helmet. ◀ Further regulations

Small buses and expensive or still relatively new cars are often broken into or stolen. The most important rule when parking a vehicle is to leave absolutely nothing behind, especially no valuables! Empty the glove box and leave it open. Take out the car radio if possible. And it is also best to leave the car in a locked car park or garage overnight. If misfortune does strike, then the police should definitely be informed. This is necessary in order to make an insurance claim! Car theft

Many town centres are subject to traffic-calming measures and parking spaces are in short supply. Cars are safest in garages and guarded car parks. No-parking signs (Zona tutelata INIZIO = start of the no parking zone, Divietato di sosta, sometimes with the addition of ambo i lati = on both sides of the road) must be obeyed. The colour markings on curbs mean: white = free parking, yellow = parking spaces reserved for certain parties, such as taxis and buses; blue = parking, but fees apply. The standard procedure is »gratta e sosta«, meaning, a card is bought from the nearest tobacconist. It is placed behind the windscreen after the day, month and time of day are scratched free. Parking is not allowed along curbs marked black and yellow. Parking

◀ Parking fees

Rental cars　In order to be allowed to rent a car in Italy the driver must be at least 21, have a credit card and have had a driving licence for at least a year. Bookings with international car rental firms can be made from home, which is generally cheaper. The local car rental offices are listed in telephone books under »Noleggio«.

Taxis　Taxis are often not fitted with a taximeter. In order to avoid misunderstandings, it is best to negotiate a price in advance for longer trips.

Trains　Delays are almost the norm and many stations are well away from town centres. The main lines largely run along the coast from Messina to Palermo and further to Tràpani as well as from Messina via Taormina and Catania to Syracuse and Agrigento. Timetable information is available from Trenitalia (►p. 73), at stations and from travel agencies. Every station kiosk will have a general timetable.

Ferrovia Circumetnea ►　A ride on the narrow gauge railway Ferrovia Circumetnea is a special experience. It runs between Catania and Giarre/Riposto station. It goes around Mount Etna in the process. The 114km/71mi journey lasts three and a half hours (►p. 223).

Town and overland buses　A dense network of town and overland buses connects all of Sicily's major towns. They usually depart from and arrive at station forecourts; more information is available from the local information offices. Tickets are available at machines or directly from the driver (**schedule information**: www.italybus.it).

Ferries ►　Tickets for town buses are available from the kiosks of the operating companies as well as tobacconists and newsagents. Ferries ►p. 76

Distances

	Agrigento	Caltanissetta	Catania	Enna	Messina	Palermo	Ragusa	Siracusa	Tràpani
Agrigento		57	167	95	265	126	133	218	180
Caltanissetta			110	38	207	127	131	161	236
Catania				85	94	207	103	60	316
Enna					183	136	136	137	245
Messina						237	202	158	346
Palermo							248	259	107
Ragusa								86	308
Siracusa									368

.?. Reggio di Calabria 4 hrs
.?. Villa San Giovanni 30 min

.?. Shipping lines
Average journey times (hours)
hrs between the mainland and Sicily and between Sicily and Sardinia

.?. Cagliari　12 hrs
.?. Genova　22 hrs
.?. Livorno　18 hrs
.?. Napoli　9½ hrs

km　Distances in kilometres

©Baedeker

.?. Cagliari 11 hrs

Travellers with Disabilities

Sicily is not an easy place to get around for those with limited mobility. It is worth looking at the website of Accessible Italy, which aims to open up Italy for foreign tourists with disabilities.

 INFORMATION FOR THE DISABLED

ITALY

▶ **Accessible Italy**
Tel. 378 94 11 11
www.accessibleitaly.com

UNITED KINGDOM

▶ **Tourism for All**
c/o Vitalise, Shap Road Industrial
Estate, Shap Road, Kendal
Cumbria LA9 6NZ

Tel. 08 45 124 99 71
www.tourismforall.org.uk

USA

▶ **SATH (Society for Accessible Travel and Hospitality)**
347 5th Ave., no. 605
New York, NY 10016:
Tel. (212) 4 47 72 84
www.sath.org

Walking

Sicily's ancient symbol, the **Trinakria**, a winged girl's head with snakes for hair, surrounded by three legs, is still to be found everywhere today. It is sold everywhere as a souvenir and also adorns the coat of arms of the autonomous »Regione Sicilia« as well as the uniform buttons of its employees. Take the invitation literally and explore the largest island of the Mediterranean on foot. **Johann Gottfried Seume**, who went on a walk from Saxony to Syracuse in 1802, said: »Those who walk see more on an anthropological and cosmic level than those who drive, and I think that everything would be better if everyone were to walk more.«

Walkers see more

Hiking on Sicily is called trekking, giving it an adventurous air. More and more Sicilians are discovering this active pastime. Local offices of the environmental organizations and the **Clup Alpino Italiano** (CAI, Italian alpine club; tel. 0 22 05 72 31, fax 0 22 05 72 32 01, www.cai.it) run organized trips. The sunny island is an excellent hiking area, not just during the »primavera siciliana«, when the island explodes in a sea of flowers. It is just as worthwhile in autumn and winter. The landscape is full of surprises. The highest mountain is also an active volcano. A drive or climb up **Mount Etna**, 3300m/10,900ft, makes its way through a wide range of climates and vegetation zones, almost like a trip from Palermo to northern Norway.

Hiking in Sicily

Buses depart from the Rifugio Sapienza up to an altitude of 2900m/ 9500ft. From here it is possible to go on excursions to the most re-cent craters in the company of authorized mountain guides. On clear days almost the whole of Sicily is visible. Nature trails on Mount Etna's eastern side run below the Rifugio Sapienza to Monte Nero degli Zappini and to Monte Zoccolaro as well as on the northeast flank around the Monti Sartorius. The forestry administration maintains an extensive trail network on Mount Etna's western side above Bronte. Maps and information are available from local tourist information offices and from the park administration in Nicolosi (information: www. parcoetna.ct.it, www.et-natrekking.com, www.si ciltrek.ch, www.apt.catania.it).

! **Baedeker** TIP

Hiking Lovers

Six particularly beautiful hiking trips are listed in this book from p. 134 onwards; for further suggestions see *Landscapes of Sicily. Walks. Car Tours. Picnics*, Sunflower Countryside Guides.

Aeolian Islands Located off Sicily's northern coast are the Aeolian or Lipari Islands, a volcanic bridge between Mount Etna and Mount Vesuvius. The seven islands of volcanic origin are all small hiking paradises in their own right. Many of the trips can also be done with children and end with a refreshing dip in the sea, which is warmed by steam in some places. Following the most recent prominent eruption there are currently no climbs up Mount Stròmboli (900m/3000ft).

Peloritani, Nébrodi and Madonie A mountain range runs along Sicily's north coast, the Peloritani in the east, followed by the Nébrodi and the Madonie. Extensive beech forests and high mountain meadows characterize the Parco dei Né-brodi, exciting rock formations rise up above Alcara Li Fusi. Marked hiking trails were and are still being set up (www.parcodeinebrodi.it). The Madonie, further west, are home to the most biodiverse forests of the Mediterranean region; outstanding karst formations are joined together by a dense network of trails. Information from the tourist offices and in Cefalù. The working group under Girolamo Lombardo at AAPIT Palermo opened up the province of Palermo for hikers and bikers in an exemplary manner, with the topographical **trail map of the Madonie natural park** (1:50,000).

The Carta dei Sentieri e del Paesaggio dell'Alto Belice Corleonese (1:50,000) corresponds to the large catchment area of the Fiume Belice. The landscape between Palermo and Sciacca is one of Sicily's little-known beauties, even though it was described by Tomasi di Lampedusa in *The Leopard* and Hollywood has made place names such as Prizzi and Corleone world famous. The Sicilian director and Oscar winner Giuseppe Tornatore filmed *Cinema Paradiso* in **Palazzo Adriano**. Surprisingly the town is just as homey in reality as it is in the film, and has still not fallen victim to tourism. Now everyone can take a look behind the scenes and explore places like the Albanian

Piana degli Albanesi or Mezzojuso, the bell-casting town **Burgio**, the eyrie Caltabellotta, or the excavations of ancient Ietas on foot. The 1613m/5292ft Rocca Busambra rises majestically like a mini alpine range above the **Bosco della Ficuzza**. The mixed oak forest is most beautiful in May, when the peonies are in bloom. The valley of the **Fiume Sosio** is a mecca for palaeontologists. The maps are reliable travel companions. In addition to roads and hiking trails they also depict the »Regie trazzere«, the old royal droving route. There are plans to transform disused narrow-gauge railway lines into cycle paths. On the backs of the maps there are countless practical tips such as addresses of agriturismi, bed & breakfast, mountain refuges, trattorias, wine cellars, oil mills and cheese dairies. The legend and all the important explanations are also given in English.

A natural gem: Pantalica Gorge

Riserva Naturale dello Zingaro
The Riserva dello Zingaro, Sicily's oldest natural reserve in the province of Tràpani, is exotic. Old mule tracks with views of the Gulf of Castellamare wind their way past dwarf palms. The entrance fee includes a trail map and a visit to the interesting natural history museums (www.riservazingaro.it). The Aegadian Islands are also part of Tràpani province. Maréttimo is particularly easily accessible with its trail network (www. egadi.com).

Aegadian Islands ▶

Southeastern Sicily
Among the natural gems in southeastern Sicily are the **Riserva Naturale Orientata Vendicari**, the gorges of **Pantàlica** and **Cassibile** as well as the cosy little river **Ciane**, which is lined by papyrus. Trail maps and information are available from the tourist information offices in the provinces of Ragusa and Siracusa (www.ragusaturismo.it, www.siracusa1.it).

When to go

Subtropical climate
Sicily has a warm, subtropical climate typical of the Mediterranean region with moist, mild winters and dry, hot summers. The cause of the seasonal weather changes is the shift of the subtropical high pressure belt along with the position of the sun. Spring, up until the end of April, is surprisingly cool and changeable, while autumn remains warm for a long time, but from mid-October the weather becomes more changeable. With 2700 hours of sunshine a year, Palermo takes first place. Between June and August the sun shines for more than 80% of the astronomically possible time.

Precipitation
Messina, with an average annual rainfall of 832 l/ m² (33.1 inches), is the wettest of the larger coastal towns. Catania, situated in Mount Etna's rain shadow, is the driest at 547 l/ m² (21.5 inches). Higher altitudes see significantly more precipitation, and above 1500 – 1800m/ 4900 – 5900ft snow can fall in the winter months. One problem for the island's water supply, particularly for agriculture, is the extent to which precipitation levels fluctuate year by year. For that reason Mount Etna is a vital water store for the island. Its flanks see two to three times as much rainfall as Catania. With 7 – 12 rainy days, October to February are the wettest months. From May to September the days are almost always dry, save for some thunder showers. The transition months of March, April and October, when the autumn weather begins, are changeable. The cause of the change in the weather is the advanced time of year, when cold air affects the western Mediterranean more often and more severely. Low pressure turbu-

? DID YOU KNOW ...?

■ In Catania the best month is November, when the average number of rainy days is five and it gets five and a half hours of sunshine a day.

lence can then develop explosively over the water, which has a temperature of up to 24°C/75°F. Torrential rainfall and severe thunderstorms are the consequence. 40–60 l/m² can fall locally in 24 hours, causing serious flooding. However, longer periods of bad weather remain the exception, even in late autumn.

The Sicilian summer, from mid-June to around mid-September, is hot and quite muggy. 30°C/85°F and more are daily occurrences in July and August up to an altitude of 500m/1600ft. Catania is the hottest place, with an average daily maximum of 32°C/90°F. The air in the streets that has heated up during the day hardly cools to a temperature of below 25°C/77°F by morning. Only on the coast does the daytime onshore wind bring mild relief. If the hot sirocco is blowing from Africa and this is coupled with foehn winds from Mount Etna, temperatures can top 40°C/104°F (Catania: abs. max. 46°C/115°F, July). Spring and autumn are a lot more pleasant, with noon temperatures of around 22–26°C/72–79°F. Near the coast the winters are mild and sunny. Daytime temperatures maintain a benign level of around 17°C/63°F, even in January. The cold time of year is significantly harsher at higher altitudes. There are even some winter sports opportunities on the Madoníe mountains, which reach a maximum altitude of just under 2000m/6500ft. Near the summit of Mount Etna sharp frosts and snow are likely from November to March.

Temperatures

Away from the extreme summer heat May, June and September are the most favourable times to go. Autumn seaside holidays should not extend beyond mid-October because of the increasing risk of rain. After this time, the sheltered coasts of Palermo and Catania are best, as they boast sunshine and mild temperatures, even during the winter months. The Mediterranean is warmest in early August, when it reaches temperatures of 25–26°C/77–79°F; it is coolest in February, at 13–14°C/55–57°F.

When to go

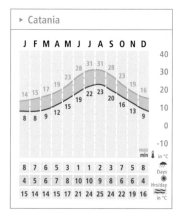

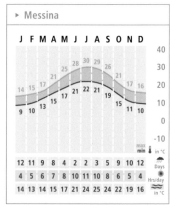

Wine

Italian wine has its origin on Sicily. Today the island is one of Italy's four major wine-producing regions, along with Emilia-Romagna, Apulia and Veneto. Two-thirds of the entire annual production (9 million hectolitres) are red wines (rosso), one-third white wines (bianco). The open wine served in pizzerias and trattorias is only a real pleasure in establishments that pay attention to quality. A less romantic option, but one that is somewhat safer, is getting a labelled bottle. **Reading the label** attentively is worthwhile, because Italian law classifies wines into different categories and requires strict controls for some of them. The most basic wines are the vini da tavola (VDT). They are just called rosso or bianco and do not state the grape, vintage or place of origin. Wines with a typical place of origin or grape are called IGT wines (indicazione geografica tipica); among the best-known are the two brands Corvo and Regaleali.

VDT ▶

IGT ▶

DOC ▶ DOC wines (Denominazione di origine controllata) are top quality. They are wines that have to come from a controlled region. There are 19 DOC regions on Sicily and these wines make up 3% of the total. Wines from controlled and guaranteed origins (**DOCG**, denominazione di origine controllata e garantita) can only be found in the Cerasuolo di Vittoria on Sicily. DOC and DOCG wines are always analysed and tasted prior to sale. There is a numbered state control strip on the neck of the bottle that guarantees that the guidelines were adhered to. Sicily's modern wines are considered the most reliable of southern Italy. In the early 1990s, when there was talk of the Sicilian wine miracle, the wine growers created a sensation with Chardonnay, Merlot and Cabernet. Since then more and more vineyards are opting for mixed grape varieties, particularly for »Nero d'Ávola«, the »black one from Avola«. One of Sicily's special features is the revived **Marsala** (white and red varieties; different dessert and aperitif wines, from dry to sweet, from old to young, sometimes sparkling) and, on a smaller scale, also the (sweet) **Passito wines** that are produced on Pantellería (Moscato) and on the Lipari Islands (Malvasia). Among the **best-known producers** are Benanti (including some strong Etna wines), COS (including a fabulous IGT Nero d'Ávola), Donnafugata (the best white wines are Chiaranda del Merlo, Vigna di Gabri; the best reds are Angheli,

! **Baedeker** TIP

Wine tour

The roots of the Sicilian Planeta family go back a long way, but they have only made their own wines since 1995. These are produced in five locations on the island and are now among the best. Visitors and wine connoisseurs are welcome and some vineyards have accommodation. **La Foresteria** near Selinunte is an attractive starting point for cultural, culinary and oenological pleasures. The food here is outstanding (there are also cooking classes) and it is naturally accompanied by excellent wines (information: www.planeta.it).

Milleunanotte and Tancredi), Duca di Salaparuta (without its own vineyards; largely good IGT wines, the most basic ones are sold under the brand Corvo), Firriato (including Santagostino Bianco and Rosso), Planeta (top-quality wines in five locations), Rapitalà (DOC Álcamò), Regaleali – Tasca d'Almerita (including a fabulous choice of IGT wines sold under the Regaleali brand), Settesoli (leading co-operative with IGT single-grape wines and blends sold under the Mandarossa brand) and Barone di Villagrande (including Etna wines). Interesting Marsala wines come from Carlo Pellegrino, Florio and Vecchio Samperi.

MISTRETTA

Tours

SICILY: ART AND CULTURE BETWEEN THE SUN AND THE SEA. THE FOLLOWING CHAPTER CONTAINS SUGGESTIONS FOR SIGHTSEEING TRIPS AND HIKES

TOURS THROUGH SICILY

Because of its location and long history, Sicily is maybe the most self-contained of the Italian regions. The following chapter makes suggestions about how to explore this »world of its own« in a vehicle or on foot.

Castellammare del Golfo, a pretty port on Sicily's north coast

Agrigento
Temple of Hera in the Valle dei Templi

Piazza Armerina
Erotic art in Antiquity: mosaics in Villa Romana del Casale

★ San Vito lo Capo   TOUR 2
★ ★
★ ★ Érice   ★ Palermo
Zingaro   Monreale   ★ Solunto
àpani
★ Álcamo   Piana   Termini   ★ ★ Cefalù
ia   degli Albanesi   Imerese
★ ★ Segesta   Vicari   ★ Imera   S. Stéfano
★ Marsala   Corleone   TOUR 4   di Camastro
★ Castelvetrano   Prizzi   Lercara Friddi
Mazaro   Pian del   Castronovo
el Vallo   Leone   Cammarata   ★ Calascibetta   Nicosia
ave di Cusa   Sciacca   Caltanissetta   ★ ★ Enna
★ ★ Selinunte   Ribera   TOUR 2   ★ Piazza   ★ Calta-
TOUR 1   ★ ★ Armerina   girone
Eracléa   Villa Romana   Grammichele
Minoa   ★ ★ Agrigento   del Casale
Licata   TOUR 3
★ Gela   Palazzolo
TOUR 1   Vittória   Acréide
★ Ragusa
★ Módica
Scicli   ★ Íspica

Milazzo
★ Tindari   ★ Messina
Sant' Ágata di Militello   Patti
★ Taormina   ★ ★ TOUR 1
©Baedeker   ★ Naxos
★ ★ Etna
★ Catania
TOUR 3
Augusta
★ Megara Hyblaia
★ ★ Siracusa
Pantàlica
★ ★ Noto
Vendicari

Noto
A Baroque gem: the cathedral Santi Nicola e Corrado

Travelling in Sicily

»Art and culture between the sun and the sea« – this is how Sicily attracts visitors to the island. The largest Mediterranean island is a classic educational destination. Even though the island's natural beauty, its sandy and rocky coasts and its almost untouched landscapes in the interior have been »discovered« in recent years, beach and walking holidays are still not the number one pursuit. A trip to Sicily is first and foremost an exploration of Greek, Roman, Byzantine, Arab, Norman, French and Spanish culture, which can be found everywhere, in the cities and villages, in the language and in people's gestures.

Mode of transport

Visitors will find it most convenient to travel in their own car. The road network is good, even though the streets through towns are often narrow and the mountain roads are winding. The **round trip of Sicily** is a classic. It provides a more or less complete picture of the island. The following towns are good alternative **bases**: Cefalù (for western Sicily), Taormina or a town near Mount Etna (for eastern and northeastern Sicily), Syracuse or one of the Baroque towns, such as Módica, Noto or Ragusa (for eastern and southwestern Sicily), Agrigento (for western Sicily and trips to the interior) and Marsala or Castellammare del Golfo (for western and northwestern Sicily). Apart from the peak season, July–August, when early reservations are a must, sufficient accommodation should be available.

i | Seaside fun ...

■ ... and/or trekking: crystal-clear water, fine sandy beaches, impressive cliffs, active volcanoes, untouched hiking paradises, the choice on Sicily is immense. You must choose ...

Hiking

Since more and more people want to explore this landscape on foot, this chapter includes six of the best walks on Sicily (p. 134 onwards).

Tour 1 Round Trip

Start and end: Messina
Duration: at least 3 weeks

Length: 1100km/680mi

The grand tour always follows the coast, apart from a couple of detours into the interior. In order to avoid putting off Sicily's capital, Palermo, to the end of the trip, it is best to do this tour anticlockwise.

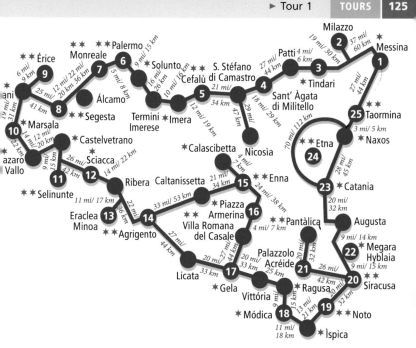

The round trip begins in Messina, which is a convenient location for those travelling by rail or car. Those arriving by boat or air can easily start the tour from either Palermo or Catania. The SS 113d runs northeastwards from ❶ ✳ **Messina**, always with views of the Strait, all the way to Punta del Faro, where it then heads westwards, past Mortelle beach, reaching the SS 113 near Divieto (34km/21mi from Messina). In Olivarella (19km/12mi) the road turns right to ❷ **Milazzo** (7km/4mi), which has ferry links to the Lipari Islands (►Lípari, Isole). Beyond Falcone the road follows a number of hairpin bends to ❸ ✳ **Tìndari** (pilgrimage church, excavations of ancient Tyndaris, 30km/19mi). The next stop is the somewhat elevated **Patti**, where a Roman villa has been uncovered (6km/4mi). After passing a few seaside resorts, continue to ❹ **Sant'Àgata di Militello** (44km/27mi), from where it is possible to take a detour south to the 1505m/4938ft Portella della Miraglia in the Nebrodi Mountains (SS 289, 30km/19mi). The coast road continues to **Santo Stéfano di Camastra** (29km/18mi), which is famed for its ceramic goods; the SS 117 branches off here, making its way through the mountains to **Nicosia** (47km/29mi). The next stage of the journey reveals views of the magnificent rocky headland of the port of ❺ ✳✳ **Cefalù**. Its old town is centred on the famous Norman cathedral (34km/21mi). Near Buonfornello the road goes under the Catania–Palermo motorway and reaches the excavation site of the westernmost Greek

From Messina to Palermo
◄ 275km/170mi

Fun on the beach in a pretty setting: Cefalu

town on Sicily, Himera (✳ **Imera**), where Syracuse and Akragas (modern-day Agrigento) successfully defeated Carthage in a battle in 480 BC (19km/12mi). The thermal baths of **Termini Imerese** at the foot of Monte San Calógero are a further 16km/10mi away. The road now passes several seaside towns, the ruins of ancient Soluntum (✳ **Solunto**; nice panoramic road around the cape) as well as **Bagheria**, once a picturesque garden suburb, now a faceless rural town. The road then finally reaches the outskirts of ❻✳✳ **Palermo** (41km/25mi), one of Europe's oldest cities.

From Palermo to Tràpani
105km/65mi ▶

Leave Palermo on the SS 186 and drive to ❼✳✳ **Monreale** (301m/988ft) with a cathedral that is famous for its mosaics (8km/5mi). Continue to Partinico (21km/13mi) on the SS 113 past **Álcamo** to the Elymian town of ❽✳✳ **Segesta** with its ancient theatre and especially its temple, located in a somewhat lonely spot (35km/22mi).

After **Calatafimi** the road reaches the provincial capital of ✳ **Tràpani** (41km/25mi), the ferry terminal for trips to the Aegadian Islands to the west (Égadi, Isole). From here, take the steep mountain road to the medieval town of ❾ ✳✳ **Érice** (751m/2464ft).

The SS 115 runs southwards from Tràpani, across flat land to the port of ❿ ✳ **Marsala** with its wineries (31km/19mi), and then south-eastwards to the pretty port of ✳ **Mazara del Vallo** (22km/14mi). After ✳ **Castelvetrano** the road reaches the ruins of the ancient Greek town of Selinunte (⓫ ✳✳ **Selinunte**), once one of the largest towns on the Mediterranean, with more than 100,000 inhabitants (35km/22mi). Rest and relaxation is available in the neighbouring   fishing and holiday town of Marinella, which has beautiful sandy   beaches. Now it is possible to choose between two different routes to the spa town of ⓬ ✳ **Sciacca** at the foot of Mount San Calógero; there is either the main road, SS 115, or the winding, but charming old road via Menfí (42km/26mi).

From Tràpani to Agrigento
◄ 200km/124mi

The final section of this leg makes its way via **Ribera** (22km/14mi) to the Plàtani River (11km/7mi), beyond which a path to the right leads to the ruins of ancient Heraclea Minoa (⓭**Eraclea Minoa**). For a break from historical sites, head for the ✳✳ **sandy beaches** around Capo Bianco (►Baedeker Tip p. 199). Past Siculiana and the port of Porto Empédocle, the road finally reaches Agrigento (⓮ ✳✳ **Agrigento**). Its ancient temples are among the most significant evidence of ancient culture (36km/22mi).

It is possible to complete this leg by taking the shorter coastal route to Gela via **Licata** (44km/27mi), but the route through the interior is preferable because of its scenic beauty and art-historical significance. The SS 640 winds its way northeastwards from Agrigento to the provincial capital of **Caltanissetta**, the centre of sulphur mining (53km/33mi), and onwards to ⓯ ✳✳ **Enna** (948m/3110ft; 34km/21mi), the »balcony of Sicily«. The nearby picturesque town of **Calascibetta** is worth a visit (7km/4mi).

From Agrigento to Enna and Gela
◄ 188km/117mi

Now turn southwards on the SS 561, passing the ancient lake of Pergusa (9km/6mi), where, according to ancient legend, the god of the underworld, Hades, abducted Persephone. Nowadays drivers compete for titles on the local racetrack. The attractive mountain road then leads to ⓰ ✳ **Piazza Armerina** (29km/18mi), the starting point for a trip to the ✳✳ **Villa Romana del Casale** with its rich 3rd and 4th-century mosaics (6km/4mi to the south). The final section runs along the SS 117b southwards to the port and industrial town of ⓱ ✳ **Gela** with its archaeological attractions (44km/27mi).

Shortly after Gela the SS 115 leaves the coast behind. It makes its way to the Baroque towns of **Vittória** (33km/21mi) and ✳ **Ragusa** (25km/16mi), then via ⓲ ✳ **Módica** (15km/9mi) and ✳ **Íspica** (18km/11mi) to ⓳ ✳✳ **Noto**, Sicily's Baroque gem (21km/

From Gela to Ragusa and Syracuse
◄ 144km/89mi

Excursions ▶ 13mi). Hikers and water lovers will find attractive excursions from Módica and Noto into the island's interior or to the coast (▶Tour 3, p. 130).

The SS 115 gets back to the coast at **Ávola**, leaving the beach at Ognina to the right, and ending in Syracuse (❷⓪ ✳ ✳ **Siracusa**) (32km/20mi), once the largest Greek town in Sicily, with magnificent reminders of its golden past.

Excursion ▶ Take the SS 124 to ❷①**Palazzolo Acréide** (697m/2287ft, 42km/26mi), a Baroque town with the remains of ancient Akrai (including a theatre and necropolis). Drive northwest for 10km/6mi towards Caltagirone, then turn right and through Càssaro and Ferla to the necropolis of ✳ ✳ **Pantálica** (32km/20mi), Sicily's largest necropolis with more than 5000 graves from the early historical period, set in picturesque landscape high above the Anapo Valley.

From Syracuse to Messina 175km/109mi ▶ This section of the round trip covers Sicily's east coast. As it leaves Syracuse, the major SS 114 road touches the plateau on which the necropolis was located, the main section of ancient Syracuse, then makes its way to the coast and passes the narrow Magnisi peninsula. Shortly afterwards, the turning to the excavation site of ancient ❷② ✳ **Megara Hyblaea** lies 15km/9mi outside Syracuse. 1km/0.5mi later there is a turning to the right, which leads to the port of **Augusta** (14km/9mi). The road now crosses the plain of Catania and the River Simeto, reaching the lively town of ❷③ ✳ **Catania** (32km/20mi from Syracuse).

Catania is a good starting point for trips to Europe's most active volcano, Mount Etna (❷④ ✳ ✳ **Etna**) or for a trip around the mountain to Taormina. This route is 112km/70mi (as against 50km/31mi for the direct route between Catania and Taormina). From Catania to Messina, accompanied by the Autostrada A 18,

 DON'T MISS

- The island's capital Palermo
- Segesta, Selinunte, Agrigento, testimonies of »Magna Graecia«
- Syracuse, a port with a significant ancient heritage
- Catania and Mount Etna, Europe's largest and most active volcano
- Taormina's breathtaking location
- The picture-book silhouette of Cefalù
- In the interior: Piazza Armerina with mosaics in the Roman Villa del Casale
- Necropolis of Pantálica
- Noto, Ragusa and Módica, Sicily's lively Baroque towns

the SS 114 touches on the »Riviera dei Ciclopi«, home to holiday resorts such as **Aci Castello**, **Aci Trezza** and **Acireale**. The road now makes its way via Giarre and Fiumefreddo to Cape Schisò with the ruins of ✳ **Naxos**, the oldest Greek colony on Sicily (45km/28mi), and to **Giardini** (2km/1mi), a seaside town and the station for ❷⑤ ✳ ✳ **Taormina** (3km/2mi). Because of its location high above the sea and the splendid Teatro Greco with views of Mount Etna, this small town is one of the highlights of a trip to Sicily. The road then follows the coast to **Messina** (6km/4mi), the round trip's starting point.

Tour 2 A Breath of the Gods: Temples, Theatres, Ruins

Start and End: Palermo
Duration: at least 8 days

Length: 500km/310mi

The first Greeks arrived in Sicily in the second half of the 8th century BC. Within just a few generations »Magna Graecia« underwent an incredible boom. This tour visits the best examples of ancient architecture, which have enchanted travellers from every era.

After an extensive exploration of ❶ ✱ ✱ **Palermo** (including a trip to the cathedral of ❷ ✱ ✱ **Monreale**) this tour makes its way along the Gulf of Carini to ❸ ✱ ✱ **Segesta**. The incomplete temple has stood majestically in a valley by Monte Bàrbaro for almost 2500 years. Those who are good on foot can walk up to the Greek theatre from here (there are also buses). ❹ ✱ ✱ **Érice** is a good place to spend the night: with its tidy streets and historic buildings high up above the sea, it is probably Sicily's most beautiful town after Taormina.

Lovely sandy beaches in ❺ ✱ **San Vito lo Capo** invite visitors to stop and spend a few restful days. A trip to Sicily's most beautiful nature

◄ Excursions

reserve, ✳✳ **Zingaro**, with its magical little bays, steep cliffs and unspoilt nature is a must (either from here or the pretty fishing village of Scopello; get there via Castellammare del Golfo).

The main route includes a detour to the island of ❻ ✳ **Mózia** in the Stagnone Lagoon, with its Carthaginian excavations. The road then continues to ✳ **Marsala**, known for its dessert wines and boasting an unexpectedly pretty old town, and to ✳ **Mazara del Vallo**, Sicily's main fishing port. One great place to stop is the ancient quarry of **Cave di Cusa**, where visitors can see the individual phases in which the column sections for the temples in Selinunte were carved. Next up is another highlight, namely the excavations of ❼ ✳✳ **Selinunte**, once one of the largest towns on the Mediterranean. There are nice sandy beaches in the neighbouring holiday and fishing town of Marinella. Beyond ❽ ✳ **Sciacca**, a significant port and Sicily's best-known thermal bath, the tour reaches the former Greek settlement of ❾ **Heraclea Minoa** with ruins of a theatre. Below the cliff is a wonderful, long ✳✳ **sandy beach** (► Baedeker Tip p. 211), the ideal place to stop and take a break before heading on to ❿ ✳✳ **Agrigento**, whose places of worship in the Valle dei Templi are among the most significant testimonies to ancient culture.

Between Agrigento and Palermo From here the tour makes its way back to Palermo through the island's interior, not on the SS 189 or the SS 121, but on the less busy SS 118. This area is one of Sicily's lesser known beauties, even though it was described by Tomaso di Lampedusa in *The Leopard* and in spite of the fact that Hollywood has made places such as ⓫**Prizzi** and ⓬**Corleone** famous around the world. ✳ **Bosco della Ficuzza**, dominated by the rock walls of Rocca Busambra and situated around 15km/9mi outside Corleone, is a refuge for rare animals and plants and also a good place to go hiking. ⓭**Piana degli Albanesi**, which was founded by Albanian refugees towards the end of the 15th century, is a popular destination for the inhabitants of the capital, particularly at weekends. From here it is another 20km/12mi to the outskirts of **Palermo**.

Tour 3 Suffering Set in Stone: Baroque Sicily

Start and end: Catania   **Length:** 400km/250mi
Duration: 7 days

In the beginning there was a disaster: the severe earthquake of 1693 destroyed Catania and dozens of towns and villages in the southeast of the island. However, the rebuilding works began just a short while later.

Catania and numerous other towns, including Noto, Módica, Grammichele, Ragusa, Scicli and Palazzolo Acréide, were rebuilt in the Baroque style, the preferred style of that period, which combines and glorifies effervescent joie de vivre and profound piety. This route visits the most significant examples of this stylistic and architectural »experiment«.

The starting point is ❶ ✳ **Catania**, the »black daughter of Etna«, which was seriously damaged during the volcanic eruption of 1669 and by the earthquake of 1693. During its reconstruction black lava stone was the preferred building material. Magnificent Baroque buildings adorn the cathedral square. There is, however, also interesting evidence of Antiquity and the Middle Ages. The route then continues along the coast, past **Augusta** to ❷ ✳✳ **Siracusa**, a town with a great past. Anyone in the mood for scenery and exercise should visit the necropolis of ❸ ✳✳ **Pantálica** (a simple trip via Floridia, Casa Valle Fame, Càssaro and Ferla, approx. 50km/30mi).

The Baroque towns now start lining the SS 115 like pearls on a necklace: ❹ ✳✳ **Noto**, which has preserved its Baroque appearance like no other town; **Ìspica**, the pretty rural town of **Scicli** and ❺ ✳ **Módica**, divided into an upper and lower town. ❻ ✳ **Ragusa** also consists of two parts, a Baroque upper town and a largely medieval lower town, where San Giorgio Cathedral can be found. It is one of Sicily's most significant Baroque structures.

Noto and Módica are starting points for wonderful trips into the island's interior, where rivers, now mostly dry, carved spectacular gorges (Italian: cava) into the foothills of the Hyblaean Mountains. The wild, romantic 13km/8mi ✳ **Cava d'Ìspica** (►Módica) was inhabited

◄ Excursions

The Baroque town of Noto welcomes the spring.

from the Stone Age until 1693. ✳ ✳ **Cava Grande del Cassibile** (▶ Ávola) attracts visitors with several idyllically located pools. Those interested in birds or a highly diverse underwater world should make a detour to the nature reserve of ❼ **Vendicari** (▶ Baedeker Tip p. 305), one of Sicily's most important wetlands, which runs all the way to **Marzamemi**, a great place to spend a few relaxing days on the coast. The small seaside towns between Marzamemi and **Pozzallo** are mainly frequented by Italian visitors. The »Baroque Route« now either follows the SS 194 via Giarratana or the SS 514 via the mountain town of Chiaramonte Gufli, known for is sausages, to ❽ **Grammichele**. This Baroque town is only 15km/9mi from ❾ ✳ **Caltagirone**, the »Città della Ceramica«, Sicily's »ceramics capital«, with its Baroque upper town. From here it is another 65km/40mi on SS 417 to **Catania**, the tour's starting point.

Tour 4 The Monti Sicani

Start and End: Vicari **Length:** 100km/60mi
Duration: driving time approx. 4 hours

This trip makes its way through the southernmost part of Palermo province along the Monti Sicani. The tour leaves the town of Vicari and heads to Santo Stéfano via Prizzi and back again via Cammarata and Lercara Friddi. There are lots of hiking opportunities en route.

Gentle rolling hills and rugged, inaccessible elevations up to 1000m/ 3300ft lie side by side here, forming fascinating contrasts. In addition this region is one of the most fertile, since it is also the wettest. Some of the mountain towns were Mafia strongholds. ❶**Vicari** lies at the foot of the remains of a mighty 11th-century Norman castle that once dominated the entire river valley of the San Leonardo. A walk to the ruin is really worthwhile for the magnificent panoramic views. The route from Vicari to Prizzi is a small country road. It leads past the **Portella della Croce** and the **Castello della Márgana**, which towers up on an inaccessible rock. The Monte Cáraci protected area is situated to the south. The pretty old quarter of the small mountain town of ❷**Prizzi** (1000m/3280ft) is a lovely place to go for a walk. At Easter, Death and the Devil walk through the convoluted streets for the »Ballo dei Diavoli«, at the end of which they are forced to flee by angels. Rugged landscapes on the one side of Prizzi, and dense oak woods on the other, provide a contrasting and exciting ambience.

A trip to the **Montagna dei Cavalli** to the south is also very worthwhile. Its untouched landscape is home to rare trees, plants and many different kinds of orchids. The main SS 118 road then makes its way to ❸**Pian del Leone**, a lake popular with migratory birds.

Through an untouched environment

Leave the SS 118 in Santo Stéfano Quisquino and take a side road to ❹**Cammarata** – it is possible to make a detour to the S. Rosalia hermitage on the way. The route runs through the Monte Cammarata protected area. The mountain of this name is the highest elevation of the Monti Sicani. En route from Cammarata to ❺**Castronovo di Sicilia** are the cliffs of Monte Cammarata and Monte Kassar, a sanctuary for geese, herons and herring gulls. Past further picnic sites and starting points for hikes, this is a good area for excursions into the nearby protected area (such as that of the Monte Carcaci with many holm oaks and downy oaks as well

as rare falcon species). The road finally reaches ❻**Lercara Friddi**, where sulphur was once mined and Sicily's best liqueurs are now made and sold (▶tip p. 172). Take the SS 189 down towards Palermo, to the starting point at **Vicari**.

Hiking route 1 Monte Venere

Start/end: Taormina/Castelmola
Walking time: 3 hrs 45 mins

Length: 7km/4mi
Elevation: 630m/2065ft ascent, 380m/1245ft descent

The trip from Taormina to Castelmola has always been a popular tourist trail and, whether enjoyed by bus or on foot, there is a lot to see. Continue on the old mule tracks and be rewarded by an even more magnificent view, usually with no other tourists around, from the 884m/2900ft Monte Venere.

Route The hike from ✳ ✳ **Taormina** to Castelmola starts at Largo S. Caterina outside **Palazzo Corvaia** (tourist office; ▶ map p. 422). Take the Via Circonvallazione behind the Roman **Odeon**, from which a marked stairway soon leads up to the **Church of Madonna della Rocca**, accompanied by fantastic views and diverse vegetation. Further towards Castelmola, follow the surfaced road for a little while, before turning left at the Casa Gigi Samperi, a ceramics workshop. The steep road and concrete steps lead to the underpass below **Castelmola** (1 hr).

It is just a few paces to the left to the town centre. The walk, however, turns right here. Cross the road and follow the steps and the road downhill for a little while to the next intersection. Keeping the Padre Pio statue and the war memorial on the left, take the road up the hill. The metal sign »**M. Venere**« shows the way. The road forks at a cemetery. Go straight on, past a large antenna. The gravel road, surfaced in places, quickly climbs between the houses of the Contrada Roccella in hairpin bends. The road narrows above the houses, turns right and almost levels out as it makes its way past open terraces. After passing two private driveways, leave the pass and turn left on to the path marked red, which opens into a flight of steps. The old **Mulattiera** (cobbled mule track) follows the ridge line. Shortly before the steps are interrupted by the street, there is a stone bench, a perfect spot for a break (1 hr 40 mins).

Now follow the narrow road uphill for a little while, past an antenna. Below the reservoir continue left, cross the street and follow the old farm road along the ridge. The pink ruins of the Bar Scalia, which was a popular destination until the 1950s, lie along the way. The pretty view remains. Cross the narrow surfaced road one last time. The next time you encounter it, follow it to the left until you reach a pass (2 hrs 5 mins). A marked path then goes right towards Forza d'Agrò, the ascent towards the summit (marked red) turns sharply to the right over slabs of rock and then on an unmistakable path. Cross the depression between the karst limestone to get to the top of Monte Venere (2 hrs 20 mins), whose summit is marked by a cairn and a triangulation point. The panoramic views are magnificent! The

Castelmola: the small mountain town seems to hover above the sea.

Peloritani can be seen in the north, the road from Messina in the east and beyond it the mountains of Calabria. Taormina and the Bay of Naxos are right below us, while the majestic Mount Etna dominates the view to the south. Return back to Castelmola via the same route. There are buses to Taormina from the piazza at the town entrance.

Hiking route 2 Monte Nero and Grotta dei Lamponi

Start/end: Piano Provenzana
Walking time: 3 hrs 30 mins

Length: 10km/6mi
Elevation: 350m/1150ft ascent and descent

✳ ✳ **Mount Etna is even more magnificent from the north than on its south side, which is also usually overrun by tourists. Piano Provenzana, a popular winter sports resort, was completely covered in lava in 2002–03. The hike around Monte Nero and to the Grotta dei Lamponi shows off the whole spectrum of the mountain's diverse variety of volcanic shapes.**

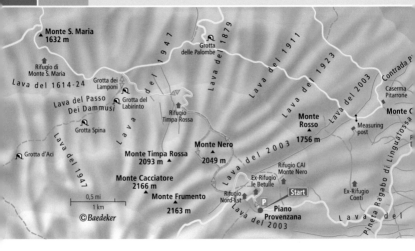

Route An off-road vehicle track runs northwards from the car park by the STAR office (four-by-four excursions towards the summit crater) in **Piano Provenzana**. Follow it through a field of black lava dating from 2002–03 with its typical rough surface, past dead white trees and to the turning marked »Monte Nero – Rifugio Timpa Rossa« (15 mins). Little cairns mark the path through the young lava layer. Keep walking towards the bare cone of Monte Nero, then cross a sandy plateau where milk vetch grows in thorny pillows. On the eastern flank of **Monte Nero** (35 mins) the path turns to the right and runs parallel to a number of small craters known as *bottoniera* (buttonhole facing).

This path meets another from the top. Follow the new one to the left, making your way along the northern flank of Monte Nero. To the right is the Alcantara Valley, beyond which are the Peloritani and Nebrodi mountains. A cairn marks the next fork (45 mins); climbing to the left is the later return route. This is a good point to shorten the walk. The walk proper continues to the right towards the Grotta dei Lamponi, crossing a further lava field and subsequently heading into the beech forest. The **Rifugio Timpa Rossa** (1 hr 5 mins) stands in a clearing. It has an open shelter room.

From the hut, take the descending forestry track through the beech forest. At the **Passo dei Dammusi** (1 hr 35 mins) this track meets the Pista Altamontana, which runs in a wide arc around Mount Etna in the west. While a'a lava is dominant around Mount Etna, the 1614–24 eruption largely brought pahoehoe lava to this area, which is a very fluid lava. The billowy surface and lava caves are typical; large hollow spaces were formed when the lava continued to flow below the surface, while the surface itself had already cooled. Follow the wide track to the left for a few steps and then turn left on to a path. Washed out colour markers and cairns show the way to the **Grotta dei Lamponi** (1 hr 40 mins). The ceiling of this huge lava cave has collapsed in two places. Explore it carefully and with torches. Without knowledgeable mountain guides it is wise to turn back at this point. Walk back along the same route, past the **Rifugio Timpasole**, back to the fork in the road on the northern flank of Monte Nero (2 hrs 40 mins). Turn right here and follow the ascending path, which is marked by widely spaced wooden pegs and occasionally also by red colour markers. This path makes its way around Monte Nero in an anti-clockwise direction. The smoking summit craters can be seen along the way. On the sandy plateau to the east of Monte Nero the circle is complete and the waymarked path makes its way back through the young lava field on to the off-road vehicle track. **Piano Provenzana** lies to the left.

A safety tip to conclude: in the event of fog, turn back and stay on the familiar route. If there are signs of a thunderstorm do not even set off to begin with!

Hiking route 3 Pantàlica

Start/end: Anaktoron
Walking time: 3 hrs 45 mins

Length: 13km/8mi
Elevation: 500m/1640 ascent and descent

Declared a UNESCO World Heritage site, , ✷ ✷ Pantàlica (▶Palazzolo Acréide, surroundings), with thousands of Bronze Age rock tombs and deep gorges, is also one of Sicily's scenic highlights. An ideal day trip from Syracuse!

From the car park below the **Anaktoron**, the royal palace of the my-   **Route**
thical King Hiblon, it is just a few steps to the small elevation with the foundation walls of the megalithic palace. The signposted path towards »Necropoli Sud. Villaggio Bizantino« initially makes its way eastwards, only to turn back west later. Past chamber tombs, another path meets up with this one from the valley to the left. This is the later return route. For now continue straight on. The River Anapo gorge lies to the left. The route forks at the previously announced **Belvedere Necropoli Sud** (20 mins). Before descending, it is worth making a little detour to the Byzantine village of San Micidiario and the necropolises of Filiporto. On the pass of Filiporto (30 mins) this walk crosses the ancient defensive trench which protected the plateau and the Anaktoron from attacks from the west.

Back at the Belvedere Necropoli Sud fork, there are steps in the rock leading down into the valley. At the next fork, keep left and join the dirt road that was visible from above as a light band. Until 1956 a narrow-gauge railway connected Syracuse and Vizzini. Heading left, it is not far to the **former station Necropoli Pantàlica** (1 hr 15 mins), with toilets next door. Now follow the old railway tracks down river

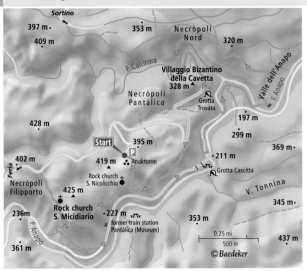

(there is the option of making a small detour to the right down to the river). Somewhat further a path branches off to the left; it is marked as »Percorsi Particolari D«. Climbing up here is the shortest way of returning to the starting point. The walk, however, continues straight ahead on the gravel road, first through a short tunnel, then over a bridge. Before the next long tunnel (1 hr 45 mins), turn left on to a path that is initially accompanied by a wooden railing.

The path follows the course of the Anapo in a semi-circle, with some mild scrambling sections. Shortly before it rejoins the dirt road, turn left to the river at a group of aspens (2 hrs). Cross to the other side over the stepping stones. The road now climbs in hairpin bends, past an abandoned farmstead, through almond and carob groves. Use the wooden ladder to climb over the fence and turn left on to the road coming from Sortino (2 hrs 20 mins). Heading eastwards as a dirt road, it turns into a narrow path that descends further between dry-stone walls. The rock tombs carved into the limestone walls look like honeycombs. Climb down the steps in the rock to reach the valley floor of the Calcinara after 2 hrs 45 mins. The clear water pours down cascades into rock pools; from the end of May onwards olean-der is in full bloom here.

There are more stepping stones to the other riverbank here, with steps leading back up to the end of a surfaced road (3 hrs).

Follow it towards Ferla all the way to a sharp right-hand turn (3 hrs 10 mins). Continue in the same direction, but leave the road to the left, following the narrow path that winds its way down the hillside in hairpin bends. This path crosses another. Take this one to the right (uphill). At the next two forks turn right to get back to the starting point at the Anaktoron (3 hrs 45 mins).

Pantalica: on the tracks of the Sicels

Hiking route 4 Riserva dello Zingaro

Start/end: Park entrance south (Scopello)
Walking time: 5 hrs 30 mins

Length: 15km/9mi
Elevation: 600m/1970ft ascent and descent

A wild mountain landscape contrasts with hidden bays and the turquoise sea as well as with exotic dwarf palms. Both swimwear and firm footwear are a must in✳ ✳ Zingaro. At the park entrance (entry fee) friendly rangers hand out trail maps. If walking with small children, it is best to follow the main path along the coast, not least because there are several places here with access to the sea. It is also easier to turn back at any time.

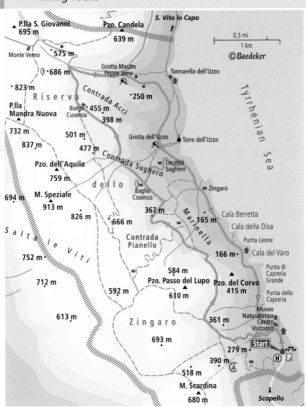

Route From the south entrance of the Riserva (►Castellammare del Golfo) there is a dirt road through a rock tunnel. It narrows until it finally becomes a clearly visible path. Leave the main path that runs parallel to the coast and turn left, in order to climb the slope in short hairpin bends above the **Centro Visitatori** (12 mins). This path meets a vehicle track from below (45 mins). Follow it to the right. It ends outside a small house. Just before that, turn left on the signposted path that climbs diagonally up the karst hillside. Keep right at the next fork, cross a valley and ignore the next turning on the left.

The path makes its way across a small plateau to the pass between Pizzo Passo del Lupo (610m/2000ft) and Pizzo del Corvo (415m/1360ft). The short, »pathless« excursion to the right up **Pizzo del Corvo** (1 hr 25 mins) is rewarded with a magnificent view: it encompasses everything from Scopello and Monte Inici to the south, the Gulf of Castellamare to the east and the mountainous backbone of the Zingaro reserve in the north and west. Sughero and Baglio Cosenza can also be made out in the north. This walk will make its way past these two abandoned settlements. Descend northwards with a view of a group of houses. Walking through wild almond and olive groves, the route now leads to **Località Sughero** (2 hrs 15 mins). The path branching off to the right leads back to the main coastal route. This route, however, continues straight on. Upon reaching the last house in the north, turn left and follow the hairpin bends up the hill, over a pass to **Borgo Cusenza** (3 hrs), which was still inhabited until the 1960s. Follow the vehicle track northwards to a valley entrance; now turn right onto the marked path that goes down into the Contrada Uzzo, past the Grotta Mastro Peppe Siino. Close to the sea this path rejoins the main path. Follow it southwards to the right. After the rugged mountain scenery the **Contrada Uzzo** feels like a green oasis. Dense dwarf palms surround the wild almond grove. In the rock wall on the right hand side is the **Grotta dell'Uzzo** (4 hrs 15 mins). This

In Zingaro Nature Park

karst cave has been a place of refuge since time immemorial. In the 1950s it was used by the bandit Giuliano and his gang as a hiding place. Past the Grotta dell'Uzzo the main path leads back to the park's south entrance. On the mountainside this is where the path from Località Sughero joins the main path. Along the way there are plenty of spots where paths lead down to the sea. At the visitor centre a path branches off left to the **Punta della Capreria** (also known as Cala della Capreria), the last of the wonderful bays. Walk back through the rock tunnel to get back to the starting point of this tour at the south entrance (5 hrs 30 mins).

Hiking route 5 Bosco della Ficuzza

Start/End: Ficuzza
Walking time: 2 hrs 15 mins

Length: 9km/6mi
Elevation: 250m/820ft ascent and descent

One of Sicily's most beautiful oak forests can be found at the foot of the proud Rocca Busambra. The hunting passion of the Bourbon King Ferdinand I saved it from being cut down. Today it is protected. The Bosco della Ficuzza is most beautiful in May, when the wild peonies are in bloom.

Route There is a large square in front of the hunting palace in **Ficuzza** (▶p. 383). Behind the façade with the coat of arms of the House of Bourbon are the no less regal cliffs of the **Rocca Busambra**. At the square's northwest corner a panel provides information for walkers. Facing away from the palace, go right past the Bar Cavaretta, over the next road and down the paved steps. This route crosses a surfaced road before meeting a gravel track from above; the former **Ficuzza station** on the left is now a **restaurant that also offers accommodation** (Antica Stazione di Ficuzza, tel. 09 18 46 00 00, www.anticastazione.it).

The railway track from Palermo into the hinterland of Corleone, closed down in 1954, has been turned into a trail for hikers and cyclists. Past the old water tower, follow this path to the right, walking away from the Antica Stazione. This path passes the Vasca Rifornimento Locomotive, a pool no longer in use, and a stationmaster's house. Before the bridge the view back to Ficuzza with the palace and Rocca Ramusa, the western continuation of Rocca Busambra, is lovely. The track now curves to the right, carving its way through the sandstone hill; it is lined by supporting walls on both sides. Shortly afterwards the path forks in the forest. The path to the left leads down to a watering hole. This walk however goes straight on a little longer, before taking the right-hand path shortly before the tunnel

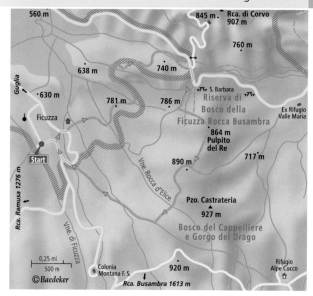

entrance, climbing to the crossing **Quattro Finaite** (50 mins). The surfaced S P 26 comes past here.

Without making contact with the provincial road, this hike continues to the right. Leave the gently ascending gravel road at the top (1 hr), turning left. Past a barrier the wide path climbs up to the Pulpito del Re. On the way there is a group of rocks on the right-hand side that makes a good place for a break. In the west, near Piana degli Albanesi, is the striking 1233m/4045ft **Kumeta**. With no views whatsoever, the **Pulpito del Re** (King's Pulpit; 1 hr 10 mins) is situated in an elevated clearing. It is a hunting seat carved into the sandstone. This is where King Ferdinand killed the game that had been driven in front of his shotgun. Today the forest of Ficuzza is home only to foxes.

Maintain the original direction and follow the narrow path uphill, which soon veers off to the right. Walking southwards, cross the forested elevation. This route leads to a clearing from which there are views of the steep cliffs of Rocca Busambra (1613m/5292ft) and Rocca Ramosa (1276m/4186ft). There is a small holm-oak wood below. Ficuzza and the hunting lodge can be seen to the right. The path now goes downhill and in **Vallone Rocca d'Elice** meets a signposted intersection (1 hr 30 mins).

The way back to Ficuzza runs downhill to the right along the opposite riverbank, between a fenced field and the stream. This route meets a gravel road from above. Follow it to the left all the way to the surfaced road. Take this road to the left, cross the bridge and, shortly afterwards, turn right at the next intersection to get back to the town in just a few minutes.

Hiking route 6 Piano Pomo and Cozzo Luminario

Start/End: Piano Sempria
Walking time: 1 hr 45 mins

Length: 3.5km/2 mi
Elevation: 325m/1066ft ascent and descent

There is an enchanting forest of large hollies on Piano Pomo, a relic from the last ice age and unique in Europe. One of the most beautiful views in the ✳ Parco delle Madonie is to be had from the Cozzo Luminario. On clear days it is possible to see all the way to Mount Etna and the Aeolian Islands.

Route Hikers will only be able to reach the Piano Sempria, the starting point for this walk, with their own vehicle. In **Castelbuono** (►Monti Madoníe) follow the S S 286 towards Geraci Siculo, in order to turn right on to the road towards **San Guglielmo** on the southern outskirts of town. The surfaced road, which is of poor quality towards the end, finishes on the Piano Sempria (1187m/3894ft). The **Rifugio Crispi**, a cosy mountain hut maintained by the Sicilian alpine club C.A.S., is a good place to spend the night. It is known for its hearty food (Rifugio F. Crispi, Contrada Piano Sempria, tel. 09 21 67 22 79, rifugiofrancescocrispi@ristorantiitaliani.it).

There is a panel at the **Piano Sempria** illustrating the course of the **nature trail** (sentiero natura). The marked path turns right into the beech forest and ascends rapidly in hairpin bends. Cyclamen and ruscus flourish in the undergrowth. This path crosses the forestry track that ascends from Piano Sempria towards Piano Pomo. This will be the later return route. There is a magnificent **downy oak** at the wayside, estimated to be more than 800 years old. The hollow

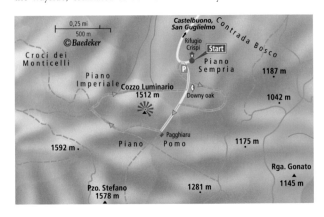

trunk houses a chapel dedicated to the Virgin Mary. The path continues to climb, then crosses a forest aisle and makes its way into a holm-oak wood. The view from a clearing (15 mins) above the Vallone Canna is lovely. To the south is Monte S. Salvatore, to the east Geraci Siculo, the Monti dei Nébrodi, and with luck Mount Etna. The path follows the terrain edge, crosses a rock sill and meets the forestry road from below. Turn left, before going through a gate and entering **Piano Pomo** (1261m/ 4137ft; 35 mins). There is a shelter

? DID YOU KNOW ...?

- Hollies can live for more than 300 years and grow up to 15m/50ft. The holly tree is evergreen and protected all over Italy. In the past its branches were hung in larders in order to keep mice away. The leaves of the lower branches have sharp thorns, while the leaves higher up are characterized by smooth edges. From April to May the trees produce either male or female flowers. Only the latter turn into berries, which ripen in winter. They are popular with birds (but poisonous for humans).

covered in rushes on this pasture, built as the shepherds did in the past. The Pagghiaru now serves as a **refuge** for the forestry workers and some of the rooms are open to hikers. Facing away from the Pagghiaru, cross the fence and turn right, quickly reaching an enchanted grove that is full of **holly trees** up to 15m/50ft tall. The wooden sign reading »Agriflori giganti« marks the entrance to the »natural cathedral«. The evergreen trees are covered in bright red berries in November. Above the hollies is a huge beech tree with the wooden sign »Faggio secolare«. The path turns sharply right here and climbs past ancient beech and oak trees and through sandstone rocks up to the **Cozzo Luminario** (55 mins), which has a summit cross (1512m/4961ft). The Madoníe Mountains are all around, the Tyrrhenian Sea is to the north. Castelbuono is down below. The piazza, corso and castle can be made out clearly. From the summit ridge the path curves to the right and descends northwards, coming across a perpendicular vehicle track at **Piano Imperiale** (1 hr), a further karst depression. Follow this track to the right. Back in the beech forest the forestry road starts descending in hairpin bends. At the next intersection (1 hr 10 mins) there are two descent options: the forestry track to the left descends rapidly, whereas the right-hand option rejoins the nature trail just before the Piano Pomo (just a few minutes). Both paths end at the Rifugio Crispi on Piano Sempria.

Destinations from A to Z

GREEK TEMPLES, ROMAN THEATRES, MOSAICS – HERE THE TEMPLE OF CONCORDIA IN AGRIGENTO – AS WELL AS SEASIDE FUN AND BEAUTIFUL SCENERY IN THE ISLAND'S INTERIOR: A HOLIDAY ON SICILY HAS ALL THIS TO OFFER.

Acireale

T 7

Province: Catania
Population: 53,000

Altitude: 160m/525ft

The lively town of Acireale towers above the sea on a lava terrace at the northern end of the Riviera dei Ciclopi.

Baroque ice-cream city with belvedere
Acireale is the successor to the Greek colony of Xiphonia, founded in 731 BC. The current townscape is characterized by the Baroque buildings around the Piazza Duomo, built after the earthquake of 1693. The square now has some high-quality ice cream parlours. Acireale is known for its **puppet theatre** (www.operadeipupi.com; ► Baedeker Special p. 342), carnival and a nativity scene from 1736, which is on display in a lava grotto during the Christmas season.

What to See in Acireale

Piazza Duomo
The cathedral square is dominated by the **duomo** (1597–1618), which features a richly ornamented Baroque portal and a neo-Gothic façade. Inside there is a meridian line surrounded by the signs of the zodiac (1843) and in the Cappella di Santa Venere a silver statue of the town's patron saint (1651). To the right next to the cathedral is the 18th-century Chiesa dei Santi Pietro e Paolo, which has an unfinished north tower, and the Baroque Palazzo Comunale (1659). The neighbouring Piazza Vigo is home to the Chiesa **San Sebastiano** (17th century) with its richly ornamented façade by Giovanni Battista Marino (1754) and integrated bell tower; the frescoes on the inside were painted by Pietro Paolo Vasta (1697–1760).

Collections
In the Palazzo Pennisi di Floristella to the left of this church there is a significant collection of ancient coins.
Further collections are housed in Pinacoteca dell'Accademia Zelantea (Via Marchese di San Giuliano 15; a library of old books as well as a bust of Caesar among other things).

? DID YOU KNOW …?

- Granita, a Sicilian speciality that's popular in summer, is made of semi-frozen water with herbal essences, coffee or the juice of lemons, oranges, figs or peaches. The granita served in Café Costarelli on Piazza Duomo in Acireale is particularly good. Beautiful and almost too big too eat are the opulent ice-cream sundaes in this long-established pasticceria.

In the south of town, between the station and SS 114, is the **Santa Venera thermal bath** (sulphurous and radioactive springs, www.terme-acirea le.com), a 19th-century neo-Classical building.
The park of the **Villa Belvedere** in the northern upper town affords splendid views of Mount Etna and the coast. There is also a sculpture of Acis and Galatea in the park.

▶ VISITING ACIREALE

INFORMATION
Via Oreste Scionti 15
Tel. 0 95 89 19 99
www.acirealeturismo.it

EVENT
Acireale's famous carnival is held in February.

GOING OUT
One of the island's largest summer-time open-air nightclubs is: Banacher, Via Vampolieri 66, Aci Castello
www.banacher.com

WHERE TO EAT
▶ Moderate
Trattoria Al Ficodindia
Piazza San Domenico 1
Tel. 09 57 63 70 24
Family-run restaurant, serving many dishes based on prickly pears, delicious liqueurs

L'Antica Osteria
Via Carpinati 30, tel. 095 60 57 56
Popular trattoria/pizzeria near Piazza Duomo

Santa Maria la Scala • La Grotta
Via Scalo Grande 46
Tel. 09 57 64 81 53; Closed Tue
Simple and good fish trattoria just a stone's throw from the harbour

Il Covo Marino
Lungomare dei Ciclopi 149
 Tel. 09 57 11 66 49, closed Mon
Excellent antipasti, outstanding fish platters, terrace and sea views

WHERE TO STAY
▶ Mid-range
Maugeri
Piazza G. Garibaldi 27, tel.
0 95 60 86 66, www.hotel-maugeri.it
45 rooms; near the cathedral, good food

Santa Caterina
Via Santa Caterina 42/b
Tel. 09 57 63 37 35, fax 09 57 63 52 74
www.santacaterinahotel.com; 20 rooms
The old town is within walking distance, comfortable rooms, top-class ristorante

Scillichenti • Il Limoneto
Via D'Amico 41 , tel. 095 88 65 68
www.illimoneto.it Quietly situated agriturismo with small apartments and a wonderful view of the countryside and the sea

Santa Tecla • Santa Tecla Palace
Via Balestrate 100
Tel. 09 57 63 40 15, www.hotelsanta tecla.it – 209 rooms; nice location above the rocky cliffs; spacious rooms

Capomulini • Parkhotel Capomulini
Viale della Fiera Franca 33
Tel. 0 95 87 75 11, www.parkhotelca pomulini.it; 103 rooms
At the small harbour; with many restaurants in the surrounding area; the seaward rooms are quiet.

Aci Trezza • I Faraglioni
Lungomare dei Ciclopi 115
Tel. 09 50 93 04 64
www.grandhotelfaraglioni.com
Rooms with sea views

▶ Budget
Bed & Breakfast Al 22
Via San Carlo 22, tel. 0 95 69 40 88
and 33 45 91 41 17
www.al22.eu – 4 rooms in the renovated old building above Piazza Duomo; breakfast on the terrace

Grotta lavica del Presepio   A nativity scene is on display in the lava grotto (on the road to Santa Maria La Scala in the northwest of town) with life-size figures made of wood and wax.

Beaches and excursions   Locals bathe near the fishing village of Santa Maria La Scala (1km/ 0.5mi to the north), from the beach of Santa Tecla (4km/2.5mi to the north), in Stazzo and in Pozillo.

Around Acireale

Aci Castello   Situated on the eastern flank of Mount Etna, the seaside resort of Aci Castello (population 18,000) is one of the region's most popular holiday destinations. It is dominated by its Norman castle (1076), which stands on a basalt rock above the harbour. **Aci Trezza** is also part of the commune. It was in this fishing village (population 2500, 2km/ 1mi to the north) with views of the bizarre Cyclopean Isles (Isole dei Ciclopi, boat connection) that Luchino Visconti filmed Giovanni Verga's novel *I Malavoglia* (1881; *The House by the Medlar Tree* ▶Baedeker Special p. 100) as *La terra trema* in 1948.

✳ **Riviera dei Ciclopi**   The legend of the giant one-eyed cyclopes is associated with the Isole dei Ciclopi, the Cyclopean Isles; the coastline north of Catania, the

A boat trip to the bizarrely shaped Isole dei Ciclopi near Aci Trezza

»Riviera dei Ciclopi« is also named after them. One of them, Polyphemus, son of the sea god Neptune, captured Odysseus and his
companions. After the giant had
eaten six of his prisoners, Odysseus
managed to blind him and escape.
Polyphemus threw rocks after him,
which landed in the sea without
striking the Greeks – these are the
Cyclopean Isles, the **Isole dei Ciclopi**.
Aci Castello, Acireale and Aci Trezza also boast a mythical origin.
Theocritus and Ovid reported that
Akis (Italian: Acis), the lover of the
nereid Galatea, was transformed
into the River Acis (modern-day
Fiume di Jaci) by the jealous Cy-

! Baedeker TIP

Museo del Palmento

The artists Cristina Amblard and Nino Carnabuci
live and work in Santa Venerina, 15km/9mi north
of Acireale. She is a potter, he is a well-known
painter. They have put their collection of
agricultural tools and rural household items on
display in their Museo del Palmento (Via
Palombaro 56; daily 9.30am–1pm after sunset,
July–Aug 1pm–4pm closed for lunch).

clops Polyphemus. George Frideric Handel was moved to produce
two different compositions by this material. In Naples in 1708 he
wrote the serenata *Aci, Galatea e Polifemo*. Ten years later he used the
same story for an English-language opera, *Acis and Galatea*.
Isola di Aci – Polyphemus's largest rock – is now home to the marine
biological station of Catania University.

★★ Agrigento · Agrigento

J 9

Province: Agrigento
Population: 60,000

Altitude: 230m/755ft

**The provincial capital close to Sicily's south coast, wonderfully situ-
ated in the hills, is one of the most worthwhile destinations on the
whole island because of its magnificent temple ruins. Many ancient
buildings form a contrast to the skyscrapers, some of which dis-
rupt the view of the higher new town. One popular nearby destination is the seaside resort of San Leone (7km/4mi to the southeast), which has a long, sandy beach.**

Tyrants, Poets and Philosophers

The town and the surrounding area were already inhabited in prehistoric times. Ancient tradition attributes the founding of Agrigento to
Daedalus, who fled to Sicily from King Minos of Crete. Akragas becomes historically tangible with its founding in 581 BC by Doric colonists from Gela and their mother city, Rhodes. It was named after
the river Akrágas, which flows through the east of the ancient town

(modern-day Fiume San Biagio) and unites with the Hypsas (now called Fiume Drago) further west. A short while after the town was founded, in 570 BC, Phalaris made himself the lord of Akragas; he had taken over the construction of the Temple of Zeus on the acropolis (in the place where the cathedral now stands), armed his construction workers and used them to subjugate the town. According to tradition, Phalaris became the epitome of a cruel tyrant. In 488 BC Theron seized power and Akragas became a flourishing town and the greatest power on Sicily after Syracuse. Together with his son-in-law Gelo of Syracuse, Theron defeated the Carthaginians at the Battle of Himera in 480 BC. Over the next 70 years the town had a political, cultural and economic golden age, as evidenced by the temples.

The poet Pindar praised Akragas, now with 200,000 inhabitants, in the 12th Pythian Ode as the »fairest of mortal cities«. At this time the philosopher **Empedocles** was active here; he mockingly commented about his fellow countrymen that they built as if they would live forever and ate as if they would die tomorrow. This shining era came to an end with the Carthaginian attack of 409 BC, to which in 406–405 BC, after Selinus and Himera, Akragas also fell victim. During the First Punic War Akragas was captured by the Romans in 261 BC, and then taken and plundered by the Carthaginians in 255 BC. In 210 BC the Romans came back; they enslaved the local population and in 207 BC replaced them by new settlers. The town was then named Agrigentum.

In AD 828, having been devastated by the Vandals and the Ostrogoths, the town fell into Arab hands. During Norman times Girgenti was known as an affluent diocese. It was not until 1927 that it was named Agrigento.

Leo von Klenze (1784–1864), the court architect in Munich from 1818, travelled around Sicily with Ludwig I of Bavaria in 1823–24. He was the first to scientifically survey and record the temples of Agrigento. The nearby port of Porto Empédocle is the birthplace of the authors Luigi Pirandello and Andrea Camilleri (▶ Famous People).

What to See in Modern Agrigento

The modern city   The starting point for looking around the modern city with its labyrinthine web of steep streets and many steps is Piazzale Aldo Moro. This is the starting point of Via Atenea, the city's main shopping street. Walk up through winding streets and flights of steps to the church of **Santa Maria dei Greci**. The Norman nave-and-aisles construction was built over the remains of a Doric Temple of Athena dating from 488 BC, which was quite small (35 x 15m /38 x 16yd). The illuminated remains of the temple, a stepped base and columns, can be seen through a glass floor in the chancel room and in the south aisle.

▶ VISITING AGRIGENTO

INFORMATION
Servizio Turistico
Piazza Aldo Moro, 92100 Agrigento
Tel. 0 92 22 03 91, fax 0 92 22 02 46
www.parcovalledeitempli.it

EVENTS
The almond blossom festival (beginning of February), the Good Friday processions, the feast of Agrigento's patron saint San Calogero (1st and 2nd Sundays in July), Pirandello celebrations (August), Feste di Persefone, classical plays in the Valle dei Templi (July–August) and the competition »Efebo d'oro« for film-music composers (September).

The choice of antipasti and other dishes in Le Caprice is vast.

WHERE TO EAT
▶ Moderate
① *Kalotta*
Piazza San Calogero
Tel. 0 92 22 63 89; closed Sun
On the outskirts of the old town, modern ambience; serves mainly fish dishes, good selection of regional white wines

② *Kokalos*
Via Cavaleri Magazzeni
Tel. & fax 09 22 60 64 27 / 28
www.ristorante-kokalos.com
Restaurant and pizzeria with views of the Valle dei Templi. Wine from the restaurant's own vineyard

San Leone · ③ Caico
Via Nettuno 35, tel. 09 22 41 27 88
afternoons and evenings, closed Tue
Popular, cosy trattoria near the beach with a veranda and recommendable cuisine. The owner is a wine lover! The emphasis is on fish dishes.

San Leone · ④ Leon d'Oro
Viale Emporium 102
Tel. 09 22 41 44 00, closed Mon
Serves mainly fish dishes and other regional specialities. Scenic views from the terrace.

San Leone · ⑤ Le Caprice
Via Cavaleri Magazzeni
Viccolo Kreta 2, tel. 09 22 41 13 64
Neat pizzeria with outside seating. There is such a large selection of very good antipasti that it would be easy to make a meal just from starters.

WHERE TO STAY
▶ Luxury
① *Villa Athena*
Via Passeggiata Archeologica 33
Tel. 09 22 59 62 88
www.athenahotels.com
31 rooms; old villa in a large garden with a unique view of the Temple of Concordia

⑥ *Baglio della Luna*
Contrada Maddalusa on SS 640

A former country estate: Foresteria Baglio della Luna

Tel. 09 22 51 10 61, fax 09 22 59 88 02
www.bagliodellaluna.com
24 rooms; country estate amidst vineyards. Nice view of the Valle dei Templi. The restaurant enjoys an excellent reputation.

▶ **Mid-range**
⑦ *Kaos*
Villaggio Pirandello on this SS 640
Tel. 09 22 59 86 22, fax 09 22 59 87 70
www.athenahotels.com
105 rooms; southwest of the Valle dei Templi, pleasant complex with a large pool; travel groups

② *Colleverde Park*
Via dei Templi 48
Tel. 0 92 22 95 55
Fax 0 92 22 90 12
www.colleverdehotel.it
48 completely renovated rooms; view of the temples from the large park and some of the rooms.

▶ **Budget**
③ *Concordia*
Via San Francesco 11
Tel. & fax 09 22 59 62 66
26 rooms; pleasant little hotel in the old town, in a street that runs parallel to Via Atenea but lower down; basic furnishing, the rooms are not particularly large, but clean and inexpensive.

④ *Belvedere*
Via San Vito 20
Tel. & fax 09 22 2 00 51
30 rooms; in Agrigento's old town, very hospitable with a small garden; some of the rooms have a view

⑤ *Terrazza sul Corso*
Via Atenea 165, tel. 092 22 65 55
www.terrazzasulcorso.it
4 rooms; friendly B & B below the old-town streets; excellently furnished rooms with balcony and guest kitchen. Nice hosts and good tips

★
Cathedral

Carry on walking upwards to get to the cathedral. It was built by the Normans on the acropolis over the ruins of the Temple of Zeus in the 11th century. It was expanded in the 13th and 14th centuries, and refurbished in the Baroque style in the 17th century. A flight of steps leads up to the main portal next to the large, incomplete 15th-century campanile. The interior of the basilica was restored in 1966 after being damaged in an earthquake. During this process an effort was made to recreate the medieval character of the nave; only the magnificent wooden ceiling of 1518 was preserved. The choir still has its lavish Baroque ornamentation. The silver shrine of the canonized Bishop Gerlando dating from 1639 is located in a Gothic chapel in the south aisle.

Take Via Fodera eastwards to the former Cistercian monastery of Santo Spirito (Mon–Fri 9am–1pm, 3pm–5.30pm, closed Sat afternoons). The façade (around 1260) is still adorned by the original Gothic pointed-arch portal and a rose window. It culminates in a Baroque pediment. The rich stucco ornamentation created by Giacomo Serpotta in around 1695 dominates the interior (stoup from the 5th century). To the right of the church are remains of the cloister, the chapter house and the refectory.

Santo Spirito

> ! **Baedeker** TIP
>
> **Cool refreshments**
> Very good ice creams and ice gâteaux, and therefore the ideal place for a treat after climbing so many steps: the family-run Caffé Concordia on Piazza Pirandello.

The collection of the **Museo Civico** exhibits paintings, sculptures and mementoes of Luigi Pirandello. Currently however the exhibits are on display in Palazzo dei Filippini (Via Atenea). The writer's plays are performed during the season (Oct–March) in the nearby **Teatro Pirandello** (Piazza Pirandello).

Ancient Sites

From the new town Viale della Vittoria leads to the church of San Biagio at the eastern end of **Rupe Atenea** (351m/1152ft; splendid view). The small church is closed. It was built in the 12th century over an ancient Temple of Demeter (480–460 BC). The foundations and parts or the northern wall can be seen behind the church apse. To the north of the building there are also two round altars, which may also have served as bothros (sacrificial pits); ritual receptacles were found inside them.

San Biagio

Steps lead down to the rock temple of Demeter and Persephone (Santuario Rupestre di Demetra) on the cliffs of Rupe Atenea. This is Agrigento's oldest temple and is believed to date back to the 7th century BC, i.e. to the time before the Greeks came here. It is a narrow rock chamber, behind which there are two caves from which water emerges. The temple offerings to Eleusinian mysteries goddess Demeter and her daughter can be seen in the Museo Archeologico.

Santuario Rupestre di Demetra

The archaeological museum has arranged the discoveries in chronological order; they contain an extensive collection of ceramics that were found in the nearby necropolises. A small bowl (6th century BC) depicts the motif of the three-legged »Triscele«, still present as »Trinakria« in the coat of arms of the autonomous region of Sicily today. Most of the black-figure and red-figure vases were imported as luxury goods from Athens. Many terracotta votive gifts, whose moulds were also found, confirm the popularity of the Demeter cult in ancient Akragas.

✷ ✷
Museo Archeologico Regionale
🕐
Opening hours:
Tue–Sat
9am–7pm
Sun, Mon
9am–1pm

Agrigento Museum

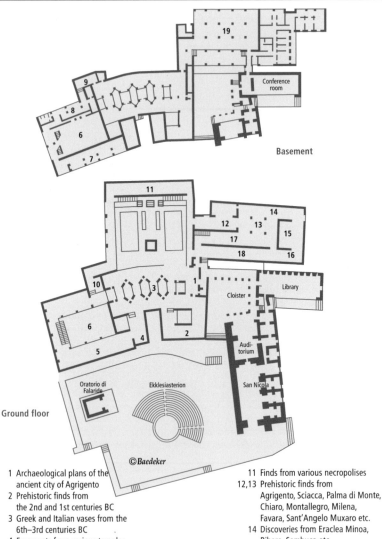

Basement

Ground floor

Oratorio di Falaride

Ekklesiasterion

San Nicola

Auditorium

Cloister

Library

Conference room

©Baedeker

1 Archaeological plans of the ancient city of Agrigento
2 Prehistoric finds from the 2nd and 1st centuries BC
3 Greek and Italian vases from the 6th–3rd centuries BC
4 Fragments from various temples
5 Votive gifts from the 6th–4th centuries BC
6 Over two floors: Temple of the Olympian Zeus, original telamon
7–9 Excavations from the Hellenic-Roman area
10 Greco-Roman sculptures

11 Finds from various necropolises
12,13 Prehistoric finds from Agrigento, Sciacca, Palma di Monte, Chiaro, Montallegro, Milena, Favara, Sant'Angelo Muxaro etc.
14 Discoveries from Eraclea Minoa, Ribera, Sambuca etc.
15 Documentation concerning about Gela
16,17 Finds from Ravenusa, Favara, Canicatti, Licata, Caltanissetta, Raffe
18 Various small finds
19 Finds not yet organized

The two-storey Sala dei Telamoni is reached via a room with capitals and gargoyles with lion heads from different temples. It is dedicated to the Temple of Zeus, which is now in ruins. In addition to a model and a reconstructive drawing there is one of the originally 38 Atlas figures, 7.65m/25ft high, two heads of further Atlases and other fragments. Further highlights are the sculpture of a kneeling warrior (presumably from the pediment ornamentation of the Olympieion, 480–470 BC), the marble statue of an ephebos (around 480 BC), a Roman child's sarcophagus and an undamaged wine bowl depicting the battle with the Amazons (5th century BC).

Next to the museum is the aisle-less church of San Nicola, built by Cistercians in the 13th century. In a chapel on the south side of this church, which is popular for weddings, is the famous marble sarcophagus of Phaedra (2nd century AD) with three scenes from the myth of Phaedra and Hippolytus. The wife of Theseus had fallen in love with her stepson Hippolytus, but had been rejected by him. Distraught, she took her own life. Theseus misinterpreted her death, accused his son of making advances to her and had him dragged to his death by Neptune's horses.

San Nicola

◄ Usually only opens for weddings and services

Behind the church is a complex that was designed as an **assembly area** (ekklesiasterion) in the 1st century BC and later turned into a small theatre. At the side is a small temple from the 2nd century AD, known as the **Oratory of Phalaris**.

At the same level as the museum is an excavated district from the Hellenistic and Roman eras (Quartiere Ellenistico Romano, from the 4th century BC to the 4th–5th century AD; daily 9am – 7pm, Mon, Sun until 1.30pm).

Ancient quarter
🕐

✱ Valle dei Templi · Valley of the Temples

Situated on a ridge at the foot of the town are the world-famous Doric temples of Agrigento, which are also a UNESCO World Heritage site. The fact that they bear names such as Heracles, Concordia and Juno Lacinia is more or less arbitrary. The temples are illuminated at night.

🕐

Opening hours: Daily 8.30am/9am until 7pm

There is access from the car park to the three structures on the eastern temple hill.

◄ The eastern temples

The Temple of Heracles, an archaic peripteros, was built around 500 BC. With a stylobate of 25.28 x 67.04m/83 x 220ft it is sizeable; it is elongated in plan, with 6 x 15 columns. Behind the cella is an opisthodomos, analogous to the pronaos, with two columns between the antae or protruding walls. The temple was destroyed by the Carthaginians in 406 BC, rebuilt by the Romans and later destroyed again by an earthquake. The fact that eight columns of the southern peristasis are standing is due to an Englishman, Alexander Herdenstel,

✱ ✱
Tempio di Ercole

Agrigento *Map*

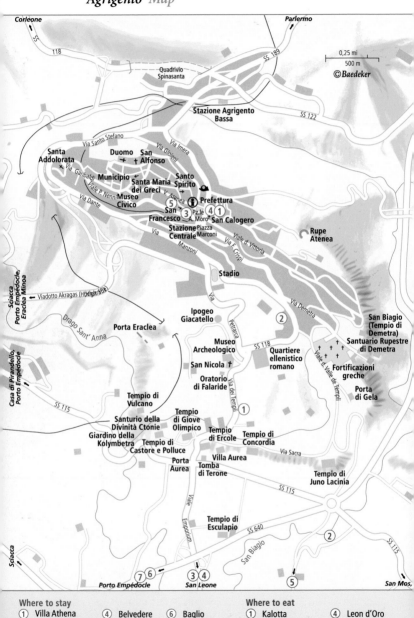

Corleone

Parlermo

Quadrivio
Spinasanta

0,25 mi
500 m
©Baedeker

Stazione Agrigento
Bassa

SS 122

Via Santo Stefano
Via Imera
Via Giolitti

Santa
Addolorata
Duomo
San
Alfonso

Via Garibaldi

Municipio
Santa Maria
dei Greci
Santo
Spirito
Prefettura

Viale P. Nenni
V. Atenea

Museo
Civico
San
Francesco
Pz.le
A. Moro
San Calogero

Via Dante

Stazione
Centrale
Piazza
Marconi

Via Manzoni
Viale d. Vittoria
Via F. Crispi

Rupe
Atenea

Stadio

Viadotto Akragas (Höchbrück)

Ipogeo
Giacatello

Via Petrarca

Via Demetra

San Biagio
(Tempio di
Demetra)

Sciacca
Porto Empédocle,
Eraclea Minoa

Drago Sant' Anna

Porta Eraclea

Museo
Archeologico

SS 118

Quartiere
ellenistico
romano

Viale d. Valle dei Templi

Santuario Rupestre
di Demetra

San Nicola

Fortificazioni
greche

Casa di Pirandello,
Porto Empédocle

SS 115

Oratorio
di Falaride

Via dei Templi

Porta
di Gela

Tempio di
Vulcano

Santurio della
Divinità Ctonie
Giardino della
Kolymbetra

Tempio di
Castore e Polluce

Tempio
di Giove
Olimpico

Tempio
di Ercole

Tempio di
Concordia

Villa Aurea

Via Sacra

Porta
Aurea

Tomba
di Terone

SS 115

Tempio di
Juno Lacinia

Viale Emporium

Tempio di
Esculapio

SS 640

San Biagio

Sciacca

Porto Empédocle

San Leone

San Mos.

SS 115

Rupe
Atenea

Where to stay
1. Villa Athena
2. Colleverde Park
3. Concordia
4. Belvedere
5. Terrazza sul Corso
6. Baglio della Luna
7. Kaos

Where to eat
1. Kalotta
2. Kokalos
3. Caíco
4. Leon d'Oro
5. Le Caprice

whose endeavours to restore the building in 1923 led to his financial ruin. The temple's original dedication is unknown; in Roman times it was dedicated to Heracles, according to Cicero, and its cult statue was a particular draw to devotees.

Gradually walk up the processional street to get to the Villa Aurea with its lavish garden, which includes the remains of necropolises from the Roman and Christian periods. Tombs can be made out further up in the rock along the town walls. Then the Temple of Concordia draws all the attention.

Villa Aurea

Together with the Temple of Hephaestus in Athens and the classical Temple of Hera in Paestum, the Temple of Concordia is among the most complete extant temples of the Greek world and is the best-preserved Doric temple in Sicily.
It was built around 425 BC, using forms that were already outdated in Greece. With a stylobate of 16.92 x 39.42m/55 x 130ft it is significantly smaller than the Temple of Heracles. 6 x 13 columns lend it

★ ★
Tempio di Concordia

Saved for posterity as a Christian church: Temple of Concordia

the classical proportions. The interior is designed in a way that was canonical in the Greek motherland: the portico, cella, opisthodomos, but without the adyton behind the cella, a feature customary in Sicily. To the left and right of the entrance to the cella, steps lead to a roof structure. The building is almost fully preserved save for the roof. It still looks quite different from the way it would have originally appeared because of the oxidized red sandstone. The temple was once covered in white stucco and then colourfully painted. The good state of preservation is due to the fact that it was turned into a Christian church under Pope Gregory the Great in the 6th century. The cella was used as the nave, and the gaps between the columns were walled up so that the porticoes could be used as aisles. Round arches in the cella walls connected the nave and the aisles (as is still the case in Syracuse Cathedral, formerly a Temple of Athena). In 1748 use as a church was abandoned and the building was restored as a temple.

★★
Tempio di Juno Lacinia

The Tempio di Juno Lacinia at the top of the temple row has almost the same dimensions and is also a peripteros with 6 x 13 columns. 25 of its columns are still upright. There is no plinth for a cult image. There is no clue as to which deity was worshipped here. The temple was destroyed by the Carthaginians (signs of burning) and was given a ramp at the eastern entrance when it was restored by the Romans. In front of it are the remains of a large sacrificial altar.

★★
The western temples

Tempio di Giove Olimpico

The Temple of Olympian Zeus (Olympeion) is now a vast mass of rubble consisting of blocks of stone and column sections, which an earthquake scattered over an area of 6000 sq m/7200 sq yd. It is difficult to get a picture of the original temple and its vast size without the plans of the reconstruction proposals now in the archaeological museum.

The tyrant Theron had the Temple of Olympian Zeus designed to commemorate the victory over Carthage near Himera in 480 BC. It was the largest Doric temple ever to be built and »the most original, but also the most fantastic creation of the Greek world« (G. Gruben). The foundation is a rectangle measuring 56.30 x 113.45m/ 185 x 370ft (ratio 1:2). On top of that is the stylobate (52.74 x 110.10m/175 x 360ft), on which there were seven columns on both ends and 14 on the sides. These columns had a (calculated) height of around 18.20m/59.70ft and a correspondingly massive lower diameter of 4.05m/13.30ft. **Goethe** commented in 1787: »The fluting of the column can be put into perspective by saying that I, standing in such a recess, would fill it as a small niche, both shoulders touching. 22 men, standing next to each other in a circle would capture the approximate periphery of such a column.«

The structure diverged completely from the canon of Greek temples. The gaps between the columns were walled up, which can still be seen from the remains of the southern side in the terrain. The ashlar

It once supported the entablature of the Temple of Zeus: an architectural Telamon.

wall was easily half the height of the columns. In addition there were niches that contained free-standing Atlas figures. These enormous statues had a height of 7.65m/25ft. Their number is calculated to have been 38. They supported the entablature and the pediments, whose reliefs must have had a height of up to 6m/20ft; according to Diodorus they depicted the battle of the Gods with the Giants and the conquest of Troy. The total height of the temple is stated to have been around 40m/130ft. The walls between the columns meant that there was no light portico around the cella; instead the entire structure was a huge closed hall with tiny entrances. It is not clear how this massive room was illuminated; E. Langlotz considered a hypaethral with a large opening in the roof, H. Drerup a Phoenician-Carthaginian columned hall. The enormous Temple of Olympian Zeus, testament to unbroken trust in the limitless possibilities of Sicily at the time, went beyond what was humanly possible; it remained uncompleted when the Carthaginians conquered Akragas in their counter-move and remained a torso. It was struck by earthquakes and its ruins were used as a quarry when the harbour of Porto Empédocle was enlarged in the 18th century.

To the west of the Temple of the Olympian Zeus is the extensive **Temple of the Chthonic Deities**, Santuario delle Divinità Ctonie. It goes back to the Sicels and was extended by the Greeks in the 6th and 5th centuries BC.

It also includes the **Temple of the Dioscuri** (Temple of Castor and Pollux), whose northwest corner (four columns and some of the entablature and pediment), imaginatively re-erected between 1836 and 1871, has become the symbol of Agrigento. It had a portico of 6 x 13 columns on a stylobate measuring 13 x 31m/42 x 100ft and was part of the final phase of this complex. The older temples have a large round altar at their centre, measuring 8m/25ft. In addition there were smaller temples and in the north of the complex two walled sanctuaries. Gottfried Gruben commented on these still rather rustic cult buildings: »Is this where, as in Eleusina, the novices were initiated into the cult? Did secret sacrificial rites take place here?«

★ ★
Tempio di
Castore e Polluce

Giardino della Kolymbetra

✳ A small sign in the western temple valley marks the entrance to the Garden of Kolymbetra. In the valley between the Temple of the Dioscuri and the Temple of Vulcan, a small lake ensured the town's water supply in Antiquity. The lake dried up, but thanks to sufficient moisture sugar cane was planted here in the 14th century and later, until well into the 20th century, fruit and vegetables were grown. Then the garden became overgrown and the area degenerated into a landfill. On the initiative of the FAI, an organization that aims to protect Italy's physical heritage, the area was turned back into a garden.

! *Baedeker* TIP

Picnic in the Garden of Eden
The Garden of Kolymbetra »is a small valley, whose magnificent fertility makes it look like the Valley of Eden« – thus an English traveller to Sicily in 1778. It is the ideal place to have a picnic; daily 10am – 7pm. Information: www.fondoambiente.it and tel. 33 51 22 90 42.

Further sights

Some of the foundations and two columns survive of the Temple of Vulcan (Tempio di Vulcano), built in around 430 BC and situated further to the northwest (beyond the modern rail tracks). Below the Temple of Heracles is the Tomb of Theron (Tomba di Terone), a tower-like mausoleum, which does not, however, have anything to do with the tyrant who died in 472 BC; it dates back to the 1st century BC. Further south, on the banks of the river Akrágas, is the Temple of Asclepius (Tempio di Esculapio, 5th century BC) with a snake pit.

Around Agrigento

Porto Empédocle

7km/4mi south of Agrigento is the small town of Porto Empédocle (population 17,000), which was founded in the 18th century and is now an industrial location and also the ferry terminal for the Pelagian Islands of Lampedusa and Linosa. Here the crime fiction author Andrea Camilleri was born in 1921 (▶ Famous People). The

Pirandello House ▶

author Luigi Pirandello (1867–1936; ▶Famous People) was born in a house in the Caos neighbourhood; on his death he was buried under his favourite pine (which has since been struck by lightning; small ⏱ museum; Mon – Fri 9am – 1pm, 2pm – 7.30pm).

Scala dei Turchi

The »Turkish Steps«, a favourite excursion, are chalk cliffs where erosion resulted in a pattern of horizontal steps, hence the name. West of these cliffs there are long sandy beaches along an impressive coastline (to get here, go west from Porto Empedocle along the coast all the way to Lido Majata, then continue on foot, or by car on the SS 115 to Realmonte and then down a cul-de-sac to the sea).

Naro

This picturesque little town (population 10,000) is situated on a hill at 520m/1705ft, 24km/15mi east of Agrigento. The crenellated town wall was built in the 13th century; in the 14th century the Chiaramonte family, as feudal lords, built a **castle** at the highest point on the site of a Saracen fort (keep, hall with mullioned windows). The ruin of the Chiesa Matrice Vecchia with its pointed-arch portal is Gothic, the new Chiesa Matrice (former Jesuit church) was built in the 18th century (sculptures by Gagini). In the town centre, where plays in Sicilian dialect are staged in summer, are San Francesco with its early-Baroque façade (pre-1635, very richly ornamented sacristy from 1721 inside). The façade of the former Benedictine church of San Salvatore remained unfinished. Inside, the dark green marble sarcophagus of Giuseppe Lucchesi is a copy of Frederick II's sarcophagus in ►Palermo. The Donna Licata and Canal Baglio neighbourhoods are home to the remains of Christian **catacombs** and the **necropolis** »Grotta delle Meraviglie«.

Palma di Montechiaro

◄ The town of The Leopard

Palma, a small run-down town (population 24,000) 31km/19mi southeast of Agrigento and not far from the south coast, was founded by Prince Carlo Tomasi di Lampedusa in 1637. The town, which has always been associated with Lampedusa, became known when Visconti made a film of the novel *The Leopard* here in 1962 (► Baedeker Special p. 100). In 1666 Giulio Tomasi di Lampedusa commissioned the Jesuit architect Angelo Italía from nearby Licata to build the main church, **Santa Maria del Rosario**. The two-storey façade, whose impact is heightened through monumental steps in front of it, as well as by its twin towers, marked »an important starting point in Baroque Sicilian architecture« (Krönig). The aisled basilica was only given its roof and dome in 1683. The Lampedusa family was also responsible for the monastery of Santa Maria del Rosario, which several of them joined. The **Castellazzo di Montechiaro**, 5km/3mi southeast of the town on a hill above the sea, was built as a defensive measure against pirates in the 14th and 15th centuries. The seaside resort of **Marina di Palma**, ruthlessly developed with concrete everywhere, is situated 5km/3mi to the south. The forbidding Torre di San Carlo dates back to the 17th century and was also commissioned by Carlo Tomasi di Lampedusa.

Sant'Angelo Muxaro

★

◄ Necropolis

This small town is situated around 36km/22 north of Agrigento above the flood plain of the Plàtani. The necropolis of the Sicani in the valley is among the most impressive in Sicily along with that in Pantálica. The cave tombs date back to the 11th–5th centuries BC and mostly have an anteroom and a vaulted main room with benches all around. The burial objects are on display in the museum of Syracuse.

The necropolis supports the theory that the Sicani capital of Kamikos of the mythical King Cocalus was located here. Cocalus received Daedalus, the creator of the labyrinth in Knossos, when he fled from King Minos. Minos followed him and came to Minoa (Heraclea Minoa) and got to the rock fort of Kamikos, which Daedalus had built for King Cocalus. The king gave Minos a friendly welcome and agreed he would hand over the fugitive; »but when he was bathing he was killed by his host's daughters, who poured boiling pitch over him. According to others he was killed by boiling water.« After that the Cretans went to war against Cocalus and besieged Kamikos for five years, but to no avail. According to ancient tradition, the mortal remains of Minos were handed back to the Cretans when Akragas (Agrigento) was founded in 583 BC. Sophocles addressed this legend in his tragedy *Kamikoi*, which only survives in fragments. Kamikos is mentioned two more times in historical sources: before 480 BC (relatives of Theron of Akragas revolted against him, were defeated and occupied Kamikos) as well as in 258 BC (the Romans took Kamikos).

> ! **Baedeker** TIP
>
> **On mule tracks**
> The energetic mayor has had the old mule tracks on Monte Castello (past Bronze Age tombs) turned into hiking trails. Cave trips (gypsum caves) are also arranged (information: www.valdikam.it).

Ávola

Province: Siracusa
Population: 31,000

Altitude: 37m/121ft

Ávola, on Sicily's south coast is, like Noto, 8km/5mi away, a Baroque town from the late 17th century. It is also the centre of almond cultivation.

Rebuilt after the earthquake

The old town (Ávola Vecchia) was destroyed so comprehensively by the earthquake of 1693 that Ávola was founded anew. The flat terrain made a regular pattern with a geometric outline possible. The shape of a hexagon was chosen.

Ávola and Around

The handsome Chiesa Matrice San Nicola is located on the large, square piazza (Piazza Umberto I); this is also where the Museo Civico is located. Four main roads emanate from this square, and there are further squares where they meet the hexagonal ring. They are adorned with flowers and fountains, especially Piazza Regina Elena, one side of which is dominated by the Baroque church of Sant'Antonio Abbate (18th century). **Swimming** is possible at Lido di Ávola (to the northeast, rocky coastline with narrow pebble and sand sections).

ÁVOLA

INFORMATION

Pro Loco
Via Ravenna 15, 96012 Ávola
Tel. 09 31 82 35 66
www.prolocoavola.it

The ruins of old Ávola, inhabited since the 2nd millennium BC and destroyed in 1693, are 8.5km/5mi northwest of modern-day Ávola (winding mountain road, good views).   **Ávola Vecchia**

Freshwater pools in the gorge of Cava Grande

Cava Grande

★ ★

⏱

For water lovers and hikers ▶

8km/5mi northwest of Ávola Vecchia, the Cassíbile River forms the Cava Grande del Cassíbile, a gorge 10km/6mi long and up to 250m/820ft deep, in which there are countless rock tombs from a Sicel necropolis that can be explored on foot (1 hr descent; in summer daily 8am – 7pm). Three idyllically situated lakes in the Cava Grande gorge are extremely popular destinations on summer weekends. They are accessible via a narrow path, carved into the rock in places. It starts at the Belvedere (the view point is situated on the SP 4, around 3km/2mi beyond Ávola Vecchia). There is a small trattoria here (closed Mon; tel. 09 31 81 12 20) as well as parking facilities.

Cassíbile

North of where the Cassíbile flows into the sea, the town of the same name occupies the site of ancient Kakyparis (on the SS 115; 10km/6mi north of Ávola). The army of Syracuse defeated the invading Athenian army near the estuary in 413 BC, and on 3 September 1943 Italy signed the armistice with the Allies in Cassíbile.

Caltagirone

P 9

Province: Catania
Population: 38,000

Altitude: 608m/1995ft

The »Capitale della Ceramica«, Sicily's »ceramics capital«, lies in a picturesque location on three hills. After it was conquered by the Arabs in the 9th century, they renamed it Qalat-al-Ghiran, »Hill of Vases«. The modern town extends on to the southern hill, while the originally medieval core, which was rebuilt in the Baroque style in the 17th and 18th centuries after being destroyed in the earthquake of 1693, can be found on the northern hill.

What to See in Caltagirone

Ceramics town

★

The main square of this hilly town is Piazza Umberto I. It is the address of the **cathedral** (18th century, renovated inside in the 19th century) and the **Palazzo Corte Capitaniale**, built in around 1600 by Antonuzzo and Gian Domenico Gagini. It is just a single-storey building with Doric pilasters at the corners and an attractive alternation of windows and doors.

Around 300m/330yd to the west is the **Chiesa San Giacomo**, originally a Norman cathedral, which was rebuilt in 1694 as a basilica. It houses a statue of St James, the town's patron saint (1518).

! **Baedeker TIP**

Watching the potter at work
There are more then 80 potteries in Caltagirone. It is often possible to watch the potters at work. There are permanent exhibits in the courtyard of Palazzo Corte Capitaniale and in Galleria L. Sturzo.

On the Piazza del Municipio, a little to the east of the cathedral square, lies the Baroque town hall as well as the former senatorial palace of 1483 and the modern **Galleria L. Sturzo**. The latter is named after the former mayor and patron of the ceramic arts, an anti-fascist and co-founder of the Christian Democrat party (1871 – 1959).

Piazza del Municipio

Leave Piazza del Municipio and climb up the stair designed by Giuseppe Giacalone in 1608; its 142 steps are covered in modern ceramic tiles. It leads to the **upper town**. The focal point at the top of the steps is Santa Maria del Monte, an 18th-century church built on the site of a 12th-century building destroyed in 1693; it contains a picture of the Madonna di Conadomini from the 13th century (replica; the original is on display only during May).

Scala

◄ Santa Maria del Monte

The Museo Civico in the old Bourbon prison, which can be reached via the Piazza del Municipio and Via Roma, is mainly devoted to the town's history (Tue – Sun, 9.30am – 1.30pm, Tue, Fri, Sat also 4pm – 7pm).

Museo Civico

VISITING CALTAGIRONE

INFORMATION

Servizio Turistico
Volta Libertini 4
95041 Caltagirone
Tel. 0 93 35 38 09, fax 0 93 35 46 10

EVENTS

»La Scala illuminata« by the large flight of steps (24 – 25 July)

WHERE TO EAT

► Moderate

La Locandiere
Via Luigi Sturzo 55
Tel. 0 93 35 82 92
closed Mon; small restaurant at the bottom of the famous steps; mainly fish dishes. Long wine list

► Inexpensive

La Scala
Scala Santa Maria del Monte
Tel. 0 93 35 77 81; closed Wed.
Pleasant trattoria right by the famous steps with fine local cuisine

WHERE TO STAY

► Mid-range

Villa San Mauro
Via Porto Salvo 10
Tel. 0 93 32 65 00, www.nh-hotels.it
92 rooms; completely modernized, comfortable hotel in the lower town

► Budget

San Michele di Ganzaria · Pomara
Via V. Veneto 84 , tel. 09 33 97 69 76
www.hotelpomara.com
40 rooms; basic family hotel approx. 12km/7mi towards Piazza Armerina. Some rooms have pretty views, pool. Excellent country fare in the restaurant

La Casa degli Angeli
Contrada Angeli
Tel. & fax 0 95 44 20 25
7 rooms; around 9km/5.5mi outside town on SP 29 towards Niscemi in a large estate; with its own wine and a magnificent panoramic terrace

Caltagirone, whose mountains provide good clay, has always been Sicily's ceramics centre.

Museo della Ceramica ✱

⏱

A bridge covered in ceramics leads to the church of San Francesco di Paola at the entrance of the magnificent, well-tended **park** (Giardino Pubblico), which is home to the ceramics museum. It demonstrates the history of ceramics in Sicily, from the prehistoric beginnings to the 21st century (daily 9am – 6.30pm).

Around Caltagirone

Grammichele ✱

Grammichele (520m/1706ft, 15km/9mi to the east; population 13,600) along with Ávola, Noto and Pachino is among those towns in southeast Sicily that were planned and rebuilt after the major earthquake of 1693. The proposal came from Carlo Maria Carafa, Principe di Butera e di Roccella, while the plans were drawn up by Michele da Ferla. As is the case in Ávola, the town is based on a hexagonal pattern, but here this was taken to extremes: even the central square with a number of gentlemen's clubs (porcupine trophies adorn the Circolo of hunters) is not a square but a hexagon. This is also the location of the town hall and the church. Six axial roads radiate from the six sides. Each leads to the periphery and meets a true square, itself a street intersection, at the centre of each of the outer districts.

Caltanissetta

M 8

Provincial capital
Population: 60,000

Altitude: 534m/1752ft

Caltanissetta, the largest town in Sicily's interior, is attractively situated above the Salso valley at the foot of Monte San Giuliano (727m/2385ft). The lively market town was the centre of sulphur, potash and magnesium mining. The name comes from the old Sicani town of Nissa, where the Arabs built a castle (qalat).

What to See in and Around Caltanissetta

Caltanissetta's men like to hang out on the central Piazza Garibaldi, the site of the Fountain of Neptune and the cathedral (1570–1622) with its twin-tower façade and frescoes by the Flemish painter Guglielmo (Willelm) Borremans (1720). The Chiesa di San Sebastiano (neo-Renaissance façade; 1891) stands opposite.
Corso Umberto passes alongside this square. At the northern end is the town hall, beyond it Palazzo Baronale Moncada (1625), a typically Sicilian Baroque building; at the end of the corso is the Jesuit church of Sant'Àgata (17th century). To the west of it is a pleasant morning market. Not far from the station, in Via Cavour, the Museo Archeologico exhibits archaeological discoveries from the surrounding area and items on local history (daily 9am – 1pm, 3pm – 7pm).

Caltanissetta

Baedeker TIP

Bookworms

The Libreria Sciascia, Corso Umberto 111, is a small, well laid-out, old-fashioned bookshop in Caltanissetta with a large Sicily section.

◄ *Museo Archeologico* ⏲

In the east of town are the 18th-century Chiesa San Domenico with a curving Baroque façade (Via S. Domenico; paintings by Filippo Paladino as well as by Guglielmo (Willelm) Borremans and, at the end of Via Angeli, in front of the hill on top of which stands the castle, is the Chiesa Santa Maria degli Angeli, where the Gothic portal recalls its 14th-century origin. The hill is dominated by the **Castello di Pietrarossa**, which was originally an Arab castle.

San Domenico

E. Basile had a large statue of Christ erected on Monte San Giuliano (727m/2385ft, 2km/1mi to the north; impressive view) in 1900.

Monte San Giuliano

This former Augustinian priory church 3km/2mi to the north was donated in around 1086 by the Norman count Roger I and his wife Adelasia after victory over the Saracens. It was consecrated in 1153 as an aisle-less building with a three-part sanctuary, whose apses are adorned on the outside with narrow pilasters. In 1859, out of grati-

Badia di Santo Spirito

VISITING CALTANISSETTA

INFORMATION

Servizio Turistico
Corso Vittorio Emanuele 109 Tel.
09 34 53 48 26

EVENTS

Magnificent procession on Maundy
Thursday with groups portraying Passion scenes;
Michaelmas market (29 September);
folklore festival (September)

SHOPPING

The (shopping) walkway above the
Mercato storico in Via Consultore
Benintente, a street that runs parallel
to Corso V. Emanuele, is an unusual
feast for the eyes, ears and the palate.

WHERE TO EAT

► Moderate

Vicolo Duomo
Vicolo Duomo 7
Tel. 09 34 58 23 31
closed Sun; good rustic dishes

Le Fontanelle
Contrada Fontanelle Nord-Ouest
Via Pietro Leone 45, tel. 09 34 59 24 37
Fax 09 34 56 11 19 – closed Mon.
Well-known agriturismo restaurant,
nice terrace; horse-riding; 5km/3mi
outside town towards San Cataldo

WHERE TO STAY

► Mid-range

San Michele
Via dei Fasci Siciliani, tel.
09 34 55 37 50, fax 09 34 59 87 91
www.hotelsanmichelesicilia.it
122 rooms; modern concrete block;
excellently furnished rooms, some
with views, right on the autostrada.
Good base for excursions

► Budget

Plaza
Via B. Gaetani 5, tel. 09 34 58 38 77
www.hotelplazacaltanissetta.it
20 rooms;. basic accommodation in
the historic centre

Bittersweet secret ►
tude for his donations, a member of the order revealed a secret recipe for an elixir made of herbs, barks, berries and citrus peel to Salvatore Averna. The crafty textiles entrepreneur and his descendants
used it to produce the Averna digestif, which is now known in more
than 50 countries.

Monte Sabucina
There is an archaeological zone on this mountain (706m/2320ft,
6km/4mi northeast, SS 122) with the remains of a town that first belonged to the Sicani, then the Greeks (6th–4th century BC); the finds
are on display in the Museo Civico in Caltanissetta.

Canicattì
The rural town of Canicattì (23km/14mi to the southwest on the SS
640, then turn left on to the SS 123, 5km/3mi, population 32,000)
lies at an elevation of 465m/1525ft in a hilly landscape with extensive
slopes where eating grapes are grown. It was probably founded by
the Arabs. Besides the Castello Bonanno there are several churches
(San Diego, Chiesa del Purgatorio) of interest.

Cammarata / San Giovanni Gémini

J 7

Province: Agrigento
Population: 6300

Altitude: 682m/2238ft

This small town and the neighbouring San Giovanni Gémini have a picturesque setting on the eastern slopes of Monte Cammarata, north of Agrigento.

What to See in and Around Cammarata

The ruins of the Castello dei Branciforti as well as the church of Santa Maria with a statue by Gagini are both worth visiting. There are attractive trails and picnic sites on the 1578m/5177ft Monte Cammarata, which with its twin summits is Sicily's highest mountain.

Cammarata

This small town with a population of around 10,000 lies at an elevation of 554m/1818ft, 20km/12mi south of Cammarata. It is famous for the »Sagra del Tataratà«, also known as the Feast in Honour of the Sacred Cross (Santa Croce), which takes place in the whole town every year on the fourth Sunday in May and during the two prece-

Casteltèrmini

An impressive medieval legacy: Castello Manfredonico in Mussomeli

ding days. It commemorates a wooden cross found here in 1667, which is said to have been used as a instrument of martyrdom during the persecution of Christians in the 3rd century. Tataratà warriors with sabres and drums as well as horsemen in historical costumes participate in the procession.

The picturesque rural town of **Mussomeli** (population 13,000) lies 27km/17mi southeast of Cammarata below the summit of Monte San Vito (895m/2936ft). It has preserved the memory of an Arab castle in its name. Here in 1370 Manfredi III Chiaramonte built the magnificent **Castello Manfredonico** (named after its builder), which towers over the town on a strategic hill (80m/260ft) 2km/1mi to the east. The building is one of the most imposing of all the castles on Sicily. The Gothic chapel and a large »Hall of Barons« survive in its interior.

Capo d'Orlando

Q 4

Province: Messina
Population: 12,000

Altitude: 18m/59ft

This inviting fishing village, which has developed into a seaside resort, is located on the eastern section of the north coast at the foot of the cape of the same name. The ancient town of Agathyrnum was probably sited on these foothills. According to Diodorus, it was founded by Agathyrnus, the son of the wind god Aeolus.

What to See in and Around Capo d'Orlando

Capo d'Orlando
On the foothills projecting to the north are the ruins of a castle and a pilgrimage church from the 16th century. To the east of the cape is a 2km/1mi stretch of coastline with bays and cliffs. Capo d'Orlando's suburb is called San Grégorio. It draws in visitors with its clear water, pebble beaches and infrastructure during the summer months that answers every imaginable childhood wish. Adjoining this suburb is the holiday village of **Testa del Monaco**.

Bay of Gioiosa Marea
East of Capo d'Orlando, beyond Testa del Monaco, is a wide bay that ends at Capo Calavà. Towns along this bay include Brolo, Gliaca and Gioiosa Marea.

► VISITING CAPO D'ORLANDO

INFORMATION
Servizio Turistico
Via G. Amendola 20
98071 Capo d'Orlando
Tel. 09 41 91 27 84
www.aastcapodorlando.it

EVENT
Procession of boats on 15 August

HOLIDAY ACCOMMODATION
Holiday accommodation, boat trips with fishermen and hikes in the nearby Parco dei Nebrodi are all organized by Carlos Vinci, Borgo S. Gregorio 8, tel. 09 41 95 51 57, mobile 33 56 59 99 41, www.maredamare.com.

WHERE TO EAT
► Moderate
San Marco d'Alunzio · La Macina
Via Aluntina 48 , tel. 09 41 79 78 48
Closed Tue – Nebrodi cuisine in a cosy family-run restaurant in a mountain village

Capri Leone · Antica Filanda
Contrada Raviola
Tel. 09 41 91 97 04

Closed Mon
Excellent Nebrodi cuisine with views of the Aeolian Islands; adjoining small hotel

WHERE TO STAY
► Mid-range
La Tartaruga
Lido San Gregorio
Tel. 09 41 95 50 12
www.hoteltartaruga.it – 38 rooms; east of the cape, large hotel, separated from the sea by a road. Excellent regional dishes served in the restaurant (open all week)

Il Mulino
Via Andrea Doria 46
Tel. 09 41 90 24 31
Fax 09 41 91 16 14
www.hotelilmulino.it
92 rooms; modern hotel near the centre and the sea

► Budget
Gioiosa Marea · Puglia
Via Umberto I 247
Tel. 09 41 30 11 77
34 rooms; very friendly ambience, lots of regulars

Naso

The small mountain town of Naso with its walnut and chestnut plantations (11km/7mi to the southeast, accessible via the winding SS 116) lies at an altitude of 497m/1630ft.
It is home to the medieval Chiesa dei Minori Osservanti. The road then continues on to Randazzo at the northern foot of Mount Etna (65km/40mi from Capo d'Orlando, ►Etna).

Frazzano

This mountain town (15km/9mi to the south) lies at an altitude of 560m/1837ft. Its San Filippo di Fragolà monastery, founded in the 5th or 6th century (rebuilt in 1090, extended between the 15th and the 18th centuries) still has the typical T-shaped floor plan (tau cross) of an Orthodox Basilian church.

Carini

H 4

Province: Palermo
Population: 34,000

Altitude: 181m/590ft

Carini is in the mountains 26km/16mi west of Palermo and is a destination with ancient origins.

Le Donne di Carini
The small settlement of Hyccara, an enemy of Segesta, was located here in ancient times. The Athenians, who were allied to Segesta, conquered it in 415 BC and enslaved its inhabitants. One of them was seven-year-old Lais, the daughter of Timandra, a friend of the Athenian Alcibiades. She came to Corinth, where she became a great hetaera (courtesan); then she went on to Thessaly, where she was stoned by jealous women in a Temple of Aphrodite. A similar fate befell Baronessa di Carini. A famous ballad laments her execution by her jealous father in 1508.

What to See in and Around Carini

Carini
There are two churches on the cathedral square, the Baroque cathedral and the Chiesa di San Vito (with a picture of San Vito, 14th century). The castle was also built in the 14th century. The great hall's fine wooden ceiling is worth seeing, as is a statue of the Madonna by Andrea Mancino in the chapel.

Grotta di Carburangeli
The unusual, 400m/1300ft-long cave is one of the best examples of underground limestone formation in Sicily. Over the course of mil-

▶ **VISITING CARINI**

INFORMATION
www.comune.carini.pa.it
www.prolocoterrasini.it

WHERE TO EAT
▶ **Moderate**
Terrasini · Primafila
Via Benedetto Saputo 8
Tel. 09 18 68 44 22; closed Mon; ambitious cuisine and elegant ambience

WHERE TO STAY
▶ **Mid-range**
Montelepre · Castello di Giuliano
Via Pietro Merra 1

Tel. 09 18 94 10 06
Fax 09 18 94 11 10
www.castellodigiuliano.it
23 rooms; the owner, a nephew of the bandit Salvatore Giuliano, decorated the castle to be reminiscent of his notorious uncle; nicely furnished rooms and outstanding cuisine

Terrasini · Hotel Cala Rossa
Via Marchesa di Cala Rossa
Tel. 09 18 68 51 53, fax 09 18 68 47 27
www.hotelcalarossa.com
68 large rooms with balcony on a nice coastline for swimming

lions of years pretty stalactites and stalagmites have formed (Carini, Via Umberto I 64; viewings require advance booking, tel. & fax 09 18 66 97 97, www.legambienteriserva.it).

Take the coastal road SS 113 from Villagrazia westwards, past the cape of Punta Raisi, to the small town of Terrasini (population 11,500), located 8km/5mi away in the coastal plain. The Villagio Turistico was built on a rock plateau here. It is a 25ha/62-acre holiday park with a water adventure park, giant flumes into the sea and bus connections to the small beach 3.5km/2mi away (Città del Mare). There is a good ornithological exhibition and a collection of colourful Sicilian carts (carretti siciliani) in **Palazzo d'Aumale** (on the coast road) (Mon–Sat 9am–1.30pm, 2pm–6.45pm, Sun until 1pm). **Terrasini**

Montelepre (10km/6mi south of Carini; population 6000) with its medieval castle was once part of the hunting ground of the archbishop of Monreale; the ancient woods are long gone now. The mountain village became known as the birthplace and base of Salvatore Giuliano (1922–1950; ► Famous People), who is also buried here. Show respect when visiting the grave!. **Montelepre**

Partinico (20km/12mi south of Carini) lies in an agricultural area and has a population of 32,000. To the south is the Lago Poma reservoir. Partinico is considered to be a Mafia centre and was the main base of Salvatore Giuliano. **Danilo Dolci** (1924–97), an author and social reformer from Trieste, also lived here for a while. The »Gandhi of Sicily« used imaginative strategies to fight against poverty, illiteracy and Mafia terrorism. **Partinico**

Castellammare del Golfo

F 4

Province: Tràpani   **Altitude:** 63m/207ft
Population: 15,000

The pretty, labyrinthine harbour town on the north coast was founded in Antiquity as the port of the Elymian town of Segesta. It owed its later boom to tuna fishing.

What to See in and Around Castellammare

An Aragonese castle was built by the harbour in the 14th century (picture p. 122). The façade of the Chiesa Madre dates back to 1726; it contains a majolica statue of the Madonna. The baths Terme Segestane (7km/4mi south) have sulphurous springs with water at a temperature of 45°C/113°F. **Castellammare**

VISITING CASTELLAMMARE DEL GOLFO

INFORMATION

Ufficio Turistico
Via Umberto I 1
91014 Castellammare del Golfo
Tel. 0 92 43 13 20
www.castellammareonline.it

GOING OUT

Open-air night clubs during the peak season

WHERE TO STAY

▶ Mid-range
Al Madarig
Piazza Petrolo 7
Tel. 0 92 43 35 33, www.almadarig.com
33 rooms; east of the castle, pleasant management, good restaurant

▶ Budget
Balata di Baida · Agriturismo Camillo Finazzo
Contrada Molinazzo , tel. 0 92 43 80 51, mobile 32 96 19 97 98 www.camillofinazzo.com; Feb–Dec, 10 rooms, lovingly run farm 5km/3mi southwest of Scopello. Signposted from the SS 187 in Balata di Baida

Scopello · Locanda La Tavernetta
Via Armando Diaz 2, tel. & fax 09 24 54 11 29, www.albergolatavernetta.it, 7 rooms; cosy guesthouse with good local cuisine

Scopello · Torre Bennistra
Via N. Roma 19, tel. & fax 09 24 54 11 28, www.hoteltorrebenistra.com Family-run ristorante-albergo, cosy rooms with sea views

WHERE TO EAT

▶ Moderate
La Cambusa
Via Don Luigi Zangara 67
Tel. 0 92 43 01 55 – At Castellammare's harbour with outside seating

Scopello · La Terrazza
Via Marco Polo 5, tel. 09 24 54 11 16 Local dishes, including seafood couscous; view of the Faraglioni

Egesta
Piazza Petrolo, tel. 0 92 43 04 09 Popular restaurant with very good fish dishes on the main square

East of Castellammare is a long **sandy beach**, but the remaining coastline is rocky. Those in the know prefer the beaches in the nearby Zingaro National Park. **Monte Inici** (1065m/3494ft) can be climbed in around three hours, a worthwhile undertaking for the view.

★ ★
Riserva naturale dello Zingaro

Hiking route 4, p. 139 ▶

Scopello (9km/6mi northwest) is an attractively situated fishing village with beach facilities as well as a former tonnara (tuna-fishing base). Zingaro National Park starts just behind the town. It has one of Sicily's most beautiful natural coastlines . Plans to construct a road between Scopello and San Vito lo Capo caused a veritable uprising in 1980, and the government had to give in. Instead, Sicily's first nature reserve was set up here in 1981. The landscape is dominated by limestone cliffs, abrupt drops and sparse vegetation. The coast is also largely rocky and, apart from a few beautiful sand and pebble bays, inaccessible. The highest elevation is Monte Speziale (913m/2995ft). The widespread dwarf palms are a special feature of this park. There are two entrances: the north entrance lies around 12km/7mi southeast of **San Vito lo Capo** (▶ Tràpani), the south entrance around 1km/0.5mi northeast of **Scopello**. Photocopies of trail maps are available at both entrances. There are various waymarked hiking trails through the park, varying in length between 7km/4mi and 14km/9mi. The simplest route runs along the coast from one entrance to the other (7km/4mi, easy, around 2 hrs without breaks and detours). The Museo Naturalistico provides information about the flora and fauna, the Museo della Civiltà informs visitors about the former living conditions in the region. The park is open all year round (daily Apr–Sept 7am–6.30pm, otherwise 8am–4pm; further information: www.riservazingaro. it). The visitor centre (Centro visitatori) can be found just beyond the entrance of Scopello.

One of Sicily's most beautiful coastlines enjoys protected status: Zingaro

This busy agricultural and industrial town (population 46,000), known for its wines, is located 11km/7mi to the southeast, near the north coast at the foot of the 826m/2710ft Monte Bonifato, on which it was founded by the Arab prince Al Kamúk in AD 828. The town gets its name from him. In 1233 Álcamo was moved to its current location by Emperor Frederick II. This is also where the poet Ciullo was born. He worked at Frederick II's court and supported his ambition of turning the Sicilian language of those days into a language of literature. The poem *Rosa fresca aulentissima* is attributed to him. The 18th-century church of Sant'Oliva, built by Giovan Biagio Amico, stands on Piazza Ciullo. It houses a statue of St Oliva by Antonello Gagini (1511); the altarpiece was painted by Pietro Novelli in 1642.

Chiesa Matrice stands on Piazza 4 Novembre; the side portal of 1499 and the campanile (featuring mullioned windows) are both

Álcamo, white wine and sonnets

from the previous structure. The current building, a vaulted basilica with a crossing dome, was a late work of Angelo Italía (1699). The interior includes Antonello Gagini's 1519 retable and a fresco cycle by the Flemish painter Guglielmo (Willelm) Borremans (1735–37). There are also some interesting sculptures by Antonello and Giacomo Gagini (16th century) in the church of San Francesco, a cycle of eight statues by Giacomo Serpotta (1724) in the Benedictine convent church of Badia Nuova and the Casa de Ballis, a patrician house dating from the 15th century.

Monte Bonifato   The views of northwestern Sicily from Monte Bonifato (826m/ 2910ft, two-hour climb; bird watching, picnic area, orchid trail) are magnificent.

Castelvetrano

E 6

Province: Tràpani
Population: 30,000

Altitude: 190m/623ft

Castelvertrano, in the hinterland of Selinunte, near the southwestern coast, is an agricultural centre where olives, wine and wood are industrially processed.

What to See in and Around Castelvetrano

Castelvetrano   The 16th-century Chiesa Madre is situated on Piazza Garibaldi. It has an elaborate portal and beautiful stucco ornamentation in its interior; in front of it is the Fontana della Ninfa from 1615 and the town hall, which houses a small archaeological collection. One of the items on display was the bronze statue of the **Selinunte Ephebe**, until it was stolen from the mayor's office in 1962. After a long odyssey the statue of the young man has found a new home in the Museo Civico (Mon – Sat 9am – 1pm, 3pm – 7pm, Sun only until 1pm).

San Domenico   The church of San Domenico, built in 1470, was adorned with stucco and frescoes by Antonino Ferraro in 1577. The donors of these works, as of the church itself, were members of the d'Aragona Tagliavia family, who had managed to become members of the aristocracy and whose tombs can be found in the choir under the dome.

▶ CASTELVETRANO

INFORMATION

Ufficio Turistico
Piazza Carlo d'Aragona
91022 Castelvetrano
Tel. 09 24 90 20 04
www.selinunte.com

The public garden **Villa Garibaldi** has a good view of the town and the surrounding area all the way to the sea.

Above the Delia River, which has been dammed to form the Lago della Trinità, is the interesting Chiesa di Santissima Trinità di Delia (4km/2.5mi west of Castelvetrano; 9am–1pm, 4pm–8pm) in the publicly accessible estate of the Saporito family. Built as a Basilian domed cross-in-square church between 1140 and 1160, the lords of the manor later used it as a burial site. The interior reveals carefully

✳ Santissima Trinità di Delia

executed masonry not covered by plaster. At the centre is a monumental marble sarcophagus, which imitates the porphyry sarcophagus of Emperor Frederick II in Palermo cathedral. The exterior has the appearance of block-like solidity, while the frames of the pointed windows and the dome reveal Arab influences.

Cave di Cusa is the name of area of Selinunte's ancient quarries, 11km/7mi southwest of Castelvetrano (3.5km/2mi from Campobello di Mazara.) Stone was quarried here until Selinunte was destroyed by Carthage in 409 BC. Ever since, pieces of stones at all stages of production have been lying around here, from stones that hewn straight from the rock to others that were almost ready for transport to Selinunte 10km/6mi away. The huge blocks, column sections and capitals of Temple G, weighing as much as 100 tons, also came from here. This quarry provides an insight into how workmen went about their business in Antiquity.

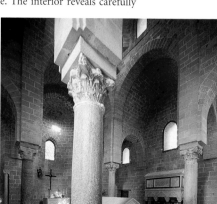

A gem: the Norman church of Santissima Trinita di Delia

The small rural town of Gibellina (population 4000) 20km/12mi north of Castelvetrano suffered such severe earthquake damage in the night of 14 January 1968 that it was decided to rebuild the town as Gibellina Nuova 18km/11mi further west. Well-known architects, sculptors and painters such as Pietro Consagra, Arnaldo Pomodoro, Oswald Mathias Ungers and Rob Krier donated works. Gibellina Nuova is thus a cultural historical monument with the highest density of modern art in the whole of Italy. The not entirely uncontroversial new town was based on English garden cities, incorporating wide avenues and two-storey terraced homes with small front gardens and green spaces, a completely atypical building style for Sicily.

Gibellina Nuova

The entrance to the town is the star-shaped Porta di Ferra gate (Pietro Consagra, 1980). During a walk through the town visitors will pass by the snail-shaped »Meeting«, a see-through building by Consagra, which is now used as a bar, social centre and meeting place, as well as by Ludovico Quaroni's church La grande Sfera, which has an Arab air. The **Museo d'Arte Contemporaneo** somewhat further north houses the vast majority of the donated art (Via Segesta, Tue–Sun 9am–1pm, 4pm–7pm). It was in Casa di Lorenzo that Francesco Venezia worked on the old façade of the former palazzo; events are held in its courtyard throughout the summer (information: IAT, Piazza XV Gennaio 1968, 91024 Gibellina, tel. 0 92 46 78 77, www. comune.gibellina.itt).

Gibellina Il Cretto
The ruins of old Gibellina were buried by the Umbrian painter Alberto Burri under white cement, creating the fascinating artwork *Il Cretto* (*The Crack*; picture p. 190). The theatre festival **Orestiadi di Gibellina** is held here between June and October (Fondazione Orestiadi di Gibellina, Baglio di Stefano, tel. 0 92 46 78 44, www.orestiadi.it).

Salemi
This small town, known for its white wines (446m/1463ft, 25km/16mi west of Gibellina; population 12,000) also suffered damage in the earthquake in 1968. Roger I built a castle here during the Middle Ages that Frederick II extended. Garibaldi proclaimed himself dictator of Sicily here in May 1860, three days after arriving in Marsala. The remains of the early Christian basilica of San Michele can be seen in the archaeological zone.

★ Catania

S 7

Provincial capital
Population: 333,000

Altitude: 10m/33ft

This city, situated in the middle of the east coast, which is flat here, is an important centre of trade and industry and also the seat of Sicily's oldest university. Catania is a fascinating, lively place with sacred and secular Baroque buildings and many monuments from Antiquity and more recent times, located in the Piana di Catania, a fertile plain between Mount Etna and the sea.

Katane under Mt Etna
Ionian Greeks from Naxos (near Taormina) founded the city of Katane in 729 BC in a place the Sicels had inhabited. The lawmaker Charondas lived here in the 6th century BC. During the first half of the 5th century the city's history became dramatic: it was under the rule of Syracuse at the time. The tyrant Hieron I moved the population to Leontinoi and populated Katane, which was then called Aitne

again in the subsequent period, thanks to high agricultural yields. In 278 BC the city took in Pyrrhus of Epirus. Conquered by the Romans in 263, it became a Civitas decumana and was henceforth part of the Roman province of Sicilia. During the empire Katane/Catania experienced a golden age, as proved by the ruins of several buildings. Overshadowed during the Byzantine era by Syracuse and during the Arab era by Palermo, Catania attained significance again

Baedeker TIP

Don't miss

Legendary almond granita from the Pasticceria Savia (Via Etnea 302–304). Another popular location is Nievski, a post-Marxist meeting place for students, Scalinata Alessi 15–17. Marella Ferrara, Italy's most outlandish fashion designer, »weaves« Sicilian terracotta and Etna lava into her ladies' wear (showroom Ferrara Couture, Via Alberto Mario, www.marellaferrara.com).

in the 12th century, when it became a trading and maritime centre under Norman rule. The **earthquake** of 1169 (15,000 deaths) created a serious rupture, as did the devastation caused by the Hohenstaufen Emperor Henry VI in 1194. The Spanish rulers from the House of Aragon developed the city (a university was founded here in 1434). In 1576 the majority of its inhabitants died of the plague. In 1669 the western part of the city was destroyed by a **lava flow**, while the rest was ruined in the **earthquake** of 1693. After such a history of unfortunate events, the city was rebuilt in the 18th century to plans by, among others, Giovanni Battista Vaccarini. Several buildings, such as Sant'Àgata, the cathedral façade, San Giuliano and the university, as well as the famous Elephant Fountain, were designed by him. The resulting city has wide axial roads and rectangular squares. Although it often feels dark because of the black lava stone used as the building material, the statement on Porta Ferdinandea (now Porta Garibaldi) from 1768, »Melior de cinere surgo« (»Reborn from my ashes more beautiful«) was quite justified.

◄ Phoenix from the ashes

729 BC	Greeks found Katane.
263 BC	Romans conquer the city.
12th century	Under Norman rule Catania is a centre of trade and seafaring.
16th–17th century	The plague, an eruption of Mt Etna and an earthquake cause great devastation.
18th century	Catania's magnificent rebirth

The university continues to ensure that the city remains young and vibrant: the magnificent Baroque streets of the Centro storico, now pedestrianized, are filled with pubs, enoteche and music clubs. Le Ciminiere, the revitalized 18th-century sulphur kilns by the harbour, have become symbols of the city's culture. Congresses, exhibitions and music events of international standard take place here.

»La Nera«, the »black city« today

What to See in Catania

Piazza del Duomo

The city centre is the traffic-free Piazza del Duomo, which got its final look in the late 17th and in the 18th century: Porta Uzeda (1696), cathedral (1730–39), Sant'Àgata (1735–67), Elephant Fountain (1736) and Palazzo del Municipio (1741) – all of them creations of Giovanni Battista Vaccarini. The model for Vaccarini's Elephant Fountain, **Fontana dell'Elefante** an elephant made of black lava supporting a small Egyptian obelisk, was Bernini's Elephant Obelisk in Rome.

✳ **Sant'Àgata Cathedral**

According to tradition, the cathedral of Sant'Àgata stands on the spot where Saint Agatha died a martyr's death (► Baedeker Special p. 406); it was previously the Benedictine Abbey of Sant'Àgata, which was made a cathedral in 1092. Between 1086 and 1090, after Catania had been conquered by the Normans (1085), construction began on the site where the Roman Achillean Baths had stood. Building materials were taken from their remains, as well as those of other ancient structures, to construct the cruciform basilica. Earthquakes in 1140 and 1169 made extensive repairs necessary, and after the 1693 earthquake the cathedral had to be completely rebuilt, retaining the original size of the nave. The three Norman lava apses, whose exteriors

The Piazza del Duomo, the heart of the »black« city at the foot of Mount Etna

Catania *Sant' Àgata Cathedral*

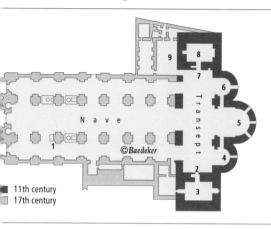

1 Tomb of Vincenzo Bellini (1801–1835)
2 Marble gate by Giovanni Battista Mazzolo (1545)
3 Cappella della Madonna
4 Cappella di Sant' Àgata
5 Presbytery, choir stalls by Scipione di Guido (1588)
6 Capella del Sacramento
7 Marble gate by Giandomenico Mazzolo (1563)
9 Sacristy with a fresco by G. Platania (1679) featuring Mount Etna's eruption of 1669

■ 11th century
▢ 17th century

are structured by blind arcades, can be seen from the courtyard of the archbishop's palace. Get to it by walking eastwards along the cathedral's northern side for around 150m/170 yd.

Some of the original building materials can be seen inside the apses of the cathedral, along with the characteristic pointed arches and corner columns. When it was rebuilt, the nave was reconstructed under the direction of Girolamo Palazzotto, while G. B. Vaccarini completed the façade in 1736. He used six columns from the destroyed Norman cathedral, which had previously come from ancient buildings. The dimensions and the proportions of the interior, crowned by a tambour dome, are impressive. It was designed as a pantheon of Catania. Visitors will sense this as soon as they see the simple tomb of the opera composer Vincenzo Bellini by the second pillar on the right. He was born in Catania in 1801, died in Paris in 1835 and was brought back to the town of his birth in 1876 (►Famous People).

From the south transept a portal designed by Giovanni Battista Mazzolo (1545), leads to the Norman **Cappella della Madonna**, which houses two sarcophagi, one Roman and one medieval, in which kings of Aragon and Constance of Aragon (d. 1363; consort of Frederick III) are buried.

The main focus of the south transept is the **Cappella di Sant'Àgata**, which is closed off by a wrought-iron gate. The marble triptych on the altar of this greatly venerated chapel was the work of Antonello Freri (16th century). The life of Saint Agatha is the main subject of the carved choir stalls (1588); there are further tombs of Sicily's Aragonese kings in the choir. In the sacristy is a contemporary depiction of the 1669 eruption of Mount Etna with the lava flow that reached Castello Ursino.

A team of scientists and engineers at the Instituto Nationale di Geofisica e Volcanologica monitor Mount Etna's every move around the clock, as here in May 2005. The INGV headquarters are located in the small town of Nicolosi.

WHEN THE EARTH QUAKES...

The flair of the south, evidence of Antiquity and good weather attract thousands of tourists to Sicily every year. One of the attractions is Mount Etna, a giant among volcanoes. It is not just the largest active volcano in Europe, it is also one of the largest in the world.

Its eruptions have always worried and threatened the people of this area. Now as then, they monitor the mountain known locally as **Mongibello** (from the Italian and the Arabic words for mountain, monte and djebel) carefully and with concern. The major eruptions have been monitored with equal care since Antiquity, when the Greek poets Pindar and Aeschylus reported such an event in 478/474 BC. During one of the most recent eruptions, in 1983, an attempt was made to weaken the volcanic forces by targeted explosions, but without the desired success. Nature was stronger.

A trip to the Etna region shows visitors the signs of devastation: old and new lava flows, meandering through the landscape. In Catania this material can also be seen in the town: at the Hohenstaufen castle (Castello Ursino), which originally stood right by the sea. During the massive eruption of 1669 the lava flow got all the way to the sea, flowed past the castle, and destroyed several villages as well as the western part of Catania and the harbour. Since this disaster, which claimed 20,000 lives, the castle has been 500m/550yd from the sea. However, the decay of volcanic material has brought **great fertility**, which is the reason why the people are loath to leave this area and why they build their homes close to Mount Etna, trying to defy whatever nature chooses to throw at them. The famous Etna wine flourishes here, as do citrus fruits, olives, figs and fruit, up to an altitude of 1000m/3300ft. It is possible to speak of a **cultivated landscape** at least up to this elevation. Chestnuts grow up to an altitude of 1600m/5250ft. The next vegetation

zone is reserved for more undemanding species, such as acacias, gorse, barberries and ferns that grow between 1500m/4900ft and 2500m/8200ft. There is no more vegetation beyond that.

Enormous forces

Southern Italy's volcanism is directly associated with the creation of the Apennines, which run along Italy from north to south and of which Mount Etna is part. Since the Early Pleistocene, Mount Etna has grown above the tectonic fault lines which run from the Lipari Islands along Sicily's east coast in a southwesterly direction, piling up huge amounts of lava and tufa. For that reason the more recent eruptions have usually occurred on the flanks, from cracks and secondary craters, of which some 300 are known. Mount Etna is currently around 3350m/11,000ft high. Its base has a diameter of 40km/25mi and it covers an area of around 1400 sq km/540 sq mi. Tectonic activity is also to blame for the frequent earthquakes that, like volcanic eruptions, have affected the people here, claiming countless lives from Antiquity to the present. A serious earthquake in the 6th century caused the ancient temples of Selinunte in the southwest of the island to collapse. However, most earthquakes take place around the tectonic fault line to the south of Mount Etna, the most far-reaching of which devastated the entire southeast in 1693.

New life from the ruins

This devastating event also had beneficial consequences, in a different way from Mount Etna's eruptions. The destruction caused by the 1693 earthquake triggered a magnificent re-building effort. It gave the entire southeast of Sicily a new face, a **Baroque face**, and new life flourished

Gibellina Il Creto – the sculptor Alberto Burri buried the town of Gibellina, destroyed in the 1968 earthquake, under a cement blanket.

again. Unlike the regions around Etna, which are characterized by agricultural activity, the large man-made landscape created here was architectural. The need for creating new housing was combined with the Baroque **need for representation**. The highly practical, political considerations of the landowners should not be overlooked either: for a village or town accommodating at least 80 families the aristocratic owner got one vote in the barons' parliament.

In 1607, long before the devastating earthquake, the Spanish viceroy Marcantonio Colonna founded a new town in the modern-day province of Ragusa, naming it **Vittoria**, after his daughter. In line with the Baroque penchant for regular construction, this planned town (i.e. not one that grew over time) is based on a grid pattern.

After 1693 the destroyed towns were generally rebuilt in the same location, from Caltagirone and Niscemi in the west to Augusta and Syracuse on the east coast, from Palagonia and Acireale in the north to Ispica, Modica and Scicli in the south, and, the biggest of them all, Catania. In some cases the destruction was so immense that it was preferred to move the town to a new location. This was the case for Avola, Francofonte, Giarratana, Grammichele and also Noto. The love of geometry always came through. Regular patterns were very popular for the street plan. An artistic hexagonal pattern was chosen for Avola and Grammichele.

Ragusa is a special case. Here, the destroyed old town was rebuilt (Ragusa Ibla) with streets that were necessarily labyrinthine because of the terrain; Rosario Gagliardi's magnificent church of San Giorgio stands here. But in addition, further up, the new town of Ragusa Superiore was built on a grid pattern (as in Vittoria). In addition to the construction of countless churches and palaces all over Sicily, all this contributed to the fundamental change in the architectural face of Sicily that happened during the Baroque age. In addition to the remains of Antiquity and the Middle Ages, 18th-century Baroque became the third major era of art and architectural history on the island.

The birthplace of Giovanni Verga (1840–1922, ▶ Famous People; Via S. Anna 8, very near the cathedral) commemorates the famous author and exponent of »Verismo« (Mon–Fri 9am–1pm).

Casa Museo Giovanni Verga

Visiting the warren that is the fish and food market will provide an exciting change. To get here, take the steps at the southwestern corner of the cathedral square. The market is one of Sicily's most colourful (Mon–Fri only in the mornings, all day Sat).

★ Fish and food market

The church of the convent of Sant'Àgata opposite the cathedral's north side (1735–67) is considered to be one of G. B. Vaccarini's main works. The block-like structure is dominated by a powerful octagonal dome and fronted by a magnificent façade, whose central portion is concave. The church is built on a central ground-plan but with nave, choir and transepts of different lengths, the longest being the nave, which also houses the matroneum (nuns'gallery).

Badia Sant'Àgata

Walk eastwards a little along Via Vittorio Emanuele, between Sant'Àgata and the cathedral, to get to the hall church of San Placido (convent) with its three-storey concave façade, a work by Stefano Ittar (1769).

San Placido

Via Teatro Massimo leads to Piazza Bellini, the address of Teatro Bellini, one of Italy's most beautiful opera houses. In 1890 the neo-Renaissance building was inaugurated with Bellini's *Norma*.

Teatro Bellini

Return to Piazza del Duomo and turn southwards to Porta Uzeda (1696), which separates the beginning of Via Etnea from the harbour district.

Porta Uzeda

Behind the magnificent gate to the left in Via Dusmet is the archbishop's palace and Palazzo Biscari, which the Paternò Castello family, the princes of Biscari, commissioned to a design by A. Amato in several construction phases between 1707 and 1763. The rich window frames of the top floor are quite striking. The builder's grandson, Ignazio Biscari, extended the palace in order to make space for his extensive collections. In 1787 Goethe visited »the museum where marble and brass statues, vases and all kinds of antiquities are gathered together« and Prince Vinzenzo, the collector's son, »presented his coin collection in special confidence« (now in the Museo Civico in Castello Ursino).

Palazzo Biscari

Castello Ursino, a defiant-looking lava building, stands on Piazza Federico di Svevia. Constructed by Riccardo da Lentini from 1239 onwards, this defensive Hohenstaufen building closely resembles the castles of Frederick II in Syracuse and Augusta. The floor plan consists of four wings around a central courtyard. There are few decorative elements; at the entrance on the north side there is a Hohen-

★ Castello Ursino

The Theatre Bellini commemorates the composer who was born in Catania in 1801.

staufen eagle seizing a hare. The castle originally stood very close to the harbour, but the large lava flow of 1669 made its way along its western side (where it can still be seen) and moved the coastline eastwards. The Castello houses the **Museo Civico** (municipal museum) with local finds and collections. It exhibits sculptures, a Hellenistic relief of Polyphemus, who was blinded by Odysseus; as well as porcelain, weapons and paintings (including from the Sicilian school of the 19th–20th centuries; daily 8.30am – 1.30pm).

Piazza Mazzini   Piazza Mazzini, a square Baroque piazza in the middle of an intersection, has remained unchanged since the 18th century. It is surrounded by porticoes, for which 32 ancient columns were used, and by buildings of the same height with pilasters.

Porta Garibaldi   From here Via Garibaldi leads to Porta Garibaldi (Porta Ferdinandea). This monumental gate was built in 1768 in honour of Ferdinand IV and his consort Maria Carolina, a daughter of Empress Maria Theresa of Austria. The architects were Francesco Battaglia and his son-in-law Stefano Ittar. They built the gate in horizontal layers of white limestone and black lava. The city side is plainer, while the more opulent outer side has concave wings and is crowned by a clock between winged figures that symbolize Fame.

Walk north from Piazza Mazzini. Via Vittorio Emanuele is just a few steps away. It too emanates from the cathedral square, placing it within the area of the ancient city. Here, on the southern slope of the former acropolis, is the Teatro Romano (entrance: Via Vittorio Emanuele 266). It was built in the 2nd century BC in place of a Greek structure. The auditorium, divided into two sections, has a diameter of about 100m/100yd. The steps are made of lava, the orchestra and seating area was covered in marble. To the west of it is the **odeon**, a small theatre also made of lava, whose orchestra lies at the same height as the theatre's upper corridor (Mon–Fri 9am–1.30pm, 3pm–7pm).

Teatro Romano

The birthplace of the composer Vincenzo Bellini (1801–35, ► Famous People; daily 9am–12.30pm, in winter until 1.30pm) is located at the corner of Via Vittorio Emanuele/Via Crociferi. Opposite it is the church of **San Francesco d'Assisi** with an impressive Baroque façade.

Museo Belliniano

A little further north, on the left-hand side of Via Crociferi, there are two significant Baroque churches. First, the Chiesa di San Benedetto, the church of the Benedictine nuns. Its special feature is the atrium with an elegant flight of steps leading up to the nave. The ceiling painting (*Glory of St Benedict*) was done by Giovanni Tuccari from Messina in 1727.

San Benedetto

Immediately above it is the Jesuit church, designed by Angelo Italía towards the end of the 18th century. It has a front of seven bays; adjoining it is that of the church of **San Francesco Borgia** (pairs of columns on two storeys). Opposite, G. B. Vaccarini built the oval church of **San Giuliano** with a convex façade and a huge cupola.

Chiesa dei Gesuiti

Turn left from Via Crociferi into Via Gesuiti, which ends in Piazza Dante. Here, where the Greek acropolis stood, the Benedictines started building the church of San Nicolò and the associated monastery in 1702; it is one of the largest in Europe and despite the long construction period was never completed. The unfinished façade is marked by pairs of large column stumps on high pedestals. A large dome covers the unadorned interior, which features a meridian from 1841 (transept), the choir stalls (18th century) and the large organ (1755–67, Donato del Piano), which was praised by Goethe. From the dome (access in exchange for a tip) visitors have lovely panoramic views all the way to Mount Etna.

San Nicolò

◄ View

The former monastery to the left of the church has a richly ornamented façade with pilasters and window decorations, as well as two pretty courtyards (four were planned).

A nice walk goes eastwards to the major north-south axis, the Via Etnea. At its lower section, not far from Piazza del Duomo, its course is interrupted by the Piazza dell'Università; this creation by Vaccarini

Other sights

is lined by the university with its bell gable (on the left side) and the Palazzo San Giuliano (1745, on the right-hand side). Not far from here, on the left side of the road, is the **Chiesa Collegiata**, a basilica whose curving façade was designed by Stefano Ittar in 1768. Further along Via Etnea crosses Piazza Stesicoro; there is a monument to Bellini here on the right-hand side (G. Monteverde, 1882), while the remains of the Roman **amphitheatre** (2nd–3rd century), which could hold 16,000 spectators, can be seen to the left. The façade in the background belongs to the Capuchin church. The **Chiesa Sant'Àgata al Carcere** somewhat higher up on the square of the same name (18th century) commemorates St Agatha, who was held captive in the dungeon (visible from inside) before her martyrdom. The church's attractive 13th-century portal was part of the cathedral façade until the earthquake of 1693. In front of the intersection of Via Etnea and Via Regina Margherita, on the left-hand side, is **Villa Bellini**, the city park with green spaces, a flight of steps and two hills with views of Catania. Adjoining it to the north is the **Botanical Garden**. The church of Santa Maria di Gesù stands on the square of the same name. It was built in the 18th century in the site of an older Renaissance building. It houses several works by Antonello Gagini; the crucifix above the main altar was made by Fra Umile da Petralia.

Museums in the cultural centre Il Ciminiere

On Viale Africa in the complex of the cultural centre of Il Ciminiere; there are two worthwhile museums. The **Museo del Cinema** (Tue–Sun 9.30am – 12.30pm, Tue, Thu also 3pm – 4.30pm) is devoted to the history of cinema and the film locations on Sicily used by directors such as Rosselini and Visconti. The **Historical Museum of the 1943 Sicily Landing** (Museo Storico della Sbarco in Sicilia 1943; Tue – Sun 9.30am – 12.30pm, Tue, Thu also 3pm – 5pm) addresses the island's history at the time when the Allies (Americans, British and Canadians) invaded the island in the Second World War.

Around Catania

Lido Plaia

The city's beach begins around 3km/2mi south of town. Sandy beaches can be found to the north between Aci Castello and Giarre-Riposto (►Acireale and ►Taormina).

Motta Sant'Anastasia

8km/5mi to the west is the picturesque town of Motta Sant'Anastasia with a Norman castle. 7km/4.5mi southwest of the city is Catania War Cemetery, where 2135 Allied soldiers who died close to Catania, especially in the fighting over the Simeto River bridgehead, were buried (follow the tangenziale from the airport towards the A19 to Palermo; the cemetery is signposted just before the A19).

Misterbianco

The small town of Misterbianco (7km/4.5mi to the west) is named after the Benedictine White Monastery (Monastero bianco), which was buried when Mount Etna erupted in 1669.

► Etna (33km/20mi to the northwest); Catania is the starting point for the train that goes around Mount Etna several times a day (Circumetnea; ►Etna)

Etna

✶✶ Cefalù

M 4

Province: Palermo
Population: 14,000

Altitude: 15m/50ft

The seaside town of Cefalù with its unmistakable silhouette is situated in the central section of Sicily's north coast. The picturesque old town with its famous Norman cathedral lies between the sea and the 270m/885ft monolith Rocca di Cefalù. In the west there is a bay several miles long with a fine sandy beach, while the Madonie Mountains begin in the hinterland. As a result it is not surprising that Cefalù has become the most popular holiday destination on the island after Taormina.

*View of Roger II's famous Norman cathedral
from Rocca di Cefalu*

Norman cathed-
ral by the sea

The town's name is self-explanatory once you have set eyes on Cefalù for the first time: Kephaloidion, from Kephalos, head, thus the Greek name of the ancient settlement at the foot of the large rock. Cefalù experienced a golden age under the Norman Roger II, who moved it to the foot of the monolith and who, in 1131, one year after being made king, founded the majestic cathedral that now dominates the town.

What to See in Cefalù

Old town

The old town's street plan dates back to the 12th century, but the majority of the buildings are 16th century. The main axis is Corso Ruggero, which runs from Piazza Garibaldi to the northern shore. There are countless stairs and streets all the way to the castle rock on the one side, while there are straight little streets leading down to the sea on the other. The Hosterium Magnum, the former residence of the Norman king (nice mullioned window) stands at the intersection with Via Amendola (Corso Ruggero 75).

Hosterium
Magnum ►

▶ VISITING CEFALÙ

INFORMATION
Servizio Turistico
Corso Ruggero 77, 90015 Cefalù
Tel. 09 21 42 10 50, fax 09 21 42 23 86

WHERE TO EAT
► **Moderate**
① *La Brace*
Via 25 Novembre 10, tel. 09 21 42 35 70
closed Mon and Tue lunchtime; bistro-style restaurant; good local cuisine

Il Trappitu

② *Il Trappitu*
Via C. O. di Bordonaro 96
Tel. 09 21 92 19 72
Tasteful, rustic decoration, terrace above the sea; extensive wine list, large selection of regional dishes

③ *Baglio di Falco*
Contrada Vallone di Falco
Tel. 09 21 42 08 20
www.bagliodelfalco.it, closed Wed, pleasant inner garden with seating under old olive trees, in the winter a fire is lit inside; approx. 2km/1mi outside town

► **Inexpensive**
④ *Trattoria Al Girotondo*
Via Gibilmanna 46, tel. 09 21 42 13 12
closed Mon; this is where the locals go. Rather inconspicuous from the outside, with a nice roof terrace (open during the summer); the pizzas have the reputation of being the best in the area.

Cefalù *Map*

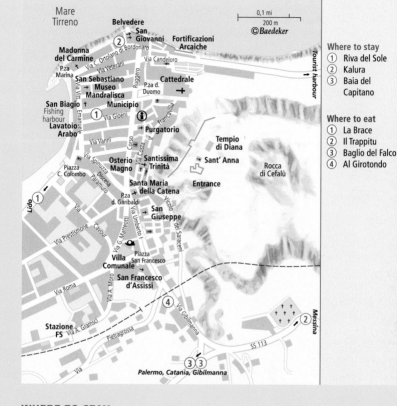

Mare Tirreno

0,1 mi
200 m
©Baedeker

Belvedere
San Giovanni Fortificazioni Arcaiche
Madonna del Carmine
P.za Marina
Via C. Ortolano di Bordonaro
Via Candeloro
Via Veterani
San Sebastiano
Museo Mandralisca
Via Vitt. Emanuele
Cattedrale
P.za d. Duomo
San Biagio
Fishing harbour
Municipio
Via Gioeni
Lavatoio Arabo
Purgatorio
Via Vanni
Tempio di Diana
Sant' Anna
Rocca di Cefalù
Piazza C. Colombo
Via Spinuzza
Via Discesa Paramuro
Osterio Magno
Santissima Trinità
Santa Maria della Catena
Entrance
Lido
Via Prestismone Cavour
P.za d. Garibaldi
San Giuseppe
Via Umberto
Vicolo dei Saraceni
Villa Comunale
Piazza San Francesco
San Francesco d'Assissi
Via A. Moro
Via Roma
Stazione FS
Via A. Gramsci
Pietragrossa
Via Gibilmanna
SS 113
Messina
Palermo, Catania, Gibilmanna
Tourist harbour
Corso Ruggero
Via Matteotti

Where to stay
① Riva del Sole
② Kalura
③ Baia del Capitano

Where to eat
① La Brace
② Il Trappitu
③ Baglio del Falco
④ Al Girotondo

WHERE TO STAY

► Mid-range

① *Riva del Sole*
Viale Lungomare 25
Tel. 09 21 42 12 30
Fax 09 21 42 19 84
www.rivadelsole.com
28 rooms; close to the centre, basic, spacious rooms

② *Kalura*
Località Caldura
Via Vincenzo Cavallaro 13
Tel. 09 21 42 13 54
Fax 09 21 42 31 22

www.kalura.it, 80 rooms – very nicely situated; long-established address above the sea with its own small bay and very nice rooms. Big choice of sporting activities.

③ *Baia del Capitano*
Contrada Mazzaforno
Tel. 09 21 42 00 05, fax 09 21 42 01 63
www.baiadelcapitano.it
39 rooms; 6km/4mi west of the old town; the comfortably furnished rooms are on the small side; the grounds are large and face the sea; the hotel has its own beach.

★★
Cathedral
🕐
Opening hours:
daily 8am – noon
3.30pm – 7pm

According to legend, Roger II had fallen into distress at sea and vowed that if he were saved, he would build a church on the beach where he was brought to safety. The building was »a symbol of gratitude for the successful, comprehensive colonization of Muslim Sicily by the Norman conquerors« (G. Cassata). The political motivation must not be neglected: Roger II made the dioceses of Palermo and Messina into archdioceses right after he was made king, and created new dioceses in Lìpari, Patti and Cefalù. Cefalù Cathedral was also meant to be the burial site of the Norman dynasty. This did not happen because the building was not yet finished when Roger died in 1154. The king was buried in Palermo; the two porphyry sarcophagi, which he had set up for himself and the queen in Cefalù in 1145, were later moved to the capital by Frederick II.

It took a long time for the cathedral to be completed (it was only consecrated in 1267); in addition the original monumental plans were altered for the more recent sections (nave). It is a cruciform basilica with magnificent transepts and choir. The west front looms over the sloping cathedral square. It features two huge, square towers, which are largely unadorned; between them is a portico designed by Ambrogio da Como in 1471. The wall above the portico is adorned by two rows of pointed arch friezes; the arches of the lower frieze intersect. Below it is the King's Door, the Porta Regum.

The **eastern building** is imposing. It can be seen by walking along a narrow path (behind the apse) up the slope to a small platform as well as from the top of Rocca di Cefalù (photo p. 195). The eastern sections are significantly higher than the nave. The semi-circular

? | DID YOU KNOW ...?

■ It says in the open book which Christ is holding in his left hand: »I am the light of the world: he that followeth me shall not walk in darkness, but shall have the light of life.« (»Ego sum lux mundi, qui sequitur me non ambulabit in tenebris sed habebit lucem vitae« John 8:12).

apse of the choir projects far to the east. It is structured by pilasters in the lower section, on top of which stand paired columns. The top section of the wall features a frieze of round arches. The frieze of intersecting pointed arches characteristic of Norman architecture was used on the side walls of the apse and on the eastern walls of the transepts. The south (left) transept is higher than the north transept and the roof of the nave because it was vaulted in the 15th century.

The nave has two rows of granite columns, whose ancient and Byzantine capitals support pointed arches. The nave and aisles have an open wooden roof structure, whose beams are richly painted. The cathedral has a font in the south aisle (12th century) and a statue of the Virgin by A. Gagini in the north aisle (1533). The triumphal arch, supported by two imposing columns, forms the boundary between the nave and the transept. It is a double triumphal arch: the higher of the two arches was part of the original plans; a lower one was built underneath it when it was decided to build the nave at a lower height than initially planned. Both transepts have a gallery. The modern glass windows by Michele Canzoneri from Palermo, a veritable master of light, are sometimes overlooked, which is a pity.

Interior

The side walls of the choir feature stucco ornamentation. The eyes are drawn to the mosaics on a gold ground here, which were part of the original structure. They are the work of Byzantine artists whom Roger II conscripted. Christ Pantocrator, the ruler of the world, in the semi-dome covering the apse, dominates this part of the cathedral. The inscription above the arch reads »Incarnate, I, creator of mankind and saviour of mankind I created, I, who am become flesh, judge over the flesh, and as God over the hearts«. The semi-circle below it is divided into four areas. The upper register depicts Mary, praying, between the archangels Raphael and Michael, Gabriel and Uriel.
The third register (next to the central window) depicts Peter and Paul, the patron saints of the Norman dynasty, between the four evangelists, as well as further apostles. The walls to the side depict prophets and saints of the Western and Eastern churches – a symbol of the state's supremacy over the Catholic and Orthodox subjects. The choir's cross rib vault is also richly decorated with cherubs and seraphs. Despite frequent restoration, the mosaics of Cefalù are considered to be the best-preserved in Sicily.

Mosaics

To the left of the cathedral is the cloister, which was closed for decades (10am–1pm, 3pm–6pm). It has pointed-arch arcades with finely worked double columns (mid-12th century).

Cloister
🕐

The modern town hall stands on the western side of Piazza del Duomo. Via Mandralisca runs next to it. The museum of the same name

Museo Mandralisca

Baedeker TIP

Le Petit Tonneau

Discover the fine differences between Marsala, Malvasia, Zibibbo, Crema di Mandorla, Passito and so on during a wine tasting, for example in the splendid enoteca in Via Vittorio Emanuele 49 (www.lepetittonneau.it).

🕐 (no. 13; daily 9am – 12.30pm, 3.30pm – 7pm) houses the private collection of the art lover Enrico Piraino, Barone di Mandralisca. It contains Greek vases (including one that depicts a tuna seller), Arab vases, coins and a shell collection. The main attraction is the mysterious *Portrait of an Unknown Man* by Antonello da Messina (1465).

San Biagio, Lavatoio ►
The church of San Biagio (13th century) and a washing area, presumably from the Arab period, can be found on Via Vittorio Emanuele.

Hiking up Rocca di Cefalù 🕐
A steep stair starts at Corso Ruggero near Piazza Garibaldi and leads up to the 270m/885ft rock of Cefalù (daily 9am – 8pm, until 5pm in winter). This is where the prehistoric and ancient settlements were located. There are the remains of a megalithic Temple of Diana (9th century BC), a cistern from the Arab period, as well as the ruined castle and the town wall from the Norman period. The view of the town's tile roofs is lovely. When the weather is good, it is even possible to see the Lipari Islands (►Lìpari, Isole). An ideal picnic place!

Around Cefalù

Gibilmanna
A winding scenic road leads from Cefalù to the pilgrimage site of Gibilmanna (population 25), situated 14km/8.5mi to the south on the slopes of Pizzo Sant'Angelo (1081m/3547ft). The **Sanctuary of Gibilmanna** (17th–18th century) is located here in a very pretty setting. On the Nativity of the Theotokos (birth of Mary, 8 September) the Santuario di Gibilmann is the destination of pilgrims from all over Sicily. An unsurfaced road leads to the observatory on **Cozzo Timpa Rosa** (1005m/3297ft) 4km/2.5mi away (views).

Pollina
The small town of Pollina is around 20km/12mi east of Cefalù, on a rocky outcrop at an elevation of 900m/2950ft. **Manna** is harvested here. A small museum shows how the bark of manna ash is turned into a compound that is used by the pharmaceutical industry. On some days the views of snow-covered Etna are splendid from up here.

Isole Égadi · Aegadian Islands

A–C 4/5

Province: Tràpani   **Population:** 4400

The three Aegadian Islands emerge from the water off Tràpani on Sicily's west coast: Favignana is the largest and the location of the only *comune*; **opposite it is Lévanzo; Maréttimo, the wildest, is the last island and less than 160km/100mi from the Tunisian coast. The islands of Formica and Maraone (uninhabited) lie between Tràpani and Lévanzo.**

Favignana and Formica are fishing ports, particularly for tuna (the »Mattanza« in May; ►Baedeker Special p. 204). Thanks to the beautiful landscape and good diving opportunities, tourism is also developing. August is an especially busy time, when the people of the nearby coastal towns come to the islands to visit the local beaches.

Tuna and tourists en masse

 ## VISITING AEGADIAN ISLANDS

INFORMATION
www.egadi.com
www.isoleegadi.it (commercial website with lots of information)

TRANSPORT
Conventional and fast ferries from Tràpani to Favignana and Lévanzo (1–1.5 hrs; speedboats 15 mins) as well as to Maréttimo (3 hrs; fast ferries 45 mins); cars can only be taken to Favignana. Trapani has a local airport (regular buses from here to the harbour).

SHOPPING
Favignana ·
Conservittica Sammartano
Strada Comunale Madonna 4
Tel. 09 23 92 19 54
All kinds of tuna specialities, including ventresca, tuna belly, mosciame, cured tuna

WHERE TO EAT
► **Moderate**
Favignana · El Pescador
Piazza Europa 38
April – Nov; tel. 09 23 92 10 35
It's all about fish and other seafood.

Maréttimo · Hiera
Via G. Maiorana 8, tel. 32 87 44 56 90
Local cuisine, in the evenings pizza too

WHERE TO STAY
► **Mid-range**
Favignana · Aegusa
Via Giuseppe Garibaldi, tel.
09 23 92 24 30, www.aegusahotel.it
15 rooms; pleasant accommodation in a palazzo; restaurant in the courtyard

Favignana · Delle Cave
Contrada Torretta (Scalo Cavallo)
Tel. 09 23 92 54 23
www.hoteldellecave.it, 9 rooms
2km/1mi to the east outside town, near the north coast; simple, stylish rooms

Maréttimo · Maréttimo Residence
Via Telegrafo, tel. 09 23 92 32 02
www.marettimoresidence.it, 75 beds
Small holiday complex south of the
town centre; run on ecological prin-
ciples; comfortable apartments, boat
trips, diving courses etc.

Levanzo · Residence La Plaza
Via Salita Poste, tel. 33 95 04 54 08
www.levanzoresidence.com
Apartments in the village with bath-
room and cooking facilities

▶ **Budget/Mid-range**
Lévanzo · Paradiso
Via Lungomare
Tel. 09 23 92 40 80
15 rooms, March – Nov
Small guesthouse with good food
above the harbour pier

Lévanzo · Dei Fenici
Via Calvario 18
Tel. 09 23 92 40 83
10 rooms; the guesthouse is just a few
metres above the Paradiso; sea views

History   With their victory over the Carthaginians the Romans ended the
First Punic War here in 241 BC. In the Middle Ages settlers from
Liguria focused on fishing and harvesting corals, which made them
wealthy. In 1860 the islands were used as a hiding place for Garibal-
di's ships before the freedom fighter sailed to Sicily's mainland on 11
May on his »Expedition of a Thousand«.

Favignana

Favignana (Aegusa in Antiquity; population 4500), just 6km/4mi
from the Sicilian coast and at 19 sq km/7 sq mi the largest island of
this group. Its highest elevation is Monte Santa Caterina (302m/
991ft) in the island's hilly eastern area. The **main town**, Favignana,
lies in a deep bay on the north coast in the shadow of Castello Florio.
The good road network (50km/30mi) makes this island suitable for
bike rides (rental facilities at the harbour); bus trips are also a good
way of exploring attractive landscapes here. A walk to Fort Santa Caterina also delivers views of the archipelago as well as of the Sicilian
coast and Érice. Another enjoyable option is to take a boat trip
around the island with its many grottoes and diving in waters that
are rich in fish but not entirely harmless. Bizarre rocky beaches can
be seen near the ancient quarries of Cala Rossa in the northeast of
the island.

Lévanzo

Lévanzo (5.8 sq km/2.2 sq mi, population 200), known as Phorantia
in Antiquity, is the smallest island of this archipelago. It is 12km/8mi
from Tràpani and 4km/2.5mi from Favignana. The highest elevation
is Pizzo di Monaco (278m/912ft). The coastline is very rugged.
Grains and wine are grown on the island and there is also livestock
farming. Pine trees were planted around Cape Minoia. The quiet

Favignana: tufa quarries on Cala Azurra

main town of Lévanzo with its low, white houses, lies on the south coast at Cala Dogana, where ships dock. The springless island has many grottoes, including the Grotta del Genovese on the west coast at a height of 30m/98ft (Stone Age pictures of animals and people). It can be accessed on foot via a mule track, or by boat (only when accompanied by the custodian, www.grottadelgenovese.it).

Maréttimo

Maréttimo (12 sq km/4.6 sq mi, population 800) is the westernmost island in this group, around 30km/20mi from Tràpani. The hilly interior culminates in Monte Falcone, at an altitude of 686m/2250ft; there are small plains around the coast. The vegetation is largely maquis. This island has freshwater springs. The coast is rich in bays and grottoes (stalactite grottoes del Cammello, della Bombarda and del Presepe). Punta Troia at Maréttimo's northeastern tip is dominated by a castle. The town of Maréttimo lies in the east of the island. The island's private accommodation is completely booked out in August, but for the rest of the year Maréttimo is an insider tip. Trails in an exemplary condition open up the island's interior.

The final act of a mattanza or the cruel end of a perfect swimmer: several men pull their half-dead catch into the boat.

MATTANZA – DANSE MACABRE IN THE SEA

The boats slowly come closer together. The fishermen sing. »E aiamola e vai avanti« calls the lead singer. »Let's start, let's go«. The others reply: »aiamola, aiamola«. They sing quietly, without haste and pull in the nets. The rectangle created by the boats gets smaller and smaller, half of the nets are brought back in. Now the men stop singing.

Suddenly the sea starts bubbling – the fish dance the »sarabanda della morte« the death dance, in the death chamber (»camera della morte«), which is now around 10m/33ft by 20m/65ft and 2m/6ft deep. Some 200 tuna fish chase through the narrow chamber, jump up or try to dive down, but the net is impenetrable. Then the »rais«, the leader, raises his hand. The men are quiet. Only the sea is raging from the thrashing fins of the captured animals. The command is given and then the men force huge hooks into the stately fish. »Prima i piccoli e poi i grandi«, »first the small ones and then the big ones«, someone calls out. Sometimes a fish manages to free itself, but it is not long before a further hook digs into its body.

Bloody spectacle

The water is dyed red with blood, and dead tuna float around, weaker animals that died of a heart attack. The men use to hooks to pull them in,

heaving them on board with their hands. It is hard work, as a tuna fish weighs on average 200kg/440lbs. In addition the men have to be very careful because the tail fins are sharp as a knife and can kill a person. Then the fish are on the boat. The men still have to remain vigilant because the death throes, which can last up to ten minutes, see the tuna thrashing around on the deck. Woe betide the man who gets caught in that! After around 15 minutes the inferno is over. Around 200 animals will be on the boats with wide eyes, as they are taken to the abattoir. Now the net of the death chamber is back down at 30m/100ft, ready for the next »mattanza«.

A tuna is a **perfect swimmer** whose body consists of up to 75% muscle, and can reach speeds of 90kph/55mph. But tuna also set records as long-distance swimmers: over a 15-year period they cover around 1.5 million km (930,000 miles) between the North Sea and the Norwegian

fjords, where they hunt, and in the waters around Sicily, where they spawn. A highly developed member of the mackerel family, the tuna has just three enemies: killer whales, mako sharks and humans.

Ancient fishing method

The people of Sicily have preyed on tuna for a long time. The fishermen of Favignana use a very efficient method for their »tonnara« (tuna fishing), which their ancestors learned from the Arabs in the 9th century. Fixed nets several miles long are anchored along the tuna's ancient migratory routes, so that a school gets caught in the confined chamber. Large fish-traps the size of harbour basins are used to drive the fish into the »camera della morte«, around which the fishing boats position themselves. The reason why all this effort is necessary is that the sought-after Atlantic bluefin tuna does not take bait before spawning. The tuna battle begins in April. The 10km/6mi of nets, 450 anchors, around 6000 stone weights and 3500 buoys to mark the nets have to be prepared and put out. That alone takes a month. Getting

them in and storing them takes another month. The »mattanza« takes place four times during the fishing season (April to mid-July), but only around 40 fishermen still do it.

Over-fishing

The times when the island lived exclusively off fishing are over. The tuna schools around Favignana have got smaller and smaller since Genoese and Neapolitan fishermen sailed the Mediterranean, finding tuna with a helicopter and an echo sounder. Today nets are only put up around Favignana and Bonagia. Without help from the state and Japanese enthusiasm for Atlantic bluefin tuna (Japan buys 90% of Favignana's tuna) these operations would have closed down a long time ago. Immediately after the »mattanza« the animals are butchered by Japanese specialists and frozen for transport to Tokyo. The islanders are left with the entrails, the bones and the tender meat around the eyes. By the way: the canned tuna sold in Italy is the less tasty albacore, and is not caught by Italian boats but by Japanese ones!

★★ **Enna**

Provincial capital
Population: 28,300

Altitude: 931m/3054ft

Situated at almost 1000m/3100ft, Enna has been considered the »navel« of Sicily since Antiquity. In ancient times there was a central Temple of Demeter (goddess of the harvest) and Persephone here. According to legend, Hades abducted Persephone from the nearby Lake Pergusa and took her to the underworld.

History The town's history is reflected in its name. In Greek it was called Enna, the Latin name was Henna; Castrum Hennae became Kasr Jânna during the Arab period, which was translated back into Italian as Castrogiovanni – and when ancient traditions were revived under Mussolini in 1927, the town got its old name of Enna back.

▶ VISITING ENNA

INFORMATION

Servizio Turistico
Piazza N. Colajanni 6, 94100 Enna
Tel. 09 35 50 08 75, fax 0 93 52 61 19
www.ennaturismo.info

EVENTS

The highlight of Holy Week (Settimana Santa) is the Good Friday procession; plays and concerts in Castello Lombardia in summer

WHERE TO EAT

▶ **Moderate**

① *Ariston*
Via Roma 365, tel. 0 93 52 60 38
Closed Sun; very good seafood dishes as well as traditional cuisine

② *Calascibetta · La Brace*
Contrada Longobardi
Tel. 0 93 53 46 99
Closed Mon; lovingly prepared local dishes

③ *La Trinacria*
Via Caterina Savoca 10

Tel. 09 35 50 20 22, closed Mon;
Basic trattoria with delicious regional treats prepared to old recipes

WHERE TO STAY

▶ **Mid-range**

① *Bristol*
Piazza Arcangelo Ghisleri 13
Tel. & fax 09 35 52 44 15
www.hotelbristolenna.it
Hotel with tidy rooms in the town centre; garage

② *Grande Albergo Sicilia*
Piazza Napoleone Colajanni 7 Tel. 095 35 50 08 50 Fax 093 55 50 04 88
www.hotelsiciliaenna.it; 80 rooms
Long-established hotel, set back slightly from the corso

③ *Località Pergusa · La Giara*
Via Nazionale 125
Tel. 09 35 54 16 87
Fax 09 35 54 15 21
www.parkhotellagiara.it; 20 rooms
On the eastern side of Lake Pergusa towards Piazza Armerina

The Sicel fort was Hellenized from the 5th century BC onwards under the influence of its trading partners Syracuse and Gela. During the First Punic War (264–241 BC), Enna, which was considered impregnable, was much fought over. In 258 BC as a result of treachery it fell into the hands of the Romans, who punished it cruelly in 214 BC when it wanted to side with Carthage. In 136 BC a great slave rebellion started in Enna: the slave leader Eunus, who proudly styled himself »Antiochus, King of the Syrians«, temporarily controlled the whole of Sicily. A monument has been erected in his honour at the base of Lombardy Castle. His reign ended when the town was starved out and taken by the Romans in 132 BC after a long siege led by P. Rupilius. That same year Rome sent a diplomatic mission to the famous Temple of Ceres (Demeter) in Enna, whose cult image was stolen by the greedy praetor Verres (73–70 BC).

◄ A Syrian Spartacus

In 535, during the Byzantine period, Enna was considered an important defensive location. The Arabs were only able to conquer it in 859 under Abbas Ibn Fadhi. Roger I moved people from his wife Adelasia's home, Lombardy, to the city. Frederick II extended the castle the most. Frederick III of Aragon was made »king of Trinacria« here in 1314, and in 1324 the parliament of barons convened here. During the period that followed Castrogiovanni gradually become insignificant. During the Second World War it was badly damaged.

Enna *Map*

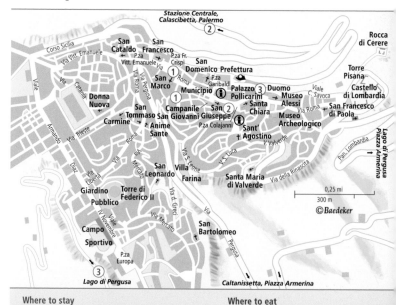

Where to stay
① Bristol ② Grande Albergo Sicilia ③ La Giara

Where to eat
① Ariston ② La Brace ③ La Trinacria

What to See in Enna

Piazza Vittorio Emanuele On the city's main square, Piazza Vittorio Emanuele, is the church of San Francesco with a 15th-century campanile. To the north is Piazza F. Crispi with its belvedere, which has splendid views of the neighbouring Calascibetta, the Madoníe and Mount Etna. The park-like complex has a fountain with a replica of Bernini's *Rape of Persephone*. **Via Roma** gradually makes its way uphill from Piazza Vittorio Emanuele. It widens to small squares in several places. Pass by the Baroque church of San Benedetto (Piazza VI Decembre) and the Catalan Gothic Palazzo Pollicarini to get to the cathedral (Piazza Mazzini).

Cathedral Built in 1317, the Chiesa Madre was restored after a fire. The extension works continued until the 17th century. Only the transept survives of the original building. The exterior of the apses dates back to the end of the 15th century. There are fantastic wooden ceilings inside the cathedral (the Battle of the Angels). Pietro Rosso from Bologna added a Coronation of the Virgin, richly adorned with stucco, in the main apse in around 1595. The capitals and bases of the columns separating the nave from the aisles are ornamented with sculptures; a few of them have inscriptions marking them as works by Gian Domenico Gagini from 1560. The pews date back to the 16th century, as do the paintings in the presbytery by F. Paladino.

The **Museo Alessi** next to the cathedral exhibits the cathedral's treasure, a coin collection as well as medieval works of art (daily 9am – 12.30pm, 4.30pm – 7.30pm).

Museo Archeologico The museum on Piazza Mazzini displays archaeological discoveries from the surrounding area (currently closed).

★ ★
Castello di Lombardia Via Roma continues as Viale Savoca and ends at Castello di Lombardia, one of the largest of the Sicilian castles (daily 9am – 8pm, only until 5pm in winter). It is named after the Lombard guard of Adelasia, the consort of the Norman Roger I; after his death, she married Baldwin I, who was installed as king of Jerusalem after the First Crusade, and died in Patti in 1118.

The castle, at the base of which a statue commemorates the slave leader Eunus, consists of Byzantine, Norman and Hohenstaufen elements. Six of the original 20 towers survive, the highest being **Torre Pisana** (95 steps; views).

Rocca di Cerere North of the castle is Rocca di Cerere, on which the famous Temple of Demeter (Latin: Ceres) was once located. Cicero wrote: »So great was the renown and the age of the cult, that the people, when they went there, seemed not to set off to a Temple of Ceres, but to Ceres herself.« The cult image stolen by Verres was so magnificent that people »either believed they were seeing Ceres herself or an image of

Castello di Lombardia

Ceres not made by human hand, but instead one that had fallen from heaven«. Today there is no trace of any of that, except for some workings on the cliff wall.

Situated on its own on a hill in a public garden to the southwest of the town is Torre di Federico II. The octagonal tower, surrounded by a partially extant octagonal wall, repeats the basic pattern of the Castel del Monte in Apulia and was modelled on Eguisheim in Alsace. It is 26m/85ft tall and has a diameter of 17m/56ft and a wall thickness of 3.5m/11.5ft. A recessed spiral staircase in the wall leads to the two upper storeys. The two main storeys have stately rooms with eight sections of rib vaulting. There used to be a 1km/0.6mi underground passage connecting Torre di Federico with Castello di Lombardia.

★
Torre di Federico II

Around Enna

The small farming town of Calascibetta (population 7000) is situated 7km/4.5mi north of Enna at an altitude of 691m/2267ft. As is confirmed by necropolises, it was already inhabited in the 11th century BC by Sicels. In 841 the Arabs founded this place, which they called Kalat Scibet, as a base for their siege of Enna. Roger I also besieged

Calascibetta

View of neighbouring Calascibetta from the Belvedere in Enna

Enna from here in 1087. Of his castle only the bell tower of the present church of San Pietro survives. This Chiesa Matrice (14th century) possesses a handwritten 14th-century Bible in Gothic script.

Lake Pergusa   10km/6mi south of Enna (SS 561), between two mountainsides covered in eucalyptus trees, is the oval Lago di Pergusa, now dry (667m/2188ft). It was once 1km/0.6mi wide, 2.2km/1.4mi long and 4.6m/15ft deep. According to legend, Persephone was kidnapped by Hades here as she was picking flowers, and taken to the underworld. Her mother, Demeter (Ceres), caused the land to wither, thereby forcing Hades to allow her daughter to return to the earth in spring and summer. It is from this legend that one of the major ancient vegetation and mystery cults developed. The racing circuit and a wire fence around the lake have taken away the latter's former magic. There are, however, plans to rectify this example of environmental destruction.

Leonforte   The town of Leonforte (population 17,000) is situated 18km/11mi northeast of Enna (on the SS 121) at an altitude of 612m/2008ft. Prince Nicolò Placido Branciforte founded the small town in the 17th century. Apart from the church of San Giovanni Battista and Branciforte Palace from 1620, the Granfontana is worth mentioning. This monumental livestock watering tank was set up on the outskirts

★
Granfontana ▶   of town at the behest of the town's founder in 1651. Located under

an arcade wall, on which several boldly designed gables rest, the water flows from 24 pipes into a vat, »a magnificent example of an artistic solution to a practical problem in Sicilian Baroque« (Krönig).

Agira

This small rural town (population 12,000; 650m/2133ft) is situated 13.5km/8mi east of Leonforte above Salso Valley. The river Salso is dammed to the east of the town, forming Lago di Pozzilo. At the start of the 4th century BC the Sicel town of Agyrion had 20,000 inhabitants and was allied to Syracuse. In 339 BC Timoleon drove out the tyrant Appolloniades and moved 10,000 Greeks here. The town's Temple of Heracles was well-known. This information comes from the historian **Diodorus Siculus**, who was born in Agyrion and lived in Alexandria and Rome in the 1st century BC. His **universal history**, written in Greek, ranges from the formation of the world to Rome's invasion of Britain in 54 BC; it is the most important source for Sicily's ancient history.

The townscape is characterized by a warren of picturesque streets with steps, Baroque churches and palazzi, including Chiesa San Salvatore on Piazza Roma in the town centre. The castle dates back to Arab times and was taken over by the Normans after the Arabs were driven out.

Eraclea Minoa

H 8

The ancient town of Eraclea Minoa, which has been investigated since 1907, lies only 35km/22mi to the west of Agrigento on a plateau to the east of the mouth of the Plàtani, the ancient Halykus.

At the foot of the bright, white chalk cliff Capo Bianco, there is a long, curving bay and a small pine wood. The small holiday village and a campsite are only overrun during the peak season. **Food and drink** are provided by Lido Garibaldi, which is situated right on the fine sandy beach (bar, ristorante, pizzeria).

★ ★
Beaches

The town was founded by Selinunte in the 6th century BC on the site of a pre-Greek settlement. The town was called Minoa, because, according to Greek tradition, King Minos of Crete landed here, in the territory of the Sicani king Cocalus, when he was pursuing Daedalus. He demanded that Daedalus

Accommodation tips

- The beach restaurant Lido Garibaldi, open all year round, also rents out apartments (tel. 09 22 84 60 61, 09 22 84 05 34, mobile 33 98 13 79 07).
- Crystal-clear water and an almost deserted sandy beach can also be found at Torre Salsa, where pitches for campers and small apartments are let (15km/9mi east of Eraclea Minoa, along the SS 115 towards Agrigento, 92010 Montallegro, tel. & fax 09 22 84 70 74 as well as 3 36 94 59 67, www.torresalsa.it).

be handed over to him, but was murdered by Cocalus in his castle in Kamikos (►p. 163, Sant'Angelo Muxaro). In around 505 BC Euryelon occupied the town, which was now called Herakleia. Located in the Greek-Carthaginian border region, the town changed owners often and in 210 BC became Roman. It was abandoned in the 1st century AD.

Excavations

During excavations parts of the 6km/4mi-long ancient town wall were uncovered, along with bastions and gates, as well as a Greek theatre (3rd century BC; quite derelict) with sea views. The nine seats with arm and back rests are of note. They were evidently meant for important people. Also of interest are public and private buildings (some of them under protective roofs) and a Greek necropolis. The antiquities collection displays local finds such as vases, terracotta figures and utility objects, reconstructed drawings and plans (daily 9am – 1 hr before sunset).

Siculiana Marina

Siculiana Marina (18km/11mi to the southeast) is a holiday resort with a long, relatively wide sandy beach and rocky coastline.

Ribera

The town of Ribera (230m/755ft; 18km/11mi to the northwest, near the SS 115, population 17,000) is a centre of orange cultivation. This is where the politician Francesco Crispi (1819–1901) was born; he was Italy's prime minister twice.

Capo Bianco, right below the ancient town of Eraclea Minoa

✶✶ Érice

Province: Tràpani   **Altitude:** 751m/2464ft
Population: 29,000

Situated on Érice (751m/2464ft), known as Eryx in Antiquity, is the quiet mountain town of the same name; it feels like an elevated bastion overlooking western Sicily. There are great views of Tràpani, its salt pits and the coast from the top. Although the evidence of Antiquity is largely gone, the medieval townscape still survives and the cobbled alleyways between uninterrupted rows of house fronts have an unmistakable atmosphere.

Mons Eryx used to be the site of a cult of an ancient Mediterranean mother goddess. She was worshipped by the Elymians, who founded a polis here; later she was equated with the Carthaginian Astarte, the Greek Aphrodite and the Roman Venus. The cult was associated with sacred prostitution involving girls known as hierodules. The location of the temple is known, but the building itself is no longer extant. According to ancient tradition, the town and temple were founded

Legend and history

◀ Heracles in Eryx

Chiesa Matrice in the picturebook town of Erice

▶ VISITING ÉRICE

INFORMATION

Servizio Turistico
Viale Conte Pepoli 11
91016 Érice
Tel. 09 23 86 93 88
Fax 09 23 86 95 44

GOOD TO KNOW

To Érice by air
The eastern outskirts of Tràpani and
Mount Eryx are connected via a
modern cableway (tel. 09 23 86 97 29,
www.funiviaerice.it).

Terra Libera
In Via S. Rocco 1, a side street of Via
Vittorio Emanuele, food and wine as
well as other goods are sold that were
produced on »terra libera«, land
confiscated from the Mafia.

EVENTS

Impressive Easter procession on Good
Friday. »Venere d'Argento«, July–Sept,
summer festival with music, dance
and theatre. »Zampogna d'Oro«, holiday with traditional instruments in
December.

WHERE TO EAT

▶ Expensive
① *Monte San Giuliano*
Vicolo S. Rocco 7, tel. 09 23 86 95 95
Closed Mon; regional specialities in a
smart ambience, garden seating in
summer

▶ Moderate/inexpensive
② *Osteria da Venere*
Via Roma 6
Tel. 09 23 86 93 62
Closed Mon; elegant dining experi-
ence in a secularized church

WHERE TO STAY

▶ Mid-range
① *Moderno*
Via Vittorio Emanuele 63
Tel. 09 23 86 93 00
Fax 09 23 86 91 39
www.hotelmodernoerice.it
40 rooms; in the town centre; the
hotel has clean rooms with stylish
furniture and a well-known restaurant.

② *Ermione*
Via Pineta Comunale 43
Tel. 09 23 86 91 38
www.ermionehotel.it
46 rooms; approx. 1.5km/1mi below
the town; basic hotel with views of
Tràpani and the Aeolian Islands

Valderice · ③ Baglio Santacroce
Contrada Santa Croce, on the SS 187
Tel. 09 23 89 11 11
www.bagliosantacroce.it, 25 rooms
Rural guesthouse dating back to the
17th century with a nice garden; the
restaurant also enjoys a good reputation.

by Eryx, a son of Poseidon and Aphrodite. He was defeated in a battle with Heracles, who however allowed him to continue to rule,
under the condition that he would hand it over to one of Heracles's
descendants. According to Virgil, Aeneas of Troy came across Mons
Eryx on his way from Carthage to Rome and built a temple there for
his mother Aphrodite/Venus.

Érice Map

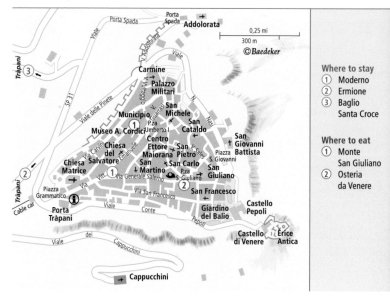

Where to stay
1. Moderno
2. Ermione
3. Baglio
   Santa Croce

Where to eat
1. Monte
   San Giuliano
2. Osteria
   da Venere

◄ A big lie

According to Thucydides (6,46), Elymian Segesta, which was later in the hands of Eryx, provoked the Athenians in 416 BC to go on their Sicilian adventure by luring them with the allegedly rich temple treasures of Eryx: »The people of Segesta had, however, contrived the following, when the first emissaries from Athens came to them ... They took them to the Temple of Aphrodite on Mons Eryx and showed them all the votive gifts, bowls, amphorae, incense burners and quite a few other objects, silver-plated, which produced a big visual impact with little monetary effort, and in all the houses they hosted the ship's crews, for which they sought out and borrowed all the gold and silver beakers in Segesta and the neighbouring Phoenician and Hellenic towns and used them to serve the men as if they belonged to them. Since almost everyone used the same ones almost all of the time and there was so much to see everywhere, it made a great impression on the Athenians and they returned home, talking about the wealth they had seen.«

In the following period Eryx was a Carthaginian base. In 260 BC Hamilcar founded Drepanon (Tràpani) from here. In 241 BC the town fell to Rome. Since the Romans believed they themselves descended from Aeneas, the Temple of Eryx, founded by Aeneas, was highly regarded and the inhabitants had a special standing. The Arabs called Mons Eryx Gebel-Hamed, the Normans Monte San Giuliano (after Julianus, who had inflicted defeat on the Saracens); this name was only replaced by the ancient one again in 1934.

What to See in Érice

Porta Tràpani The outline of the town is the shape of a triangle. The winding road ends at the southwestern corner, outside Porta Tràpani, one of the three Norman city gates that interrupt the town walls.

Baedeker TIP

Almond pastries

Érice is known for its sweet almond pastries. A large selection is available from the guardians of the old recipe, such as: Maria Grammatico (Via Vittorio Emanuele 14) and Caterina Silvestro (Pasticceria San Carlo, Via San Domenico 18 and Via Guarnotti 52).

Castello Pépoli Walk through the park with its lavish greenery, which was named after the Norman balio (governor), to get to the medieval Castello Pépoli. It stands in the site of the ancient acropolis and was renovated in the 19th century (now a luxury hotel).
To the east, where the Temple of Aphrodite used to stand, is **Castello di Venere**, the Castle of Venus, from the 12th–13th century (magnificent views; daily 9am–2 hrs before sunset).

San Giuliano Walk northwest along Via Roma to Piazza San Giuliano with a church of the same name, which was built under Roger I in 1076 and restored in the 17th–18th centuries.

San Carlo, San Pietro Via Filippo Guarnotti leads to the church of San Carlo (17th century); and immediately to the right of it is the church of San Pietro (1363, renovated in the 18th century) as well as the neighbouring San Rocco institute, a former monastery.

Centro Ettore Majorana The road opens up into Piazza S. Domenico with the church of San Michele, which was dedicated in 1486 and which, like San Rocco, is now used by the Ettore Majorana centre. This research centre was opened in 1963 and named after the Sicilian nuclear physicist who disappeared without trace in 1938 (in 1975 Leonardo Sciascia wrote *La scomparsa di Majorana*, *The Mystery of Majorana*, which addresses the scientist's fate). The research centre published, among other things, the Érice Manifesto against the nuclear arms race in 1982.

San Giovanni Battista Not far to the east, on the piazza of the same name, is Chiesa San Giovanni Battista. The eastern gate in the Gothic-Norman style is all that survives of the original fabric. The church houses works by Antonello Gagini (1531) and Antonio Gagini (1525).

At the highest point of Erice, where the Elymians once worshipped their goddess, lies the Castello di Venere, also known as Castello Normanno.

Walk southwest along Via Cordici, Via Fontana and Via Salerno to get to the Gothic church of San Martino (1339, refurbished in 1682 and 1858). Now turn back to **Piazza Umberto I**, the town's central square. This is the address of the town hall with the Museo Comunale A. Cordici. It exhibits local discoveries from the Punic and Roman cultures, including a fine head of Aphrodite from the 4th century BC, evidence of the cult that surrounded this goddess (Mon – Fri 8.30am – 1.30pm, Mon, Thu also 2.30pm – 5.30pm, closed Sat and Sun).

San Martino

◀ Museo Comunale A. Cordici

🕓

The Chiesa del Carmine lies to the north, near Porta Carmine and Palazzo Militari, whose façade is characterized by ornaments in the Plateresque style. Both buildings were constructed by the priest Bernardo Militari in 1423.

Chiesa del Carmine

Follow Via Rabata in a southwesterly direction. The Elymian town wall was built 3000 years ago. The road leads to the main church (Chiesa Matrice) and immediately afterwards to Porta Tràpani, the town's southwestern entrance.

Town wall

Chiesa Matrice, dedicated to the Assumption of the Virgin, features a lovely rose window at the front and is the town's most significant building. It was constructed in 1314 with stones from ancient buildings at the behest of Frederick of Aragon, who had the campanile built two years earlier in 1312 as a defensive tower (can be climbed). In 1426 the church façade was given a Gothic porch. The interior was renovated in the 19th century.

Chiesa Matrice

★★ Etna

Mount Etna is Europe's largest and highest volcano. Its base has a diameter of around 40km/25mi and it covers an elliptical area of almost 1400 sq km/540 sq mi. It has a gently sloping plateau at 2900m/9514ft, on top of which stands the summit cone, whose elevation changes as a result of volcanic activity but currently stands at 3369m/11,053ft.

Fertile fiery mountain

The volcano first formed in the early Pleistocene, over tectonic fault lines that run from the Lipari Islands via the Sicilian east coast all the way to the Hyblaean Mountains, building up large amounts of lava and tufa. The eruptions of the stratovolcano usually occur at cracks in the flanks and at side craters (more than 400). Precipitation seeps into the porous tufa and emerges as springs lower down, which, together with the mineral-rich soils, allows intensive agriculture and horticulture. There are rings of different vegetation zones around the mountain. A drive to the summit is like a trip from Palermo to North Cape (▶Baedeker Special p. 188).

*A threatening and fascinating natural spectacle:
Mount Etna's lava flows making their way towards the valley*

The Greeks associated the volcano with the myth of Typhon and Enceladus, who, in the battle of the giants, were trapped under Mount Etna by the gods. They also moved the **forge of Hephaestus** and the cyclopes here. They called the mountain »Aitne« (»fiery mountain«). The Sicilians combined the Italian and Arabic words for mountain, monte and gibel, and call it Mongibello, »mountain of mountains«. The area was declared a **nature park** in 1987 (park administration in Nicolosi, ►below). The remains of an ancient building at an altitude of 2917m/9570ft **(Torre del Filosofo)** were completely buried in the 2002–03 eruptions. The current settlements have encroached very close to the mountain, completely disregarding the danger. In the north and west people live just 15km/9mi from the main crater.

! Baedeker TIP

A guided walk up the volcano

A guided hike up Mount Etna is both safe and highly interesting. One choice is the Swiss mountain guide and vulcanologist Andrea Ercolani (Guida Vulcanologica, Via Marconi 27, Sant'Alfio, tel. & fax 09 59 96 89 92, www.siciltrek.it; further suggestions on p. 113 and p. 135).

 VISITING ETNA

INFORMATION

Linguaglossa · Pro Loco
95015 Linguaglossa
Piazza Annunziata 5, tel. 0 95 64 30 94
www.prolocolinguaglossa.it
Information about excursions up the volcano

Nicolosi · Servizio Turistico
Via Martiri d'Ungheria 36/38
Tel. 0 95 91 15 05, fax 09 57 91 45 75
www.aast-nicolosi.it

Nicolosi · Parco dell'Etna
Via del Convento 45 A
Tel. 0 95 82 11 11, fax 0 95 91 47 38
www.parcoetna.it

Randazzo · Ufficio Turismo
95036 Randazzo, Piazza Municipio 17
Tel. 09 57 99 00 64
www.prolocorandazzo.it

Zafferana Etnea · Pro Loco
95019 Zafferana Etnea, Piazza Luigi
Sturzo 1, tel. 09 57 08 28 25
www.zafferana-etnea.it
Also information about Mount Etna excursions

WHERE TO EAT

► **Expensive**
San Giovanni la Punta · ① Giardino di Bacco
Via Piave 3, tel. 09 57 51 27 27
Closed for lunch and Mon; elegant, with a nice garden and good food

► **Moderate**
Nicolosi · ② Grotta del Gallo
Via Madonna delle Grazie 40
Tel. 0 95 91 13 01
Closed Mon outside the peak season; garden restaurant in a nice location

Randazzo · ③ S. Giorgio e il Drago
Piazza S. Giorgio 28
Tel. 0 95 92 39 72
Closed Tue; trattoria with traditional dishes, outside seating in summer

Randazzo · ③ Veneziano
Via Romano 8a, tel. 09 57 99 13 53
Closed Sun evening and Mon; family-
run trattoria, traditional cuisine

Sant'Alfio ④ Case Perrotta
Loc. Perrotta, Via Andronico 2
Tel. 0 95 96 89 28, www.caseperrotta.it,
closed Mon; 8km/5mi outside or
town, popular agriturismo restaurant
with nice rooms

WHERE TO STAY
▶ Luxury
**San Giovanni La Punta · ① Villa
Paradiso dell'Etna**
Via Viagrande 37
Tel. 09 57 51 24 09, fax 09 57 41 38 61
www.paradisoetna.it
35 rooms; long-established luxury hotel

▶ Mid-range
Mascalucia · ② Azienda Trinità
Via Trinità 34 Tel. & fax 09 57 27 21 56
www.aziendatrinita.it, 8 rooms;
friendly apartments in a magnificent
garden with a pool and views of
Mount Etna, outstanding cuisine

Linguaglossa · ⑥ Il Nido dell'Etna
Via G. Mateotti
Tel. 0 95 64 34 04, fax 0 95 64 32 42
www.ilnidodelletna.it
Family-run hotel on the outskirts of
town. The ambience is tastefully
modern. Etna views and very good
restaurant

Linguaglossa · ⑥ Valle Galfina
Contrada Valle Galfina
Tel. 34 88 62 97 54 and 095 64 77 89
www.scilio.com; 7 rooms
Agriturismo with views of Mount Etna
in vineyards, 1km/0.6mi south of Linguaglossa; flawless rooms and cuisine

Nicolosi · ③ Biancaneve
Via Etnea 163

Tel. 0 95 91 11 76, fax 0 95 91 11 94
www.hotel-biancaneve.com
80 nice rooms, ideal for trips to Mount
Etna, situated above Nicolosi at 900m/
2950ft

Nicolosi · ④ Corsaro
Piazza Cantoniera Etna Sud
Tel. 0 95 91 41 22, fax 09 57 80 10 24
www.hotelcorsaro.it
12 rooms; 300m/330yd from Rifugio
Sapienza; comfortable rooms with a
restaurant

**Zafferana Etnea · ⑤ Primavera
dell'Etna**
Località Airone, Via Cassone 86
Tel. 09 57 08 20 10, fax 09 57 08 16 95
www.hotel-primavera.it
57 rooms; large complex with spacious
rooms, good restaurant

▶ Budget
Linguaglossa · ⑥ Villa Refe
Via Mareneve 42 , tel. & fax
0 95 64 39 26 – Eight clean rooms

Nicolosi · ③ Etna Garden Park
Via della Quercia 5
Tel. 09 57 91 46 86, fax 09 57 91 47 01
www.etnagardenpark.com; 24 rooms
Hotel in the town centre

Randazzo · ⑦ Scrivano
Via Bonaventura 121
Tel. 0 95 92 11 26, fax 0 95 92 14 33
www.hotelscrivano.com, 30 rooms
Centrally located on the SS 120;
comfortable rooms and a restaurant

Randazzo · ⑦ Antica Vigna
Contrada Monte La Guardia
4km/2.5mi outside Randazzo
Tel. 34 94 02 29 02, fax 0 95 92 33 24
www.anticavigna.it, 15 rooms; agriturismo with comfortable apartments
on a nice vineyard; much of the food
served is organic.

Etna Map

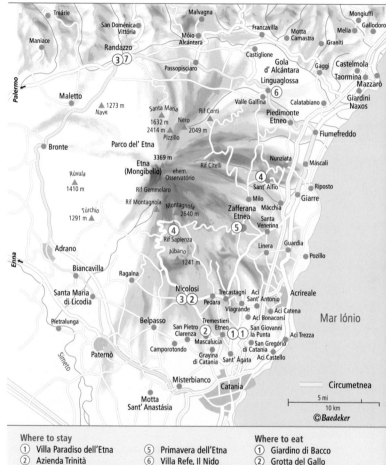

Where to stay
1. Villa Paradiso dell'Etna
2. Azienda Trinità
3. Biancaneve, Etna Garden Park
4. Corsaro
5. Primavera dell'Etna
6. Villa Refe, Il Nido dell'Etna, Valle Galfina
7. Scrivano, Antica Vigna

Where to eat
1. Giardino di Bacco
2. Grotta del Gallo
3. S. Giorgio e il Drago, Veneziano
4. Case Perrotta

Mount Etna's eruptions have endangered its surroundings time and time again. There have been around 150 major eruptions. Devastating ones in Antiquity occurred in 479, 425, 396 (lava flows all the way to the sea), 141, 135, 126, 122 (Katani was destroyed), 50, 44, 38 and 32 BC, as well as AD 40. In recent times there were serious eruptions in 1669 (destruction of Catania), 1893 (Silvestri Crater was formed), 1910, 1911 (Northeast Crater was formed), 1923, 1928, 1971, 1981, 1983 and 1986. Two new craters were formed during the

Eruptions

eruption in autumn 1989. In 1992 the lava flow halted just outside Zafferana Etnea. The 2002–03 eruptions made headlines. A number of new cones were formed below the summit on this occasion. It was in the news again most recently in 2011, when Catania's airport had to be closed temporarily.

On the Volcano

Preparation

Hiking route 2, p. 135 ▶

Climbing Mount Etna is one of the major highlights of a trip to Sicily; it is relatively easy, but it is important to carry protection against the cold, the wind and the rain, even in summer. High hiking boots will provide protection against small stones and sand. Contact-lens wearers should be aware of the fact that there is fine ash in the air and conditions can get very windy.

Etna – south side

Leave Catania on the Strada Etnea via Gravina (8km/5mi, to the right is an eruption crack from 1381) and past the 1669 lava flow to **Nicolosi**. This village, home to many mountain guides (700m/2300ft, population 5300), is located on Mount Etna's southern slopes. Because of its climate it is a great summer destination or a base for excursions up the mountain. It is also home to the **park administration** (▶p. 219). The museum (Museo Vulcanologico Etneo, Via C. Battisti 32) exhibits minerals, different kinds of lava rock, products made of lava and examples of rural buildings. The craters of the Monti Rossi (949m/3114ft), now covered in pine trees, are not far away. It was a powerful lava flow from these craters that reached Catania in 1669. When driving to the summit region, watch out for the different vegetation zones and also for the lava flows of the 19th and 20th centuries. The views of Mount Etna and the sea from the belvedere in **Trecastagni** (586m/1923ft, 5km/3mi to the east, population 4000) are stunning. The Chiesa Madre with a sculpture by Gagini is also worthwhile.

There is a well-built road from Nicolosi, past the turning to the Grande Albergo Etna (1715m/5627ft), to **Rifugio Sapienza**, a ref-

The eruptions of Mount Etna make the soil fertile

uge run by the alpine club at an altitude of 1935m/6348ft (restaurants and souvenir shops). Those not wanting to go any higher can visit the Crateri Silvestri, which formed during an eruption in 1893. From here there is a cable car up to the mountain station of La Montagnola (2500m/8200ft), where visitors switch to a four-by-four operated by SITAS (www.funiviaetna.com) to drive up to an altitude of 2900m/9500ft in good weather (those with asthma or heart complaints should exercise the necessary caution). Mountain guides point out the most recent eruption crater and decide whether the weather allows a climb to the main crater.

Linguaglossa (information: Pro Loco, ►p. 219) is the starting point for a drive up Etna from its northern side. It is the starting point of the 20km/12mi panoramic road Mareneve towards Piano Provenzana (1800m/5900ft, hiking and winter sports area).   **Etna – north side**

Trip Around Mount Etna

A trip in the diesel-operated narrow-gauge Circumetnea railway offers impressions of contrasting landscapes. From the station of Catania Borgo in Via Cardonda at the top end of Via Etnea, the 110km/68mi journey takes 3.5 hours to go three quarters of the way around Europe's largest volcano to Giarre/Riposto (connecting trains here to Messina and Catania) and back to the east coast. After leaving behind Catania's sprawling suburbs, the train makes its way through orchards and vineyards, past the pistachio groves of Bronte and through several bizarre lava fields with views up to the summit craters. The journey can be interrupted at will, for example in friendly Etna towns like Randazzo and Linguaglossa (information: tel. 0 95 54 12 50, www.circumetnea.it; only Mon–Sat).   **Ferrovia Circumetnea**

The most comfortable way to explore the landscape around Mount Etna is on the Circumetnea

FERTILE MOUNTAIN OF FIRE

✳ ✳ **The volcano is located on the fault line between the African and the Eurasian continental plates. The Earth's crust is in constant motion here: magma can emerge along this line of weakness. Mount Etna is thus one of the most active, if not the most active volcano in the world.**

① Bubbling forces

The first eruptions of Mount Etna occurred around 700,000 years ago. Mount Etna in its current form developed around 3000 years ago. It is estimated that in the past 400 years, it has brought more than a billion cubic metres of lava to the surface. Every year around 25 million tons of carbon dioxide emerge from its craters and cracks, making it one of the world's greatest polluters.

② Magma feed

Mount Etna obtains its fiery freight from the upper mantle, at a depth of 70–120km/45–75mi. Towards the summit the molten mass is distributed through countless cavities. From here there are several volcanic chimneys transporting it to the surface. The uppermost magma chamber is located just 2–3km/1–2mi below the summit.

③ Summit

Mount Etna has four constantly active main craters, of which the 300m/100ft northern crater only formed in 1979. New secondary craters form all the time or cracks open up allowing lava to flow out. The first reported outbreak drove out the Sicani from the east coast in 1500 BC.

④ Mount Etna does not just bring destruction

The rapid decomposition of lava into fertile soil has allowed the people around the mountain to harvest high yields of wine, oranges and lemons for millennia. Cold lava is a sought-after material for new buildings. The black stone obtained from the lava mass has shaped the appearance of many towns around the volcano.

⑤ Glowing lava flows

Like luminous rivers the lava flows push their way towards the valley, destroying everything in their path. Some are up to 15km/9mi long, others end just 250m/225yd beyond where they emerged. Nobody can stop them. At best they can be diverted, by creating walls of earth for example.

⑥ Empedocles and the volcano

According to legend, the Sicilian philosopher Empedocles hoped to become immortal by jumping into the volcano's crater. »O give yourself to nature before she takes you«, Hölderlin has him proclaim before he vanished where »the Earth's fire gushes from the depths of a mountain«. But instead of gaining divine attributes, his body evaporated in the silicate, which had a temperature of more than 1000°C/1800°F.

Mount Etna is one of the world's largest air polluters.

During the 2002–03 eruption, fountains of lava shot up to 200m/ 650ft into the air.

Decorative: the black lava rock contrasts nicely with the light, pastel stones; here the church of Santa Maria in Randazzo.

© Baedeker

Prickly pears also grow well on the fertile soil.

Nothing can stop the glowing lava flows. They destroy everything in their path.

Paternò Paternò, an ancient Greek settlement (255m/837ft, population 44,000), is situated 20km/12mi northwest of Catania on the southwestern slopes of Mount Etna, in the midst of citrus fruit plantations; one variety of blood orange is even named after the town. The Simeto River meanders in the west. In the Middle Ages the town was founded by the Normans. On the rock that towers above it, Roger I had a castle built in 1073, which he passed on to his daughter Flandrina and her husband Henry del Vasto from Lombardy; from their descendants it came into the hands of Bartolomeo De Luca, count of Paternò, in 1193. It was altered in 1900. Chiesa Madre (Santa Maria dell'Alto), built in 1342, is nearby. A further church, Santa Maria della Valle (1072), has a wonderful Gothic portal.

The small town of **Belpasso** (551m/1808ft, 5km/3mi to the northeast) owes its grid pattern to its reconstruction in 1695 after the devastating earthquake of 1669.

Biancavilla Biancavilla (3km/2mi outside Adrano) was founded by Contessa Entellina (1450), again by degli Albanesi (1488; ▶ p. 350) and finally in 1489 by Albanian refugees. The Albanian Madonna dell'Elemosina is venerated in the Chiesa Madre.

Adrano This town (560m/1837ft, population 32,500), a centre of citrus fruit and grape production, is situated on a lava terrace on the southwestern slopes of Mount Etna. Until 1929 it was called Adernò, then it was given its ancient name again. It comes from the Sicel god Adranus. Under Roger I (1060–91) a Norman **castle** was built here on Saracen ruins in 1070. Like the defensive structures in Paternò and Motta Sant'Anastasia, it was meant to secure his hold over Catania. It is a rectangular keep, which was altered in the 14th and 16th centuries (chapel with remains of frescoes); it now houses a worthwhile archaeological museum (Tue–Sat 9am–1pm, 4pm–7pm, Sun 9am–1pm). The neighbouring Chiesa Madre, whose nave is separated from its two aisles by 16 lava columns, also dates back to Norman times. In 1980 Europe's first solar power station was inaugurated somewhat to the southwest of Adrano in Euryalos. The joint Franco-German-Italian project consisting of 182 mirrors is no longer in operation.

Museuo di Adrano ▶ ⏱

Approx. 6km/4mi to the northwest of Adrano is a medieval bridge, the **Ponte dei Saraceni**, which spans the Simeto River (the last 2km/1mi of dirt road are a challenge for vehicles).

Ponte dei Saraceni near Adrano

A detour leads to Centùripe, originally a Sicel settlement. This small farming town is magnificently located on top of a mountain between the valleys of the Simeto and the Dittaino (18km/11mi southwest of Adrano, population 6600, views of Mount Etna!). A local pottery industry developed here in the early 3rd century BC, with vivid, strong colours that were achieved through combining encaustic with tempera. Frederick II destroyed the town in 1233 after a rebellion. In 1548 it was re-founded. The Museo Archeologico (in the town hall) exhibits, among other things, a black Attic vase decorated with figures such as the strange motif of Heracles playing a lyre (530 BC), terracotta sculptures as well as the characteristic pottery from Centùripe itself, such as Dionysus with the personified grapevine (Ampelos). Most discoveries from Centùripe are, however, in the Archaeological Museum of Syracuse (▶Siracusa). The **Castello di Corradino** (on Piazzale Belvedere in the southeast of town) is not a medieval building, but the remains of a Roman mausoleum. Further ancient remains can be found nearby: in Vallone Difesa there is a Roman building that is believed to be a seat of the Augustales, whose function it was to maintain the imperial cult; there are baths in Vallone dei Bagni and a Hellenistic house in Contrada Panneria. Finally, parts of the town wall survive here and there.

Centùripe
◀ An ancient pottery

Back on the main route around Mount Etna, you pass by the »pistachio town« of Bronte (760m/2493ft, population 20,000). From here it is 13km/8mi north to the former Benedictine abbey of Maniace,

Bronte

Randazzo was built on an old lava layer.

Abbazia or also **Castello di Maniace**. The names goes back to the Byzantine general George Maniakes, who defeated the Arabs here in 1040 (his name also lives on in Castello Maniace in Syracuse). In 1799 Ferdinand IV gave the abbey together with the town of Bronte to the Admiral Horatio Nelson as a fief out of gratitude for his help; Nelson thus became Duke of Bronte. After a visit to the small church, the pretty garden is a nice place to stop and take a break (Tue–Sun 9am–1pm, 3pm–5pm, until 7pm in summer).

Randazzo

Randazzo was built on the northern slopes of Mount Etna in a dominating position above the Alcàntara Valley on an old lava layer (765m/2510ft, population 11,500). Although only 15km/9mi away from the main crater, this town was spared the volcano's eruptions in historical times. It suffered severe damage in the Second World War however.

There are three parish churches in its centre, which has a medieval feel, because there were three Christian congregations in Randazzo until the 16th century:

! *Baedeker* TIP

Randazzo Pasticciere

A visit to Pasticciere Santo Musumeci either before or after looking around the town of Randazzo is a must (opposite Chiesa Madre di Santa Maria on the square of the same name). The biscuits, sweet treats and gateaux are a delight, so forget about counting calories here.

Greek, Latin, and also Lombard. The Chiesa Madre di Santa Maria is a 13th-century (Latin) church made of cut lava stone. The impressive apses date back to the 13th century. The portals and windows were altered into the Catalan Gothic style. The (Greek) Chiesa di San Nicolò was built in the 14th century; the transept and the apses are original. It houses sculptures by Antonello and Giacomo Gagini as well as a 15th-century triptych. The Palazzo Finocchiaro, opposite, was built in the early 16th century and is a fine example of a transitional Gothic/Renaissance building. The façade's fascia features a Latin inscription. The (Lombard) Chiesa di San Martino has an elegant campanile with mullioned windows as well as crenellation (14th century). It houses a marble font from 1447; the crucifix in the south apse dates back to 1546 and the marble tabernacle in the north apse dates back to the 15th century. The Palazzo Reale (13th–14th century) on the main road, Via Umberto I, was once the residence of Charles V.

The tranquil town of Linguaglossa (550m/1804ft, population 5500) is the starting point of the panoramic Mareneve (sea and snow) road, which leads to the less visited northern slopes of Mount Etna and further up to the plateau Piano Provenzana (1800m/5905ft, 5.5km/3.5 mi). In summer the town is a starting point for trips to the summit and tours with off-road vehicles to around 2900m/9500ft. The tourist information office houses a small Etna museum. The cemetery on the road to Piedimonte Etneo is worthwhile for its impressive Art Nouveau mausoleums.

Linguaglossa
✷
◄ Panoramic road

The pretty town of Zafferana lies 24km/15mi north of Catania on the eastern flanks of Mount Etna (574m/1883ft, population 7300). Its location amid gardens on the edge of vineyards make it a popular, refreshing place to visit in summer; it has both sea views and is at the same time a good starting point for hikes and trips to the Etna region. During the major eruption of 1992 Zafferana was miraculously spared: the lava flow stopped 800m/900yd outside town.

Zafferana Etnea

Gela

N 10

Province: Caltanissetta
Population: 77,000

Altitude: 45m/148ft

Gela, once one of Sicily's most significant Greek colonies, has changed a lot since petroleum was discovered here in 1956. Oil refineries, oil rigs and new housing developments dominate the townscape. There is not much evidence of its great past. The archaeological museum is definitely worth visiting for its exhibits.

▶ VISITING GELA

INFORMATION

AAST
Via Pisa 75, 93012 Gela
Tel. 09 33 91 37 88

WHERE TO STAY

▶ **Mid-range/Budget**

Sileno
① Contrada Giardinelli
on the SS 115
Tel. 09 33 91 11 44
fax 09 33 90 72 36
www.alberghiinsicilia.com/sileno.php
88 rooms; a box but of a good
standard, popular with business
travellers

② *Stella del Mediterraneo*
Località Falconara on the SS 115
Tel. & fax 09 34 34 90 04
www.stelladelmediterraneo.it
12 rooms; around 20km/12mi to the
northwest, lovingly run, small hotel
next to Castello Falconara

WHERE TO EAT

▶ **Moderate**

① *Casanova*
Via Venezia 89–91
Tel. 09 33 91 85 80
Closed Sun evenings, Mon and in
August; local cuisine in a pleasant
atmosphere

Gelo the tyrant Gela was founded in 690 BC by settlers from Rhodes and Crete. The town was named after the river Gelas (modern-day Torrente Gattano). It flourished; in 581 BC the citizens founded Akragas (Agrigento) and in around 550 BC built a treasury in Olympia. In 505 BC Cleander, son of the Olympic victor Pantares, asserted himself as tyrant here with the help of Sicel mercenaries. After seven years he was replaced by his brother Hippocrates (498–491 BC), who conquered large parts of eastern Sicily. After his death the commander of his cavalry, Gelo (491–478 BC), assumed rule of Gela, which was for a short while Sicily's most powerful town, until Gelo occupied Syracuse, moving his residence as well as most of the inhabitants there. Together with this father-in-law Theron of Akragas, he defeated the Carthaginians in the Battle of Himera (Imera). The Greek tragic playwright **Aeschylus** spent the last years of his life in Gela and was buried here in 456 BC. When the Athenians invaded in 415–413, Gela supported Syracuse. Soon afterwards, in 405 BC, the city was destroyed by Carthage on its great campaign of destruction, suffering the same fate as Selinunte and Agrigento.

It was rebuilt in 340 BC by Timoleon of Syracuse, but Gela only had a few decades left: in 311 BC Agathocles of Syracuse attacked the town, killed 4000 inhabitants and had them buried in mass graves (some of which have been found). In 284 BC the Mamertines destroyed the town completely. The site remained barren until Frederick II founded the town of Terranuova on the site in 1230. In 1928 the town got its old name of Gela back. On 10 July 1943 Allied forces landed near Gela and Licata.

Gela *Map*

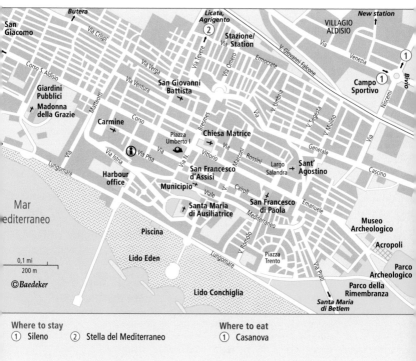

Where to stay
① Sileno   ② Stella del Mediterraneo

Where to eat
① Casanova

What to See in Gela

The centre of this industrial town lies somewhat above the coast. The main road is Corso Vittorio Emanuele with Piazza Umberto I, which is dominated by the neo-Classical façade of the **Chiesa Matrice** (18th century, façade renovated in 1844).

Piazza Umberto I

The museum, which exhibits discoveries from Gela and the area around Caltanissetta, can be found at the southeastern end of the corso. Its outstanding architectural fragments deserve special mention. There is a terracotta horse's head from a temple acroterion (end of the 6th century BC), a sandstone burial stele with an exact replica of a temple roof (1st half of the 5th century BC) as well as a remarkable numismatic collection with more than 5000 coins from the archaic period (before 490 BC), silver and gold coins from the 5th century BC; the coins from Gela depict the Gelas river god, a bull with a human head (daily 9am – 7pm; the Zona Archeologica closes 1 hr before sunset).

★
Museo Regionale Archeologico

⊙

✳
Zona Archeo-
logica Acropoli,
Parco della
Rimembranza

Immediately adjoining the museum is the easternmost of the two ancient districts: the Zona Archeologica Acropoli and the Parco della Rimembranza on the hill »Molino a vento«. This is where the town's residential quarters, which Timoleon built in around 340 BC, were excavated. The park, which makes up the southern side of the acropolis, possesses the remains of two Doric temples; one was probably dedicated to Athena (6th century BC), the other to the chthonic deities Demeter and Persephone; there is a column in front of it (5th century BC).

Bagni Greci

The western archaeological zone is located at the opposite end of the corso, 3km/2mi away. When the corso forks, follow Via Manzoni (left) and a short while later Via Europa (right). Near the hospital the remains of public baths, a horseshoe-shaped complex from the 4th century with clay pools and seats, were found on the site of a necropolis (5th century BC).

Capo Soprano

A few hundred metres to the west is Capo Soprano. There is a sign pointing out the entrance to the large archaeological area on the southern side of Viale Indipendenza. Large parts of the ancient town fortifications were found on this cape under 13m/43ft sand dunes. The crenellated wall is the largest and best-preserved of its kind. It dates back to the 5th century BC and was given its current appearance after the Carthaginian destruction of 405 BC, when Timoleon re-founded Gela in 340 BC. What is special about it is that two techniques were used in its construction: the lower sections, most at risk

Around 2500 years old: the town walls on Capo Soprano

The grand castle of Castellucio

during attacks, were built out of exactly cut limestone blocks (up to 4m/13ft high); for the upper sections unfired clay bricks were used, which are now protected from weathering by glass panes. The wall, which changes direction several times, survives to a height of 7–8m/23–26ft. The complex is illuminated at night. There are good views of the small harbour (Porticciolo) and the beach towards Agrigento from the wall.

Around Gela

The sizeable castle of Castelluccio (7km/4.5mi to the north) dates back to the 14th century and is situated in a conspicuous position above the SS 117b.

Castelluccio

Butera lies 19km/12mi to the northwest of Gela at an altitude of 402m/1319ft on a mountain ridge in the hinterland of the Gulf of Gela, not far from the south coast. It was founded by the Arabs; after they were forced out the Normans built a fine castle here in 1096.

Butera

The coastal road reaches the 14th-century crenellated castle by the sea after around 20km/12mi; the long **sandy beach** is much visited at weekends and during the holidays.

Falconara

The port of Licata, a town of trade and industry (population 41,300), 33km/20mi northwest of Gela, is situated on the site of ancient Phintias, which was founded by the tyrant of the same name from Agrigento in 280 BC in order to give a new home to the inhab-

Licata

itants of Gela, which had been destroyed by the Mamertines. According to inscriptions and coins, the inhabitants continued to call themselves Gelan.

The present town was founded in the Middle Ages and flourished, fortified under Aragonese rule, in the 16th and 17th centuries. On 10 July 1943 American troops landed here and near Gela. Licata achieved literary fame as the home town of Lara Cardella. The 17-year-old got onto several bestseller lists with her first publication, *Volevo i pantaloni* (1989; *Good Girls Don't Wear Trousers*). In her book she describes the nature of the Sicilian macho and the oppression of women. »I asked Mother if I could [wear trousers] and her unwitting reply, ›Good girls don't wear trousers. They're for men, or sluts‹ gave me my next idea. Easy, I thought. If I couldn't become a man, I'd become a slut. Before I go any further, let me tell you the local definition of a slut. A slut is any woman that doesn't dress and behave in the way that is considered proper. [...] ›Slut‹ is just a convenient label, a licence for gossip, and you could even say these women fulfil an important social function.«

◀ Good Girls Don't Wear Trousers

There is a small museum with ancient discoveries near the town hall in Via Dante. The church del Carmine dates back to the 18th century (Giovan Biagio Amico). It contains the former monastery and a 16th-century cloister as well as the remains of an earlier 14th-century building. The **Castello Sant'Angelo**, built in 1615, towers above the town. Remains of the ancient town of Phintias were found here. There are several pleasant **beaches** in and near the town.

! *Baedeker* TIP

Eating well

Regardless of any literary fame, Licata has not become one of the top ten places to visit on Sicily. That makes the commitment of chef Pino Cuttaia all the more pleasing. He runs his restaurant La Madia here. Fish, seafood and artichokes are the mainstays of his fine regional cuisine (category: expensive, closed Tue and Sun evenings; Corso F. Re Capriata 22, tel. 09 22 77 14 43, www.ristorantelamadia.it).

Ravanusa

The archaeological museum of Ravanusa (24km/15mi north of Licata) has a good exhibition of ancient ceramics (Corso della Repubblica, next to the bar Curti Vella, Mon – Fri 8.30am – 1.30pm). The small ceramics town of **Riesi** (330m/1083ft, population 18,000) 11km/7mi away, is the headquarters of the Waldensian Servizio Cristiano, which works for creating better living conditions (with guest house; Via Monte degli Ulivi 6, tel. 09 34 92 81 23, www.serviziocristiano.org).

Isola, Isole ...

▶ see names of island groups, e.g. Aegadian Islands

Lentini

R/S 9

Province: Siracusa
Population: 27,700

Altitude: 56m/184ft

Lentini lies at the northern edge of the Hyblaean Mountains (Monti Iblei), around 30km/20mi south of Catania. According to legend, this is where the Laestrygonians lived, the giant cannibals whom Odysseus met on his adventures (Odyssey, verse 10).

What to See in and Around Lentini

The plain of Leontinoi was already known for its fertility in Antiquity. Citrus fruits are grown there today too. Like Naxos, whose inhabitants founded Leontinoi, and Katani, which was founded at around the same time, ancient Leontinoi was a settlement by Ionian Greeks. It later had conflicts with Gela and Syracuse. It was the home of the orator Gorgias (b. around 480 BC), who made impassioned speeches in Athens asking for support against Syracuse; Plato dedicated a dialogue to him. It was also the home of Giacomo (b. around 1210), the notary of Frederick II and a significant poet. In the Chiesa Madre (17th and late 18th century), built above a hypogaeum from the early Christian period (3rd century), there is a Byzantine icon of Mary. The archaeological museum (Via del Museo) exhibits discoveries from the region from the time of the Sicels onwards.

Lentini

The ancient town of Leontinoi was situated 3km/2mi to the south in the valley of San Mauro and on the hills Metapiccola and Colle San Mauro. The remains of this town can be seen in the archaeological

Leontinoi

 VISITING LENTINI

WHERE TO STAY

► Agriturismo

Casa dello Scirocco
Contrada Piscitello, between Lentini and Carlentini
Tel. & fax 33 94 90 77 43
www.casadelloscirocco.it
Old manor set among orange groves. Services available include excursions, cooking classes and trips on horseback.

Tenuta di Roccadia
Contrada Roccadia

south of Carlentini
Tel. & fax 0 95 99 03 62
www.roccadia.com
16 rooms in a former monastery; wide selection of sports, ceramic courses etc; excellent food

Il Giardino del Sole
Contrada Masseria San Demetrio, north of Lentini, tel. 33 89 44 41 22
www.ilgiardinodelsole.it
Reconstructed farm between oranges, figs and olives with 9 rooms, typical regional cuisine

zone (on the road to Carlentini), and include the town wall with several towers (7th–5th century BC), the Syracuse Gate in the south, the agora and a Greek temple. Outside the town walls is a necropolis from the 4th–3rd century BC, and in the surrounding area there are remains of cave churches from the 7th century and the Norman period. The walls of the Grotta del Crocifisso feature the remains of frescoes from the 11th–15th centuries. To the north of what is now the archaeological zone, Frederick II built a castle on the site of an ancient building.

Carlentini
Carlentini (228m/748ft, 3km/2mi south of Lentini, population 13,000) goes back to Emperor Charles V, who founded it in 1551. People living in malarial areas moved here.

Biviere di Lentini
The Biviere, dammed to make a huge fish pond by the Knights Templar in the 12th–13th century, was drained in the 1920s in order to fight malaria. In the 1970s the natural basin at the foot of the Monti Iblei was flooded again in order to irrigate the large orange groves. It is now one of Sicily's most important bird sanctuaries.

Francofonte
The rural town of Francofonte (281m/922ft, 13km/8mi to the southwest, population 14,000) is known for its orange plantations. At the centre of town is the Chiesa Madre with works by Spagnoletto, as well as the Baroque Palazzo Comunale.

Palagonia
Palagonia (200m/656ft, 26km/16mi northwest of Lentini, population 14,000) is located where the Monti Iblei end and the plain of Catania begins. 1.5km/1mi outside town, on the SS 385, is the hermitage of San Febbronia with a small basilica and Byzantine frescoes (6th–7th century) in the apse. The 385 continues to ►Caltagirone (28km/17 mi).

Militello in Val di Catania
This small town (413m/1355ft, population 8900), rebuilt in the Baroque style after the 1693 earthquake, was declared a UNESCO World Heritage site in 2002 because of its beautiful townscape and its Baroque churches. The church of San Benedetto and the adjoining former Benedictine monastery (town hall), which was built before the earthquake, are both worth visiting. The church of San Nicolò now houses the museum of the same name and exhibits liturgical objects and a few paintings.

Vizzini (619m/2030ft, population 8000) is one of the places in the Monti Iblei that was rebuilt in the Baroque style (in 1669) after the

! **Baedeker TIP**

La Mostarda
The people of Militello are proud not just of their pretty town but also of their local sweets, and especially of Mostarda, fruits candied in mustard-flavoured syrup. Every year during a weekend in October this treat is celebrated during the »Sagra della Mostarda e del Ficodindia«.

severe earthquake of 1693. Thanks to Giovanni Verga (1840–1922, ►Famous People) it went down in literature and the world of opera. The Sicilian author mainly focused on simple farmers and fishermen in his realistic regional novels. *Mastro Don Gesualdo* is set in Vizzini, as is the story *Cavalleria rusticana* (Alfio, for example, comes from Licodia, which is just a few miles southwest of Vizzini), which Pietro Mascagni (1863–1945) set to music in his successful opera. A nice example of Vizzini's new Baroque appearance is the church of **San Giovanni Battista**, which has a three-storey façade adorned with columns. The façade rises up steeply at its centre, and the church is topped by a tall tambour dome. The church has columns with fine white stucco ornamentation.

⋆ ⋆ Isole Lìpari · Lipari Islands

O – W 1/2

Province: Messina
Population: 12,600

Altitude: Sea level–962m/3156ft

The Lipari Islands or Aeolian Islands (Isole Eólie) emerge from the Tyrrhenian Sea between 30km/20mi and 80km/50mi off Sicily's north coast. They are of volcanic origin, which is demonstrated by fumaroles, hot springs and sulphurous springs as well as the still-active volcano Stròmboli. In the past criminals were banished to the islands. These days people come here especially to experience their pristine character, as well as for their beaches with volcanically heated seawater and for climbing and hiking.

It is not just the dormant volcanoes that shaped the mountainous, rugged coastlines; the sea has played a major role. The archipelago, rising up from a depth of 4000m/13,000ft, consists of seven main islands, of which Vulcano is the closest to Sicily proper. North of it are Lìpari and Salina; Filicudi and Alicudi lie to the west, while the islands of Salina, Panarea and Stròmboli lie to the northeast.

Seven beautiful islands

The islands vary in size from 3.4 sq km/1.3 sq mi with 270 inhabitants (Panarea) and 37.6 sq km/14.5 sq mi and 11,000 inhabitants (Lìpari), while the maximum elevations range from 420m/1378ft (Panarea) to 962m/3156ft (Salina). The total population of these seven islands, which also include a number of smaller islets and rocky outcrops, is around 12,600. Since only Vulcano and Salina have springs and the cisterns only supply the islands with non-drinking water, the drinking water comes by tanker from Messina.

According to Greek and Roman mythology, these islands were the seat of Aiolos (Aeolus in Latin). The son of Hippotes was, as Homer

Islands of the wind god

▶ VISITING LIPARI ISLANDS

INFORMATION

Servizio Turistico
Corso Vittorio Emanuele 202
98055 Lìpari
Tel. 09 09 88 00 95
Fax 09 09 81 11 90
www.aasteolie.191.it
www.portaledelleeolie.it

Rooms, holiday flats and houses
Rooms and apartments are let on
Lìpari by Enza Marturano, fax
09 09 88 05 92, www.enzamarturano.it.
Holiday flats and houses on Filicudi: A
Tana, tel. 34 73 60 95 and
34 97 89 17 28, www.atana.it
On Salina: Didyme Viaggi, Santa
Marina, Via Risorgimento 196, tel.
09 09 84 33 10, fax 09 09 84 30 78,
didymeviaggi@tiscalinet.it

TRANSPORT
High-speed ferries (aliscafi and catamarani) and car ferries (traghetti)
between the islands and Milazzo; in
summer also regular connections to
Palermo, Messina, Reggio Calabria
and Naples.
By plane and boat: the best airport is
Catania; Giunta buses to Milazzo from
here between April and September.
On the islands: the number of cars and
motorbikes allowed on the islands is
strictly limited, and is only worth it, if
at all, on Lìpari and Salina (information from the tourist office).

WHERE TO EAT
▶ Expensive
Lìpari · ① Filippino
Piazza Municipio
Tel. 09 09 81 10 02
www.filippino.it. Closed Mon in winter; below the acropolis with views of
the sea and excellent island cuisine

Lìpari · ② E Pulera
Via Diana 51
Tel. 09 09 81 11 58, www.pulera.it
Only open in summer; small menu
with typical island dishes; in a wonderful garden with jasmine and stone
tables; very friendly service

Lìpari · ③ La Nassa
Via Franza 36, tel. 33 55 26 29 66
www.lanassavacanze.it
Closed Mon, Apr–Oct
Family-run restaurant for gourmets,
with a small garden and roof terrace;
also nice holiday flats

Stròmboli · Punta Lena
Via Marina, tel. 0 90 98 62 04
Apr–Oct; much-acclaimed food on the
eastern end of Ficogrande Bay with
views of Strombolicchio

▶ Moderate
Lìpari · ④ Kasbah Café
Via Maurolico 25; only open in the
evenings.
Café and restaurant with garden seating; tasty antipasti as well as pizzas;
also a popular music bar

Salina · Mamma Santina
Santa Marina
Via Sanità 40, tel. 09 09 84 30 54
www.mammasantina.it – Try the spaghetti with 14 herbs; also recommended as a place to stay.

▶ Inexpensive
Lìpari · ⑤ Pescecane
Corso Vittorio Emanuele 223
Tel. 09 09 81 27 06
Tables outside; very good pizzas

Stròmboli · La Lampara
Via V. Emanuele 27
Tel. 0 90 98 60 09 – Popular pizzeria;

Vulcano · Maria Tindara
Via Piano 38, tel. 09 09 85 30 04
Local cuisine; also a few rooms to let

WHERE TO STAY
▶ Luxury
Lìpari · ① Villa Meligunis
Via Marte 7, tel. 09 09 81 24 26
www.villameligunis.it, 32 rooms
The central building is an old palazzo, comfortably furnished rooms in modern buildings, roof terrace

Stròmboli · La Sirenetta Park Hotel
Loc. Ficogrande, Via Marina 33
Tel. 0 90 98 60 25, fax 0 90 98 61 24
www.lasirenetta.it
55 rooms; comfortable hotel complex by the sea; definitely ask about special offers during the off-peak season

▶ Mid-range
Lìpari · ② Giardino sul Mare
Via Maddalena 65
Tel. 09 09 81 10 04, fax 09 09 88 80 15 0
www.giardinosulmare.it, 46 rooms
Near the harbour Marina Corta overlooking the sea, to which there is access; saltwater pool, terraces; restaurant with a terrace

Lipari · ③ Gattopardo Park
Viale Diana, tel. 09 09 81 10 35
www.gattopardoparkhotel.it; 47 rooms
Somewhat above the centre; rooms in bungalows or in the main building of an 18th-century mansion

Filicudi · La Canna
Contrada Rosa
Tel. 09 09 88 99 56, fax 09 02 50 99 29
www.lacannahotel.it; 10 rooms
Panoramic location and a good restaurant

Popular pizzeria on Stromboli: La Lampara

Panarea · Oasida Pina
Via San Pietro, tel. 090 98 33 24
www.panareadapina.it; 12 rooms
Classy bungalows around a green courtyard with a thermal shower and a pool; the Ristorante Da Pina next door is legendary.

Panarea · Tesoriero
Via C. Lani 3, tel. 0 90 98 30 98
Fax 0 90 98 30 07, www.hoteltesoriero.it – 11 spacious rooms above the harbour, nice roof terrace

Salina · Signum
Loc. Malfa, Via Scalo 15
Tel. 09 09 84 43 75, fax 09 09 84 41 02
www.hotelsignum.it; 30 rooms
Nice building in a vineyard on the north coast; with an excellent restaurant and pool

Salina · B & B La Praia di Rinella
Loc. Rinella, Via Rombo 41, tel.
09 09 80 90 82, 34 72 81 45 22
www.lapraiadirinella.com – Small B & B owned by the photographer Francesco Iannello at the harbour; breakfast served on the sun terrace.

Hotel Signum on Salina

www.eolianhotel.it; 88 rooms
Nice hotel with a main building and smaller surrounding buildings in a lavish garden. With a restaurant and panoramic terraces.

Vulcano · Conti
Loc. Porto Ponente, tel. 09 09 85 20 12
www.contivulcano.it; 67 rooms – Nice house on the sea; family-run establishment

▶ Budget

Lìpari · ④ La Dolce Vita
Contrada Monte,
mobile tel. 360 96 99 60 and
360 69 97 72
www.ladolcevitalipari.it; 4 rooms
March–Dec – Agriturismo with great views of Vulcano on the western slopes of Monte Giardina; the pretty Spiaggia Valle Muria is just a short walk away. Recently renovated, cheerful rooms.

Lìpari · ⑤ Enzo il Negro
Via Garibaldi 29
Tel. & fax 09 09 81 31 63
www.enzoilnegro.altervista.org
14 basic rooms very near the harbour Marina Corta

Strómboli · Miramare
Via Vito Nunziante 3
Tel. 0 90 98 60 47, fax 0 90 98 63 18
www.miramarestromboli.it; 12 rooms
Pretty little complex on the waterfront road from Ficogrande (inexpensive in the off-peak season)

Vulcano · Eolian Hotel
Loc. Porto Ponente, tel. 09 09 85 21 51

Alicudi · Ericusa
Loc. Perciato, tel. 09 09 88 99 02
www.alicudihotel.it; 20 rooms – the only hotel on Alicudi, with basic rooms and a restaurant

reported (Odyssey, 10), made the keeper of the winds by Zeus. Very much later the Sicilian historian Diodorus remarked that this happened because he taught the sailors how to use their sails and predicted the change of the winds as an omen for an upcoming volcanic eruption. He lived happily with his wife, six sons and six daughters on the inaccessible floating island of Aiolia. He offered hospitality to the lost Odysseus and his men for a month and put the winds in a leather sack, but the curious seafarers opened this sack as they sailed on, whereupon the storms blew them back to the island of Aiolia,

Lipari: view of Vulcano from Belvedere Quattrocchi

whose master gruffly sent them packing. According to Virgil (Aeneid 1, 52), Aiolos ruled with a sceptre over the winds that raged in a cave on the island of Lipara.

These islands have seen human activity since Neolithic times, when the inhabitants used volcanic glass obsidian to make weapons and tools; they also exported their products. **History**

In around 575 BC a group of Doric colonists from Knidos and Rhodes came here under their leader Pentathlos and settled on the Lipari Islands. During their battle with the Etruscans they created a strong fleet. Since they were allied with Syracuse, their islands were attacked and plundered by the Athenian fleet in 427–425 BC. Contested by the Greeks and the Carthaginians for a long time, the islands were ultimately conquered in 252 BC by the Romans, who exploited the alum deposits and hot springs.

Subsequently the islands became a hiding place for pirates. In around AD 836 they were conquered by the Arabs and then by the Normans in 1080. In 1544 the admiral of the Ottoman sultan Suleiman the Magnificent, the formidable Hayreddin Barbarossa, plundered Lìpari and enslaved the population. This caused Charles V to build the citadel on Lìpari as a protective measure for the new settlers.

Capers and pumice

For a long time now the population has had sources of income other than farming (Malvasia di Lìpari, capers), fishing and working in pumice quarries. Pumice is now sought-after to make »stone-washed« jeans. Tourism has created a noticeable boom. Between 1880 and 1960 more than a third of the population emigrated to Australia and America. Today their descendants are returning and investing in tourism.

✱ Lìpari

Main island of Lipari

Information: www.lipari.com ▶

Lìpari (up to 602m/1975ft, 37.6 sq km/14.5 sq mi, population 11,000), the ancient Lipara, is the largest and most populated of this island group. It is of volcanic origin. Its maximum elevation is Monte Chirica, at 602m/1975ft; south of it is Monte Sant'Angelo, at 594m/1949ft. Monte Pelato in the northeast reaches an altitude of 476m/1562ft, Monte Guardia in the south is 369m/1211ft. The west coast drops off steeply. In the east and north there are narrow, flat coastal strips.

Lìpari Map

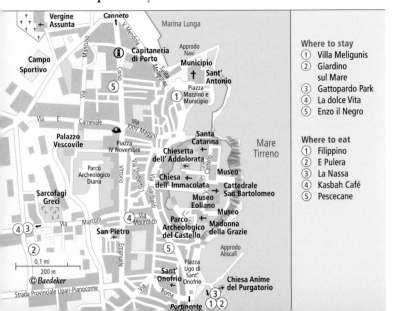

Where to stay
1. Villa Meligunis
2. Giardino sul Mare
3. Gattopardo Park
4. La dolce Vita
5. Enzo il Negro

Where to eat
1. Filippino
2. E Pulera
3. La Nassa
4. Kasbah Café
5. Pescecane

© Baedeker

Lipari's castle hill

The **main town of Lipari** (population 5000) lies on the east coast. The castle hill is at its centre, embraced by the Marina Lunga and the Marina Corta. The ancient acropolis was replaced by a medieval castle (13th century) and the fort that Charles V built in the 16th century after the island was plundered by Hayreddin Barbarossa. To the west of the castle hill is the **new town** with the long, straight Corso Vittorio Emanuele; this is Lìpari's main street, lined by shops, cafés and restaurants.

Via Concordato (steps) leads directly to the cathedral of San Bartolomeo, which was built by the Norman king Roger II in the 12th century and converted to the Baroque style in 1654. The modern bronze door depicts the town's plundering by Corsairs. Inside the church is a life-size silver statue of the patron saint. The Norman cloister with original animal capitals was only rediscovered a few years ago.

San Bartolomeo

The interesting archaeological museum is housed in several buildings around the cathedral. The former bishop's palace (10th century) contains the prehistoric collection, the building to the left the classical department (Mon – Fri 9am – 1.30pm, 3pm – 7pm, Sat, Sun only until 1pm). The most significant Stone and Bronze Age island cultures and their far-reaching trade connections are depicted chronologically by means of ceramic and burial discoveries. The spectrum of Neolithic obsidian tools (5th–3rd millennium BC), to which Lìpari owed its first economic boom, are particularly interesting. The yield from the bothros of Eolos, a container for votive objects made

★
Museo Archeologico
◔

of lava stone (550 BC) was extremely rich. In the **pavilion of the smaller islands** opposite the bishop's palace, the discoveries from all the other Lipari Islands are on display. The neighbouring building has a **volcanic department**, in which the islands' geological structure and volcanism are explained.

Classical department ▶ The building to the left of the cathedral contains further discoveries from the necropolises of Lìpari and Milazzo. Among the exhibits of outstanding significance are colourful vases by the »Lìpari painter« (1st half of the 3rd century BC), an Attic bowl with red figures by the Pan painter (480–470 BC), Sicilian-Greek ceramics and bowls with mythical motifs, including one featuring Hippolytus driving a chariot with four wild horses, who are scared by a sea monster that tips over the chariot, burying it beneath itself. Then there are the depiction of Hercules's wedding with Deianira, bowls from Paestum with mythological scenes from the mid-4th century BC and a unique collection of clay statues with character masks of Middle Comedy and New Comedy (4th–3rd century BC).

Archaeological zone In front of the museums are uncovered layers documenting the site's ancient settlement (informative panel). The archaeological zone was set up at the southern end of Via Castello. It features a small theatre in ancient form as well as Greek and Roman sarcophagi. Most of them have come from the Diana district, where Greek settlers created a necropolis on the site of a Neolithic village in the 6th century BC; this necropolis was later used by the Romans too. The views of Marina Corta from the archaeological zone are lovely.

Island round trip A well-built ring road (27km/17mi) runs all the way around the island. Driving north from Lìpari, it is 3.5km/2mi to Canneto, the centre of pumice quarrying; it is possible to walk through the obsidian fields and pumice quarries of Forgia Vecchia and Rocche Rosse from here. A kilometre north of Canneto is the start of Spiaggia Bianca, the main beach on Lìpari. It is not white, consisting of dark pebbles and pumice rubble. Continuing along the east and north coasts, it is 6.5km/4mi to Acquacalda. From the long beach of dark pebbles, the views of the island of Salina are stunning. Now the road leaves the coast and makes its way via Quattropani (5km/3mi), on a plateau, to the farming village of Pianoconte 4km/2.5mi away. Just outside this village there is a right-hand turn into an access road to the thermal baths of **San Calògero**, where visitors will find a 60°C/140°F sulphur bicarbonate spring and a spa from 1887. During construction works Roman baths and an almost 4000-year-old »Myce-naean» sauna were discovered. At the **Belvedere di Quattrocchi** near the cliffs there is a picture-perfect view of Vulcano. It is a 2km/1mi walk down to the bay of Spiaggia Valle Muria. In some places the beach consists of fine, dark lava sand, and steam emerges from the sea. The main road now turns east, back to the town of Lìpari (9.5km/6mi southeast of Quattropani).

The best beaches for swimming are around Canneto (Spiaggia Bian-ca), Acquacalda and Spiaggia Valle Muria (▶above). There are diving schools at Marina Corta. Fishing co-operatives organize boat trips to the rocky outcrops off the island's south and west coast (Faraglioni, Pietra del Bagno).

Beaches

◀ Boat trips

◀ ✳ Vulcano

Vulcano, the southernmost of the Lipari Islands (21 sq km/8 sq mi, up to 499m/1637ft), is separated from its larger neighbour, Lìpari, by a 1km/0.5mi channel (Bocche di Vulcano). In Antiquity the island

Popular resort

The dormant Gran Cratere on Vulcano

was called Hiera Hephaistou, but also Therasia and Thermessa. To-day it is a popular resort because of its mud baths and seawater that is warm all year round (population 467).

Dormant volcanoes ► Vulcano largely consists of the volcanoes Gran Cratere (391m/1283ft), Monte Saraceno (481m/1578ft) and Monte Aria (499m/1637ft). The latter two became dormant early on. Gran Cratere had its most recent major eruption in 1889–90. Today it has fumaroles. There is a particularly high density of these sulphurous emissions on Piano delle Grande Fumarole on the southeastern slopes. Between Gran Cratere and Monte Aria in the east and Monte Saraceno in the west, there is a green plateau (freshwater springs) criss-crossed by deep valleys.

According to Pliny, it was not until historical times – 183 BC – that the small crater island of Vulcanello (123m/404ft) emerged from the sea north of Vulcano. It became dormant in the 19th century. It is connected to the main island via a narrow isthmus. There are settlements at either end, Porto di Ponente (in the west) and Porto di Levante (in the east, quay). The 500m/550 yd main beach of fine lava sand lies close to Porto di Ponente. At the eastern end there are hot springs whose sulphurous mud is said to have healing properties.

Destinations The island's only road (8km/5mi) goes to the sprawling rural town of Piano (grilled chicken) and ends in Gelso at a tiny sandy beach (fish trattoria). The waymarked one-hour climb up to Gran Cratere with its sulphurous gases is worthwhile but not entirely risk-free. Vulcano also has lovely sea grottoes, including the Grotta del Cavallo in the west.

✳ Salina

Caper island Salina, the archipelago's second-largest island (26.8 sq km/10.3 sq mi, population 2150) consists of eight dormant volcanoes. It is easy to recognize because of its two main peaks, to which it probably owes its ancient name of Didyme (twins): Monte Fossa delle Felci (962m/3156ft) and Monte dei Porri (850m/2789ft) to the west of it, separated by Valdichiesa Valley.

Salina is the only island that is not part of the municipality of Lìpari. It has three municipalities itself: Santa Marina Salina in the middle of the east coast, with the district of Lingua at its southern end; Malfa on a plateau on the north coast with a western district of Pollara; Leni in the valley between the main mountains near the south coast with the nearby district of Rinella, a centre for diving. The single-storey houses with their roof terraces and pergolas are characteristic of the island. The movie *Il Postino* was filmed on Salina (1994; ►Baedeker Special p. 100).

Vegetation Salina has water, which makes it very fertile. The lavish flora gives it a friendlier, less bizarre feel than its neighbours. Maquis grows at

A nice sandy beach in Rinella, the centre of underwater sports on Salina

higher elevations, further down there are prickly pears, capers and vineyards on terraced slopes. The **capers** of Salina are famous for their aroma, and the gold-to-amber **Malvasia** – there is a naturally sweet version, a passito with greater sweetness and a highly alcoholic liquoroso – sells for top prices.

A 17km/11mi U-shaped road connects the island's towns (good bus network). The pilgrimage church of Madonna del Terzito (1630) in the pretty Valdichiesa to the west of Leni and the crater of Pollara by the sea are both worthwhile destinations.

Island round trip

For those who like climbing volcanoes and enjoy the outdoors, the island with its marked hiking trails is a paradise. Beaches can be found near Lingua and Santa Maria Salina (pebble) as well as near Rinella (sand). There is diving in Pollara, in Punta to the north of it and in Rinella, where visitors will also find sconcassi (hydrogen sulphide emissions). It is possible to take a boat from Malfa to the impressive arch near Punta del Perciato and Faraglione di Pollara.

? DID YOU KNOW ...?

■ Maybe it comes from Asia Minor, maybe from the Sahara: the thorny caper bush, Capparis spinosa. Its flowers are as beautiful as orchids, but when the capers flower it is too late to harvest them. It is all about the dark green buds, which are laboriously picked by hand, then marinated in sea salt and finally sold, preserved in salt, vinegar or oil. The big caper festival Sagra del cappero takes place every year in Pollara on the first weekend in June.

✳ Filicudi

A refuge for stressed city dwellers

The 9.5 sq km/3.7 sq mi island of Filicudi, the ancient Phoenicusa, is one of the western Lipari Islands. It is separated from its neighbours, Alicudi and Salina, by water more than 1000m/3300ft deep and rich in fish. It is a rugged cone with three extinct volcanoes, Fossa delle Felci (773m/2536ft), Montagnola (383m/1257ft) and Torrione (280m/919ft). There is a small plateau and the Capo Craziano peninsula (174m/571ft; photo p. 18) in the southeast. Rocks, small islands and cliffs (including the 85m/279ft Canna) as well as individual green terraces shape the appearance of this landscape, three-quarters of which is protected. During a boat trip it is possible to visit several sea grottoes, including the large Grotta del Bue Marino on the southwest coast.

A Bronze Age settlement with oval houses and a small rock necropolis (18th–13th century BC) was discovered on the Capo Graziano peninsula in the southeast; prehistoric settlements also existed in Piano del Porto. As was the case in Antiquity, the 245 inhabitants mainly live in the southern part of the islands: in the ports of Filicudi Porto and Pecorini as well as in Valdichiesa, which was named after a church dedicated to Saint Stephen.

✳ Alicudi

Alicudi, the ancient Ericusa (heather), is the westernmost of the Lipari Islands, 16km/10mi west of Filicudi. The almost circular 5.2 sq km/2 sq mi island has the outline of a blunt cone. The highest eleva-

It's a quiet life on the small island of Alicudi

tion is the 675m/2215ft Filo dell'Arpa (also known as Timpone della Montagnola). Its western slopes consists of corroded lava, while figs, almonds and grapes are grown on terraces on the eastern slopes. Instead of roads there are steps and instead of cars there are mules. Burial discoveries from the 4th century BC confirm that the island was inhabited in Antiquity.

Boats dock in **Alicudi Porto** in the southeast of the island. A good half of the population (100) are people from Germany and northern Italy who wanted to make new lives for themselves. Alicudi has only had electricity since 1990; the island's only hotel is open during the summer months.

✳ Panarea

Panarea, 15km/9mi northeast of Lipari, is the smallest, but finest of the Lipari Islands (up to 420m/1378ft, 3.4 sq km/1.3 sq mi, population 270). Together with the uninhabited rocky islands of Basiluzzo, Spinazzola, Panarelli, Lisca Bianca, Lisca Nera, Bottaro, Dáttilo and Le Formiche it forms an archipelago, the remainder of a volcano that is partially under water. The volcanic environment expresses itself through fumaroles (Conca della Calcara in the north, where the ground reaches temperatures of almost 100°C/210°F) as well as through healing springs with water that has a temperature of 50°C/122°F (in the village of San Pietro). On the western side of Panarea the cliffs drop off steeply to the sea. Panarea's eastern side is covered in green, aromatic maquis. During the summer months this island is a retreat for Italy's in-crowd; Panarea is a hiking paradise with a culinary edge.

Fashionable natural gem
◀ Information: www.ama panarea.it

The village of Panarea consists of the districts of Ditella (north), San Pietro on the eponymous Cala (central; this is where the Aliscafi dock) and Drauto (south). It is possible to climb the 420m/1378ft Timpone del Corvo from San Pietro and Ditella, while Drauto is a good starting point for a visit to the **prehistoric settlement** with 23 oval huts from the 14th to 13th centuries BC, which was discovered in 1948 on the rocky Punta Milazzese jutting out to the south above the picturesque bay of Cala Junco.

The best swimming bay is Cala Junco at the foot of Punta Milazzese. A family-friendly sandy beach can be found in Caletta dei Zimmeri. The clear water, rich in fish, attracts divers. A boat trip to the rocky island of **Basiluzzo** (165m/541ft, 3.5km/2mi to the northeast) is also worthwhile. The ruins of a Roman villa are quite interesting and the remains of a Roman harbour basin can be seen on the sea floor at the docking site.

◀ Leisure

✳ Strómboli

Strómboli, the Isola di Fuoco (Fire Island; up to 924m/3031ft, 12.6 sq km/4.8 sq mi, population 650) in the far northeast of this island

Vulcanissimo!

realm, is famous for the archipelago's only volcano that is still active, the mountain that has guided seafarers at night as the »fire of the sea« and a gigantic lighthouse since Antiquity. Its summit is Serra Vancura (924m/3031ft); the eruptions occur at an altitude of around 700m/2300ft. The last major eruptions occurred in 1930, 1971, 2002–03 and 2007. At short intervals the volcano flings hot lava into the sky. The lava either plummets back into the crater or tumbles to the sea down the northwest slope in the Sciara del Fuoco. Since there are no settlements here, there is no danger to the population.

A great contrast to the black wall of the Sciara del Fuoco is the lavish vegetation with maquis, palm trees, fruit trees and large rhododen-drons on the island's eastern side.

The town of **Stròmboli** in the northeast of the island consists of two villages: San Bartolo and San Vincenzo with the church of the same name. The mooring site Ficogrande lies between the two. On the other side, the southwest coast, is the small town of Ginostra, which can only be reached by boat. The low, single-storey buildings with roof terraces and pergolas are typical here too.

Playing with fire on Stromboli, yet nevertheless highly worthwhile:
a guided hike to the edge of the crater

The strenuous climb up the volcano takes a good three hours. Start at such an hour that you can observe the spectacle in darkness. There is a route from San Bartolo to the former observatory at Punta Labronzo and onwards over rubble fields to the crest around 250m/820ft away from the crater. Find a protected spot from which to observe the volcano here (only with a guide; can be booked through Magmatrek, Via Vittorio Emanuele, tel. 09 09 86 57 68, www.magmatrek.it).

Climbing the volcano

A boat trip to Ginostra is a great way to see the wild, rugged south coast. The night-time spectacle of glowing chunks of lava being flung into the sea is impressive to watch on the north coast. 2km/1mi to the northeast of Stròmboli, the basalt cliffs of **Strombolicchio** emerge from the sea. More than 200 steps lead up to the terrace at the lighthouse on this cliff (43m/141ft).

Boat trips

★ Marsala

C 6

Province: Tràpani
Population: 83,000

Altitude: 12m/39ft

This lively Baroque town on Sicily's west coast owes its founding to the Carthaginians, its name to the Arabs, its world-famous wine to the Englishman John Woodhouse and its patriotic fame to Garibaldi.

Sicily's western tip, at Cape Boeo, just 140km/85mi from Tunisia, has always been used for orientation by ships. After losing their base of Motya (▶ Mózia) in 397 BC, this is where the Carthaginians founded the town of Lilybaeum, extending it to create a great sea fort. When Rome and Carthage made peace after the First Punic War in 241 BC, it went to Rome. Its first bishop was Pascasinus, who was forcibly taken to north Africa along with some of the population by the king of the Vandals, Genseric, in AD 440; upon his return Pope Leo the Great asked him to take part in the Council of Chalcedon. When the Arabs arrived in nearby Mazara in 827, they called the town Mars-al-Allah (port of God), which is where the town's current name comes from. The Normans also developed the town, which was fortified under Roger I. Charles V, however, had the harbour filled up during his not very successful campaign against the Algerian pirates in 1541. Consequently Marsala lost its significance to Tràpani and only experienced a turnaround when the Englishman John Woodhouse from Liverpool started producing Marsala wine in 1773. Marsala soon outdid port in popularity. Soon after 1806 another Englishman, Benjamin Ingham, opened a similar factory, and by

History

► VISITING MARSALA

INFORMATION

Pro Loco
Via XI Maggio 100
91025 Marsala
Tel. 09 23 71 40 97

GOING OUT AND WINE TASTING

During the summer months, Lungomare is where the nightlife is. Very good and affordable wine is available from Cantina Pellegrino (Via Fante 39, tel. 09 23 71 99 11, www.carlopellegrino.it, guided tours Mon–Fri 9am–12.30pm, 3pm–6pm).

WHERE TO EAT

► Moderate

① *Divino Rosso*
Via XI Maggio/
Largo A. di Girolamo 1
Tel. 09 23 71 17 70
Closed Mon; elegant restaurant and enoteca in an attractive palazzo; drink an aperitif at the bar before deciding whether to eat indoors or out.

② *Garibaldi*
Piazza dell'Addolorata 35
Tel. 09 23 95 30 06
Closed Sat; cosy trattoria in the old town behind Chiesa Madre; typical seafood dishes – one speciality is couscous with fish

WHERE TO STAY

► Mid-range

① *President*
Via Nino Bixio 1
Tel. 09 23 99 93 33
Fax 09 23 99 91 15
www.presidentmarsala.it

128 rooms; this quite central hotel is a good option for business people, travel groups and individual travellers.

② *Villa Favorita*
Via Favorita 27
Tel. 09 23 98 91 00
Fax 09 23 98 02 64
www.villafavorita.com
87 rooms; nice villa in a park; the complex also has small bungalows; a good restaurant

1814 there were four British wineries in Marsala and several in Mazara – appropriately the town's patron saint was Saint Thomas Becket of Canterbury!

A thousand Redshirts ► On 11 May 1860, Giuseppe Garibaldi landed with his thousand badly equipped, but highly motivated guerrillas to start his famous victory campaign against the Bourbon troops.

On the same day 83 years later, on 11 May 1943, air-raids caused devastating damage.

Marsala Map

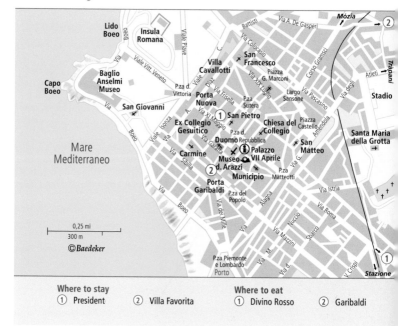

Where to stay
① President ② Villa Favorita

Where to eat
① Divino Rosso ② Garibaldi

Marsala is made of Grillo, Damaschino, Inzolia and Catarratto grapes. Boiled must (concia) and various flavouring agents are used, following old company traditions, to produce a dessert wine whose alcohol content ranges from 13 to 16%; it bears the quality seal SOM (Superior Old Marsala). Annual production of around 3 million hectolitres is shared by British and local companies such as Florio, Rallo and De Bartoli. There are several different quality grades: Marsala Fine is made after it is stored for four months in holm-oak barrels, Marsala Superiore requires aging for two years, and the final grade, Vergine or Soleras, is only given to wines aged for five years
The wineries (baglio) lie between Cape Boeo and the harbour. They are open to visitors who want to look around and taste some of their wines (information from tourist offices). These days around Marsala, Álcamo, Salemi, Menfi and Castelvetrano a light white is produced which has made Sicilian wine successful around the world.
Tip: wine tasting and sales in, for example, Enoteca La Ruota, Lungomare Boeo 36A (tel. 09 23 71 52 41, next to the archaeological museum). For anyone wanting to know more, the winery Montalto maintains a small **wine museum** around 5km/3mi south of Marsala (Enomuseo with adjoining restaurant; Contrada Berbaro, tel. 09 23 96 96 67, www.cantinemontalto.com).

Marsala wine

What to See in Marsala

The heart of Marsala is the **Piazza della Repubblica** on the long axis that runs through the town from the northwest to the southeast (Via Vittorio Veneto – Via XI Maggio – Via Calatafimi). On one of the ends of the rectangular piazza is the 16th-century Palazzo VII Aprile with an airy round-arch loggia and a dominant central tower. On one of the sides is the imposing façade of the cathedral of San Tomaso. It is a Norman columned basilica, which was completely refurbished in the 18th century. It houses several works by the Gagini family.

San Tomaso

Museo degli Arazzi

The group of eight large **Flemish tapestries** from Brussels that were once kept in the church are famous. After undergoing thorough restoration, they have been on display in the Museo degli Arazzi since 1984 (Via Garraffa 57; Tue – Sat 9.30am – 1.30pm, 4.30pm – 6pm, Sun only until 1pm).

The tapestries, made between 1565 and 1570, address topics from the First Jewish-Roman War, which ended with the destruction of Jerusalem by Titus in AD 70. The precious pieces came from Archbishop Antonio Lombardo of Messina, who was born in Marsala and who had been to Madrid twice on diplomatic missions and received the tapestries as gifts from Philip II of Spain, as Flanders was part of his empire at the time. He left them to his home town of Marsala. He himself was buried there in 1596 in the church known as the Chiesa Madre.

Carry on a little from the tapestry museum to a small square with the late Baroque façade of the **Chiesa del Purgatorio** (1701), which is now used as the Santa Cecilia concert hall. Via Garibaldi runs from Piazza della Repubblica in a southwesterly direction, first to the Municipio (in a

San Tomaso, a Norman cathedral with a decorative Baroque façade

Spanish palazzo from 1576) and past it to the **Porta Garibaldi** (formerly Porta di Mare), which was built in the 17th century in the form of a Roman triumphal arch. Right next to it is the Baroque church of Sant'Addolorata.

Leave the Piazza della Repubblica in a northwesterly direction along Via XI Maggio to reach the abbey church of San Pietro (1569) with its large tower and a pinnacle covered in majolica. The grotto below the church has a Roman mosaic.

San Pietro

The **Porta Nuova** was built at the end of the road in 1789. Piazza Vittoria lies in front of it. Adjoining it to the north is the narrow rectangular park of Villa Cavalotti, which is bordered by remains of a Spanish bastion.

The area to the northwest, towards Cape Boeo, is undeveloped; it is the site of the ancient town of Lilybaeum, some of which, namely the **Insula Romana**, has been excavated. One of the ruins is a small bath-house with mosaics (Mon – Sat 9am – 1pm and 3pm to 1 hour before sunset; information in the Archaeological Museum).

! **Baedeker TIP**

Antichi Sapori

Many different wines, but also sauces, sweet treats, herbs, spices and other essences – basically almost all of the traditional Italian »sapori« (flavours, tastes) can be bought here. It is possible to try some of them first: Enoteca Antichi Sapori, Via XI Maggio 10 in the pretty old town.

This interesting museum lies on the coast road right by the cape (Lungomoare Boeo; Tue – Sun 9am – 7pm, Mon 9am – 1.30pm). It used to be the feudal seat (baglio) of one of the Nobili of Marsala. On display in the left-hand hall are discoveries from Marsala (Lilybaeum), Mózia and the surrounding area; at the centre of the room are mosaic floors and a large model of Roman Lilybaeum.
The right-hand hall is dominated by the remains of a 35m/120ft Carthaginian ship dating back to the 3rd century BC. It was found in the sea near Mózia and then reconstructed.

Museo Archeologico Baglio Anselmi
★
◀ Nave Punica

This plain building with a portal from 1555 to the south of the museum replaced an early Christian church dating from the 5th century. The baptismal font from the first church is still extant. According to local tradition, it was part of the ancient oracle of the sibyl of Lilybaeum.

San Giovanni

To the west of Cape Boeo is a single Roman column. The inscription commemorates Scipio Africanus, who set sail from here in 146 BC on his campaign to destroy Carthage, and Garibaldi's arrival on 11 May 1860. Finally, Salvatore Fiume's **wine fountain** is worth a mention (1982; Piazza F. Pizzo south of the station).

Roman column

Between Marsala and Tràpani

Via del Sale
There are several salt pans along the approx. 30km/20mi salt road between Marsala and ▶Tràpani (runs parallel to SS 115). Sea water evaporates in the shallow pools, leaving a layer of crystallized salt behind. The »harvest« is piled up to make salt hills, which are then covered in tiles. More information about this ancient method of salt extraction is available in the salt museum **Mulino Salina Infersa**. Some of the windmills are in operation during the week. They pump the salt water from one pool into the next (Contrada Ettore Infersa; May–Sept daily 9.30am–1pm, 3pm–sunset). The **museum shop** sells Sicilian sea salt with a pink flamingo on the box. There is a pleasant café-ristorantino, Mamma Caura, next door, as well as one of the two quays for boat trips to ▶Mózia, and a canoe rental shop.

www.saline
ettoreinfersa.com ▶
🕐

✷ Mazara del Vallo

D 7

Province: Tràpani   **Altitude:** 8m/26ft
Population: 51,500

The old port of Mazara del Vallo at the mouth of Fiume Mazaro on Sicily's southern west coast is one of Italy's most important fishing ports.

History
After ▶Selinunte was founded, Phoenician Mazara became its port. In 409 BC Hannibal captured the town at the start of his campaign against the Greek towns in southern Sicily. Further destruction was caused by the Romans in the First Punic War (264–241 BC). The conquest by the Arabs began here in 827. They made Mazara the main settlement of one of their three Sicilian provinces, the Val di Mazara, which encompassed western Sicily (besides Val di Noto in the southeast and Val Démone in the northeast). They were replaced by the Normans in 1072. Roger of Hauteville set up his provisional government here and created the first quasi-parliamentary assembly of nobles in European history in Mazara.

What to See in Mazara

Harbour
The river harbour has been the town's economic centre since Antiquity. The life of the fishermen, largely Tunisian migrant workers, takes place all around it. Further south is the spacious basin of the new harbour (ships to Pantellería and Porto Empédocle).

San Nicolò
Regale
On the east side of Porto di Canale, in a somewhat elevated position, is the small Norman church of San Nicolò Regale, a square structure from the 11th or 12th century. Its floor plan is based on that of By-

The life of the fishermen of Mazara del Vallo takes place all around the harbour

zantine churches, as was the case with Trinità di Delia near ►Castelvetrano. Each of the exterior walls features three stepped blind arches around the windows. There are three apses around the choir. The church is crenellated all around the top. The dome in its interior is supported by four columns with ancient capitals.

The quarter around Via Bagno, north of this church, dates back to the Arab period. Today Kasbah is mainly home to people from north Africa who migrated here in the 1960s.

Kasbah

Carry on along the coast in a southeasterly direction from the new harbour to get to the mouth of the Mazaro. Here, with a broad façade and a richly ornamented portal, stands the former palace of the Knights of Malta (16th–17th century), which is now the town hall (Municipio).

Palazzo dei Cavalieri di Malta

The Museo Civico on Piazza San Bartolomeo (former Jesuit college, 17th century; daily 10am–12.30pm) exhibits local discoveries from Roman times and a collection of paintings.In 1988 fishermen netted the statue of a satyr between Sicily and Tunisia. The bronze statue (4th or 3rd century BC) is missing its tail, more than half of its arms and its left leg. This depiction of Dionysus's companion, whirling around on one leg, is possibly a statue, famous in Antiquity, by **Praxiteles** (Piazza Plebiscito, daily 9am–6pm).

Museums
🕐
◄ Museo del Satiro Danzante

🕐

The neighbouring church of Sant'Ignazio was built between 1701 and 1714 using an oval floor plan over a pre-existing building.

Sant'Ignazio

▶ VISITING MAZARA DEL VALLO

INFORMATION

Ufficio Informazione
Piazza Santa Veneranda 2
91026 Mazara del Vallo
Tel. & fax 09 23 94 27 76

WHERE TO EAT

▶ Expensive

① *Pescatore*
Via Castelvetrano 191
Tel. 09 23 94 75 80
Closed Mon; fish prepared in all kinds
of ways and spicy pasta dishes

▶ Moderate

② *La Bèttola*
Via Maccagnone 32
Tel. 09 23 94 64 22
Closed Sun; popular restaurant,
mainly fish dishes

WHERE TO STAY

▶ Luxury

① *Kempinski Giardino di Costanza*
Via Salemi km 7, 100
Tel. 09 23 67 50 00
Fax 09 23 67 58 76
www.kempinski-sicily.com
91 rooms; this hotel, opened in a large
park right by the sea in 2005, provides
every imaginable creature comfort
and relaxation opportunity in the
hotel's own spa.

▶ Mid-range

② *Hopps*
Via G. Hopps 29
Tel. 09 23 94 61 33, fax 09 23 94 60 75
www.hoppshotel.it
188 rooms; even though external
appearances may be deceptive, it is a
good option with a pretty courtyard.

Piazza della Repubblica Turn right down a street behind Sant'Ignazio to get to Piazza della Repubblica. The rectangular, generously proportioned piazza is dominated by the San Vito Fountain (Ignazio Marabitti, 1771) and surrounded by imposing Baroque buildings, including the bishop's palace (1596; altered in the 18th century) and the church seminary (Seminario) with its two-storey arched halls (1710).

Santissimo Salvatore This columned basilica with a cruciform floor plan was founded by the Normans. Built in around 1086, it was extended in the Baroque style in 1696 and given a new façade in 1906. The remains of the original external decoration can still be seen at the eastern apse. The westwork and crossing dome that were added in the later remodelling dominate the square.

The clear internal proportions and the painted interior are impressive. The main feature of the choir is a sculpture group of the Transfiguration, a work by Antonello Gagini or his son Antonino (1537). The Catholic church only made the Transfiguration of Jesus a universal feast in 1457, while it has always been a popular motif in Byzantine art. Its presence in Mazara has been explained by the fact that the Greek prelate Bessarion (1449–58), who had fled when the Turks occupied Constantinople, was the bishop of Mazara, even though he resided in Rome, and gave an icon of the Transfiguration

Mazara del Vallo *Map*

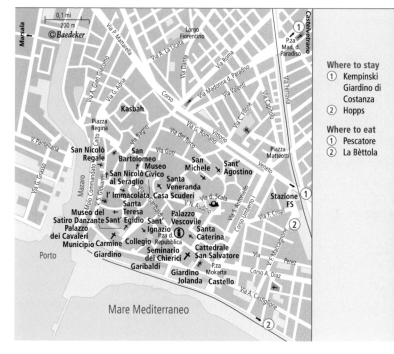

Where to stay
① Kempinski
    Giardino di
    Costanza
② Hopps

Where to eat
① Pescatore
② La Bèttola

to his cathedral. A sarcophagus in the cathedral's northwest corner resembles that of Emperor Frederick II in Palermo. This one is not, however, made of imperial porphyry, but of green marble. The 3.15m/10ft wooden crucifix (after 1200) in the chapel in the apse in the northern part of the transept is probably the oldest of many painted crucifixes in Sicily.

Villa Garibaldi

The park around Villa Garibaldi runs parallel to the coast road. The ruin of a Norman **castle** can be found at its southeastern end, where the park borders on Piazza Mokarta; an inscription commemorates the fact that Count Roger built Mazara Castle in 1072.

Santa Caterina

Via Giuseppe runs from Piazza Mokarta back to Piazza Plebiscito, part the cathedral's eastern apse. On the right-hand side here is Piazza Santa Caterina with the church of the same name (it houses a statue of Saint Catherine by Antonello Gagini, 1524).

Santa Veneranda

Via di San Michele ends in a square on which the Benedictine convent church of Santa Veneranda stands. It is an attractive circular, domed structure with a short nave and transepts (probably after

1651); in around 1750 the church was given a tall twin-tower façade, which was built diagonally to the church in order to fit in with the piazza.

Tonarella Just over a mile south of the town is a nice sandy beach.

Around Mazara del Vallo

Cave di Cusa The ancient quarries of Selinunte (15km/9mi to the east) can be reached by taking the SS 115 to Campobella di Mazara train station, crossing the railway line and then making a sharp right turn (►Castelvetrano). The **Chiesa Trinità di Delia** is also very interesting (►Castelvetrano).

✷ Messina

V 3

Provincial capital	**Altitude:** 3m/10ft
Population: 243,000	

Messina, the island's third-largest city, is the »gateway to Sicily«: this is where visitors travelling by train and car set foot on Sicilian soil for the first time, welcomed by the large statue of the Madonna della Lettera in the harbour, which bears an inscription on the pedestal reading »Vos et ipsam civitatem benedicimus« (»We bless you and your city«) – a quote from a letter that, according to legend, Mary sent to the city's Christians.

Messina's natural harbour, its situation on the Strait of Messina, which is just 3km/2mi wide at this point, and its proximity to the mainland are all factors that have shaped the city's history since Antiquity. These days Messina, situated between the sea and the Peloritani Mountains, is a modern city with wide streets, many skyscrapers and large squares, a centre of trade and transport. It is thriving, despite all the vicissitudes that nature and history have subjected it to, from the 1908 earthquake to the Allied bombs of 1943.

Strait of Messina The Strait of Messina, Lo Stretto di Messina, is, geologically speaking, a trench that formed around 600,000 years ago, causing Sicily to become an island. The funnel-shaped nature of the strait, which becomes very narrow around Messina, means the tidal currents are stronger here than anywhere else in the Mediterranean. They switch every six hours and reach speeds of up to 10kph/6 mph. This has two consequences: the seawater, constantly in motion and thus rich in oxygen, attracts large quantities of plankton, which in turn brings in schools of fish, making the strait a good place for fishing. On the other hand these changing currents used to cause problems for shipping. This is reflected in the ancient myth of the sea monsters **Scylla and Charybdis**, mentioned in Homer's Odyssey. Scylla stole the men from the ships and Charybdis sucked down every sailor who came too close to her. This myth is alive in the place name Scillia on the Calabrian shore and the whirlpool Cariddi off Sicily's northeastern corner. The trench of the Strait of Messina also means that this is an incredibly active **earthquake zone**.

In 1985 the Italian government decided to **build a suspension bridge** over the strait. Technical problems and a lack of funding have delayed this ambitious project by many years. Now at least there is a schedule for its construction (▶Baedeker Special p. 74).

Even before the Greeks arrived, this strategically favourable place was inhabited, namely by the Sicels. The location became known to history in 730 BC, when Greeks arrived from Chalcis on Euboea. They also founded the town of Kyme (Latin: Cuma) west of Naples as the first Greek settlement on Italian soil. They named the new settlement

Cultural bridge-head

◀ continued on p. 266

Messina, the »gateway« to Sicily

► VISITING MESSINA

INFORMATION

Servizio Turistico
Piazza Cairoli 45
98100 Messina
Tel. 09 02 93 52 92
Fax 0 90 69 47 80
www.comune.messina.it

TRANSPORT

Train and car ferries to Villa San Giovanni and Reggio di Calabria; speedboats to Villa San Giovanni, Reggio di Calabria and the Lipari Islands; ferries to Calabria and Malta; airport Aeroporto dello Stretto (Reggio di Calabria);
narrow gauge railway Circumetnea from Giarre-Riposto via Randazzo to Catania

GOOD TO KNOW

Messina's most important shopping street is Viale San Martino between Piazza Cairoli and Viale Europa; everything from designer goods to bargains can be found here and in the shops in the side streets.

EVENTS

Procession of the giants Mata and Grifone on 14 August; Vara procession on 15 August in honour of the Madonna della Lettera

WHERE TO EAT

► Moderate

① *Le Due Sorelle*
Piazza del Municipio 4
Tel. 09 04 47 20
Closed Sat lunchtime and Sun; small gourmet restaurant with a large selection of wines

Capo Peloro · ② Lilla Curro
Via Lido Ganzirri 19 Tel. 090 39 50 64, closed Mon

Excellent cuisine in simple rooms, reduction to the essential: fish dishes

► Inexpensive

③ *Trattoria del Popolo*
Piazza del Popolo 30
Tel. 090 67 11 48; closed Sun
Hearty regional, tasty cuisine, served in arcades.

④ *Trattoria al Padrino*
Via Santa Cecilia 54–56
Tel. 09 02 92 10 00; closed Sat evening and Sun. Cucina messinese, popular with locals. The dishes are not on a menu but are recited.

WHERE TO STAY

► Mid-range

① *Jolly Hotel dello Stretto*
Via Garibaldi 126
Tel. 0 90 36 38 60, fax 09 05 90 25 26
www.medeahotels.com, 96 rooms
Good middle-of-the-road hotel; centrally located and therefore not entirely quiet; nice views of the Strait.

► Mid-range/Budget

② *Paradis*
Loc. Contemplazione
Via Consolare Pompea 335
Tel. 0 90 31 06 82, fax 0 90 31 20 43
www.hotelsparadis.it; 88 rooms
A new building at the Lungomare in the north of the city; view of the Strait.

③ *Villa Morgana*
Loc. Ganzirri
Via Consolare Pompea 237
Tel. 0 90 32 55 75, fax 0 90 32 55 77
www.villamorgana.it; 13 rooms
On the outskirts of Ganzirri, a small hotel with a garden, approx. 10km/6mi outside Messina

Messina Map

Milazzo   Torre Faro   Museo Regionale

opuccini   Via Palermo

Margherita

Regina

L.go Cailler   Fiera di Messina

Santa Lucia   Fata Morgana

La Maria La Nuova   Via P.za Casa Pia

Santa Maria dei Angeli   P.za S. Vincenzo

aria Santissima di Pompei   Osservatorio Meteorologico   San Giuliano

Prefettura   Fontana del Nettuno

San Giovanni di Malta   Via S. Giovanni di Malta   P.za Unità d' Italia

San Francesco d' Assissi   Aquario

Villa Mazzini

Mare Ionio

Reggio di Calabria, Villa San Giovanni

Isole Lipari (only Aliscafi)

0,25 mi   400 m
©Baedeker

Cristo Re   Teatro Vittorio Emanuele   Forte San Salvatore

Monte Vergine   Colonna Votiva

Monte di Pietà   Annunziata   Via S. Camillo

antuario Montalto   Municipio   P.za Antoniello

Duomo   Porto

Fontana di Orione   Santissima Annunziata dei Catalani

SS Salvatore

P.za Masuccio   Università   Laterna Raineri

P.za Maurolico   Museo Zoologico   Santa Maria Alemanna

armine   Palazzo di Giustizia   Santa Caterina Valverde   Sant' Elia   Dogana   Via L. Rizzo   P.za Cavallotti   Citadella

P.za Popolo Sardo   Piazza Cairoli   Piazza Repubblica   Stazione Marittima

Stazione Centrale

Piazza Cairoli   Cannizzaro

Stretto di Messina

alazzo Gallo   Catania   Catania

Via S. Raineri

Where to stay
① Jolly Hotel dello Stretto
② Paradis
③ Villa Morgana

Where to eat
① Le Due Sorelle
② Lilla Curro
③ Trattoria del Popolo
④ Trattoria al Padrino

On 7 October 1571 the fleet of the Holy League, under the command of Don John of Austria, defeated the larger Turkish fleet near Lepanto

THE NAVAL BATTLE OF LEPANTO AND THE ROSARY

Don John of Austria, the son of Emperor Charles V, was born in Regensburg on 24 February 1547. Entrusted with military and administrative tasks by his half-brother Philip II of Spain, he achieved fame and distinction during his short life. He died from the plague at 31.

His main achievement was victory over the Ottoman fleet in the naval battle of Lepanto on 7 October 1571, a large operation for which he used his fleet in Messina. The **European powers** had long hesitated before deciding to launch an attack on the Ottomans. In 1453 Constantinople fell, which brought the thousand-year-old Byzantine Empire to an end. In the 16th century the Ottomans conquered not just Rhodes, the stronghold of the Knights Hospitallers, but also Egypt and other parts of northern Africa, all the way to Tunis and Algiers. There was a further direct threat to Europe from another side: the conquest of Hungary and Romania and the first siege of Vienna in 1529.

The only Mediterranean power that still posed a counterbalance was Venice, but even this naval republic suffered painful losses. The brutality with which the Turkish general Lala Mustafa Pasha treated the Venetian lawyer Marcantonio Bragadin was met with disgust and outrage. Finally Venice, Spain and the Papal States joined forces in the Holy League and sent their fleets to sea.

Victory despite being outnumbered

The Ottoman fleet had left its base in Naupactus, Venetian Lepanto, and had made its way westwards into the Gulf of Patras. Here, near the island of Oxeia, the two fleets met on 7 October 1571. A murderous battle ensued, claiming around 40,000 lives. The Spanish poet Cervantes had his left hand mutilated. This last-ever major naval battle involving galleys ended with the triumph of the Holy League over the Ottoman fleet, which outnumbered the victors. Ali Pasha, the Ottoman commander, committed suicide in face of this defeat. The battle was called the **Battle of Lepanto**, after his official headquarters (Lepanto/Naupactus). Don John of Austria, the young commander of the European allies, returned, glory

now his. Just a year later a monument was erected in his honour in Messina, where he had set off from on his glorious endeavour.

Creation of the rosary

This battle was hugely significant. After the unsuccessful sieges of Vienna (1529) and Malta (1565), the myth of the invincible military power of the Ottoman Empire was broken. This success was not just attributed to Don John of Austria, but also to his heavenly support. According to legend, the Virgin Mary effected the victory through her intercession. That was the reason why Pope Pius V introduced the Feast of the Rosary in 1572.

The **rosary**, a sequence of prayers in honour of the Virgin, is based on the Hail Mary, which, after the Lord's Prayer, was the most widespread prayer at the time. The sections of this prayer sequence are understood symbolically as a wreath of spiritual roses. A Lord's Prayer, ten Hail Marys and one Gloria Patri form one decade. The rosary consists of 15 decades, each of which is accompanied by a mystery: five joyful mysteries, five sorrowful mysteries and five glorious mysteries – analogous to the Annunciation and Nativity, the Passion, and

the Resurrection. The rosary quickly became established and widely adopted.

Brotherhoods of the rosary

On the anniversary of Lepanto, 7 October or the first Sunday in October, the Feast of the Rosary is held. In the Middle Ages brotherhoods formed that were active in the social field. Even today they organize and fund, among other things, the elaborate processions of Sicilian saints' days, especially during Holy Week. Brotherhoods of the rosary are dedicated to feasts of the rosary. They have their own oratories (places of prayer and worship), including the **Oratorio del Rosario di Santa Cita** in Palermo. It is certainly worth visiting, not because of the likenesses of notable representatives of this brotherhood in the vestibule, or because of C. Maratta's Madonna of the Rosary on the high altar, but because of the stucco works by Giacomo Serpotta in the main room (around 1700). The entrance wall features a depiction of the Battle of Lepanto; the Virgin Mary, making her intercession, can be seen above the ships. The artist thereby recognizes the historical root of the Feast of the Rosary and captures a historical event and a pious legend, creating a higher reality.

in Sicily after the shape of the headland surrounding the harbour: **Zankle** (sickle). At the start of the 5th century BC, after the collapse of the rebellion of the Ionian cities against the Persians (494 BC), refugees from Miletus and Samos also moved to the town. It then took in many Messenians who had fled their Peloponnese home because of Sparta's bellicose policies towards its neighbours. Anaxilas, also from Messenia, made himself the tyrant of Rhegium in Calabria, then conquered Zankle shortly after 490 BC and called it **Messana/Messene**, which developed into modern-day Messina. In 426 BC Messina joined the Athenian side, but soon switched back to Syracuse. In 396 it was destroyed by the Carthaginians, and in 395 BC rebuilt by Syracuse. In 289 BC, after the death of the tyrant Agathocles of Syracuse, it fell to his bodyguards, the Mamertines (sons of Mars), who killed the entire male population and used the town as a base to tyrannize the whole of Sicily. In 264 BC the Mamertines triggered the First Punic War by asking Rome for help. In 263 BC Messina became a Roman »civitas foederata« and subsequently experienced a golden age as a Roman trading centre.

730 BC	The Greeks found the town
263 BC	Messina becomes a Roman civitas foederata and a successful Roman trading centre
1302 – 16th century	The House of Aragon has its residence here
1908	Earth and sea quake: 60,000 deaths, extreme devastation
1943	Serious bombing by the Allied forces

Messina was also a flourishing city during the three centuries of Byzantine rule (535–843). After that the Arabs took over (843–1061), followed by the Normans (1061–1194). The Normans promoted the Greek Orthodox Basilian abbey of San Salvatore dei Greci as a place that taught the West about eastern religion and Byzantine culture. Towards the end of the rule of the House of Hohenstaufen (1194–1266), Messina, Milazzo and Taormina founded a free state in 1255, which ended again in 1266 with the reign of Charles of Anjou. The Spanish House of Aragon, which came to power after the Sicilian Vespers of 1282 (▶ Baedeker Special p. 42), preferred to live in Messina. It was only in the 16th century that Palermo became the residence of the kings and viceroys again.

Chronicle of disasters ▶
Messina's good times came to an end with an unsuccessful rebellion against the Spanish rule (1674–78). There were a number of disasters in the subsequent period: in 1743 plague (40,000 victims), in 1785 an earthquake (12,000 deaths), in 1823 terrible flooding, in 1847–48 rebellion against the rule of the Bourbons of Naples and bombardment by the troops of Ferdinand II (»Re Bomba«), in 1854 cholera

(15,000 deaths), in 1894 earthquake, in 1908 (28 December) another earth and sea quake (60,000 deaths, nine-tenths of the buildings destroyed), in 1943 aerial bombing by the Allied forces that destroyed more than half of all the buildings.

What to See in Messina

Two factors have shaped the modern cityscape: after the destruction of 1785, Messina was rebuilt on a regular, spacious plan. After the disaster of 1908 it was rebuilt again on the same plan in the Art Nouveau style, while preserving and rebuilding a few significant buildings. However, the heart of the city had shifted southwards from the cathedral square to the traffic hub of Piazza Cairoli, the starting point of Viale San Martino. This is also where the department stores, elegant boutiques and cafés can be found. Of course the cathedral square is much more significant from an architectural and historical perspective.

Cityscape

The Piazza del Duomo is the historical centre thanks to the cathedral and the **Fountain of Orion**. Giovanni Angelo Montorsoli, a pupil

Piazza del Duomo

Piazza del Duomo, Messina's historic centre

of Michelangelo, created the fountain in 1547–51 in honour of the legendary founder of the city. The pathos of its figures puts it in stark contrast to the severe silhouette of the cathedral; on its left side is a Baroque Marian column by Giuseppe Buceti (1758).

★★
Cathedral

The cathedral, originally built by the Normans, was begun in 1160 and consecrated in 1197. After it was rebuilt following the 1908 earthquake, efforts were made to recreate it true to the original. Some parts were preserved, such as the sculpted portals of the 15th and 16th centuries; other parts had to be reconstructed, such as the 60m/197ft **campanile**. It houses one of the world's largest astronomical clocks (1933), by the Ungerer company of Strasbourg; every day at noon the figures start moving and depict scenes from Messina's history, such as the handing over of the legendary letter by the Madonna. Like all Norman cathedrals in Sicily, inside the cathedral is a columned basilica built in the shape of a cross, with three apses and an open, colourfully painted roof, giving it a truly monumental sense of space. The arcades have pointed arches. The mosaics in the apses depicting Christ enthroned are reconstructions, as are the apostle al-

Messina *Cathedral*

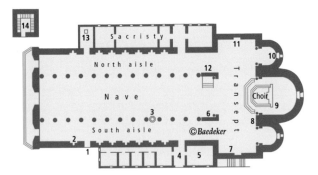

1 Portal (designed by Polidoro da Caravaggio; built by Domenico Vanello, 16th century)
2 John the Baptist, sculpture by Antonello Gagini (1525)
3 Chancel (designed by Polidoro da Caravaggio; built by Domenico Vanello, 1539)
4 Entrance and vestibule
5 Cathedral treasure
6 Tomb of five bishops (early 15th century)

7 Organ (1948) with five manuals, 170 registers and 16,000 pipes, tomb from 1195 and access to the crypt
8 Tomb of Archbishop Guidotto De Tabiatis (Goro di Gregorio, 1333)
9 Choir stalls (16th century, reconstruction)
10 Cappella del Sacramento with an original mosaic from the 14th century (Virgin with Child, as well as the kneeling Queen Leonora etc.)

11 Tomb of Archbishop Antonio La Lignamine by Giovanni Battista Mazzolo
12 Tomb of Archbishop Bellorado by Giovanni Battista Mazzolo (1513)
13 Baptistery, entrance portal by Polidoro da Caravaggio, font (16th century)
14 Campanile with carillon (1933)

tars in the aisles. The sculpture of John the Baptist at the first altar on the right was made by Antonello Gagini (1525). Do not miss a visit to the cathedral's treasure chamber (Mon–Sat 9am–1pm, ⊙ summer also Mon–Fri 4pm–7pm). The gold-embroidered cloak, dating from 1668, adorns the altar Madonna every 3 June.

The second significant church is the Santissima Annunziata dei Catalani (Piazzetta dei Catalani). It was the only one to survive the 1908 earthquake. It was built in the second half of the 12th century under Norman rule. The east side dates back to this time; the main apse between the transepts is distinguished by its delicate architectural composition with blind arcades on small, graceful columns and multi-coloured construction material. The west end with its three portals dates back to a 13th-century alteration. In the interior, ancient columns with different capitals support raised arches. The nave has a barrel vault, while the aisles feature groin vaults.

★ ★
Santissima Annunziata dei Catalani

A bronze monument by Andrea Calamecca on Piazzetta dei Catalani commemorates Don John of Austria, the son of Charles V; Don John set off from Messina in 1571 for the naval Battle of Lepanto, where he defeated the Turks (▶Baedeker Special p. 264). The monument was dedicated just one year later.

Piazzetta dei Catalani

Walk south along Via Garibaldi, which runs in a north-south direction parallel to the harbour. Just beyond Via I Settembre is the ruin of the church of Santa Maria Alemanna (12th–13th century), the chapel in the hospice of the Teutonic Knights.

Santa Maria Alemanna

Go via the Piazza del Duomo to the city hall on Piazza Municipio and to Teatro Vittorio Emanuele. Further north on Via Garibaldi, the city park Villa Mazzini and **Fontana del Nettuno** (1557), like the Fountain of Orion a work by Montorsoli, are two sights of interest. Via della Libertà starts at this fountain and runs northwards away from town to the exhibition complex of the Fiera di Messina (every August) and to the museum.

Piazza Municipio

◀Villa Mazzini

The museum exhibits art that survived the disaster of 1908 (Viale della Libertà 465; Thu–Tue 9am–1.30pm, Tue, Thu, Sat also 4pm–6.30pm, in winter 3pm–5.30pm). The most important treasures are the two-storey St Gregory polyptych, which was painted in 1473 and damaged in the earthquake of 1908 (hall 4), and two important works by Caravaggio, which the painter, who was wanted for manslaughter, produced during his short asylum in Sicily in 1608–09: *The Adoration of the Shepherds* and *The Raising of Lazarus* (hall 10).

★
Museo Regionale
⊙

A very pretty, busy panoramic road starts under the name of Viale Italia to the west of the university and continues to the west of town

Panoramic road

under changing names (V. Principe Umberto, V. Regina Margherita), following the former fortification before ending in the north at the coast road. It passes the Botanical Gardens, the Santuario di Montalto and the votive chapel of Cristo Re.

Peninsula

The remains of the **citadel** of 1681, the fort of San Salvatore, which is named after the famous 12th-century Greek monastery supported by the Normans and destroyed in the 16th century, and, at the tip, the »Madonnina« of 1934, with the abovementioned inscription »Vos et ipsam civitatem benedictimus« (»We bless you and your city«), can be found on the peninsula that protrudes into the harbour bay from the west.

Excursion to Reggio di Calabria

✳
National Museum

(currently closed) ▶

🕐

This destination is situated on the Italian mainland. It is only half an hour from Messina by high-speed ferry. The National Museum not far from the harbour houses the two **bronze statues of Riace**, which were found in 1972 by amateur divers. They were probably made by Phidias in the 5th century BC. Other remarkable exhibits are the bronze »Philosopher's Head« from Porticello (late 5th century) as well as paintings by Mattia Preti and Antonella da Messina (Piazza de Nava; Tue – Sun 9am – 7pm; www. museonazionalerc.it).

North of Messina

Capo Peloro

The northbound coast road passes fishing villages with poetic names such as Paradiso, Contemplazione, Pace and Grotta; then Ganzirri with a salt lake in which mussels are farmed.

Punta del Faro ▶

Finally the road reaches the cape with the old lighthouse (Faro, 12km/7 mi) next to the enormous pylon that was built to support the cable across the Strait but is no longer in use. The mainland is only 3km/2mi away at this point (views). It is possible to continue westwards via Acquarone to Spartà, where a side road turns left and makes its way back to Messina via Castane di Furie through pretty mountain scenery (18km/11mi).

Scala

Once in Scala (6km/4mi west of Messina on the SS 113 towards Palermo), walk to the ruins of the Gothic church Santa Maria della Scala. 4km/2.5mi further along, at the Portella San Rizzo is the watershed of the **Monti Peloritani** at an altitude of 465m/1526ft. A pretty panoramic road leads southwestwards to the Santuario di Dinnamare at **Monte Antennamare** (1127m/3698ft).

Gesso

In the Capuchin church in Gesso there is a remarkable altarpiece by Antonio Catalano the Elder (1560–1630) depicting the adoration of the shepherds (Chiesa die Cappuccini; on the SS 113, 18km/11mi northwest of Messina).

Rometta, on the northern side of the Peloritani Mountains, made a name for itself when for a long time it resisted Arab conquest of the island, which began in 827 with the occupation of Marsala. It was the last bastion to fall in 925. The small Chiesa del Salvatore, a Byzantine-style church with a central ground plan, is an architectural monument. **Rometta**

Between Messina and Taormina

To get to Mili (12km/7mi south of Messina on the SS 114) go to Mili Marina, then turn right into the Mili Valley. Shortly before the entrance to the town, at an elevation of 199m/653ft, is the monastic chapel of Santa Maria, one of several examples of Norman churches in this region. It is a aisle-less structure with a three-part domed sanctuary. Santa Maria is a former church of the Basilians, Greek Orthodox monks who were assisted by the Normans and received a confirmation of their intention to build from Count Roger I in 1092. **Mili**

Continue southwards on the SS 114 to Itála Marina, then turn right to **Itála** (altitude: 210m/689ft; 2.5km/1.5mi from the coast). 1.5km/1mi beyond the town is a Norman church, Santi Pietro e Paolo, which was commissioned by Roger I after a victory over the Saracens; it was then given to the Basilian order. The exterior is decorated with interlacing Lombard bands. The interior is a columned basilica with pointed-arch arcades and a vaulted sanctuary. The dome, supported by squinches, was reconstructed in the restoration of 1930.

Santi Pietro e Paolo: a Byzantine gem in Casalvecchio Siculo

Ali Terme   The town of Alí Terme (population 2300, approx. 30km/20mi south of Messina, 5km/3mi south of Itála Marina), situated in fertile landscape by the sea, is known for its sulphurous springs.

Sávoca   The picturesque mountain village of Sávoca (on the SS 114 until just beyond Santa Teresa di Riva) is one of the locations of Francis Ford Coppola's Mafia epic *The Godfather*. A ruined Norman castle and a 14th-century church are both of interest. Underneath the church the mummified corpses of the former Nobili are on display in wall niches.

Casalvecchio Siculo   Casalvecchio Siculo is situated 6km/4mi beyond Sávoca, at an altitude of 383m/1257ft in the valley of the Agrò (dry in the summer months). On its northern bank, in the midst of olives and oranges, is one of the most fascinating examples of late Byzantine sacred architecture (photo p. 271). The church of Santi Pietro e Paolo was part of a Greek Orthodox Basilian monastery and probably built under Roger II in 1116, then renovated in 1172 under William II. The structure is all of a piece, with multi-coloured exterior walls (red bricks, gold-brown limestone and black lava); these have narrow pilasters, which split at the top and turn into a Lombard band. The top of the rectangular building is crenellated. Despite its length, the unadorned interior is not a basilica (i.e. with an elongated nave flanked by aisles) in the manner of the »Latin« West. Instead, as was the Eastern Orthodox custom, there is a narthex between two (only half preserved) stair towers, beyond which it is built on a central plan with an area in the shape of a Greek cross and the three-part sanctuary.

★

Santi Pietro e Paolo ►

The central area has a larger dome supported by squinches, the sanctuary by a smaller one of the same type.

Sant'Alessio Siculo   The popular seaside town of Sant'Alessio Siculo is a starting point for a trip to Forza d'Agrò (►Taormina).

Milazzo

T 3

Province: Messina
Population: 33,000

Altitude: Sea level

Milazzo, a ferry terminal and fishing port, is situated on a narrow headland that reaches far into the gulf of the same name. Most visitors do not see much of this pretty old town because they go straight to the Lipari Islands.

History   Greeks from Zankle (Messina) founded the town of Mylai in 716 BC. Not far from there the Romans achieved their first naval victory when they defeated the Carthaginian fleet in 260 BC. In the Middle Ages the Norman kings built a castle that was extended by Frederick

● VISITING MILAZZO

INFORMATION

Servizio Turistico
Piazza Caio Duilio 20, 98057 Milazzo
Tel. 09 09 22 28 65, fax 09 09 22 27 90,
www.aastmilazzo.it

TRANSPORT

Main ferry terminal to the Lipari
Islands. Daily Giuntabus to Catania
airport (www.giuntabus.com)

WHERE TO EAT

► Expensive
① *Piccolo Casale*
Via Riccardo d'Amico 12
Tel. 09 09 22 44 79
Closed Mon; unassuming from the
outside, but the best restaurant in town

► Moderate
② *Al Castello*
Via Federico di Svevia 20
Tel. 09 09 28 21 75, closed Tue
The good food is ample reward for
the effort of getting up here.

WHERE TO STAY

► Mid-range
① *Riviera Lido*
Strada Panoramica, Loc. Corrie
Tel. 09 09 28 34 56, fax 09 09 28 34 57
www.hotelrivieralido.it; 49 rooms
2km/1mi outside town; comfortable,
with views of the bay and of refineries

② *Petit Hotel*
Via Dei Mille 37
Tel. 09 09 09 28 67 84 www.petit-
hotel.it, 9 rooms
An eco-friendly little hotel by the
harbour, the food served in the small
but good restaurant is also organic

► Budget
③ *Jack's Hotel*
Via Colonello Magistri 47
Tel. 09 09 28 33 00
Fax 09 09 24 12 17
www.jackshotel.it, 13 rooms
Approx. 400m/450yd from the har-
bour; pleasantly furnished rooms

II and then again by the Spanish in the 15th–16th centuries (tel.
09 09 23 12 92, guided tours Tue–Sun 9.30am, 10.30am, 11.30am, ☉
5pm, 6pm and 7pm). Here in 1860 Garibaldi defeated the Bourbon
troops who had established themselves in the castle.

Milazzo and Around

The modern **lower town** by the harbour was largely built after 1860.
The charming **upper town** is home to the magnificent castle, which
was expanded by Frederick II and later by the Spanish in the 15th
and 16th centuries (the Great Hall is an interesting feature) and the
old cathedral, which was designed by Camillo Camilliani from Flor-
ence at the end of the 16th century. The church of San Papino
(1629) possesses a crucifix by Fra Umile da Petralia. All three northbound roads lead to **Capo di Milazzo** 6km/4mi away, which has a
78m/256ft lighthouse. The views of the Lipari Islands and Mount Etna are very good.

Milazzo

Milazzo Map

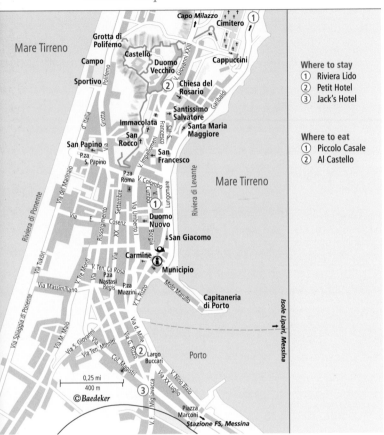

Where to stay
1. Riviera Lido
2. Petit Hotel
3. Jack's Hotel

Where to eat
1. Piccolo Casale
2. Al Castello

Santa Lucia del Mela The wine-making town of Santa Lucia del Mela (12km/7mi south of Milazzo) is situated 215m/700ft above the valley of the Torrente Floripotena, on the northern slopes of Monte Melia in the **Peloritani Mountains**.

The old Casale was popular with Frederick II; he gave it church privileges. Of the castle that was rebuilt in 1322, a triangular tower and a round guard tower survive. The large Jewish community was forced out by the Spanish in 1492. The Chiesa Madre, dedicated to Santa Lucia, has a nice Renaissance portal from the end of the 15th century. The church was altered in the 16th and 17th centuries. The tympanum depicts the Madonna with child between Saint Lucia and Saint Agatha. There is a large panel of the Madonna with Child (around 1400) in the church of the Annunziata.

Novara di Sicilia in the Peloritani Mountains

The town of Roccavaldina (approx. 20km/12mi southeast of Milazzo) in the Monti Peloritani lies at an altitude of 341m/1119ft and can be reached via Monforte Marina. In 1509 the aristocratic Valdina family acquired the castle and had the building expanded to truly palatial proportions in around 1600, probably by Camillo Camilliani from Tuscany, who was also responsible for the old cathedral in Milazzo. In 1623 Pietro Valdina was ennobled as Marchese della Rocca. Ever since, both the family and the town have been called Roccavaldina.

Roccavaldina

The town with its hot springs Ciapazzia and Fonte di Venere is part of the commune of Terme Vigliatore and situated on the broad sweep of the Gulf of Patti (approx. 18km/11mi southwest of Milazzo). Ruins of a Roman villa from the 2nd century AD have been uncovered in San Biagio (2km/1mi to the west on the SS 113). Rooms with fine mosaic floors are grouped around a large peristyle. The key to the excavated villa is available from the butcher's on the main road.

Castroreale Terme

◄ Spa in the Venus springs

The town of Castroreale (16km/10mi southeast of Castroreale Terme) lies at an altitude of 394m/1293ft in the Peloritani Mountains and can be reached via an attractive road via Barcellona Pozzo Grotto. In addition to Baroque churches there is the tower of a castle dating from 1324.

Castroreale

The town of Novara di Sicilia (650m/2133ft, 20km/12mi south of Terme Vigliatore), which is worth visiting for its medieval townscape, is the starting point for those wishing to climb Rocca di Novara (1340m/4396ft), the highest peak of the Peloritani Mountains.

Novara di Sicilia

★ Módica

Q 11

Province: Ragusa
Population: 55,000

Altitude: 381–449m/1250–1473ft

Módica, situated in a picturesque location on the southern slopes of the Hyblaean Mountains (Monti Iblei) 15km/9mi southeast of Ragusa, originated as the Sicel town of Motyka. In the Middle Ages, under the rule of the aristocratic Cabrera and Enriquez families from Spain, it was the main town of the county of the same name.

Baroque pomp in the gorge

Módica suffered quite serious damage in the 1693 earthquake. Some of the older buildings were unharmed, but the town had to be largely rebuilt. As a result the appearance of the lively lower town, situated in a narrow valley, as well as the upper town, on a rocky promontory, is fascinatingly Baroque.

What to See in Módica

Módica Bassa
Museo delle Arti e Tradizioni Popolare ►

In Via Leva in the **lower town** is the Palazzo de Leva with a portal that combines a zigzag ornament of Norman origin with plant motifs (around 1400). The folk museum in Palazzo Mercredi exhibits traditional Sicilian tools.

 VISITING MÓDICA

INFORMATION

Ufficio Turistico Comunale
97015 Módica, Corso Umberto 72
Tel. 09 32 75 92 04
www.modicaonline.it

WHERE TO EAT

► **Expensive/Moderate**
① *Fattoria delle Torri*
Vico Napolitano 14, tel.
09 32 75 12 86, closed Mon.
Trattoria in a former dairy; very good food, local products

► **Moderate/Inexpensive**
② *I Baccanti*
Via Grimaldi 72
Tel. 09 32 94 11 33 and 32 91 04 82 72
A feast for the eyes and the palate

③ *Hostaria San Benedetto*
Via Nativo 30, tel. 09 32 75 48 04
Closed Tue – a wonderful trattoria in every regard in the upper town

WHERE TO STAY

► **Mid-range**
① *Palazzo Failla*
Via Blandini 5 , tel. & fax
09 32 94 10 59, www.palazzofailla.it
Elegant small hotel in a sophisticated palazzo; expensive ristorante

► **Budget**
② *Bristol*
Via Risorgimento 8b, tel. & fax
09 32 76 28 90, www.hotelbristol. it;
27 rooms; small hotel with a garden; around 3km/2mi outside town

The Chiesa del Carmine was built in the 15th century; its façade features a portal and a rose window in the Gothic style (15th century); the marble Annunciation group inside the church was sculpted by Antonello Gagini (1528–30).

Chiesa del Carmine

The Chiesa Santa Maria di Betlem in Via Marchese Tedeschi has a special feature, namely the Cappella del Sacramento (also Cappella Cabrera) with late Gothic and Renaissance elements (around 1500).

Santa Maria di Betlem

The Chiesa di San Pietro (around 1720; Corso Umberto) is a pure Baroque building. The exterior staircase leading up to it increases the impact of its hillside location. The opulent two-storey façade has a broken pediment and rusticated pilasters, while gesturing statues of saints are grouped together to form a Baroque set-piece.

San Pietro

Módica Map

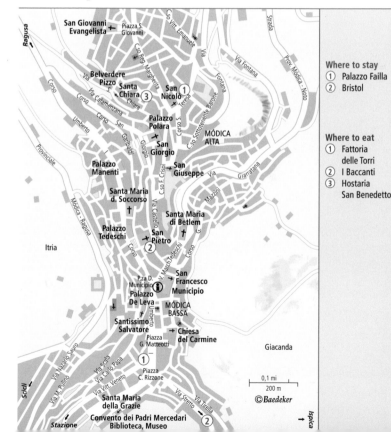

Where to stay
① Palazzo Failla
② Bristol

Where to eat
① Fattoria delle Torri
② I Baccanti
③ Hostaria San Benedetto

Salvatore Quasimodo At the station building at the southern end of the lower town a marble panel commemorates Salvatore Quasimodo (1901–68), the town's most famous son. He was awarded the Nobel Prize for Literature in 1959. His birthplace at Via Posterla 84 contains a museum that with exhibits relating to his life and works (Tue – Sun 10am – 1pm, 4pm – 7pm).

Convento dei Padri Mercedari, Museo Civico A former monastery in Via della Mercé, also in the south, houses the library and the municipal museum for archaeological discoveries, an ethnographic collection and paintings from the 18th and 19th centuries.

Módica Alta ★ **San Giorgio ▶** The **upper town** is dominated by the church of San Giorgio, which was given its current face between 1720 and 1738. A staircase with 250 steps leads up to it, beginning at Corso Umberto next to San Pietro. The façade with its five portals culminates in a high central tower, which further emphasizes the church's elevated position. It is clearly related to the church of the same name in nearby ▶Ragusa, and like that church, it is the work of Rosario Gagliardi. There is an 8m x 6m//26 x 20ft retable in the choir, which was created for the building previously on this site by the painter Bernardino Niger in 1573 in the late Renaissance style.

Around Módica

Scicli (population 26,000), situated in a depression among hills between Módica and the south coast, is a little-known Baroque gem with churches and palaces built after the earthquake of 1693. The Chiesa Madre was built as the church of Sant'Ignazio for the Jesuit college and follows the tradition of this order with the basilica floor plan and a two-storey front elevation with three portals and pilasters. The two low side towers are, un-

Baroque highlight: San Giorgio

usually, slightly set back. The church of the Carmelites was also built for a religious order, as was the associated monastery (now the magistrate's court). The façade has similar characteristics to the Chiesa Madre; its narrower single-tower design corresponds to its interior without aisles. San Bartolomeo has a high, tower-like façade, a style not uncommon in southeastern Sicily. The middle is emphasized by three columns that flank the portal, by the statue of the saint in the large niche of the top floor and the dome over the bells. The lavishly ornamented building was dedicated in 1763. There is an artistic nativity scene inside (16th century). The Descent from the Cross (17th century) is a work by the Calabrian Mattia Preti. The Palazzo Beneventano from the late 18th century is a feast for fans of the Baroque. This is true for the grotesque heads on the balcony corbels, but also for the incredibly imaginative corner pilasters.

Marian sanctuary

The Santuario di Santa Maria delle Milizie, which goes back to a building from classical Antiquity, is located 5km/3mi southwest of Scicli, to the right above the road to Donnalucata.

Donnalucata

The seaside resort of Donnalucata (6km/4mi south of Scicli) has a good beach; 2km/1mi to the west is the beach Plaia Grande with holiday facilities.

Sampieri

Sampieri is a fishing village 9.5km/6mi southeast of Scicli. The coastal road connects it to the small town of Cava d'Aliga on Punta del Corvo (sandy bay between cliffs, 4km/2.5mi to the west) and to Marina di Módica (6km/4mi to the east; 22km/14mi southeast of Módica), a seaside resort with a good sandy beach.

Marina di Módica

Pozzallo

The port of Pozzallo (approx. 20km/12mi south of Módica; population 17,700; ships to Malta) lines a pretty bay on the south coast. Thanks to the clean sea here and the combination of dunes and forest, this region is popular with holidaymakers. To the west of the old town is a modern harbour, from which the ferries to Malta depart. A medieval tower built by the counts of Módica in the 14th century as protection against pirate attacks is worth seeing. There are access roads to the beaches that lie outside town, e.g. Spiaggia di Raganzano, Spiaggia delle Pietre Nere, Santa Maria Focalla, Marza as well as to Lido Otello.

Ìspica This small farming town (population 15,500; 18km/11mi southeast of Módica) is situated at 170m/558ft on a white limestone bastion and was founded shortly after the earthquake of 1693. It was called Spaccaforno until 1935. There are several Baroque churches, including the basilica of Santa Maria Maggiore, which has elaborate stucco ornamentation and frescoes by Olivio Sozzi in its interior, as well as the Chiesa Madre (around 1750), which is dedicated to St Bartholomew and dominates the Piazza Maria Josè. At the northeastern edge of town is the wild, romantic **Parco Archeologico della Forza** at the entrance to the Cava d'Ìspica. The gorge is a nice place for gentle walks (4 hours on foot), but the northern end of the Cava is more interesting from the archaeological perspective.

✱
Cava d'Ìspica East of Módica (or 16km/10mi northwest of Ìspica), the deep, 13km/8mi-long gorge Cava d'Ìspica winds its way through the Monti Iblei (in summer daily 9am–7pm, otherwise Mon–Sat 9am–1.30pm). There are countless caves in the cliffs, often several of them, one above the other. Some were created in the Stone Age; they were later used as tombs by the Sicels. In the early Christian era they served as catacombs, and in the Middle Ages they were inhabited. The Grotta di San Nicola (with remains of Byzantine painting), the Grotta di Santa Maria (6th century) and the Christian rock tombs »u campusantu«, »urutti caruti« and »urutti giardina«, as well as the »Castello« are particularly interesting. Ask about a guided tour at the houses near the entrance to the valley.

✱ ✱ Monreale

H 4

Province: Palermo
Population: 37,000

Altitude: 310m/1017ft

Monreale is a town on the slopes of Monte Caputo above the Conca d'Oro 8km/5mi southwest of Palermo; it is also the seat of an archbishop. The magnificent cathedral, with its cycle of mosaics on a gold ground and its cloister, is the most significant monument of Norman art in Sicily. More than any other work, it reflects the idea of the Norman kingdom as the highest temporal as well as religious authority.

History Monreale's architectural history is closely connected to the political configuration at the coming-of-age of the Norman king William II. William, born in 1154, became king when his father, William I, died in 1166. When he was declared an adult at age 18, he governed independently from 1172 until his early death in 1189, i.e. for 17 years. There were tensions between the crown and the papacy, analogous to what is known in the history of the Holy Roman Empire as the Investiture Contest. The English archbishop of Palermo, Walter of the Mill, blatantly took the papal position. At his behest Roger II was not buried in Cefalù Cathedral as he had willed but in Palermo, which was under the control of the archbishop himself. The church authority thereby emphasized the demand that the Sicilian regal power derived from the pope and that he, Walter of the Mill, had to confirm the royal dignity. Therefore it was necessary to assert the authority of the king, as William's grandfather Roger II had done, following the example of the Byzantine emperors, whose supremacy over the Patriarch and the clergy was undisputed.

William II reacted unequivocally and with the means of his time, emphasizing the theocratic character of his rule by having a large royal park built on an elevation above Palermo, hence the name Monreale, royal mountain, which included a Benedictine monastery and a palace. The abbot became the bishop and already by 1183 archbishop. The king endowed his establishment with privileges and extensive estates so that Monreale was richer than the archdiocese of Palermo. In addition he declared that Monreale, already largely completed by 1185, would be the place where members of the dynasty would be buried.

A masterpiece of medieval architecture: the cathedral and cloister in Monreale

▶ VISITING MONREALE

INFORMATION
Ufficio Informazioni Turistiche
Piazza Guglielmo II, tel.
09 16 56 46 79, www.monreale.net

TRANSPORT
AMAT bus 389 (www.amat.pa.it) and
buses operated by AST (www.azien-
dasiciliani trasporti.it) between Palermo (Piazza Indipendenza) and
Monreale

WHERE TO EAT
▶ **Moderate**
Bricco & Bacco
Via B. d'Acquisto 13

Tel. 09 16 41 77 73, closed Mon
Just a stone's throw from the cathedral (opposite the Banca di Sicilia);
many starters and meat dishes (no
pasta); very good value for money

▶ **Expensive**
Il Trogoletto
Via Benedetto D'Acquisto
Tel. 09 16 41 90 23
Top-quality tableware and fine table-
cloths, outstanding food and a view of
Palermo and the gulf to boot

WHERE TO STAY
▶Tips p. 291

✳✳ Cathedral

Opening hours:
Daily 9am – 1pm
2.30pm–5.30pm

Exterior

The cathedral is a basilica built in the shape of a cross. It is of sizeable dimensions (102m/112 yd long, 40m/44yd wide, 35m/115ft
high). The western elevation is a twin-tower façade typical of Norman architecture (the north tower was never completed), in front of
which there used to be an atrium on the site of what is now Piazza
Guglielmo II. A portico was placed between the towers as well as on
the northern side in the 18th century. The still original **east end** with
its three apses (photo p. 286) makes the strongest impact. Its interlacing pointed blind arches and their high-contrast decoration of
light limestone tufa and black lava marks the liturgical importance
which this part of the church has on the inside too. The views towards Palermo and the bay of the same name are very attractive
from the courtyard of the neighbouring building.

Note the two **bronze portals**. The west portal, a work by Bonnano
Pisano dating from 1186, measures 7.80m/26ft by 3.70m/12ft, making it the largest bronze portal of its time. It depicts biblical scenes in
42 images. Four reliefs form the base, depicting fantastical animals,
the symbols of foolishness. The smaller north portal by Barisano da
Trani (from around the same time) depicts saints and evangelists on
28 fields.

The interior

Inside, two rows of nine mostly ancient columns with rich Corinthian capitals support pointed-arch arcades between the aisles and the
nave. The nave has a beautifully painted open roof structure that was
faithfully reconstructed after a fire in 1811. It is likely that there were

Christ Pantocrator in the cathedral's choir

plans for a dome supported by a tambour over the crossing, but they were never carried out. Apart from a few repairs, the marble floor dates back to the time of the cathedral's construction.

Sanctuary

The sanctuary, separated by a rood screen and, befitting its significance, set slightly higher, is almost as long as the nave. In line with Byzantine Orthodox tradition, it consists of three spaces: the choir between the prothesis and diaconicon. The king's throne (left) and the bishop's throne (right, one step lower) stand in front of the crossing columns in the nave under mosaic images of William II.
In the south aisle of the sanctuary are the tombs of the Norman kings: the porphyry sarcophagus of William I (1154–66) and the marble sarcophagus in which William II (1166–89) has lain since the original brick box was removed in 1575. The tombs of William I's consort Margaret and his sons Roger, Duke of Apulia, and Henry, Prince of Capua, are in the north aisle of the sanctuary. The urn containing the heart of Louis IX of France (Saint Louis), who died on crusade in Tunis in 1270, stands on the north wall.

Side rooms

Access to the Cappella del Crocifisso (17th century) and the cathedral treasury is via the north aisle of the sanctuary. The entrance to the staircase leading to the church roof (180 steps, views) is at the west end of the southern aisle.

CATHEDRAL AND CLOISTER IN MONREALE

✳✳ **With the construction of Monreale, William II primarily wanted to demonstrate to the pope his claim to power. The cathedral and the cloister survive. They are a treasure trove of the Middle Ages.**

🕐 Open:
Cathedral: daily 9am–1.30pm, 2.30pm–5.30pm

🕐 Cloister:
Tue–Sun 9am–4.30pm, Mon only until 1pm

① The cathedral's eastern façade
The cathedral's eastern side with its three apses reflects the builder's desire to use decor with an oriental feel: intersecting pointed blind arches and inlay made of black lava and yellow stones from Monte Pellegrino.

② Western façade
The left-hand tower was never completed. Behind the wrought-iron gate (18th century) are bronze doors by Bonanno Pisano dating from 1186; the picture areas depict biblical scenes.

③ The interior
Precious gold-ground mosaics cover all of the interior walls, which have an area of more than 6000 sq m/7000 sq yd!

④ Royal tomb
To the left of the sanctuary are the sarcophagi of the royal family, on the other side those of William I and William II.

⑤ Cloister
Arabic pointed arches rest on 228 double columns. They are smooth, or decorated with zigzag fluting or mosaic bands. There is a square fountain in one corner. Among the masterpieces of the Romanesque period are the capitals with their scenes from the Christian and Islamic world, a colourful mix of the religious and the secular.

⑥ Up high
The view into the square cloister from the church roof is fantastic.

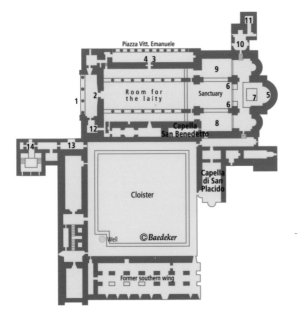

1 Portico with three arches (Ignazio Marabitti, 1770)
2 Western portal (Bonannno Pisano, 1186)
3 Portico (Gian Domenico and Fazio Gagini 1547-59)
4 Northern portal (Barisano da Trani, 1179)
5 Eastern apses
6 Bishop's throne and royal throne
7 High altar
8,9 Norman tombs
10 Capella del Crocifisso
11 Access to the cathedral treasure
12 Access to the cathedral ro
13 Entrance to the cloister
14 Entrance to the belvedere

Piazza Vitt. Emanuele

Room for the laity

Sanctuary

Capella San Benedetto

Capella di San Placido

Cloister

Well   ©Baedeker

Former southern wing

50 ft
20 m

No one pair of columns is like another. Here one of the groups of four in the courtyard's corners.

The capitals are also a world of their own: they depict plants, animals, people, goblins, dragons and other fabled creatures.

The mosaics in the transept tell stories from the life of Christ, from the Annunciation to the Crucifixion; here Rebecca's journey.

Monreale is a particularly popular spot to get married. The newly-weds emerge from the cathedral after the ceremony.

© Baedeker

Mosaics (plan p. 288–289)

The magnificence of the precious mosaics on a gold ground is overwhelming. They cover all the walls, measuring more than 6000 sq m/64,000 sq ft! What artists from Constantinople, together with local mosaic craftsmen, created here in the short period from 1179 to 1182 is unique. Countless biblical creatures and scenes emerge from the mystically shimmering gold ground, an entire cosmos of pictorial tales and proclamations.

Overview

The nave deals with scenes from the Old Testament, while the aisles depict Jesus's miracles. The transept is dedicated to the life and passion of Christ as well as to Christ after the resurrection, and to the apostles Peter and Paul. The choir is dominated by Christ Pantocrator, the »ruler of all things«, who has his place above his mother Mary.

Mosaics in the nave

The images in the nave are always arranged in a clockwise direction, as was the case in the Cappella Palatina (▶ Palermo). As there, the sequence starts on the southern nave wall at the eastern end with the top row: the story of Creation until Adam in the Garden of Eden. On the narrow western side is the Creation of Eve; the northern wall features the Fall of Man, the expulsion from the Garden of Eden, Cain, and Noah being instructed to build the ark.

Returning to the opposite side again, the sequence continues on the lower row (left to right): Noah's Ark, Abraham and the three angels. The western central row shows Lot and the destruction of Sodom (with saints Cassius and Castus in between). Abraham's story is continued on the northern wall with the preparation of Isaac for sacrifice. This is followed by Isaac and Jacob all the way to Jacob wrestling with the angel.

Transept

The transept portrays the world of the New Testament. The eastern sides are reserved for the apostles Paul (left) and Peter (right); under the images of their martyrdom they are depicted as timelessly enthroned figures. The two apostles are also depicted in the choir between the transept and apse.

At the southern crossing arch there is Zacharias, the Annunciation, the Visitation, and the Flight to Egypt. The continuation is to be found opposite on the arch on the north side: the Magi, the Massacre of the Innocents. There is also the Baptism of Jesus and the Marriage at Cana.

Now back to the opposite side again, where the southern wall depicts the Temptation, Transfiguration and the beginning of the Passion (Gethsemane) of Christ. The northern wall continues the Passion with the Crucifixion and adds the Resurrection appearances of Jesus all the way to Whitsun.

Byzantine artists and local mosaicists created an overwhelming tapestry covering all the walls.

At the threshold to the choir, William II is depicted twice on the crossing columns: as he is crowned by Christ (left, above the king's throne; photo p. 39) and as he hands over a model of the church of Monreale, which he commissioned, to the Virgin Mary (right, above the bishop's throne). Like his grandfather Roger II in the coronation mosaic in the Martorana in Palermo (photo p. 38), the king is wearing the regalia of Byzantine emperors, yet the inscription is not Greek (as it is with Roger), but Latin, a hint at the gradual separation from Byzantium and the growing influence of Latin culture.

At the base of the apse are effigies of saints Clement of Rome, Peter **Apse** of Alexandria, Sylvester and Thomas Becket. (Archbishop Becket of Canterbury was murdered in 1170, just a decade before the mosaics in Monreale were made and was canonized as early as 1173.) In the central register Mary on a throne is the main character, between the archangels Michael and Gabriel and the apostles Peter and Paul. The image programme culminates in the apse's semi-dome with the monumental image of Christ Pantocrator, whose majestic appearance dominates the entire space. His right hand raised in blessing, he holds in his left hand the open book with the words »I am the light of the world.«

Monreale Mosaics

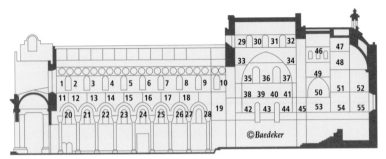

Northern wall
1 Eve and the serpent
2 Fall of Man
3 Adam and Eve are ashamed of their nakedness
4 Expulsion from the Garden of Eden
5 Adam and Eve at work
6 Cain and Abel make a sacrifice
7 Cain kills Abel
8 God asks Cain about his brother
9 Lamech kills Cain
10 God announces the flood to Noah
11 God demands a sacrifice from Abraham
12 Sacrifice of Isaac
13 Rebecca with the camels at the water hole
14 Rebecca's journey
15 Isaac sends hunting
16 Isaac blesses Jacob
17 Jacob's flight
18 Jacob's dream
19 Jacob's fight with the angel
20 Healing of the hunchback
21 Healing of the man with dropsy

22 Healing of ten lepers
23 Healing of two blind men
24 Expelling the money changers from the temple
25 Jesus and the Woman taken in Adultery
26 Healing of the lame man
27 Healing of the lame and blind
28 Mary Magdalene washes the feet of Jesus
29 The Magi
30 The Adoration of the Magi
31 Herod's order to kill all the male children
32 Boys are killed in Bethlehem
33 Wedding in Cana
34 Jesus is baptized
35 Crucifixion
36 Jesus is buried
37 The torments of Hell
38 An angel and the sleeping guard in front of the empty grave; Jesus and the apostles on the road to Emmaus
39 Supper at Emmaus
40 The two apostles after Jesus's disappearance

41 Return of the two apostles to Jerusalem
42 The miraculous catch of fish
43 The Ascension
44 Descent of the Holy Spirit
45 Christ crowns William II
46 Jacob and Zacharias
47 Two cherubim
48 Archangels Raphael and Michael
49 Malachi, Jonah, Ezekiel and Moses
50 Baptism of Paul and his argument with the Jews
51 Philip, Bartholomew and Luke
52 James, Peter and Archangel Michael
53 Paul flees to Damascus, gives letters to Timothy and Silas
54 Agatha, Anthony, Blaise
55 Stephen, Peter of Alexandria and Saint Clement

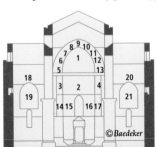

Eastern wall

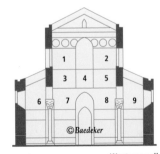

Western wall

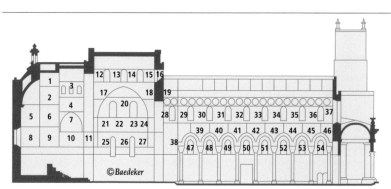

©Baedeker

Southern wall
1 Two cherubim
2 Archangels Gabriel and Uriel
3 Isaiah and Habakkuk
4 Jeremiah, Amos, Obadiah, and Joel (from left to right)
5 Gabriel, Paul and Andrew
6 Mark, Thomas and Simon the Zealot
7 Peter raises Tabitha from the dead; meeting between Peter and Paul
8 Sylvester, Thomas of Canterbury and Martin
9 Hilary, Benedict, Mary Magdalene
10 Argument between Peter and Paul and the Sorcerer; Fall of the Sorcerer
11 William II hands Mary the model of the church and consecrates the cathedral to her
12 Annunciation to Zacharias
13 Zacharias leaves the temple
14 Annunciation

15 Visitation
16 Birth of Christ
17 Joseph's dream
18 Flight to Egypt
19 Jesus is circumcized; Jesus among scholars in the temple
20 The Temptations of Christ
21 Jesus and a Samaritan woman
22 Transfiguration of Jesus
23 Raising of Lazarus
24 The apostles bring Jesus a donkey
25 Washing of feet
26 Jesus on the Mount of Olives
27 Betrayal of Jesus by Judas
28 Creation of Heaven and Earth
29 Creation of light
30 Separation of the waters and the land
31 Creation of plants and trees
32 Creation of stars
33 Creation of fish and birds
34 Creation of animals and Adam
35 Day of rest on the seventh day of creation

36 God leads Adam into the Garden of Eden
37 Adam in the Garden of Eden
38 Building of the Ark
39 The animals enter the Ark
40 Noah sends out the dove
41 Noah and the animals leave the Ark
42 God's promise to Noah
43 Noah's drunkenness
44 Tower of Babel
45 Three angels appear to Abraham
46 Abraham serves the three angels
47 Jesus drives out a demon
48 Healing of the lepers
49 Jesus heals a man with a shrivelled hand
50 Peter is rescued from the water
51 Jesus raises a widow's son
52 Jesus heals the woman with an issue of blood
53 Jesus raises Jairus's daughter
54 Jesus heals Peter's mother-in-law, Feeding of the Five Thousand

Eastern wall
1 Christ Pantocrator
2 Virgin and Child, surrounded by archangels Michael and Gabriel and saints Peter and Paul
3 John
4 Matthew
5 Nathan
6 Daniel
7 Elijah
8 David
9 Christ Emmanuel
10 Solomon

11 Samuel
12 Gideon
13 Elisa
14 Martin
15 Stephen and Peter of Alexandria
16 Pope Sylvester and Thomas of Canterbury
17 Nicholas
18 Martyrdom of Paul
19 Paul on a throne
20 Crucifixion of Peter
21 Peter on a throne

Western wall
1 Creation of Eve
2 God leads Eve to Adam
3 Lot and the angels
4 Casius and Castus in Rome
5 Destruction of Sodom
6 Feeding of the Five Thousand
7 Collapse of the Temple of Apollo as a result of prayers by Cassius and Castus
8 Exorcism by St Castrense
9 Healing of the hunchbacks

✷ ✷ Cloister

🕐
Opening hours:
Tue – Sun
9am – 4.30pm
Mon only until
1.30pm

The entrance to the famous cloister, the most significant remains of the former Benedictine abbey, lies to the right of the cathedral façade. The abbey's ruined southern wing also survives. The cloister is a square measuring 47m/153ft on each side. There are 26 arches on each of the four sides, opening up to a lavish garden. They are supported by a total of 228 double columns with double capitals. These columns are either smooth, or encrusted with coloured stones. No two pairs of columns are alike. All the corners have four little columns with reliefs on their shafts. In the southwest corner is a fountain chapel with an oriental feel and particularly richly ornamented columns; in the middle the water runs down a column with a zigzag pattern and figurative decoration at the top. The double capitals have even more imaginative designs than the columns: they depict plants, animals, people, acrobats and archers, griffins and other fabulous creatures as well as biblical subjects, including scenes from the Passion of Christ (the women at the tomb). The wealth of decorative as well as narrative elements can only be appreciated fully when real time is taken to walk around. One particularly noteworthy capital is the 19th on the western side, which depicts William II handing over the model of the church to the Madonna; then there is the capital supported by four columns in the cloister's northeastern corner with the following masterfully composed subjects: Annunciation, Visitation, an angel appears to Joseph, the birth of Christ, the proclamation to the shepherds, the Magi.

Belvedere
(currently closed) ▶

Leave the cloister and walk left along the façade, through the next entrance, to get to the Belvedere, a small park with huge rubber trees on a terrace, from where nice views are to be had of the Conca d'Oro and the Bay of Palermo.

Further sights

On Piazza Vittorio Emanuele, to the left of the cathedral, is the town hall (Municipio), which is located in part of the former royal palace. It houses a sculpture (1528) attributed to Antonello Gagini as well as the painting *The Birth of Christ* by Matthias Stomer (17th century). Via Umberto I runs northbound to the Church of the Mountain (Chiesa del Monte), which is decorated with stucco ornamentation by artists from the circle of Giacomo Serpotta. Directly next door is the collegiate church, which was built in 1565 and altered in the 17th century. The stucco ornamentation is by Serpotta, the paintings by Marco Benefial (1722, in the nave) and by Matthias Stomer (in the presbytery).

Take Via Roma southbound from Piazza Vittorio Emanuele, past the church of Sant'Antonio to the Collegio di Maria, built in 1880 to a design by the architect of the opera house in Palermo, G. B. Filippo Basile.

Around Monreale

Huge flumes and lots of other watery entertainment are on offer in the Acqua Park just outside Monreale (Contrada Fiumelato, Via Pezzingoli 172, tel. 09 16 46 02 46; in summer daily 9.30am – 6.30pm; www.acquaparkmonreale.it).

Acqua Park

A 9.5km/6mi winding roads leads from Monreale up to the airy San Martino delle Scale (507m/1663ft, population 350), which is named after the extensive Benedictine abbey, a popular destination for daytrippers. According to tradition, this abbey was founded by Pope Gregory the Great (590–604). The buildings were refurbished by G. Venanzio Marvuglia 1770–86. The church, in front of which stands a fountain by Ignazio Marabitti (18th century), has a font dating from 1396, choir stalls from 1591 and sculptures and paintings from the 16th–18th centuries by Filippo Paladino, Giuseppe Ribera, Pietro Novelli and Paolo de Matteis.

San Martino delle Scale

An ancient custom is still alive in San Martino: like their ancestors before them, the inhabitants catch pigeons and sparrows in winter in order to release them again on Easter Monday to welcome spring.

Starting from the road between Monreale and San Martino there is a short **panoramic walk** to Pizzo del Corvo, »Crow Hill«, atop which stands a Norman castle.

San Giuseppe Jato

San Giuseppe Jato lies 22km/14mi southwest of Monreale (on the SS 186 to Damiani, then on to the former Mafia stronghold of San Giuseppe Iato and San Cipirello). Iaitia (Latin: Ietum), an ancient Greek town mentioned by Diodorus, was uncovered here. It was probably founded in the 5th century BC and continued to exist until it was destroyed by Frederick II in the 13th century, when it was known as Iato.

The remains of the town wall, the agora and the Temple of Aphrodite, the Greek theatre and residential buildings (Zona Archeologica Antica Iato) are located in outstanding landscape. The excavation finds are exhibited in the Museo Civico of San Cipirello; there are, for example, a lion and several colossal statues.

! **Baedeker TIP**

Accommodation tips

The anti-Mafia organization Libera Terra (»free land«) runs agricultural businesses on confiscated Mafia land, where wine, vegetables and cereals are grown, and it is all organic, too, of course. Two of them offer farm stays: Agriturismo Portella della Ginestra, on S P 34, km 5, Piana degli Albanesi, tel. 032 32 13 25 97, and Agriturismo Terre di Corleone, Contrada Drago, north of Corleone, on S S 118, tel. 033 37 99 32 91. Information about this and similar projects: www.liberaterra.it.

The Casale dello Jato is a nicely laid out farm with seven flats. In the restaurant ingredients from the surrounding area are made into wonderful dishes following ancient recipes (Località Percianotta on S P Serralombardi to Scassabarile, tel. 09 18 58 23 09, www.ilcasaledellojato.it).

✳ Monti Madoníe

The Madonie Mountains are the western continuation of the Monti Nébrodi and the highest section of the mountain range that runs parallel to the north coast. Around Pizzo della Carbonara and Monte San Salvatore, between Castelbuono and Polizzi Generosa, they are between 1979m/6492ft and 1912m/6273ft high.

The Madoníe drop very steeply towards the north coast, while to the south they slope gently towards the interior. The limestone massif is a sparsely populated agricultural region. In 1989 a large part of this mountain range was made a nature park, the Parco Regionale delle Madoníe. Since the higher elevations are hard to access, the vegetation is lavish. Large broad-leaf woods flourish here with trees such as cork oaks, holm oaks, beeches and elms, but also hollies that grow up to 15m/50ft tall. At lower elevations olive and almond trees, grapes, vegetables and cereals are grown. Most of the villages were founded in the Middle Ages, when the coastal inhabitants fled to the hinterland from Saracen pirates.

> ## ❗ *Baedeker* TIP
>
> ### Tips for on the go
> Along the way there are a few small hotels, trattorias and signs to agriturismo businesses (farm stays), where guests are given a warm welcome and often spoiled with regional specialities (information: tourist offices in Cefalù and Palermo, www.agriturismosicilia.com and from the park administration in Petralìa Sottana; the park administration also has a Carta dei Sentieri del Paesaggio, a map with hiking trails and addresses).

The drive on winding, scenic roads provides a lot of variety. On Piano della Battaglia (1680m/5510ft) and Piano degli Zucchi (1105m/3625ft) it is even possible to pursue winter sports. Nevertheless only a few tourists ever visit the hinterland.

Hiking route 6, p. 144 ►

Through the Monti Madoníe

Targa Florio The most difficult and oldest automobile endurance race on earth, the Targa Florio, was named after its sponsor Vincenzo Florio. It was held in the hinterland of the Tyrrhenian coast between 1906 and 1997 (excluding both world wars). The Circuito delle Madoníe was originally 150km/93mi long. The start and finish were located between ►Termini Imerese and Buonfornello, just beyond where the SS 120 turns off the SS 113 coast road. The following route through the Circuito delle Madoníe follows a large stretch of the Targa Florio.

Cerda This small rural town (274m/899ft, population 5300) is the **globe artichoke** (carciofi) »capital«. During the season, from February to April, the Trattoria La Nasca 2 (Contrada Canna, tel. 09 18 99 10 55, closed Thu) serves hearty artichoke dishes at low prices. On the road

▶ VISITING THE MADONÍE

INFORMATION

Parco Regionale delle Madonie
90027 Petralìa Sottana, Corso Agliata
16, tel. 09 21 68 40 11
www.parcodellemadonie.it

GOOD TO KNOW

The Madoníe are the centre of
Equiturismo: many agriturismo businesses offer riding lessons and hacks.

WHERE TO EAT

▶ Moderate

Castelbuono · Nangalarruni
Via delle Confraternite 7
Tel. 09 21 67 14 28; closed Wed. Good
regional cuisine, e.g. fungi and game
dishes; in a side street off Corso
Umberto in the historic centre

Collesano · Agriturismo Arione
Contrada Porretti, tel. & fax
09 21 42 77 03, mobile 39 34 94 17
52 42, www.agriturismoarione.it
For walkers and visitors to the
Madoníe this is an ideal country inn
serving rustic Sicilian cuisine.
(6 guest rooms)

Collesano · Casale Drinzi
Contrada Drinzi, outside town towards Isnello, in a green setting
Tel. 09 21 66 40 27; open all week
Hearty dishes in a pleasant, rustic
atmosphere. Local ingredients, good
pizzas, excellent meat dishes, good red
wines. Basic guest rooms.

*Isnello · Rifugio Orestano
del Club Alpino Siciliano*
Località Piano Zucchi
Tel. & fax 09 21 66 21 59
www.rifugiorestano.com; 31 rooms
Rustic cuisine, including tasty local
salami and ham prepared using old
recipes; outstanding views

WHERE TO STAY

▶ Mid-range

Castelbuono · Villa Levante
Contrada Farbaudo, Via Isnello
Mobil 33 56 39 45 74
www.villalevante. it
Discerning agriturismo on a wonder-
ful estate

▶ Inexpensive/Mid-range

Castelbuono · Milocca
Contrada Piano Castagna
Tel. 09 21 67 19 44
Fax 09 21 67 14 37
www.albergomilocca.com
54 rooms; nice rural hotel in the
hinterland of Cefalù, set at an altitude
of around 500m/1640ft on the road
up to Piano Sempria

Petralìa Sottana · Monaco di Mezzo
Contrada Monaco di Mezzo
Tel. 09 34 67 39 49
www.monacodimezzo.com
Agriturismo; 5 apartments with
kitchens, pool; local dishes served in
the restaurant

Piano Battaglia · Baita del Faggio
Loc. Acque del Faggio
Contrada Fontanone del Faggio
Tel. 09 21 66 21 94
www.baitadelfaggio.it
23 rooms and a cosy restaurant at an
altitude of 1400m/4600ft between
Piano Zucchi and Piano Battaglia

Isnello · Park Hotel Piano Torre
Contrada Montaspro
Tel. 09 21 66 26 71
Fax 09 21 66 26 72
www.pianotorreparkhotel.com
26 rooms; nice destination hotel,
lovely view of the sea and the
mountains; good base for hikes

to Caltavuturo it is worth taking a side trip to **Sclafani Bagni**, baths popular for their sulphurous water. Leave the SS 120 in the medieval town of **Caltavuturo** with its ruins of a Norman castle and drive to the farming village of **Scillato**.

Polizzi Generosa Polizzi (915m/3002ft; population 3700) is situated on the brow of a hill around 30km/20mi south of Cefalù: it is the starting point for great walks in the mountains and the home of the flamboyant Milanese fashion designer Domenico Dolce (b. 1958; Dolce & Gabbana), whose father was a tailor here. The town was given the sobriquet »Generosa« in around 1234 by Frederick II. The Chiesa Madre has reliefs by Domenico Gagini (1482) and an old Dutch triptych, one of the main works of the »Master of the Embroidered Foliage« from Brussels (15th century). The »Ave Regina« by Walter Frye, who worked at the Burgundian court in around 1450, was identified on the sheet of music of a singing angel The mountain road towards **Pizzo della Carbonara** (15km/9mi to the north) goes to the Rifugio Giuliano Marini, which lies on the northern side of the mountain (1979m/6493ft).

Petralia Soprana The »upper Petralìa« towers prettily atop a rocky peak at 1147m/3763ft and is the highest comune in the Madoníe Mountains (population 3500). The crucifix carver Francesco Giovanni Pintorno, known as Fra Umile, was born here (1580–1639; monument on the piazza; one of his wooden crosses is in the Chiesa Madre). The Chiesa SS. Salvatore, a former mosque to the east of the Piazza del Duomo, was transformed into a church and consecrated under Roger I. The characteristic circular floor plan was maintained in the 18th-century renovations. The church of Santa Maria di Loreto (15th century, restored in the 18th century in the Rococo style) stands on the site of the former Norman castle. The views from the Belvedere u Castru behind it are splendid.

Petralia Sottana This small town (1000m/3280ft, population 3000) lies somewhat lower down on a rocky outcrop above the valley of the Imera Meridionale. The main town of the Monti Madoníe goes back to the Roman Petraea, in whose territory the Norman count Roger I had a castle built in 1096. The »Wedding Procession« and the mime festival »Corteo Nuziale e Ballo Pantomima della Cordella« take place here in August, the feast of the Madonna dell'Alto in September. The inhabitants make a living knotting rugs, a traditional craft that has be-

In the Madonie Mountains: in the background the town of Gangi at an altitude of more than 1000 m / 3300 ft

come rare; a more recent employer is the administration of the Parco delle Madoníe. The Chiesa Matrice was given its final look during the Baroque period; there is a 15th-century Catalan Gothic portal and a campanile with pointed-arch arcades. The aisled interior contains ancient columns; the valuable triptych dates back to the 15th century. The Chiesa della Trinità or della Badia also has a pointed-arch portal (15th century). The stone retable inside, by Gian Domenico Gagini (approx. 1503–67), depicts the front of a temple in whose triangular pediment one can see an image of God the Father. The wall is divided into five bays by richly ornamented pilasters; massive cornices separate the three storeys. Gagini placed 23 scenes from the life of Christ in the resulting fields.

Gangi

The remote little mountain town of Gangi (approx. 20km/12mi to the east, population 7100) started as a Sicel settlement. Some of the rock caves, which were probably made by the original inhabitants, survive, but they are now fronted with façades and can therefore not be made out. The town is dominated by the Gothic campanile of the Chiesa di San Nicola (14th century). The Chiesa Madre (17th century), the Norman Gothic Torre Ventimiglia on Piazza del Popolo as well as a few palaces, including Palazzo Bongiorno (18th century) are of interest.

Geraci Siculo

After this detour, return and make your way to Geraci Siculo (1000m/3280ft, population 2000) on the SS 286. The town, founded by the Arabs in the 9th century, was the seat of the Ventimiglia, a noble family, in the Middle Ages. Anyone with an interest in falcons should visit the rebuilt falconry.

Castelbuono A genuine insider tip for some rest and relaxation and a starting point for wonderful walks in the holly woods at Piano Pomo is Castelbuono (423m/1388ft, population 9000) at the foot of Pizzo della Carbonara (1979m/6493ft). During Byzantine times the place was called Ypsigro, and under the Arabs, Ruqqat Basili. The town is home to not one, but two costume festivals, the »Ntaccalora e lu triunfu di la manna« in May and the »L'Arrucata di li Ventimiglia« in August, and is dominated by the castle, which was built in 1316 in the style of the Hohenstaufen fortresses; it was the seat of the counts, since 1595 of the House of Ventimiglia. It houses the Cappella di Sant'Anna with stucco ornamentation by Giuseppe Serpotta (1683), and the Museo Civico with archaeological collections. In 1350 the Chiesa Matrice Vecchia was built. It has a double nave with aisles, and a retable by Pietro Ruzzolone. The Chiesa Matrice Nuova has a painted crucifix that dates back to the time around 1500 (also on the piazza). The Chiesa San Francesco houses the burial chapel of the Ventimiglia family, an octagonal structure with an elaborate portal, dating back to around 1500.

Isnello Isnello is a popular starting point for hikes and in winter for the ski station Piano Battaglia (1648m/5407ft). The remains of a medieval castle dominate the mountain village. The cathedral of San Nicolò was built in the 15th century; the wooden crucifix in the Leonardo chapel (to the right of the entrance) in the late medieval Chiesa San Michele was made by Fra Umile da Petralia. The village of **Gratteri** (14km/8.5mi to the west) is worth a detour, as it is sited like a balcony with wonderful view. A worthwhile panoramic walk around Monte Puraccia begins here.
Go past **Collesano** (20km/12mi to the west; Chiesa Madre 15th–16th century), a further holiday resort, and Campofelice di Roccella to get to the starting point of this round trip through the Monti Madoníe.

★ Mózia · San Pantaleo

C 5

Province: Trápani	**Altitude:** Sea level

Mózia, the Carthaginian settlement of Motya, lies on the small, circular island north of Marsala that is now known as San Pantaleo. It belongs to the foundation of the Whitaker family, who became wealthy by selling Marsala. They initiated the excavation of the ancient site.

Coming from ►Marsala, take the coastal road 10km/6mi northwards **Getting here** to Contrada Spagnola, then turn towards the sea. There are two places where ferries depart: the Imbarcadero storico quay with a small nature conservation office, as well as the second departure location 500m/550yd away at Saline Ettore e Infersa (bus number 4 from Marsala stops here). The crossing takes ten minutes.

The location of the island, which measures just 600 x 700m/ **History** 650 x 770yd, in the middle of a lagoon protected against the open sea by the elongated Isola Grande, was the reason why a Phoenician settlement was located here as early as the 8th century BC. In addition to ►Palermo and Soluntum, it served Carthage, when it had to retreat in the face of Greek colonization, as a base in western Sicily for centuries. In 397 BC Motya was conquered by Dionysus I of Syracuse. In 396 it was won back by the Carthaginians, but then voluntarily abandoned and replaced by the powerful sea fort of Lilybaion (modern-day Marsala). These days wine is grown on the island, which was named after St Pantaleon in the Middle Ages.

Mózia San Pantaleo

★ Excavations

Excavations were undertaken for the first time in 1906 by Joseph Whitaker. Since then a picture of this ancient town has developed. It is the only one in Sicily with remains from the Carthaginian period. During a tour visitors will see sizeable sections of the 2.5km/ 1.5mi town wall with its 20 towers and bastions; further in the heart of the island is the museum, in the south the Casa die Mosaici, built after the destruction of 397 BC, which features early Hellenic black and white pebble mosaics (from around 300 BC) as well as the south gate and an artificial inland port (**Kothon**) measuring 40 x 50m/ 45 x 55yd, which served as a docking site.

Discovered on the west coast were two necropolises with small stone ◄ Necropolises tombs for the urns containing the cremated remains, and, to the south, the sacred compound (known as »Tophet«) with the remains of a small Temple of Baal. This is where the first-born sons and, later, small animals were sacrificed.

The excavation area of Cappiddazzu is further north. It has a monu- ◄ Cappiddazzu mental Temple of Tanit, Carthage's chief goddess. Sizeable remains of the foundations and some ashlar masonry as well as individual mosaics survive. There is an ancient road with two lanes leading from here to the nearby north coast. The Sicilian historian Diodorus reported that there was a route from the island to the mainland (at modern-day Birgi) and to the necropolis there; this route is now just under water, but is still used by the farmers of Birgi from time to time. It begins near the **Porta Nord**, of which impressive fragments remain. This northern gate, along with two flanking towers and three successive double gates, was a powerful defensive structure. To the right there are seven stone box tombs arranged in an east-west direction.

north coast ►

Museum
Opening hours:
Daily 9am – 1pm
in summer also
3pm – 6.30pm

The discoveries of Motya, of the necropolis near Birgi on the mainland and some of the ones from Lilybaeum are on display in an archaeological museum in ►Palermo, others in the museum in ►Marsala and the remainder in the museum on the island itself. Opposite the entrance is a large relief with two lions defeating a bull. The quantity of Carthaginian tombstones and ceramics is considerable. The most significant museum exhibit is a **marble statue** that was discovered in 1978. Somewhat larger than life, it is perfectly preserved apart from its arms and feet. It is the statue of a youth in a tight-fitting pleated gown; he is wearing a wide band around his chest, which, like the gown itself, is reminiscent of Carthaginian influences. While the body hinted at through the gown seems softer, the head has been worked in the manner of the »severe style« of classical Greek sculpture; the crown of the head is only roughly modelled and has been fitted with bronze rods – clear signs that a metal object (helmet, crown?) was once here. Interpretations have included a senior magistrate, a priest or a deity (maybe Heracles/Melquart). What is certain is that the work was made of Greek marble in the second quarter of the 5th century BC – i.e. at the same time as the sculptures for the Temple of Zeus in Olympia – by a Greek sculptor for a Carthaginian client.

The Youth of Motya, a masterpiece from the 5th century BC

On the road close to the coast towards Birgi there are **salt pans**, which continue all the way to ► Tràpani with their gleaming white salt flats and windmills. This old method of obtaining salt through evaporation is in demand again, especially in more refined cuisine.

Nicosìa

O 6

Province: Enna   **Altitude:** 700m/2300ft
Population: 15,000

Nicosìa, built on several summits, is a characteristic mountain town. It developed around a (now ruined) Norman castle that Count Roger I built after he defeated the Arabs here in 1062.

What to See in and Around Nicosìa

In the town centre is the cathedral of San Nicola, whose Gothic façade and campanile with mullioned windows and painted beams date back to its foundation. The aisled interior contains sculptures by Gagini, pews from 1622 and a crucifix by Fra Umile da Petralia (17th century). In the 13th-century church of Santa Maria Maggiore, which was given a Baroque overhaul after a landslide in 1757, there is a marble polyptych by A. Gagini (1512, *Story of the Holy Virgin*) as well as the throne of Charles V. The Dominican church of San Vincenzo Ferreri has a ceiling fresco by the Flemish painter Guglielmo (Wilhelm) Borremans dating from 1717: it depicts the Holy Trinity crowning Saint Vincent Ferrer.

Nicosìa

Sperlinga (population 14,000) is **carved into the rock** of a bare ridge 10km/6mi to the northwest at an altitude of 750m/2460ft. It is dominated by a massive Norman castle that is accessed via a steep set of steps, also carved into the rock. An inscription on the archway reads »Quod Siculis placuit sola Sperlinga negavit« (»Sperlinga alone refused what pleased the Sicilians«) – a reference to the fact that this town gave the persecuted French a place of refuge after the »Sicilian Vespers« of 1282. There are several residential caves around the castle, some of which were still in use in the 1960s.

Sperlinga

? DID YOU KNOW ...?

■ There are more than 200 castles on Sicily. The most significant are those built by Frederick II, including the tower in Enna. The castle in Sperlinga is fascinating. It looks more like an architectural molehill: the entire sandstone hill was hollowed out with passages and rooms from Neolithic times onwards. The town's name comes from spelunca, the Latin word for cave.

Troina, 26km/16mi west of Nicosìa and one of the highest towns on Sicily (1120m/3675ft, population 9700) can be visited on a round

Troina

tour through the Nebrodi Mountains. Somewhat to the south there was a Sicel town in Antiquity, which may have been called Engyon. In 876 the Arabs took Troina; in 1062 they were replaced by the Norman count Roger I. He chose Troina to be his residence at first, and later it became the base for Norman military campaigns. In 1088 Roger I and Pope Urban II met here (at the second encounter in Salerno ten years later, Count Roger was granted the apostolic legateship). There is a 15th-century Norman tower and the Chiesa Madre (Neoclassical façade). The main church on the town's highest point – a spot with far-reaching views – is one of the earliest Norman churches on Sicily, because it was in Troina that the Normans founded the first Latin bishopric in 1080 (Messina: 1096). The only medieval remains are the transept walls and the bell tower. The apses have been demolished. The reservoir **Lago di Ancipa** (7km/4.5mi to the northwest) fills the valley of the Troina River.

► Norman eyrie

Cesarò

The mountain town of Cesarò (1150m/3773ft, 20km/12mi northeast of Troina) possesses the ruins of a castle that belonged the noble Roman Colonna family, who owned Cesarò as its fief. Immediately to the west of town is the mountain village of San Teodoro.

★ ★ Noto

S 11

Province: Siracusa   **Altitude:** 105m/344ft
Population: 24,000

Noto is one of the most beautiful Baroque towns in Sicily and a UNESCO World Heritage site. However, it is difficult to preserve as such, a fact proved by the scaffolding that can be seen all around.

The Sicel settlement of Neetum (modern-day Noto Antica) was located around 20km/12mi from the coast at around 400m/1312ft above the valley of the Arsinaro. From the Arab period onwards, southeastern Sicily was named after the town of Val di Noto. Noto replaced Syracuse as the provincial capital and kept this leading role until 1865. The earthquake of 1693 destroyed the town so comprehensively that, upon the suggestion of Count Landolina from Syracuse, it was abandoned and re-founded closer to the coast – unfortunately on the edge of a plateau that is not geologically stable, as the most recent earthquake of 1990 proved. In 1703 the architects Rosario Gagliardi, Paolo Labisi, Antonio Mazza and Vincenzo Sinatra created the town plan to which Noto owes its uniform appearance. The basis of the plan is a rectangular grid pattern with three main axes that run along the slope at different heights in an east-west direction: Via Ducezio, Corso Vittorio Emanuele with two imposing squares and Via Cavour. A further axis, running perpendicular to

► Rebirth after disaster

▶ VISITING NOTO

INFORMATION

Ufficio Informazioni Turistiche
Piazza XVI Maggio
96017 Noto
Tel. 09 31 83 67 44
Fax 09 31 57 37 79
www.comune.noto.sr.it

EVENTS

Primavera Barocca on the third Sunday in May with concerts and a historical procession. The highlight is the L'Infiorata, a carpet of flowers in Via Nicolaci.
End of July to mid-August: classical music festival

WHERE TO EAT

▶ Moderate

① **Trattoria del Crocifisso**
Via Principe Umberto 48
Tel. 09 31 57 11 51
Closed Wed; recommended family-run establishment in the upper town; regional, seasonal dishes

② **Trattoria del Carmine**
Via Ducezio 1
Tel. 09 31 83 87 05
www.trattoriadelcarmine.it
Closed Mon; popular family-run business that has won several awards

WHERE TO STAY

▶ Mid-range

① **Della Ferla**
Via Antonio Gramsci 5
Tel. 09 31 57 60 07
Fax 09 31 83 63 60
www.hotelferla.it
15 spacious rooms near the station

Lido di Noto · Villa Mediterranea
Viale Lido
Tel. 09 31 81 23 30
Fax 09 31 81 23 30

www.villamediterranea.it
15 rooms; small hotel with a garden by the sea

Contrada Porcari · Masseria degli Ulivi
Tel. 09 31 81 30 19 www.masseriadegliulivi.com; 16 rooms
Luxuriously refurbished estate north of Noto with every creature comfort (east of the SS 287)

▶ Budget

② **Al Canisello**
Via Pavese 1
Tel. 09 31 83 57 93
fax 09 31 83 77 00
www.villacanisello.it
6 rooms; in a somewhat hidden location at the southwestern end of town, in the wings of a former farm; nice garden

③ **Villa Ambra**
Via F. Giantommaso 14
Tel. & fax 09 31 83 55 54
www.roomsambra.com
8 rooms in comfortable surroundings, 10-minute walk to the town centre

Marzamemi · La Conchiglietta
Via Regina Elena 9
Tel. 09 31 84 11 91,
www.laconchiglietta.it
17 rooms; small hotel close to the sea

Portopalo · Villaggio Turistico Capo Pássero
Via Tagliamento 22, tel.
09 31 84 20 30, www.capopassero.it
Basic apartment village

Portopalo · Hotel Jonic
Via V. Emanuele 19, tel. 09 31 84
27 23, www.jonichotel.com
12 clean, large rooms with sea views

! Baedeker TIP

Excellent dolci and granita
In the well-known café Sicilia, run by the brothers Carlo and Corrado Assenza, the menu lists a large number of classic and new dolci, ice creams and granita, jams and other sweet temptations (Corso Vittorio Emanuele 125).

these roads (Via Principe Umberto), runs up the hill. This grid pattern was filled with churches and palaces that are evidence of the individual diversity possible while maintaining stylistic unity; thanks to the region's light limestone tufa that was used as the construction material, they feel festive and cheerful.

What to See in Noto

Corso Vittorio Emanuele
Welcomed by an extensive park (Giardino Pubblico), leave the car park in the east of town westwards and walk along Corso Vittorio Emanuele to get to the heart of the town, to Piazza del Municipio. On the way, stop to look at Porta Nazionale or Reale (by Orazio Angelini, a student of Canova; 1843) and the first monumental set of buildings, the Franciscan church of San Francesco or Chiesa dell'Immacolata by R. Gagliardi (1734) with the adjoining convent. The church façade is comparatively simple, in line with the order's tradition (the same is true for the aisleless interior with its pilasters), but its impact is heightened by its position above a large flight of steps.
To the left of San Francesco is the imaginatively designed rear façade of the monastery of Santissimo Salvatore, which now houses the **Museo Civico** (entrance on Piazza del Municipio). It exhibits an archaeological collection as well as modern art.

Piazza del Municipio
The town hall and the cathedral stand opposite each other on Piazza del Municipio. The town hall is at the square's southern end in Palazzo Ducezio, named after the Sicel leader Ducetius. Vincenzo Sinatra built the elegant palace in 1746.

Cathedral of Santi Nicola e Corrado
Looking through the arcades that open up the palace façade, you will see the cathedral of Santi Nicola e Corrado, which stands majestically atop a flight of steps on the other side of the road. Completed in 1770 and an episcopal church only since 1844, it stands out because of its magnificent twin-tower façade. The splendid portal (1982, by G. F. Pirrone) depicts the life of Saint Conrad, whose silver urn is housed in the chapel of the south aisle. The interior is topped by a large crossing dome, which collapsed in March 1996 together with the aisles (rebuilt in 2006). To the right next to the cathedral is the bishop's palace, adjoining it the former abbey church of Santissimo Salvatore. Opposite is the church of Santa Chiara with a block-like façade and an oval interior (R. Gagliardi).

Chiesa dell Collegio
Further along the corso in a westward direction, passing the Jesuit church of Chiesa dell Collegio (c. 1740, probably by R. Gagliardi) we

Noto Map

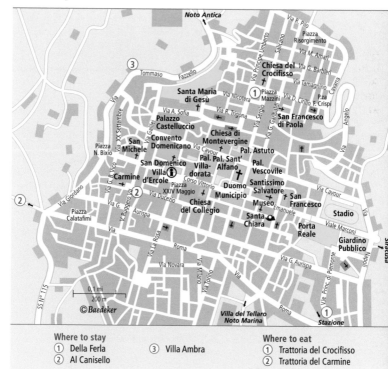

Where to stay
① Della Ferla
② Al Canisello
③ Villa Ambra

Where to eat
① Trattoria del Crocifisso
② Trattoria del Carmine

come to Piazza XVI Maggio with a Hercules fountain (tourist information) and the Chiesa di San Domenico. Begun in 1737 to designs by R. Gagliardi, it has an imposing convex façade, behind which there is an aisled interior with a central dome supported by a tambour. The Teatro Comunale Vittorio Emanuele in the southwest of the square was only built in 1860.

Return to the junction with Via Nicolaci (left), where the Palazzo Villadorata by P. Labisi (1737) attracts attention with its elaborately sculpted balcony supports.

Palazzo Villadorata

At the northern end the road is completed by the Chiesa di Montevergine, a building with a concave façade by V. Sinatra (1762). To the right, next to the neighbouring Palazzo Astuto, is the stepped street to the upper town.

Chiesa di Montevergine

Via Salicano leads to Piazza Mazzini, whose north side is dominated by Chiesa del Crocifisso. The building was constructed in around

Upper town

Original façade ornamentation on Palazzo Villadorata

1715. The two lions supporting columns in the portal of the incomplete façade date back to Roman times. There is a medieval lion in the church (in front of the first pillar on the right) and on the altar of the south transept a marble Madonna della Neve by Francesco Laurana (1471). The choir is dominated by a monumental cross.

Around Noto

Noto Antica The ancient town that preceded Noto, Noto Antica, is situated 16km/10mi to the northwest (SS 287 towards Palazzo Acréide; after 10km/6mi to the left past the pilgrimage monastery of Convento di Scala). It was abandoned after the devastating earthquake of 1693. A walk amid the ruins and the scent of maquis is a relaxing outing.

San Corrado di Fuori The place of pilgrimage dedicated to the patron saint of Noto, San Corrado di Fuori, is located 5km/3mi north of Noto, on SS 287.

Lido di Noto The sandy beach of the small seaside resort 7km/4.5mi southeast of Noto, also known as Noto Marina, stretches all the way to Eloro.

Eloro (2km/1mi south of Lido di Noto) is the ancient Helorus at the mouth of the Tellaro. Some of the ancient town survives in the form of town walls (6th–5th centuries BC), the theatre, a Temple of Demeter as well as the 9m/30ft column of a Hellenic tomb, the Colonna Pizzuta.

Eloro

▶Ávola, 8km/5mi northeast of Noto.

Ávola

There was a prehistoric village of the 2nd millennium BC here, in which tombs and cult objects of the Castelluccio culture (named after the location) were found (exhibited in the museum in ▶Syracuse; to get here from Noto 7km/4.5mi southwestwards on SS 115, then turn right heading northwest for a further 16km/10 mi.)

Castelluccio

The mosaics of the late Roman villa (4th century AD), returned after many years from Syracuse, are serious competition for the World Heritage site of ▶Piazza Armerina. They depict mythological and hunting motifs (to get here, take the country road from Noto to Pachino, 2km/1mi beyond the bridge over the Tellaro turn right to the Caddeddi estate, signposted; daily 9am–8pm).

★
Villa del Tellaro

⊙

12km/7mi south of Noto, from the ruins of the ancient Helorus, an 8km/5mi stretch of protected coastline (Riserva di **Vendicari**; with hiking trails and swimming bays) runs almost all the way to Marzamemi. Rare wading birds can be seen in the dunes, wooded areas and on the Pantani, salty lagoons. The main entrance is located on the road to Pachino.

> ## ! *Baedeker* TIP
>
> ### Sandy beaches and snorkelling
>
> A paradise for birds, fine sandy beaches, crystal-clear water as well as various waymarked hiking trails make the nature reserve of Vendicari, north of Marzamemi, in front of Isola di Capo Pássero and Isola delle Correnti a great place to visit (Apr–Oct 9am–6pm, otherwise only until 5pm, www.oasivendicari.net).

The small holiday resort of Marzamemi, 5km/3mi to the northeast of Pachino, was discovered by the director Luchino Visconti in the 1970s. There is an old tonnara (tuna processing factory). Fishing is still an important source of income.

Marzamemi

The **Grotta Calafarina** lies along the attractive stretch of coastline in which Stone Age tools were found. The next town is Portopalo, which is prettily situated on Cape Pássero. It is the harbour of an important fishing fleet. The coast with its strong current is rich in fish, which makes the town popular with divers. There is a holiday village above the cliffs. The town does not have a long beach, but it does have small bathing bays. The swimming and diving are good on the Isola di Capo Pássero (fishing boats go there in the summer) and approx. 6km/4mi to the south, opposite the Isola delle Correnti.

Portopalo

Marzamemi, discovered by Luchino Visonti as a filming location

Pachino The town in the far southeastern corner of Sicily (6.5km/4mi north of Portopalo, population 21,400) lives from making wine. The now-so-popular cherry tomatoes, pomodorini di Pachino, also grow here. Together with Ávola, Grammichele and Noto, it is one of the planned new towns of the Baroque period. It has an grid street pattern around a square central piazza, where the church of Santissimo Crocifisso stands (18th century).

✳ Palazzolo Acréide

Province: Siracusa   **Altitude:** 670m/2200ft
Population: 9000

The small Baroque town of Palazzolo, 35km/22mi west of Syracuse, is attractively situated in the Monti Iblei above the river valleys of the Tellaro and the Anapo. It took over from the ancient Akrai, which has been partially excavated to the southwest of town.

Akrai was the first colony to be set up by Syracuse in 664 BC. In the 12th century the Normans modernized the settlement and from then on it was called Palazzolo. In 1693 it fell victim to the devastating earthquake.

▶ VISITING PALAZZOLO ACRÉIDE

INFORMATION

Ufficio Informazione
Piazza del Popolo 7
96010 Palazzolo Acreide Tel.
09 31 47 21 81
www.palazzolo-acreide.it

EVENTS

Free & outdoors: an international student theatre festival takes place in the ancient theatre at the end of May (www.festivaldeigiovanipalazzolo.it).

WHERE TO EAT

▶ **Moderate**
Da Andrea
Via Maddalena 24, tel. 09 31 88 14 88 closed Tue; small restaurant with regional specialities and pizzas

WHERE TO STAY

▶ **Mid-range/Budget**
Senatore
Largo Senatore Italia, tel. 09 31 88 34 43, www.albergosenatore. com, 21 rooms; friendly, modern medium-sized hotel

Palazzolo Acréide and Around

From Piazza del Municipio with its Neoclassical town hall, a staircase leads up to the magnificent church of San Sebastiano (1609). Next to the town hall, at the start of Corso Vittorio Emanuele, is the Baroque Palazzo Judica, which contains particularly beautiful examples of the imaginatively designed balcony corbels of Sicilian Baroque palaces. The Chiesa dell'Immacolata at the end of Corso Vittorio Emanuele houses a Madonna and Child by Francesco Laurana (1470). San Paolo (Piazza Roma) probably derives from a design by Vincenzo Sinatra (1750). The remarkable façade features free-standing columns, an atrium accessed through wide round arches, an excessively high bell tower in the middle and opulent sculptural decorations (Epiphany and 12 Apostles). Nearby (Via Annunziata) is the church of Santissima Annunziata with a richly adorned portal, surrounded by twisted columns with Corinthian capitals, in the incomplete façade. The **Casa Museo** (Via Machiavelli 19; daily 9am – noon, 3.30pm – 7pm) is worth visiting. Antonino Uccello (1922–79) compiled an ethnographical collection in this attractive »house of memories«, including farming tools and household items, traditional costumes and crafts.

Palazzolo Acréide

The remains of the ancient town lie immediately south of Palazzolo on Acremonte hill (daily 9am to 1 hour before sunset). Recent excavations have uncovered a large road, which is crossed by near-parallel side streets. To the east of this main road is the most significant building, the **theatre** (views of Mount Etna), which was probably built in the 3rd century BC under Hiero II of Syracuse and renewed in Roman times. It only held around 700 spectators; twelve rows of seats of the Cavea are preserved, as well as the stone floor of the

★
Ancient Akrai

orchestra and the foundations of the skene. In the last week of May,

Plays ▶ students from all around the world put on ancient tragedies and comedies – unconventional and eminently watchable! Next to the theatre stands a smaller structure with rows of seating as in the theatre: the bouleuterion, the building that housed the council of citizens. Residential caves and tombs from the Byzantine period can be seen in the two ancient quarries of Intagliata and Intagliatella. There is a relief with sacrificing heroes preserved on the wall of the Intagliatella quarry. Have the custodian take you to the »life-sized« **Santoni**. They presumably date back to the 3rd century (and are located outside the complex on the road to Ragusa). The twelve weathered stone pictures are part of the cult of Cybele and depict the ancient Mother Goddess from Asia Minor surrounded by other figures, including Castor and Pollux, Hermes, Marsyas and priests in Phrygian dress.

Akrai: a stage for the past 2300 years

Giarratana The town of Giarratana (582m/1909ft; 14km/8.5mi southwest of Palazzolo Acréide on the country road to Chiaramonte Gulfi) is dominated by the basilica of Sant'Antonio (1783), which has the crowned Spanish double-headed eagle above the main portal. A staircase and terrace increase the impact of the façade, which is heavily structured with pilasters and columns; it elegantly terminates in the triple arcade of the bell storey.

Buccheri Go via »Paese museo«, the »museum village«, **Buscemi** (on the SS 124, 7km/4.5mi northwest of Palazzolo; with an educational folklore trail, Itinerario Etnoantropologico; guided tours with advance booking, tel. & fax 09 31 87 85 28) to get to Buccheri (15km/9mi northwest of Palazzolo Acréide). The small town boasts two Baroque churches: the Chiesa della Maddalena, built in 1709 to a design by Michelangelo di Giacomo, is a basilica with a richly ornamented façade, whose gable was expanded into a wide bell frame. Sant'Antonio Abbate towers atop a high staircase. The façade is defined by the tower-like, three-storey central section and the columns flanking it. It culminates in a narrower section housing the bells, which in turn is topped by a dome.

Ferla, northeast of Palazzolo Acréide (540 mm/1772ft), has a few interesting Baroque churches. The forceful façade of Sant'Antonio Abbate was never completed. The rich interior is an octagonal central space topped by a dome with the four arms of the nave, choir and transepts leading away from it, and four choirs in the diagonal too. San Sebastiano is a basilica with a crossing dome. The imaginatively designed portal culminates in the figure of the young martyr Sebastian between two devout women and two Roman legionaries. **Very good ice cream** and home-made confectionery are available in the Pasticceria Nuova Dolceria opposite San Sebastiano.

Ferla

There is an access road from Ferla to the fascinating rocky necropolis of Pantàlica (33km/21mi northeast of Palazzolo Acréide). The famous Sicel necropolis with around 5000 rock tombs is situated in the **Monti Iblei** (Hyblaean Mountains), a stunning landscape with rocky ground covered in maquis above the gorges of the Anapo and Calcinara rivers (Pantàlica can also be accessed from Sortino, but the road between Ferla and Sortino is interrupted). Well-made, signposted trails, some of which are carved into the limestone, guide visitors to the rock tombs. The oldest were made in around 1270 BC, the most recent in the 8th century BC, before the associated Sicel town was abandoned in around 730 BC. The oldest sections of the necropolis can be found in the north and northwest, the two more recent ones (Necropoli di Filiporto and Necropoli della Cavetta) in the south. During early Christian times some of the rock tombs were inhabited and some were made into chapels.

Pantàlica
UNESCO World Heritage site

 Baedeker TIP

Like honeycombs in stone
The Sicel capital was once located on the plateau in the hinterland of Syracuse. Trails and steps carved into the rock make their way through the magnificent landscape. There are maps at the entrances; for a hiking suggestion, see p. 137ff. (take sufficient food and water).

The settlement associated with this necropolis, the Sicel capital, was situated in the middle of the individual sections of the necropolis, high up above the **Anapo Valley** and the **Cava Grande** of the Calcinara river. Only the **Anaktoron** of this settlement has been excavated, a palace dating from around 1100 BC, whose floor plan is often compared to the megaron form of Mycenaean origin. The remains of a bronze smithy were discovered in one of the rooms of the Anaktoron (there is a car park below the Anaktoron, which is also where the walk down to the Anapo gorge begins).

The sensational discoveries from the necropolis of Pantàlica are in the archaeological museum of Syracuse (▶ Siracusa). In addition to bones, archaeologists discovered ceramics and metalwork, which suggest that the Sicels traded with Mycenaean Greece, as well as a gold treasure from Byzantine times.

★ ★ Palermo

I 4

Provincial capital
Population: 656,000

Altitude: 14m/46 ft

The porphyry tomb of the Hohenstaufen emperor Frederick II, red domes from mosques atop Norman churches, the mystical golden sheen of Byzantine mosaics, beautiful palaces, gardens with palm trees and Italy's largest opera house: Palermo, Sicily's chaotic, lively capital in the Golden Shell (Conca d'Oro) at the foot of Monte Pellegrino, has plenty of tourist attractions in store.

Despite the noticeable rise in affluence over the past decade, wealth and privation still exist side by side here – a world of contrasts, an amalgam of the heterogeneous. Palermo also has the lowest per capita income in the whole of Italy, high youth unemployment, Mafia building speculation and an unsightly ring of apartment blocks all around the city, deprived neighbourhoods with ruins from the Second World War right in the centro storico. Nevertheless Palermo is a fascinating city that thrusts visitors into the midst of life. The colourful shimmer of freshly caught fish, pyramids of the fruits of the cherry laurel, blood oranges, medlars, mandarins and pale green snake gourds, neatly piled up every morning, as well as the oriental sounds of the old-town markets of Vucciria and Mercato del Capo, the punching and stabbing of the wooden puppets in the puppet theatre shows in the evenings: often the people and their southern ways are more exciting than the monuments of glorious days. This city at the heart of the Mediterranean combines African and northern elements to produce something Sicilian.

The heights and the depths: Sicily's capital

> ! **Baedeker TIP**
>
> ### Between art and kitsch
> **Via Bara all'Olivella**, a narrow street between the Archaeological Museum and the opera, is a bazaar. Old puppets, modern plastic carretti and Mafia folklore can be found here. The wood and papier-mâché artist **Paolo Seminara** creates miniature masterpieces of the greatest precision; he has won many awards for his work (Via Bara all'Olivella 60, tel. 0 91 33 38 40).

The name Palermo comes from the Arab word baerm, which in turn derives from the Greek Panormo (all-harbour). The name therefore expresses three historical eras that shaped the city. It has its origin in a time when the Carthaginians had one of their most important cities on Sicily here; in those days the people spoke of Ziz (the flower) and Machanat (camp).

◄ The orange groves of the Golden Shell

Mahannad (the big field) refers to the fertile Conca d'Oro, surrounded by mountains, which is still used for growing oranges and

◄ Phoenicians and Carthaginians

← *The cathedral points the way in Palermo's labyrinth of streets and roads.*

lemons wherever the expanding city has not reached. In the 7th century BC the Phoenicians founded a settlement on the harbour bay; later it was a Carthaginian base during their conflicts with the Greeks. In 480 BC Hamilcar anchored here before his campaign against Mimera; in 260 BC Hannibal had his base here during the First Punic War. In 258 the Romans tried to conquer the town, but to no avail. In 254 they then did manage to take Panormo/Panormus in a combined land and sea operation. During the Roman period, Panormus, with its Greek, Carthaginian and Roman population, remained one of the island's most significant cities. Setbacks were suffered in the 5th century AD, when the Vandals and the Ostrogoths conquered Palermo. The town also remained without special significance after Belisarius conquered it for Byzantium in AD 535.

7th century BC	Phoenicians found a settlement on the harbour bay.
AD 831	Saracens conquer Panormus. As Balerm it becomes the capital of the emirs of Sicily.
1072–1194	The Normans conquer the island, Palermo becomes the capital.
1198	Four-year-old Frederick II is crowned in Palermo
1266–1860	A succession of rulers; in 1860 Palermo is taken by Garibaldi; union with Italy

Succession of rulers ▶

The city only became significant in AD 831 when the **Saracens** conquered Palermo under their general Ibn el Athir. It took over from Syracuse as the dominant city, and as Balerm was made the capital of the emirs of Sicily. Travel reports compared it to Baghdad and Cordoba because of its many mosques and palaces as well as its irrigation systems. The population rose to more than 100,000. Apart from the descendants of the indigenous population, Arabs, Jews, Greeks and Africans lived side by side.

On 5 January 1072 the **Norman** conquest began under Roger I of Hauteville and his brother Robert Guiscard, the start of a new era. Roger II and William II turned Palermo into the glorious capital of the Monarchia Sicula in the 12th century, building churches and palaces; they ruled with religious tolerance over Christians, Muslims and Jews.

In 1194 the **House of Hohenstaufen** took over from the Normans, led by Emperor Henry VI, the husband of Constance, heiress of the Norman kings. As was the case under the Normans, various nationalities and religions were represented at his court. Here emerged the Sicilian school of poetry, which for the first time wrote in the vernacular. After the death, in 1250, of Frederick, who had resided in Apulia in his later years, the decline began. In 1266 Charles of Anjou, the brother of the French king, became the ruler of Sicily with the help of the pope. But just 16 years later in 1282 the »Sicilian Vespers« be-

Sicilian Vespers ▶ gan in Palermo in front of the church of Santo Spirito. This uprising

◀ Sicilian Vespers

forced out the French (▶ Baedeker Special p. 42). Palermo, along with the rest of Sicily, went to the kings of Aragon, who were represented by viceroys.

In the 18th century the dynasties of Savoy (1713–20), Habsburg (1720–30) and Bourbon (from 1730) took over in succession. The discrepancy between rich barons and the poor masses led to a revolt in 1773 (as it had in 1647). Attempts at reform, such as those by viceroys like Caràcciolo (1782–86), did not make lasting improvements. During the Napoleonic era the British occupied the island (1806–15). Ferdinand IV of Naples lived twice in exile here, before becoming King of the Two Sicilies in 1815 as Ferdinand I. In 1821,

Palermo Overview

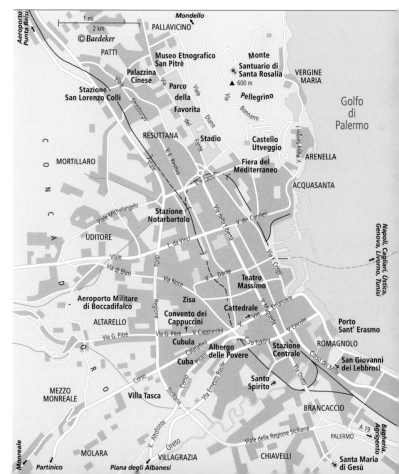

1837 and 1848 there were rebellions against the Bourbon regime. In May 1860 Garibaldi took Palermo in a four-day battle, whereupon it joined Italy.

From January to March 1943 Palermo was the target of Allied bombing. In 1946 Rome gave the island of Sicily the rights of an autonomous region. Since then Palermo's population has increased because of rural exodus; the harbour was expanded and industry has grown. Nevertheless Palermo has the lowest per capita income of all Italian provincial capitals. In addition to a university, Palermo is home to several cultural institutions.

VISITING PALERMO

INFORMATION

Ufficio Turistico
Piazza Castelnuovo 34
90141 Palermo
Tel. 09 16 05 83 51, fax 0 91 58 63 38
www.palermotourism.com
At the airport: tel. 0 91 59 16 98

Punti d'Informazioni stands on Piazza Bellini, Piazza Indipendenza, in Via Cavour and Via Vittorio Emanuele

EVENTS

The whole of Palermo is transformed into a spectacle during »U Festinu«, the festival of the city's patron saint Santa Rosalia from 9 to 15 July. It features magnificent processions, concerts in squares and a splendid firework display.
Great operas in the splendour of the belle époque are performed in Teatro Massimo (Nov–May, tel. 09 16 05 31 11, www.teatromassimo.it).

GOING OUT

Movida Palermitana: the once lethargic city has acquired a lively night life. Fashionable venues are the cultural centre Lo Spasimo (Via Spasimo, tel. 09 16 16 48 66), Discoteca Kandinsky with its palm tree courtyard (Discesa Tonnara 4) and the streets around the

Museo Archeologico. Further cultural centres are Cantieri Culturali alla Zisa (Via Paolo Gili 4, tel. 09 16 52 49 42), Kursaal Kalhesa (Foro Umberto I., www.kursaalkalhesa.it) and Nuovo Montevergini, which is also home to an ambitious theatre festival (www.palermoteatrofestival.com).
The daily newspapers provide information about restaurants and current events, for example Giornale di Sicilia and La Repubblica as well as the brochures Agenda and Lapis Palermo (available from tourist information offices).

TRANSPORT

Airport (Aeroporto) Falcone e Borsellino, 30km/20mi to the west, taxi ride to the centre approx. 40 euros; regular bus connection and the metro to the central station (Stazione Centrale).
There are orange AMAT buses (tickets from tobacconists, newsagents and central ticket offices, e.g. at the central station) on Palermo's main streets, such as Via Roma and Viale della Libertà. City buses go to places such as the Capuchin monastery (no. 327); Monreale (389; both from Piazza Indipendenza); Mondello (806) and up Monte Pellegrino (812, both from Politeama / Piazza Sturzo).

The main attractions are best reached on foot. There are tickets valid for up to two days allowing entry to all the museums and monuments.
(Multi-storey) car parks: central station: Piazza G. Cesare 43; harbour: Via Guardione 81, Via Stabile 10; centre: Via Abela 13, Via Agrigento 42 and Via Belmonte 18.

SHOPPING

Via della Libertà is a swanky shopping street with showrooms of almost all the top labels. Food and excellent wine from Centopassi Vineyard, grown on land confiscated from convicted Mafiosi, is available in the shops »*I sapori ed i saperi della legalità*« on Piazza Castelnuovo 13, www.libera terra.it. Coppolas, flat caps that look like something out of a film, just more colourful and available without having to pay protection money, can be bought between the opera and the Archaeological Museum in La Coppola Storta (Via dell'Orologio 25, www.lacoppola.com).
Colourful food markets are all over the place in the streets of the old town. The best-known market is in Vuccirìa (p. 330). Fresh fish, fruit and vegetables as well as meat are loudly advertised on Ballarò (p. 320). The most traditional market is in the Capo district around Piazza dei Beati Paoli, where it is also possible to buy soft rolls stuffed with spleen, baked chickpeas, flatbread and fried arancine (balls of rice).
Palermo's architectural highlights, recreated in terracotta, are available in Città Cotte di Vizzari, Corso Vittorio Emanuele 120.

WHERE TO EAT

▶ Expensive

① *Osteria dei Vespri*
Piazza Croce dei Vespri 6, tel. 09 16 17 16 31, www.osteriadeivespri.it; closed Sun; princely pleasures

A fitting setting for large operatic performances: Teatro Massimo

in Palazzo Ganci; Lucchino Visconti filmed the famous ball scene in *The Leopard* on the piano nobile

② *Il Charleston*
Via Generale Vincenzo Magliocco 15 Tel. 091 45 01 71 – People come here for the elegant atmosphere and to be seen, quite apart from the food.

▶ **Moderate**
③ *Antica Focacceria San Francesco*
Via A. Paternostro 58
Tel. 091 32 03 64; closed Mon.
Traditional restaurant, serving, among other things, Palermo's classic, bread with spleen and ricotta, pizza and cucina siciliana

④ *Osteria Paradiso*
Via Serradifalco 23, tel. 36 09 41 155 Closed Sun – particularly popular with locals, good fish restaurant east of Piazza Castelnuovo

⑤ *Cibus*
Via Emerico Amari 64, tel.
091 32 30 62; open all week
This restaurant between the harbour and Teatro Politeama changes from being a bakery, a food shop, a wine shop and a restaurant over the course of the day. Large selection of wines, good regional specialities

Sferracavallo • ⑥ *Delfino*
Via Torretta 80, tel. 0 91 53 02 82 closed Mon; popular restaurant, 12km/7mi northwest of Palermo, excellent fish dishes in a simple ambience

▶ **Inexpensive**
⑦ *Mensa del Popolo*
Via Mariano Stabile 58
Tel. 0 91 32 59 43 – Pizzeria and trattoria that is also popular with the locals, in a side street of Via Roma

⑧ *Pizzeria Bellini*
Piazza Bellini 6, tel. 09 16 16 55 91 closed Mon; despite a great location with views of the red domes of San Cataldo, the quality and the prices remain acceptable

⑨ *Il Mirto e la Rosa*
▶Baedeker Tip p. 329

WHERE TO STAY
▶ **Luxury**
① *Ai Cavalieri*
Via S. Oliva 8, tel. 0 91 58 32 82 www.aicavalierihotel.it; 39 rooms.
Well-maintained hotel, in a quiet, central location. All the major sites can be reached on foot

② *Centrale Palace*
Via Vittorio Emanuele 327
Tel. 0 91 33 66 66, fax 0 91 33 48 81 www.centralepalacehotel.it; 94 rooms; in the historic centre, comfortable rooms and a great roof terrace

▶ **Mid-range**
③ *Grand Hotel Piazza Borsa*
Via dei Cartari 18 (Piazza Borsa), tel. 091 32 00 75 www.piazzaborsa.com and www.costadegliulivihotels.it
Wonderfully central location, elegant hotel in a building designed by Art Nouveau architect Ernesto Basile; with the very good restaurant Kemonia

④ *Posta*
Via A. Gagini 77, tel. 0 91 58 73 38 www.hotelpostapalermo.it; 27 rooms
Pleasant family-run hotel, modern and functional interior, quiet

⑤ *Letizia*
Via Bottai 30, tel. & fax 091 58 91 10 www.hotelletizia.com; 13 rooms
Over the years this place has become more and more refined; great location

in the old town, a stone's throw from Piazza Marina

▶ **Budget**

⑥ *Cavour*
Via Alessandro Manzoni 11
Tel. & fax 09 16 16 27 59; 10 rooms
www.albergocavour.com – Very clean one-star hotel by the station, rooms with and without en-suite bathrooms, pleasant family atmosphere

⑦ *Cortese*
Via Scarparelli 16
Tel. 0 91 33 17 22
Fax 0 91 33 17 22
www.hotelcortese.net; 25 beds
Basic accommodation in the birthplace of Count Cagliostro in the labyrinthine old town near Ballarò market

West of Quattro Canti

The starting point is Piazza **Quattro Canti**, »Four Corners«, built between 1608 and 1620 by the Roman architect Giulio Lasso; it is also known as Piazza Vigliena. It was the intersection between the two most important streets in Palermo at the time: Cassàro (now Via Vittorio Emanuele), which runs from the Norman palace to the harbour, and Via Nuova, ceremonially begun in 1608 (later given the name of the Spanish viceroy Maqueda). Lasso placed a concave palace façade at each of the four »corners«; behind one of them is the **church of San Giuseppe dei Teatini**. Between two vertical rows of windows he built a fountain on the ground floor as well as sculptures on three storeys, which are flanked by columns in the sequence of the classical Greek orders: Doric at the bottom, above it Ionic, and Corinthian at the top. Since their completion occurred after 1620, the sculptures above the four seasons (they adorn the fountain) depict the Spanish kings after 1516: Charles V, Philip II, Philip III and Philip IV. The patron saints Cristina, Ninfa, Oliva and Àgata can be found at the top.

> ❗ *Baedeker* TIP
>
> **Out and about in Palermo**
> If you are good at haggling, a carriage ride is also an affordable way of exploring Palermo (Calesse from Teatro Massimo and Norman palace) or there is the Ape Calessino, the successor of the classic tricycle (tel. 38 81 16 47 72, 32 76 28 64 97).

San Giuseppe dei Teatini

The basilica of San Giuseppe dei Teatini was built between 1612 and 1645 to a design by Giacomo Besio (dome dating from 1725); the fresco inside the dome, *The Triumph of Sant'Andrea Avellino*, was painted by Guglielmo (Willelm) Borremans (1724). Paintings by Pietro Novelli and the late 18th-century scagliola interior are also of note. The convent buildings now house the Geological Museum and the University Library. The neighbouring **Palazzo Belmonte Riso** houses the Museo d'Arte Moderna e Contemporanea (Museum of Modern and Contemporary Art; Via V. Emanuele 365; tel. 091 32 05 32).

◄ www.palazzoriso.it

Palermo Map

Porto

heto

china Sammuzzo

Barchina Trapezoidale

Molo Sud

Ustica, Cagliari, Livorno,
Napoli, Genova, Tunisi

Capitaneria
di Porto

750 ft
300 m
©Baedeker

La Cala

Archivio   Porta
di Stato   Felice
Santa Maria
Santa   della Catena   P.za
Maria   S. Spirito
Porto   Vittorio   della Cala
Salvo   Emanuele
Museo delle
Piazza   Marionette
Giardino   Palazzo
Garibaldi   Chiaramonte
Bottai   Marina
5   Villa
Palazzo   Santa Maria   La Pietà   a Mare
Mirto   dei Miracoli
Francesco   Palazzo Abatellis
ssisi   La Gancia   Galleria Nazionale
Via   P.za d.
Santa   Kalsa
Teresa
P.za
KALSA   S. Euno
Via d. Spasimo
La Magione   Santa Maria   Villa
alazzo   P.za   dell' Spasimo   Giulia
iutamicristo   Magione
Lincoln
Via Abramo Lincoln
Giardino
Tropicale   Solunt. Bagheria
Abramo   Orto
Botanico
Via Archirafi
Stazione
Centrale
Corso dei Mille
Via Tiro a Segno Nazionale
Ponte dell' Ammiraglio,
San Giovanni dei Lebbrosi

Where to stay
1. Ai Cavalieri
2. Centrale Palace
3. Grand Hotel
   Piazza Borsa
4. Posta
5. Letizia
6. Cavour
7. Cortese

Where to eat
1. Osteria dei Vespri
2. Il Charleston
3. Antica Focacceria
   San Francesco
4. Osteria Paradiso
5. Cibus
6. Delfino
7. Mensa del Popolo
8. Pizzeria Bellini
9. Il Mirto e la Rosa

Highlights *Palermo*

Chiesa del Gesù The oldest Sicilian Jesuit church stands on Piazza Casa Professa. Construction started in 1564. It was then lavishly adorned with reliefs and sculptures made of stucco and marble in the 17th and 18th centuries. In the apse there is a Holy Trinity in the centre, flanked by two marble groups by Gioacchino Vitagliano (1704): Abigail kneeling before David (left), Abraham and Melchizedek (right), two of the paintings in the second chapel on the right are by P. Novelli. The church was reconstructed after serious bomb damage in 1943. The city library is housed in the former monastery buildings.

Mercato Ballarò ✳ It is possible to immerse yourself in the everyday life of the people just a few steps away on Ballarò Market (all around the piazza of the same name), which features stalls with fruit and vegetables piled high.

Piazza Bologni Via Vittorio Emanuele opens up into Piazza Bologni, which is surrounded by the Baroque palaces of the aristocracy and is also home to a monument to Emperor Charles V by Scipione Li Volsi (1631; anti-Luther inscription). Opposite is the Rococo **Palazzo Belmonte-Riso** by Giovanni Venanzio Marvuglia (1784). Not far from here, close to the cathedral, is the National Library (1586).

✱ ✱ Cathedral

This monumental structure stands on the site of a Christian basilica of the 6th century, which was then replaced by a mosque. In Norman times, archbishop Walter of the Mill (Gualterius Offamilius) from England decided that a new church should be built that would embody the archbishop of Palermo's claim to power (which caused William II to build »his« cathedral in ▶ Monreale just 8km/5mi away). Construction of the extremely elongated basilica began in 1170/1172 (consecration in 1185). Later on, the cathedral was altered several times, in the 14th and 15th centuries in the Gothic style, but particularly between 1781 and 1804 when Ferdinando Fuga redesigned the interior in a cool Neoclassical style, while adding the dome and a second transept.

Norman cathedral

🕐

Opening hours:
9am – 5.30pm
in winter there is a
lunch break

www.cattedrale.
palermo.it

Externally, the cathedral has maintained the original character of the Norman cathedral in its pure form on the east side: the three apses are structured by interlocked round arches, and cambered crenellation. The southern side, which faces the square, is the actual main façade; it was given a highlight in the **Catalan Gothic portico** of 1453, now the entrance. One of its columns (with a Kufic inscription) comes from the mosque. The pediment depicts God in majesty, while the Virgin Mary is represented above the portal (mosaic on a gold base, 13th century). The bell-tower on the western side dates back to the 12th century (1840 in its current form). The **Loggia dell'Incoronata** to the left of the western façade, on which kings showed themselves to the people after their coronation, was also built in the 12th, then altered in the 15th century.

Exterior

Palermo *Cathedral*

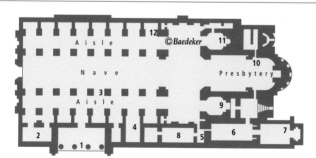

1 Portal by Antonio Gambara
  (1429/30)
2 Royal and imperial tombs
3 Stoup by Giuseppe Spadafora
  and Antonio Ferraro
  (1553)

4 Chapel with the urns of
  the city's patron saints
5 Vestibule of the sacristy
6 Sacristy of the priors
7 New sacristy, altar by
  Antonello Gagini (1503)

8 Cathedral treasure
9 Cappella di Santa Rosalia
10 Bishop's throne
11 Ciborium
12 Marble statue by
  Francesco Laurana (1469)

Porphyry Hohen-staufen tombs

🕐

Opening hours:
9.30am – 5pm
in winter only until
3pm

The main attraction in the cathedral is the monumental royal mausoleum of the Hohenstaufen dynasty (since 2004 there has been an entry fee). There are four sarcophagi made of porphyry, a material that had hitherto been permitted only for Roman and Byzantine emperors because of its purple colour and had to be imported from Islamic Egypt.

The first king to be laid to rest here was Roger II (d. 1154). Against his wishes he was not buried in »his« cathedral in Cefalù, but here in a simple sarcophagus. The two artistically more impressive sarcophagi, which he had set up in Cefalù, were brought to Palermo Cathedral in 1215 at the behest of Frederick II. They are the final resting places of Frederick II (d. 1250) and his father Henry VI (d. 1197). The fourth sarcophagus is that of Frederick II's mother Constance (d. 1198), one of Roger II's daughters. The four sarcophagi are in two rows: the left-hand sarcophagus in the front row is that of **Frederick II**. Supported by four lions, the triangular end depicts the Norman hoop crown, while the lid shows medallions of the Virgin Mary and Christ Pantocrator between the evangelists' symbols. This site is greatly revered by German visitors and is usually decorated with flowers. The fact that Sicilian aristocratic families also revered Frederick II and considered the form of his sarcophagus to be perfect is evidenced by several replicas (Cathedral of Mazaro del Vallo, Chiesa Santissimo Salvatore in Naro), though they also realized that a certain discretion was appropriate and chose green marble instead of the imperial porphyry. To the right, next to it, is the sarcophagus of Henry VI, in the back row on the left is the tomb of Roger II and to the right of it that of Constance. In addition there are two wall tombs: the one on the left is that of William I de la Roche (d. 1339), a son of Frederick II of Aragon; to the right is the tomb of Frederick's first wife Constance of Aragon (d. 1222); she rests in a sarcophagus dating from classical times with the touching inscription »Sicaniae regina fui Constantia coniunx augusta hic habito nunc Federice tua« (»Sicily's queen was I, Constance, the emperor's consort, now I live here, Frederick, yours«).

The sarcophagi were opened in 1781 and 1998–99. The embalmed bodies of Frederick II and his wife Constance were found in good condition and surrounded by precious burial gifts, which are now part of the cathedral treasure.

Chapel of Santa Rosalia

A further attraction, apart from a metal meridian in the floor, is the chapel of Saint Rosalia (to the right of the choir) with a silver reliquary (1625), which can, however, only be seen during the saint's festival in July.

*On its eastern side the cathedral →
reveals its Norman origins most clearly.*

★★
Cathedral treasure house

The cathedral treasure house possesses liturgical gowns and gold-work as well as fragments of Henry VI's burial gown, but first and foremost the precious crown of Constance of Aragon; it has the shape of the kalimavkions of Byzantine emperors and is richly adorned with strings of pearls and gems. This was probably the crown with which Frederick II was crowned emperor on 22 November 1220 by Pope Honorius III – he placed it in Constance's tomb.

Palazzo Sclàfani

Opposite the archbishop's palace is Via P. Novelli, which leads to Palazzo Sclàfani (seat of the military headquarters). Mateo Sclàfani built it in 1330 in the Gothic style, with Arab and Norman elements mixed in. In 1435 a hospital was set up in the palace and soon afterwards it was adorned with the fresco *The Triumph of Death* (now in Palazzo Abatellis).

Villa Bonanno

A relaxing way to get to Piazza del Parlamento is by strolling through the park of Villa Bonanno, which has lots of palm trees. Along the way is the monument to Philip IV of Spain (1605–65), featuring rich figurative ornamentation; after the damage caused to it by the unrest of 1848, it was fitted with a statue of Philip V (1683–1746). Bear in mind that this is the oldest part of Palermo. Here the front of Palermo's most significant non-religious building, the Norman palace, lies ahead.

Palazzo dei Normanni · Palazzo Reale

Sicily's seat of government

🕐
Opening hours:
Mon – Sat
8.30am – 1pm
2pm – 5pm
Sun until 5pm

On the hill on which the Phoenicians, Romans and Byzantines settled, the Arabs built the palace of their emirs in the 9th century – the al-Qasr, after which the road from here to the traditional harbour was named (Cassàro). They were succeeded by the Norman rulers, and then by Frederick II from the house of Hohenstaufen, under whom the residence reached its greatest splendour. During the period that followed, the palace underwent a long period of decline, until the Spanish viceroys developed it as a residence from 1555 onwards. Sicily's **regional parliament** has had its seat here since 1947.

Torre Pisana

This is the wide northeastern front of the Palazzo dei Normanni. While most of the building visible here was constructed in the 16th century, a particularly striking component survives from its original Norman period: the high Torre Pisana with its clean ashlar blocks and pointed blind arcades. The treasure chamber used to be located on the ground floor. It is the last of four massive towers; inside is a square room 15m/50ft high.

On the top floor viceroy Caramanico had an observatory built for the astronomer Giuseppe Piazzi in 1791; its dome can be seen above the Palazzi dei Normanni.

Cortile Maqueda

Enter the palazzo (entrance on Corso Re Ruggero) to get into a square courtyard surrounded by three-storey round-arch arcades,

Palermo *Palazzo dei Normanni*

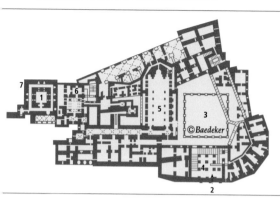

1 Torre Pisana
2 Entrance
3 Cortile Maqueda
4 Stairs
5 Cappella Palatina
  (first floor)
6 Appartamenti Reali
  (second floor)
7 Porta Nuova
  (16th century)

N

50 ft
20 m

the Cortile Maqueda; it was created in 1600 by the viceroy Maqueda. The stairs lead up to the heart of the palace, the Cappella Palatina on the first floor and the Appartamenti Reali on the second floor.

★ ★ Cappella Palatina

Cappella Palatina, the royal chapel, was commissioned by Roger II immediately after his coronation in 1130 and consecrated in 1140. The mosaics in the chancel were presumably completed in 1143. Those in the nave were created under William I (1154–66). In around 1350 the mosaics were restored under Louis of Aragon (further restorations in the 15th and 16th centuries). In 1800 Ferdinand of Naples donated a mosaic for the new entrance. Later construction work has meant that the royal chapel is no longer free-standing, but is surrounded on three sides. Only the chapel's long southern side is freely accessible. Located here is a colonnade with mosaics from the early 19th century, which replace older pictures; they address the story of David, and show a crowned man (symbol of Palermo) with medallions, which depict the ruling couple, Ferdinand of Bourbon and Maria Carolina. The harmony of the interior remains unaffected despite all the changes – it is a harmony that results from the combination of the three heterogeneous elements of Latin basilica, Byzantine domed structure and mosaic ornamentation, as well as an Arab stalactite ceiling.

Roger II's royal chapel

The chapel, a columned basilica, immediately captivates its visitors through the mystical half-light with its golden sheen. The nave's wooden ceiling has been adorned with stalactites in the Arab style, each of which are painted with countless small scenes. At the west end (to the left of the entrance) is, as one pole of the Norman view of kingship, the elevated marble site of the royal throne, behind which is a mosaic of Christ Pantocrator between the apostles Peter and Paul (c. 1350).

From here look along the narrow nave to the other pole: the chancel, also elevated, with its three apses and the dome above its central square. On the right-hand side in front of it is a marble paschal candle-holder (4.5m/14.5ft tall); its rich reliefs feature figural and floral motifs; the central one of the five sections depicts Christ with Roger II kneeling before him. Behind it is the ambo (pulpit), supported by columns adorned with reliefs and inlays and topped by Corinthian capitals. Its lecterns depict a lion and an eagle, the symbols of the evangelists Mark and John.

Mosaics The mosaics are striking. They cover all of the interior walls. Those in the nave and aisles feature Latin inscriptions and tell stories from the Old Testament (nave) and the New Testament (aisles). The depiction begins on the southern wall of the nave and then continues in a clockwise direction: southern wall, top row (left to right): Genesis to the creation of Eve, northern wall, top row: Fall of Man to the construction of Noah's ark, southern wall, bottom row: the dove and the ark to the story of Abraham and the three angels, northern wall, bottom row: Lot and the people of Sodom to Jacob's wrestling with the angel.

Christ Pantocrator in the dome of Cappella Palatina

The aisles depict scenes from the Acts of the Apostles with Paul and Peter. While the mosaics of the nave are sequential, the images in the sanctuary dome are arranged around Christ at the centre. Christ Pantocrator (Lord of All) is surrounded by a Greek inscription, which describes heaven as His footstool. Below him are angels and archangels, prophets and kings of ancient Israel. The evangelists are in the four corner niches, fully in line with the Byzantine Orthodox custom. Deviating from this custom, Christ is depicted a second time in the semi-dome of the main apse, below him the Mother of God (18th century, the difference in quality between this and the 12th-century mosaics is striking!). In addition the choir features further New Testament motifs such as the Annunciation, the Nativity of Christ, the flight to Egypt, Baptism, Transfiguration, Ascension and Whitsun. It reflects the religious attitude of the Norman kings that the Crucifixion is missing.

Appartamenti Reali

The private royal quarters are located on the second floor of the Palazzo dei Normanni. A guided tour includes the beautiful mosaics depicting plants, animals and hunting scenes in Sala di Ruggiero (Hall of Roger) as well as the Sala di Erocle (Hall of Heracles, 1560–79), in which the regional Sicilian parliament meets; the frescos were painted by Guiseppe Velazquez in 1799.

Porta Nuova

Adjoining the Palazzo dei Normanni to the west is the Porta Nuova, the handsome gate that was built in 1535 as the southern end of the Cassàro; it was renovated after being struck by lightning in 1761. The magnificent external face is characterized by colossal herma pilasters (Africans commemorate Emperor Charles V's victory at Tunis) and a loggia under the pyramidal roof.

Palazzo Orléans-Aumale

To the southwest of the Palazzo dei Normanni is Palazzo Orléans-Aumale, named after Henri Eugène d'Orléans, the fifth son of the French king Louis Philippe and Duke of Aumale (1822–97), who died here in exile (now the seat of the provincial government). Adults are only allowed in the attractive gardens when accompanied by children.

★★
San Giovanni degli Eremiti

To the south of the Palazzo dei Normanni is the idyll of the former church of San Giovanni degli Eremiti. Even before you enter the tranquil complex, the bright red Moorish domes will draw you in. And was indeed once the location of an Arab mosque, which was in turn built on the remains of a Benedictine monastery. Under the Normans it was Christianized again. In 1132 Roger II commissioned the cubic church crowned by five domes. It was originally used as a funerary chapel for the court. The interior is austere and unembellished. Geometric shapes such as circles and the hemisphere of the dome enhance the simple rectangle of the building. The two smaller spaces to the left and right of the sanctuary are topped by domes.

Opening hours:
Tue–Sun
9am – 7pm

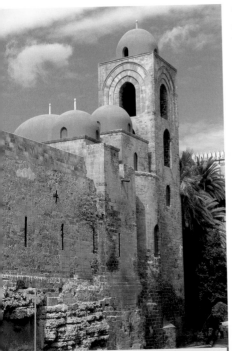
San Giovanni degli Eremiti

The tower stands above the northern transept. There is a passageway from the southern transept to the sacristy, the former anteroom of the mosque with remains of frescoes on the wall. The courtyard in front was originally a cemetery; the remains of the cistern can be seen below the courtyard.

Adjoining the church is the **cloister**, at the centre of which stands an Arab fountain. The pointed arches rest on slender marble double columns. Together with the lavish vegetation (capers, pomelos, medlars, touch-me-nots) this gives the cloister an unmistakeable atmosphere.

Turn right into Via Benedittini. The **Porta Mazara** can be found where this road meets Corso Tuköry. It is one of the Palermo's oldest city gates. It was built in the 12th century, incorporating an older surrounding wall. The gate (in the garden of the Institute of General Pathology) has the feel of a triumphal arch and is adorned with blind arcades at the sides. There are three coats of arms on the outside: Aragon at the top, below it the city's coat of arms as well as that of a noble family.

North of Quattro Canti

Sant'Agostino Take Via Sant'Agostino from Via Maqueda to get to the church of the Augustinian canons, which was built in the 13th century and altered in the 17th and 18th centuries. The façade with its pointed-arch arcade and rose window dates back to the 14th century. The interior of the elongated hall church was adorned with rich sculptures by Giacomo Serpotta, the »plaster-of-Paris Bernini«, in the years after 1711 (Mon–Sat 7am–noon, 4pm–6pm, Sun only until noon). In the northeastern corner of the cloister (1560), the façade of the chapter house (around 1300) remains extant.

Teatro Massimo On Piazza Giuseppe Verdi (taxi stands, post office) Giovanni Battista Basile and his son Ernesto built the monumental opera house with

3200 seats between 1875 and 1897. It was inaugurated on 16 May 1897 with Verdi's *Falstaff*, and has been one of the most significant Italian musical stages ever since. It was closed for 23 years because of safety issues, but after comprehensive refurbishments was opened again for productions in 1998 and can be visited during the day (photo p. 315, information ►p. 314). The statue representing Lyric Poetry was made by Mario Rutelli (1850–1931).

At the junction with Viale della Libertà is Piazza Ruggero Settimo, named after the president of Sicily's short-lived republic in 1848. The square is the centre of urban life. It is the location of the **Politeama Garibaldi**, a multi-purpose cultural building built by Giuseppe Damiani Almeyda between 1867 and 1874. The façade, in the shape of a Roman triumphal arch, is topped by a bronze quadriga by Mario Rutelli (1874).

Piazza Ruggero Settimo

Leaving Piazza Ruggero Settimo behind, take Via E. Amari to get to the **harbour** with the Marittima train station and the piers for the hydrofoils and ferries.

! *Baedeker* TIP

Meat, fish, vegetarian
Il Mirti e la Rosa in the heart of the old town is one of the city's most highly praised restaurants; the prices are low, the quality is high, regardless of whether the dishes are meat, fish or vegetarian. The best option is to order a taster menu and be surprised (closed Sun, Via Principe di Granatelli 30, tel. 091 32 43 53).

Follow Via Crispi south-eastwards from the harbour to get to the church built by the merchants of Genoa between 1571 and 1591. This interesting Renaissance building is a cruciform basilica; it has a rectangular floor plan and an octagonal tambour dome. The altarpiece of Saint Luke painting the Madonna was created by Filippo Paladino in 1601.

San Giorgio dei Genovesi

A little further to the southwest of San Giorgio, in Via Squarcialupo, is the former Dominican church of Santa Zita, which was founded in 1369, refurbished by merchants from Lucca between 1586 and 1603, and adorned with a late Baroque façade in the 18th century (interior by Antonello Gagini, 1517; Mon–Sat 9am–1pm).
To the left of the church is the **Oratorio del Rosario di Santa Zita**, prayer house of a rosary fraternity(Mon–Sat 9am–1pm). It is richly adorned with stucco work by Giacomo Serpotta, such as the entrance wall with its large nested stucco curtain, into which depictions of the naval battle of Lepanto have been worked (►Baedeker Special p. 264). The altarpiece *Our Lady of the Rosary* was painted by Carlo Maratta in Rome in 1695.

Santa Cita

Just a stone's throw from here is Piazza di San Domenico, bounded in the west by Via Roma. It features an Immacolata column, built here in 1724. The church of **San Domenico**, which goes back to the

Piazza di San Domenico

13th century, was given its final appearance during its Baroque renovation between 1636 and 1640; the powerful twin tower façade was only added in 1726. The rich interior includes a marble Pietà by Domenico Gagini (around 1460) and a large Rococo organ (1781). The parliament convened by Ruggero Settimo met in San Domenico in 1848; after that the former Dominican church became a Sicilian pantheon. The politicians F. Crispi and R. Settimo, the poet G. Meli and the painter P. Novelli as well as the astronomer G. Piazzi are buried here.

Museo del Risorgimento

Walk through the cloister of San Domenico (14th century, entrance to the left of the church) to get to the Museo del Risorgimento, which has exhibits about the Italian unification movement, including Sicily's constitution of 1812, information about the revolutions of 1821 and 1848 as well as Garibaldi's »Expedition of the Thousand« (1860).

Oratorio del Rosario di San Domenico ☉

To the left behind San Domenico is the Oratorio del Rosario di San Domenico (Via Bambinai 16, Mon – Sat 9am – 1pm). In 1578, this building, as well as the Oratorio del Rosario di Santa Zita, was lavishly adorned with stucco by Giacomo Serpotta. The highlight is *Our Lady of the Rosary with Saint Dominic* by Anthony van Dyck (1628).

✳ Vucciria

Colourful food stalls line the streets of Palermo's old quarter. The best-known market is the Vucciria, which is held every morning (apart from Sundays) and late afternoon below Piazza S. Domenico along the streets Via Cassari – Argenteria and the surrounding area.

Not far away, in Via Roma, is the church of **Sant'Antonio Abate**, which was built in the 14th century over an older Norman building. The interior features two attractive stoups from the 16th century by Camillo Camilliani.

Sant'Ignazio all'Olivella

Leave Piazza San Domenico along Via Roma in a northwest direction to Piazza Olivella to get to this basilica, built by Antonino Muttone for the fraternity of Saint Filippo Neri, starting in 1585. It was given its magnificent dome in 1732. Damaged during the Second World War, the church was subsequently restored. On the other side are the monastic buildings of the fraternity of Saint Filippo Neri with their

Colourful market in Vucciria, →
Palermo's old quarter

two cloisters. They have housed the Archaeological Museum since 1866.

★ ★ Museo Archeologico

Opening hours:
Tue – Fri
8.30am – 1.30pm
3pm – 6.45pm
Sat – Mon
8.30am – 1.30pm

The Museo Archeologico possesses the world-famous metopes of Selinunte, making it one of the most significant Italian collections of antiquities. It is housed in the former monastery of San Filippo Neri. The **small cloister** (17th century) and the hall to the right display discoveries from underwater archaeology. Two neighbouring rooms feature Egyptian and Phoenician pieces, including the Palermo stone, whose hieroglyphic inscription contains a list of Egyptian pharaohs of the Old Kingdom (3238–2990 BC), a Punic torso from Motya (6th century BC), two anthropomorphic sarcophagi from Pizzo Cannita, ancient Soluntо, and a votive column from Lilybaeum dedicated to Baal.

Ground floor

Tip
The museum is being restored. At times sections are closed. Some exhibits are on display in Albergo delle Povere (Corso Calatafimi 213). ▶

The **large cloister** has a colossal statue of Zeus (2nd century BC) and architectural fragments from Soluntum; while the Hall of the Twin Steles has a collection of double-headed votive steles (6th–4th century BC), of which around 10,000 were found in the Temple of Zeus Meilichius near Selinunte. The Ettore-Gabrici hall displays terracotta ornamentation from Temple C in Selinunte with the central figure of Gorgo Medusa (550 BC) in the reconstruction by Ettore Gabrici.
Exhibited in the Pirro-Marconi hall are the simas of the Temple of Himera with lion's heads spouting water (480 BC).

★ ★
Hall of Selinunte

The metopes of Selinunte are a fascinating collection of Greek sculpture. The oldest pieces are located to the right: the four Salinas metopes with the gods of Delphi (Artemis, Leto, Apollo), a sphinx, the abduction of Europa as well as Heracles with the Cretan Bull (around 575 BC). In addition there are two more recently discovered metopes, which were used in fortifying the acropolis of Selinunte (a deity on a cart, making sacrifices before goddesses).
On the left wall are two Daedalian heads (around 600 BC) and a giant torso from Temple G (late 6th century BC). The lower portions of two metopes survive from Temple F (Dionysus defeats a giant, Athena fights Enceladus). The three metopes from Temple C (around 575 BC) are magnificent: Apollo's quadriga seen from the front, Perseus kills Medusa, Heracles carries the defeated Cercopes on a pole.
The back wall is dedicated to Temple E with the reconstruction of parts of the pronaos frieze, in which the art of Selinunte reached its classical climax (470–460 BC). The metopes depict Heracles fighting the Amazons, the wedding (hieros gamos) of Zeus and Hera, Artemis with Actaeon being turned into a stag, Athena and the giant Enceladus.

The Casuccini collection takes visitors back to ancient Tuscany, while the following rooms feature Etruscan pieces from Chiusi.

Palermo Museum

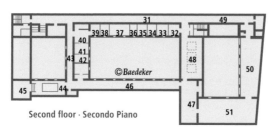

Second floor · Secondo Piano

Second floor
◄–42 Prehistoric collection

43–47 Greek, Apulian, Campanian
and Sicilian ceramics

48 Mosaics and frescoes
49–51 Ceramics

First floor · Primo Piano

First floor
◄5,19 Collection of significant
finds arranged
by place
◄–18 Finds from the necropolis
in Selinunte

20 Clay sculptures from Sicily
and Greece
21 Vessels from various eras
22 Korai, terracotta statues
from Selinunte
23 Art bronzes

24 Greek marble sculptures
25 Roman sculptures
26 Discoveries from
the necropolis in Panormo
27–30 Small containers, gold and
silver works, coins

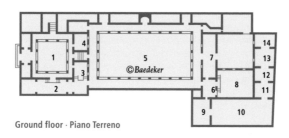

Ground floor · Piano Terreno

Ground floor
1,2 Underwater discoveries
3,4 Egyptian and Phoenician
discoveries

5 Inscriptions and sculptures from
Tyndaris and Soluntum
6 Hall of the twin steles
7 Hall of the Greek inscriptions

8 Ettore Gabrici Hall
9 Pirro Marconi Hall
10 Hall of Selinunte
11–14 Etruscan collection

Quiet oasis: the courtyard of the Archaeological Museum

First floor The north and west corridors of the first floor have exhibits arranged by their place of discovery. These locations include the Punic sites of Panormos (Palermo), Soluntum, Motya and Lilybaeum, Elymian sites (Segesta, Monte Jato, Poggioreale) and Sicani sites (Castronovo). The department of clay sculpture contains votive statues from the Temple of Demeter Malophoros in Selinunte.

The hall of bronzes (of Etruscan, Greek and Roman origin) features a life-sized bronze ram from Hellenistic times, which used to guard the Castello Maniace in Syracuse along with a counterpart. A Pompeiian fountain sculpture depicts an athlete defeating a bull. In the hall of Roman sculptures there is a late Roman floor mosaic from Lilybaeum with seasonal motifs (3rd century AD).

Second floor The second floor is home to the prehistoric collection. The copy of several graffiti from the Addaura cave is interesting. The extensive ceramics collection has vases from Corinthian, Ionian, Laconian, Attic, Etruscan and Italian origin.

East of Quattro Canti

The Piazza Pretoria, very near Quattro Canti, which can be reached ✱
via a few steps from Via Maqueda, is dominated by a monumental **Piazza Pretoria**
fountain, the **Fontana Pretoria**, which was created by the Florentine
sculptors Francesco Camilliani and Angelo Vagherino in 1544–55 for
viceroy Don Pietro de Toledo. He did not accept it and in 1573 the
city of Palermo acquired it. Ever since then it has remained in its
current location in front of the senate, where it is the dominant architectural feature with its circumference of 133m/145yd and its
height of 12m/39ft. Its naked male and female figures were frowned
upon by the population for a long time.

Not far away is the 17th-century church of San Matteo. The four **San Matteo**
statues on the dome pillars were made by G. Serpotta (1728). The
square's south side is taken up by the **senatorial palace**, which is
now the city hall (municipio). Based on a building from 1463 and altered during the Baroque period (as demonstrated by the statue of
Saint Rosalia from 1661, by Carlo d'Apriles), the municipio was giv-
en its current façade in 1875 by G. D. Almeyda.

The neighbouring square, Piazza Bellini, is home to three churches. **Piazza Bellini**
The Chiesa di Santa Caterina was built as a hall church for Dominican nuns between 1566 and 1596; in the 17th and 18th centuries its
interior was altered with lavish Baroque decorations (Santa Caterina
on the high altar by A. Gagini, 1534). Two significant buildings from
the Norman period are far more interesting than this church, however: the churches of La Martorana and San Cataldo, which lie next
to each other.

The Baroque façade (1728–30) could easily mislead visitors into ✱✱
thinking Santa Maria dell'Ammiraglio (Admiral's Church) is much **La Martorana**
more recent than it is: it was founded in 1143 by George of Antioch,
the »admiral of admirals« of the Kingdom of Sicily under Roger II, ⏱
an Orthodox Christian who spoke Arabic. Today the liturgy follows Opening hours:
the Uniate Greek Orthodox rite once more. Mon – Sat
The exterior reveals Arab influences with its blind pointed arcades, 8.30am – 1pm
and even the campanile that was rebuilt after the earthquake damage 3.30pm – 7pm
of 1728 has an Arab-Norman character. However, the fundamental Sun 8.30am – 1pm
architectural idea is Byzantine; in line with the dominant architectural type since the middle Byzantine period, the structure was designed
as a domed cross-in-square church: the nave and transepts are of
equal length, the dome above the central square is supported by four
columns and the choir features three apses. The nave and transepts
have barrel vaults, while the lower, small corner rooms have groin
vaults. The original building had to endure significant alterations. By
1200 the narthex, vestibule and campanile were added. In 1435 King
Alfonso of Aragon donated the church to the Benedictine nuns of

Palermo La Martorana

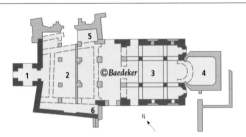

1 Campanile
2 Former Norman courtyard (expanded 16th/17th century)
3 Former Norman church
4 New chapel (17th century)
5 Mosaic: Holy Virgin blesses George of Antioch
6 Mosaic: Christ crowns Roger II

the nearby convent, which was founded in 1194 by Aloisa Martorana; ever since then the church has commonly been known as La Martorana. In the 17th century the narthex and the open atrium were incorporated, turning a church with a central ground plan into an irregular structure. The nave was pulled down along with its mosaics in 1683–86, and replaced by a larger rectangular space. In addition the nuns had the interior covered in frescos.

★★
Mosaics

Nevertheless, the most precious part of the church, the cycle of mosaics on a gold ground, the oldest in Sicily (around 1150), remains extant. It originally adorned all of the wall and vault space above a 4m/13ft pedestal with porphyry and serpentine incrustations. The Christ Pantocrator at the centre of the dome with the inscription »I am the light of the world« dominates. He is surrounded by four archangels, their hands concealed by cloths. At the imperial court in Byzantium, this was an expression of reverent obeisance. Below them an inscription was discovered, which Amari recognized as being the words of a Byzantine hymn translated into Arabic, a fact representative of the polyglot culture of those days.

The dome's tambour has depictions of prophets, while the four squinches show the evangelists. The Annunciation is depicted in the triumphal arch. The side apses feature the parents of Mary, Joachim (left) and Anne (right); the lost mosaic of the nave probably depicted Mary in the orans (supplicant) position. As is unsurprising for a church dedicated to the Virgin Mary, there are two further Marian subjects: the Nativity of Christ and the Death of the Virgin in the barrel vault, which adjoins the central square in the west. Christ stands next to the deathbed, holding the soul of the deceased, in the form of a small child, in his hands. The remaining areas are adorned with prophets, apostles and saints.

In the vestibule of the narthex (the original west wall), the founder of the church, George of Antioch, had himself depicted on the right; to the left Christ crowns Roger II – a motif previously reserved to the emperors of Byzantium, thereby demonstrating the claim of the Norman kings against both Byzantium and the pope (photo p. 38).

Immediately next to La Martorana is the church of San Cataldo, with its bright red domes and delicate crenellation. It too was founded by a Norman admiral. When William I succeeded his father Roger II, he chose Maio of Bari in place of George of Antioch as admiral. The man from Apulia dedicated his church to a saint from his home, Bishop Cataldo from Taranto, and chose the »Latin« floor plan of a basilica with a nave and two aisles. The long elevation is emphasized by three Arab domes over the raised nave. The Arab-Norman character is also evident in the cubic exterior with three pointed windows on each side, which are flanked by blind arches, and the fine crenellation around the top.

The austere ashlar masonry of the exterior walls is also reflected in the interior, which is, apart from the beautifully ornamented inlays in the floor and the capitals of the four ancient columns, completely unembellished.

★
San Cataldo
🕐
Opening hours:
Daily 9.30am – 1pm
Mon – Sat
also 3.30pm – 6pm

They bear the signature of Arabic architects: La Martorana (back) and San Cataldo (front)

Piazza della Rivoluzione The small Piazza della Rivoluzione (east of Via Roma) commemorates the rebellion against the Bourbons in 1848 and the fact that twelve years later, in 1860, Garibaldi first showed up in Palermo. The square features a fountain with the »Genio di Palermo«, one of the city's emblems.

Palazzo Scavuzzo

Palazzo Aiutamicristo There are two palaces on Via Garibaldi: Palazzo Scavuzzo, built shortly after 1500 in the late-Gothic and Renaissance styles, and the generously proportioned Palazzo Aiutamicristo (»Help me, Christ«). Built in 1490 by Matteo Carnelivari for the merchant Guglielmo Aiutamicristo from Pisa, it was already expanded in 1494 by Nicolò Grisafi and altered towards the end of the 16th century. It was the residence of Emperor Charles V and later of his son Don John of Austria, the victor of the Battle of Lepanto (1571). The courtyard with its two-storey loggias and crenellated top floor is impressive (entrance Via Garibaldi 23).

La Magione Santissima Trinità Behind Palazzo Aiutamicristo, turn left into Via Magione to get to Piazza Magione. The Chiesa La Magione (Santissima Trinità) in a garden of palm trees, a noble Norman church, was mentioned for the first time in 1191, as a daughter church of the Cistercians of Santo Spirito. Emperor Henry VI gave it to the Teutonic Knights in 1191, from which it gets its name La Magione, meaning »house« (of a religious order, mansio). After suffering serious damage in the Second World War, the church was rebuilt. There are three portals with rounded-ashlar blocks, a style that was taken over from the orient during the time of the crusades. Above them are blind pointed-arch arcades, which also adorn the other exterior walls. The nave and two aisles of the interior are separated by columns under pointed arches. To the left of the church is the northern wing of the cloister, with its double columns and pointed arches from the 12th century.

Galleria d'Arte Moderna The collection in the nicely restored **Palazzo Sant'Anna** contains paintings and sculptures from the 19th century with a local bias, including works by Francesco Lojaconoa and Franz von Stuck, and from the 20th century: Carlo Carrà, Felice Casorati, Mario Sironi, Arturo Tosi, Renato Guttuso and Gino Severini (Via Sant'Anna 21, www.galleriadartemodernapalermo.it, Tue–Thu, Sun 9.30am–6.30pm, Fri, Sat until 11pm).

San Francesco d'Assisi North of Piazza della Rivoluzione is the church of San Francesco d'Assisi, which has Gothic arcades and an open roof structure. The interior is adorned by eight allegorical statues by G. Serpotta (1732), carved choir stalls (1524) and the richly decorated Mastrantonio chapel (left aisle) with reliefs by Francesco Laurana (1468).

Nice place to take a break, →
such as in Antica Focacceria: San Francesco d'Assisi

Oratorio di San Lorenzo The Oratorio di San Lorenzo to the left of the church was built in around 1550 and richly adorned with stucco by Giacomo Serpotta in 1699. The motifs include the stories of saints Francis and Lawrence. The altarpiece of 1609, painted by Michelangelo da Caravaggio (*Nativity of Christ*), was stolen in 1969.

Santa Maria della Catena The church of Santa Maria della Catena on the coast road is a reminder of the fact that the harbour (cala) could be closed off with a chain here in the past. The building (1500–40) is a good example of the mix of late Catalan Gothic elements with those of the Italian Renaissance. The portal sculptures were done by Vincenzo Gagini in the 16th century. A vestibule with three segmental arch arcades leads into the basilica, which was given a Baroque refurbishment in the 18th century. The church frequently puts on concerts.

✳
Puppet Museum The interesting Puppet Museum is not far away (Via Butera 1, Mon – Fri 9am – 1pm and 3.30pm – 6.30pm; tel. 0 91 32 80 60; ▶Baedeker Special p. 342).

La Cala The old harbour, La Cala, was originally much bigger than the current harbour basin now frequented by fishing boats and yachts. It was guarded by an Arab and later Norman fort that is no longer extant. The modern harbour is quite a bit further north.

Porta Felice Porta Felice, build in 1582 under viceroy M. Collona and his wife Felice Orsini, completes the Cassarò and is the counterpart to Porta Nuova (▶above, Palazzo dei Normanni). This is where the popular **waterfront promenade** of the Foro Italico begins (panoramic views).

✳
Palazzo Lo Steri Chiaramonte The palace is situated to the south of Santa Maria della Catena. It was built by the Chiaramonte, a noble family from Agrigento, in the 14th century, when they experienced the pinnacle of their power but also their downfall. Work began in 1307 under Manfredi I Chiaramonte, count of Módica and seneschal of the kingdom, and continued until 1380. The second storey remained uncompleted. In 1396 Andrea Chiaramonte was decapitated in front of his palace following his rebellion against King Martin I of Aragon. Lo Steri later served as the residence of the viceroys (1468–1517), as the headquarters of the Inquisition (around 1600) and as a courthouse (1799). Today it is part of the faculty of architecture. The imposing structure (40m/ 44yd square) has four wings and surrounds a square courtyard. The ground floor has a closed-off feel, while the first floor has mullioned windows. The wooden ceiling in the main hall (14th century) survives. It features motifs from history and legend.
The palace stands on Piazza Marina and the small park of **Giardino Garibaldi**. Huge rubber trees and their aerial roots attract all the attention here.

Some rooms of the palace of the Lanza princes (17th century) still have their original furnishings, giving a good impression of the domestic lives of aristocrats in the late 18th century (Via Merlo 2; Mon–Sun 9am–7pm).

Palazzo Mirto

The palazzo at the eastern end of Via Alloro was commissioned in 1490 by Francesco Abatellis, a dignitary at the court of Ferdinand of Aragon. The architect was Matteo Carnelivari, who also designed Palazzo Aiutamicristo. The result is a square block with a richly decorated portal and a courtyard that is completed on one side with a double-storey loggia. The palace, built using Catalan Gothic elements, was a Dominican priory between 1526 and 1943, and houses the Galleria Regionale della Sicilia (modernized by Carlo Scarpa), which exhibits works from the Middle Ages and the modern era (open: Tue–Sun 9am–1.30pm). One of the collection's main works is the fresco **The Triumph of Death** in the palace chapel (hall 2), created by an unknown painter in around 1400 for the hospital in Palazzo Sclàfani. The palazzo also possesses Moorish ceramics (13th–16th century; hall 3), sculptures from the Gagini family (halls 5, 6) and the idealized portrait of Eleonora of Aragon (hall 4), who died in 1405, which was painted by **Francesco Laurana** in around 1480. The Renaissance painter **Antonello da Messina** has three panels in this collection, depicting the church fathers St Augustine, Gregory the Great and St Jerome, but his main work here is the *Annunziata* (1474; hall 10), depicting the Virgin Mary in a precious blue gown. The triptych of Malvagna by the Flemish painter Jan Gossaert, known as Mabuse (1510; hall 13) is worthy of note.

★
Palazzo Abatellis, Galleria Regionale della Sicilia

Antonello da Messina: »Annunziata«

The Gothic Chiesa La Gancia (also Santa Maria degli Angeli) is to be found to the right of Palazzo Abatellis (built c. 1490 as a hospital church for the Franciscan order). The coffered wooden ceiling dates back to the church's founding days. There is also an Annunciation by Antonello Gagini (on the pilasters of the presbytery).

La Gancia, Santa Maria degli Angeli

To the left of Palazzo Abatellis the Dominican architect Andrea Cirincione built this hall church for Dominican nuns in 1678–84. The

La Madonna della Pietà

Brave heroes in shining armour, ready to fight evil

They come alive in his hands: Pupparo Mimmo Cuticchio at work.

TEATRO DEI PUPI – HEROES ON STRINGS

It is known that the »teatro dei pupi« has existed on Sicily since the first half of the 19th century. It developed from the tradition of the »cantastorie«, an almost extinct genre performed by street singers, who recited great chivalrous epics.

The puppet theatre uses the subjects of Charlemagne and his heroic noble paladins. It tells of the era of the court of Count Roger in Palermo, taking ideas from the legends of King Arthur and the Knights of the Round Table as well as from the Spanish epic El Cid and the fight against the Moors. Like the cantastorie, the opera dei pupi reduces to historical and legendary events to their most exciting, eventful scenes and makes a strict separation between **good and evil** – between goodies and baddies. Phoenicians, Greeks, Carthaginians, Romans, Vandals, Goths, Arabs, Normans, the French, Spaniards – the island lost battles against invaders around a dozen times and had to bow to their will. But in the puppet theatre it was possible to fight against the centuries-old Sicilian trauma of being eternally defeated and for Sicily to be victorious for once. What better enemy than those whom the Sicilians always believed to be the »real infidels«, namely the **Saracens**. But before the bloodthirsty Saracens, in ridiculous oriental clothes, can be ruthlessly defeated by brave Christian knights in shining precious armour at the end of the performance, there are moving love scenes between a comely knight and a beautiful maiden, magicians and monsters are battled, and a nasty Mussulman tries to abduct a pretty Christian princess.

The **teatro dei pupi** is an art form that developed among the people, one that lived in and with the people: taxi drivers, merchants and waiters always knew what was currently happening

in these multi-part plays. Like soap operas, the audience knew the individual characters and identified itself with them, thereby feeling with them through the different events: sometimes it was moved, sometimes outraged, sometimes it egged on its »heroes« by shouting out encouragement and sometimes it loudly booed the villains.

Exhausting spectacle

But spectators could not be pleased by the plot alone. The movements of the pupi had to be right too. This requires great skill from the puppeteer, who had to handle the puppets, which are about 1m/3ft tall and weigh around 20kg/45lbs, with the help of iron bars. The »puparo«, the puppeteer, is a real artist: artistic director, director, speaker, costume designer, set designer, carpenter, tailor and smith in one. In recent years the teatro dei pupi has seen a revival. Tourist interest in this popular spectacle has contributed to this development, as has a new-found local interest in all popular forms of artistic expression.

The **art of puppeteering** is alive and well in Palermo. In addition to performances in the interesting puppet museum and the Museo Etnografico Pitre, there are privately run theatres: in the shadow of Teatro Massimo, for example, the Cuticchio family regularly has its knights defeat the Saracens (Via Bara all'Olivella 95, tel. 0 91 32 34 00). The same thing happens in Teatro Argento (Via P. Novelli, tel. 09 16 11 36 80), in Teatro Ippogrifo (Vicolo Ragusi, tel. 0 91 32 91 94) as well as in the Munna in Monreale (Cortile Manin, tel. 09 16 40 45 42). Acireale (www.operadei-puppi.com) and Syracuse are also known for their puppet shows.

Although the performances are all in Italian, visiting a play is well worthwhile even for people who do not understand the language. The performances are action-packed and it is possible to follow what is going on in general.

two-storey columned façade in the style of the Roman Baroque is a work by Giacomo Amato. The interior is richly adorned by stucco works by Giacomo, Giuseppe and Procopio Serpotta. The large ceiling fresco, *Glory of the Dominican Order*, is a work by Antonino Grano (1708). The neighbouring Chiesa di **Santa Teresa** stands on the site of the Arab harbour castle built in AD 937.

Santa Maria dello Spasimo At the southern edge of the Kalsa neighbourhood, the incomplete late Gothic Spanish church (1503), which was in the past used as a theatre, a plague hospital and a poor house, has now become a **cultural centre**. Open-air concerts and plays are put on here.

Villa Giulia »In the public garden, immediately by the road, I spent the most enjoyable hours in tranquillity. It is the most wonderful place on earth.« (Goethe on 27 April 1787). The park (daily 9am–6pm, in winter Mon–Sat 9am–5pm, Sun only until 2pm) goes back to a Rococo garden created by Niccolò Palma in 1778. At the centre is a fountain with a sundial; for a second fountain Marabitti made the sculpture of the Genius of Palermo (18th century). Next to Villa Giulia is the **Botanical Garden** (Orto Botanico), which was laid out

Presumably Palermo's oldest Norman church: San Giovanni dei Lebbrosi

in 1789. Its monumental entrance with Doric columned halls on both sides and a central dome was built by the Frenchman Léon Dufourny in 1789. More than 10,000 plants from all around the world flourish outside and in eight greenhouses here.

At the southern end of Via Abramo Lincoln is the central station. To the right of it is the small monastery church of **Sant'Antonino** dating from the 17th century; in the last chapel to the right is a wooden crucifix painted by Fra Umile da Petralia and Fra Innocenzo da Palermo, c. 1639.

Stazione Centrale

Outside the City Centre

Corso dei Mille, the extension of Via Garibaldi, begins east of the central station; it runs in a south-easterly direction. It was here that on the night of 26 to 27 May 1860 Garibaldi's »Expedition of a Thousand« encountered Bourbon forces for the first time in Palermo. The Corso crosses the Oreto River, which is spanned by the **Ponte dell'Ammiraglio**, the city's oldest bridge. It got its name from Roger II's admiral, George of Antioch, who donated it in 1113. The bridge spans the river in seven arches that are smaller towards the banks.

Southeastern Palermo

Just over half a mile further, on the left-hand side, is the church of San Giovanni dei Lebbrosi (Corso dei Mille 382). The dating is unclear: according to prevailing opinion, the church was built by Robert Guiscard and his brother Roger I in 1071 during the siege of the Arab-held city, making it Palermo's oldest Norman church. Originally dedicated to John the Baptist, it was named after a leper hospital. Frederick II gave the church and the hospital to the Teutonic Knights of La Magione (up until the 18th century). The Baroque elements were removed during restoration works in 1930. The unadorned, austere building with two Moorish domes has an asymmetrical façade, since there is a tower at the left-hand side. The eastern section of the nave is somewhat wider than the western section and is completed by three semi-circular apses. Two rows of robust octagonal pillars supporting round arches structure the basilica's interior.

San Giovanni dei Lebbrosi

Go westward from the central station on Corso Tuköry and turn left into Via del Vespro to the cemetery of Sant'Orsola. On it stands the Chiesa del Vespro (Santo Spirito), only open to the public in the mornings, in front of which the »Sicilian Vespers« began in 1282 (▶ Baedeker Special p. 42). It was built in 1173–78 by Archbishop Walter of the Mill (Gualterius Offamilius) as the oratory of a Cistercian monastery outside the old city wall. It was subsequently altered several times, particularly when viceroy Domenico Caràcciolo had the monastery pulled down in 1782 in order to make space for the new cemetery. During restoration works in 1882, in honour of the

Southern Palermo
✷
◀ Chiesa del Vespro, Santo Spirito

600th anniversary of the Sicilian Vespers, the later interior additions were removed. A striking feature on the north side is the colourful façade. Also striking is the east end, where the crossed arches of the three apses are made of lava. The south side is simpler, because the cloister adjoined here. The location of former monastic buildings can still be made out on the southern transept. The basilica's interior, characterized by Cistercian austerity, features two rows of round columns supporting pointed arch arcades. A pointed arch separates the elevated choir. The roof structure is open.

Santa Maria di Gesù
Turn back along Via del Vespro to Via Filicuzza and follow it southwards to get to a small cemetery on the northern slopes of Monte Grifone with the church of the priory of the Conventual Franciscans, founded in 1429 (4km/2.5mi south of the centre). The tomb of the founder, Bishop Beato Matteo del Gatto of Agrigento, can be seen inside; the priory complex possesses an attractive cloister from the founding days. A friar takes visitors to the belvedere (views!).

Above the monastery (Via Conte Federico) are the remains of **Favara Castle** or Maredolce, one of Roger II's summer residences. It was a complex with four wings (maybe dating back to Arab origins), which was surrounded on three sides by a lake. The northwestern side, adorned with blind arcades, is the best-preserved. The interior of this wing possesses a small groin-vaulted, domed chapel.

! **Baedeker TIP**

Visiting the anti-Mafia centre

Father Pino Puglisi worked with children and young people in the Quartiere Brancaccio in order to prevent them falling under the influence of the Mafia. The fact that this youth work threatened the power of the clans was demonstrated by his murder in 1993. The Centro Padre Nostro commemorates the committed priest and continues his work. In talks with the staff visitors will find out a lot about the work in the anti-Mafia centre (Via Brancaccio 461, tel. 09 16 30 11 50, www.centropadrenostro.it; Mon – Fri 9am – 8pm). The feature film by Roberto Faenza (*Alla luce del sole*, *In the Light of the Sun*, 2005) tells Puglisi's story.

Cuba Palace
When **Cuba Palace** (Corso Calatafimi 94) was completed in 1180 under King William II, it lay outside the city towards Monreale in a park with an artificial lake. Now Cuba Palace (Arabic »cubat« means »vault«) lies in the grounds of a barracks. It is a rectangular building, whose walls are adorned by pointed blind arcades. The interior features the remains of Arab stalactite decoration. Boccaccio described its original beauty in the sixth tale of the fifth day in his *Decamerone*.

La Cubula
The park of Villa Napoli dates back to Norman times; it can be reached via the entrance to a residential apartment block. The pavilion with the »small dome«, the »Cubula«, stands in a lemon grove (Corso Calatafimi 575, bus stop Villa Napoli). It was built around

the same time as Cuba Palace. It is a square structure with a small red dome, which opens to all sides with pointed arch portals with stepped archivolts and Moorish ornaments.

Turn from Corso Calatafimi into Via Pindemonte, which opens up into Piazza Cappuccini. This is the site of a Capuchin priory that is known for its catacombs. These underground tunnels were dug into the tufa after 1599 and used until 1881 for burials. Those who do not shy away from the macabre spectacle can look at around 800 mummified bodies, arranged by gender and class. Even the clothes, in a state of decay, still reveal the origin and profession of the deceased, because until the last century, many mummies were regularly given new clothes by their relatives. The bodies were brought to the Colatoio, a small, dry air-tight room, washed with vinegar after eight months and placed dressed into the wall niches or laid in open coffins.

Convento dei Cappuccini

🕐
Opening hours:
Daily 9am – noon
3pm – 5.30pm

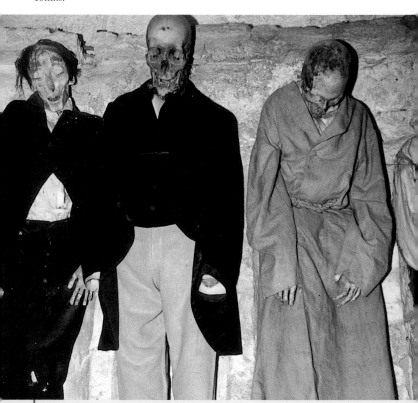

Mummified bodies in Convento dei Cappuccini

★
La Zisa

🕐
Opening hours:
Mon–Sat
9am–7pm
Sun until 1pm

The now beautifully restored palace, built by kings William I and William II between 1165 and 1180, can either be reached from the Capuchin priory or from Palazzo dei Normanni, as well as by bus 124. The complex, known as al-Aziz (glorious) in Arabic, is an Islamic-Norman pleasure palace. The three-storey building is rectangular, with the entrance on the long side, while the narrow sides feature central projections with 16th-century crenellation. There was once a bridge from the central entrance to a pavilion island in an artificial lake. Behind the portals a corridor runs straight through the building as a vestibule for the rooms beyond. The main room is the central room or fountain room with mosaics and a stalactite vault; there is an elevated fountain at the back wall, from which the water flowed down over an angled wall, which had a cooling effect. The water then flowed through the room and into the lake in front of the façade, a motif that is also widespread in Arab palace architecture. Inside the palace there is a **Museum of Islamic Art**.

Cantieri Culturali alla Zisa

In the immediate vicinity, in former factory grounds, the »**Cultural Building Site**« (Via Paolo Gili 4, tel. 09 16 52 49 42) was set up. Exhibitions, concerts, ballets and plays are staged here.

Northern Palermo

Parco della Favorita

On the southwestern slopes of Monte Pellegrino Ferdinand IV of Naples built an exile residence with an extensive park for himself and his wife, Maria Carolina, when he had to retreat to Palermo to escape French troops in 1798–1800 (now a park with tennis courts, a football stadium and a race track as well as three busy through roads). Palazzina Cinese (Favorita) was designed by Venanzio Marvuglia to match the Chinese look which was fashionable at the time. Inside, there are a Chinese, a Turkish and a Pompeiian salon (view of the park and of Monte Pellegrino from the roof terrace). The former estate buildings house the **Museo Etnografico Pitrè** set up by folklorist Giuseppe Pitrè. It exhibits traditional costumes, painted farm carts (carretti), tools, puppets, and figures from nativity scenes as well as ceramics (currently closed; the exhibits are temporarily on display in Palazzo Travallo, Via delle Pergole 74).

Città dei Ragazzi

🕐

The »Children's City« is an educational playground and experience park for all age groups (Viale Duca degli Abruzzi 1, tel. 09 16 71 43 73; Apr–Sept, Tue–Sun 10am–8pm).

Villa Igiea

Villa Belmonte

En route to Monte Pellegrino there are two beautiful villas and gardens open to the public. Leave the city centre on Via Monte Pellegrino and then take Via Bonanno. Turn right towards the coast onto Via Cardinale Rampolla. Where it becomes Via Papa Sergio I on the left, Villa Igiea (now a hotel with an Art Nouveau ballroom by Ernesto Basile) lies to the right, by the sea, and Villa Belmonte to the left, on the slopes of Monte Pellegrino(casino built in 1800 by Venanzio Marvuglia for Giuseppe Ventimiglia, Principe di Belmonte).

Northern Surroundings of Palermo

The former fishing village of Mondello is just 12km/7mi north of Pa-   **Mondello**
lermo, in a bay between Monte Gallo (581m/1906ft) and Monte Pellegrino (609m/1998ft). It was »discovered« by Palermo's affluent inhabitants in the early 20th century, whereupon it became a summer
getaway. It possesses an artificial harbour and a 2km/1mi sandy
beach (getting there: there are three roads from Palermo, frequent
buses, one night bus after 10pm).

At Punta di Priola, to the southeast, there are several caves, including   **Caves**
Addaura Grotto, in which carvings and other prehistoric remains
were discovered. The depictions of animals and plants resemble
those of Lascaux (France) and Altamira (Spain). Other good options
are boat and bus trips to Capo Gallo, the fishing village of Sferracavallo and the seaside resort of Isola delle Femmine (opposite the island of the same name).

Palermo's summer resort: Mondello

✷
Monte Pellegrino

Goethe praised this seaside mountain in northern Palermo as being the »most beautiful promontory in the world«. People have lived here since the earliest times, when the mountain was called Heirkte: in 278–277 BC Pyrrhus took it from the Carthaginians, in 248 BC Hamilcar occupied it and held back Roman attacks for three years. In the 17th century it was associated with the name of St Rosalia and became one of Sicily's major **places of pilgrimage** (hence Monte Pellegrino, Pilgrimage Mountain, but the derivation may also be from the Arabic Djebel grin, the nearby mountain).

There is a winding panoramic road leading to the pilgrimage chapel of **Santuario di Santa Rosalia** (429m/1407ft, 14km/8mi from the city centre). The road continues to the viewpoint, which features a statue of Rosalia (458m/1503ft). A staircase leads to the Baroque façade (1625), which stands in front of the Cave of Rosalia, which is 25m/27yd deep. The grotto contains a glass shrine with a sculpture of the saint inside (sculpture 18th century; daily 7.30am – 12.30pm, 2pm – 7pm). Goethe's description can be read in German and Italian on a plaque (▶ Baedeker Special p. 406). Countless votive gifts are testament to the people's firm faith. Every year Palermo's patron saint is celebrated between 13 and 15 September.

It takes half an hour to climb to the summit of Monte Pellegrino from the Santuario (antenna on top, 609m/1998ft; **magnificent view**).

Southern area around Palermo

Monreale

▶Monreale (8km/5mi southwest)

Carini

▶Carini (26km/16mi to the west)

Piana degli Albanesi

This convivial town, 24km/15mi south of Palermo (720m/2362ft, population 6300), can be reached via a panoramic road. It was founded in 1488 by Greek Orthodox Albanians who had fled from the Turks. Other Albanian villages are Contessa Entellina (1450) and Biancavilla (1489). The town is the seat of a Greek-Catholic bishop for the Albanians living in Italy. Up until the 19th century all public offices were held by Albanians. The local dialect still survives today, as do the local customs and the precious traditional costumes that are still worn for church festivals, such as Easter, Epiphany and Saint George's Day (23 April). Services are held in Albanian, Greek and Italian. The cannoli stuffed with ricotta and candied fruits are famous all over Sicily.

In the Uniate church of San Giorgio, an iconostasis separates the nave from the sanctuary, as is the Orthodox custom. In the church of San Demetrio (16th century) there are late-Byzantine icons as well as an apse adorned by Pietro Novelli. The large **reservoir** of Piana degli Albanesi to the south of town supplies Palermo with drinking water.

The small town with its medieval castle is situated around 32km/ 20mi southeast of Palermo (approx. 30km/19mi from Piana degli Albanesi). A few miles to the north, by a bridge, there is an Arab bathhouse (**Bagni di Cefalà**, presumably from the 11th century). This complex, built in the vicinity of the Cefalà River and a hot spring, is considered a unique building of Arab culture in Sicily. There are bands of ornamentation around the exterior walls featuring Kufic inscriptions. The building contains three deep pools in a hall (barrel-vaulted ceiling) measuring 14 x 6.50m/4 x 21 ft. The back of the room is separated by two columns supporting three arches. The building was used for livestock for a long time, then it was restored and it is now accessible to the public.

Cefalà Diana
◄ Saracen baths

East of Palermo

Modern speculative building made this town the victim of urban sprawl. It is located 12km/7mi east of Palermo (80m/260ft, population 54,000; getting there: A 19 or SS 113 towards Cefalù) set in a well-irrigated landscape of lush vegetation. The aristocracy of Palermo built villas in Bagheria in the 17th and 18th centuries, as they wanted to reside in a manner befitting their status, and in a beautiful location but away from the seat of the viceroys.

Bagheria

◄ Baroque monster and concrete

The trend began when Giuseppe Branciforte, Principe di Butera, disappointed that his hopes of becoming a Spanish viceroy in Sicily had not worked out, chose to build **Villa Butera** as a castle-like manor house in the middle of a large garden (1658, Corso Butera). Not far away is **Villa Villarosa**, which is a good 130 years younger. It was built by the architect Giovanni Venanzio Marvuglia between 1790 and 1792. As a Neoclassical structure with colossal Corinthian columns, it marks the final chapter of period styles represented in Bagheria.

The most elaborate complex is **Villa Valguarnera** (Piazza Garibaldi), which has a stately drive, an oval courtyard flanked by columned halls and the concave façade of the casino. The Dominican architect Tommaso M. Napoli built it in 1714 for Principessa Anna Valguarnera.

> ! **Baedeker TIP**
>
> **Living like a Gattopardo**
> At the end of the 18th century the counts Pilo di Capaci had a villa built amid orange trees near **Santa Flavia**. The utility rooms have been turned into comfortable accommodation (Agriturismo Villa Cefala, SS 113 no. 48, tel. 0 91 93 15 45, 34 77 51 93 90, www.tenuta cefala.it). Very good cuisine, mainly traditional, is served in **Trattoria Don Ciccio** (Via del Cavaliere 87, Bagheria, tel. 0 91 93 24 42; closed Wed and Sun).

Villa Cattólica by Francesco Bonanni, Principe di Cattólica, was built shortly after 1700. Since 1974 the villa has been home to the Galleria d'Arte Moderna with works by the painter Renato Guttuso (d. 1987, ►Famous People), who was born in Bagheria in 1912, and other contemporary painters (on the SS 113; Tue – Sun 9.30am – 2pm,   ☉

Villa Cattólica

The walls of Villa Palagonia are populated by bizarre characters.

3pm–7.30pm; www.museoguttuso.it). Tommaso M. Napoli was also the architect of **Villa Palagonia,**, commissioned by Ferdinando Gravina, Principe di Palagonia in 1715. The building has an elliptical floor plan. The convex entrance façade corresponds to the concave centre of the garden side with its elaborate staircase. The bizarre, monstrous stone sculptures on the walls and portals all around the main building have aroused much criticism (daily 9am–1pm, 4pm–7pm, in winter 3.30pm–5.30pm, www.villapalagonia..it).

Solunto ✱ This very interesting excavation site near Sicily's north coast is around 18km/11mi east of Palermo and 3.5km/2mi northeast of Bagheria on the eastern slopes of Monte Catalfano (374m/1227ft), from where the views are outstanding. Besides Motya (▶Mózia) and Panormos (▶Palermo), Solunto was one of the three sites to which the Carthaginians withdrew in western Sicily, to get away from Greek colonization in the 8th–7th centuries BC. In 397/396 BC Dionysius I of Syracuse destroyed this Punic town, which was presumably located in the plain near what is now Cozzuo Cannita. In the middle of the 4th century BC Solunto was refounded by its inhabitants in its current location on the hillside. It grew rapidly, especially since the

Carthaginians defeated the tyrant of Syracuse, Agathocles, in 307 BC and allowed his soldiers to retreat to Solunto. In 254 BC the town became Roman. It remained in existence until around AD 200, when it was abandoned. Excavations have been taking place since the 19th century. A walk through the **excavations** reveals a characteristic Roman town (exhibition by the entrance). Regardless of its slope (with a height difference of up to 60m/197ft) it is based on a regular chequerboard pattern (Hippodamian grid). Walking up from the museum, visitors first reach the southern end of the via decumana. It is almost 6m/20ft wide and possesses some original brick paving. The side streets are only 3m/10ft wide and surfaced with large stone slabs. One exception is cardo maximus, which climbs from its intersection with the decumanus (181m/594 ft) to the left to a height of 217m/712 ft. The houses on either side of the decumanus feature a peristyle around which residential rooms with floor mosaics and frescos are arranged; the simple buildings on the outskirts of town mostly do not have a central courtyard. Since the town did not have any springs, water supply was managed via cisterns.

🕐
Opening hours:
Mon – Sat
9am – 5.30pm
Sun only until 1pm

Follow the main road. The first site on the left is the **Ginnasio**; however, regardless of its name it is not a gym, but a particularly elaborate Hellenistic-Roman residence with an atrium and peristyle, of which six columns and the entablature have been re-erected. Beyond the cardo maximus is the elongated, narrow **agora**. In front of a row of buildings there a Punic-style altar on this square. On the left-hand slope there are a small building with semi-circular steps (**Bouleuterion**), in which the council of citizens met, and a **theatre**, which was built into the hillside (nice view). Both buildings are believed to date back to the 4th century BC; they were renovated in Roman times. »Solunto is so far the only place in Sicily where a mixed Greek-Carthaginian culture could be sensed.« (Margot Klee). While the houses have a Greco-Roman feel, the cult sites (Astarte statue) demonstrate a clear Punic influence.

Solunto *Map*

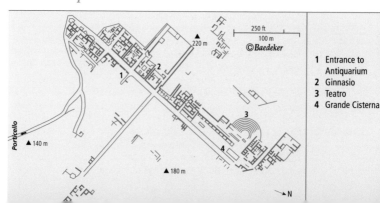

250 ft
100 m
©Baedeker

▲ 220 m
▲ 140 m
▲ 180 m

Porticello

1 Entrance to Antiquarium
2 Ginnasio
3 Teatro
4 Grande Cisterna

N

Santa Flavia The fishing and holiday village of Santa Flavia is 2km/1mi southeast of Solunto in a pretty bay. To the south of it, on Cape Solanto, there is a castle dating back to the time of the Norman king Roger II. It was later used to process the fish that were landed at the quay.

Porticello The northbound **coast road** leads to the fishing villages of Porticello (daily morning fish market) and Sant'Elia, then to Cape Zafferano (226m/741ft) and the steep cliffs of Cape Mongerbino and the fishing village of Aspra (bathing beach).

Pantellerìa

C/D 11/12

Province: Tràpani
Altitude: 836m/2743ft

Size: 83.5 sq km/32 sq mi
Population: 7800

Pantelleria lies completely isolated between Sicily and Africa – 102km/63mi off Sicily's west coast and only 84km/52mi from Tunisia. The island is of volcanic origin and is dominated by the Montagna Grande (836m/2743 ft), whose extinct crater is surrounded by several lateral craters.

Pantelleria The main town of Pantellerìa (population 5000) has a natural harbour on a bay on the northwest coast, dominated by the medieval Castello Barbacane. The airport is located 4km/2.5mi to the southeast, below Monte Sant'Elmo. Splendid panoramic views, all the way to the African coast, can be had from its summit, but those from that of 836m/2743ft Montagna Grande are finer still. Further **destinations** in the island's interior are San Vito (south of the airport), Vale di Ghirlanda (southeast of Montagna Grande) and Khamma (on the eastern side of the island).

✱
Heads of Caesar ▶ The chance discovery of excellently preserved marble heads of the Julio-Claudian imperial family in an open cistern on the acropolis in 2003 was an archaeological sensation. Today they can be seen in Barbacane Fortress by the harbour. A 40km/25mi ring road touches several small towns. 4km/2.5mi to the south of the main town of Pantellerìa are the Neolithic settlement of Mursia and the tombs (sesi), similar in character to the nuraghe in Sardinia. After passing the island's southern end (Balata dei Turchi) via the small port of Scauri, the road reaches the »rear of the island« (Dietro Isola). It subsequently makes its way back to the main town along the east coast. Along the way it passes Punta Levante and Cala dei Cinque Denti (Bay of the Five Teeth). A **boat trip** from the main town or from Scauri on the southwest coast is worthwhile. The trips go to interesting sea grottoes such as Grotta dello Storto and Faraglione Dietro Isola, which rises around 3m/10ft out of the sea.

▶ VISITING PANTELLERÌA

INFORMATION

Pro Loco
Piazza Cavour 1, tel. 09 23 91 18 38
www.pantelleria.it
Information also from the tourist
information office in Tràpani

TRANSPORT

There are several ferries a week
between Trapani and Pantelleria
(www.siremar.it, www.usticalines.it),
in summer there are also fast ferries –
when the sea is stormy, the boats turn
back. Inexpensive flights from Palermo and Trapani (www. flyairone.it,
www.meridiana.it). Rental vehicles at
the airport (www.pantelleriairport.it)
and in the main town.

SHOPPING

The very sweet zibbibo grapes are
used to make Passito di Pantelleria,
one of the best Mediterranean dessert
wines. Dunnafugata, one of the most
renowned producers, runs guided
tours on the vineyard from the

beginning of July to the end of
September (www.donnafugata.it).

WHERE TO EAT

▶ Inexpensive

Il Cappero
Via Roma 31, tel. 09 23 91 26 01
Mid-May–mid-Oct; located centrally
in the main town, popular with the
locals

WHERE TO STAY

▶ Mid-range

Mursia • Cossyra
Contrada Mursia , tel. 09 23 91 12 17
www.mursiahotel.it; 155 rooms
Two hotels nicely situated on the sea,
with all creature comforts such as
pools and an excellent restaurant

Blue Moon
Via Don Errera, Pantelleria (town)
Tel. 09 23 91 27 85
www.pantelleriahotel.it; 12 rooms
Modern hotel by the harbour with a
small spa area

Apart from beaches and pools, the island's leisure activities are sup-
plemented by particularly beautiful diving grounds, claimed by some
to be the most beautiful in the Mediterranean (there are several diving bases).

**Beaches, under-
water sports**

Patti

R 4

Province: Messina
Population: 13,600

Altitude: 157m/515 ft

**The cathedral city of Patti lies on the eastern section of Sicily's
north coast between Cefalù and Milazzo, on a terrace with views
of the Lipari Islands.**

▶ VISITING PATTI

INFORMATION

Servizio Turistico
Piazza G. Marconi 11
98066 Patti
Tel. 09 41 24 11 36
Fax 09 41 24 11 54

WHERE TO EAT

▶ Moderate
La Capannina
Mongiove di Patti
Via Catania
Tel. 09 41 31 76 30
North of the centre; signposted. The
search is worth the effort: large
selection of pizzas and fish dishes.

Al Gambero Rosso
Bivio per Montagnareale
Tel. 09 41 24 02 28
Closed Tue; somewhat west of the
centre, on the road to Montagnareale. Very popular restaurant »tipo
sferracafallo« (►p. 316), which is all
about the fish.

WHERE TO STAY

▶ Mid-range
Hotel Club La Playa
Via Plaia 3
Marina di Patti
Tel. 09 41 36 13 98
Fax 09 41 36 13 01
www.laplaya-hotel.it
70 rooms and apartments; right on
the sea (small beach), large pool.
Good base for visiting Tindari

Story of a humiliation The city developed from a Benedictine monastery founded by Roger
I in 1094. It is associated with a famous historical figure: Roger's
third wife, Adelasia of Montferrat. Adelasia is also associated with
San Fratello (►p. 378), which her Lombard troops founded in the
11th century. After the death of Roger I on 4 January 1101, she became regent for her six-year-old son Roger II until he came of age in
1112. In 1112 the crusader king Baldwin I, though still married to an
Armenian princess, successfully courted her, for her treasures but also for the political significance of Norman Sicily. In return, marriage
with Baldwin gave Adelasia the rank of queen. The marriage contract
was negotiated in 1113, and Adelasia made it a condition that the
crown of Jerusalem should go to her son Roger II should this marriage remain without issue. »In the summer of 1113 the countess set
out from Sicily in such splendour as had not been seen on the Mediterranean since Cleopatra sailed for the Cydnus to meet Mark An-
tony. She lay on a carpet of golden thread in her galley, whose prow

Baedeker TIP

Ostriches in the Nébrodi

In Patti's picturesque hinterland, south of San Piero di Patti, is the 200ha/500-acre Daino estate, a family-run business offering agriturismo, with oak and hazel woods and olive groves, a small carp lake, red deer, ostriches, peacocks, horses and donkeys. The restaurant in the lovingly restored stables serves regional cuisine, largely made with produce from the estate and served with their own wine. The 25 apartments and rooms are a wonderful place to stay. Il Daino, C. da Manganello San Piero di Patti, tel. 09 41 66 03 62, fax 09 41 66 05 40, www.ildaino.com.

was plated with silver and with gold« (Runciman), nine further ships carried her Arab bodyguard and her personal treasures. But just four years later, in 1117, Baldwin had the marriage annulled, having spent Adelasia's rich dowry. Adelasia, »shorn of her wealth and almost unescorted, sailed angrily back to Sicily« (Runciman). She died in Patti the following year (1118, sarcophagus in the south transept of the cathedral).

During the construction of the motorway the remains of a late Roman villa were discovered, which had been buried by an earthquake in the 10th or 11th century. The main building consisted of a large peristyle as well as two halls. The floors were covered in mosaics, created by artists from northern Africa. Parts of a bathhouse were also discovered. The excavation and restoration works are ongoing (daily 9am–1 hr before sunset). **Late Roman villa** ☉

Around Patti

The associated seaside resort of Marina di Patti, 3km/2mi to the north, with a sandy beach, rocky coastline and hotels, is a good place from which to go on boat trips to nearby grottoes and the Lipari Islands (►Lìpari, Isole). **Marina di Patti**

►Tìndari (10km/6mi to the east) **Tìndari**

The small town in the northeast of Sicily (population 5000) has an outstanding location on the western slopes of Monte Burello (960m/ 3150 ft) above Torrente Elicona. An altar relief in the Chiesa Madre depicts the life of St Nicholas (Gagini school). The castle was built by Frederick of Aragon (1302–11). **Montalbano di Elicona**

Isole Pelágie · Pelagian Islands

D–F 11–13

Province: Agrigento   **Population:** 5500

The Pelagian Islands of Lampedusa, Linos and the uninhabited Lampione are Sicily's southernmost island group, 160–200km/ 100–125mi from Sicily's south-western coast and just 110km/70mi from Tunis.

Almost Africa | Poor in vegetation and springs, surrounded by crystal-clear water, tropical-looking bays for swimming and a **colourful underwater world**, the islands have been a popular summer destination for beach and diving tourists from northern Italy only for a few years. They are also an **involuntary landing site** of the clandestini, refugees from northern Africa travelling by boat.

Lampedusa | Lampedusa, a narrow island elongated in the east-west direction, is 21 sq km/8 sq mi in area; its highest point is Albero Sole in the

Lampedusa: fishing still plays a big role in the islanders' lives today.

⏵ VISITING PELAGIE ISLANDS

INFORMATION

www.isola-lampedusa.it
www.isoladilampedusa.it
www.lepelagie.com (travel agency
with good service)

TRANSPORT

Boat connections from Porto Empédocle (Agrigento), 7 hrs to Linosa and
9 hrs to Lampedusa
Flights from Palermo, Aeroporto di
Lampedusa, tel. 09 17 02 06 19.
There is an island bus, also rental cars,
scooters and motorboats.

WHERE TO STAY

▶ **Mid-range/Luxury**
Lampedusa · Baia Turchese
Contrada Guitgia
Via Lido Azzurro
Tel. 09 22 97 04 55
Fax 09 22 97 00 98
www.lampedusa.to/baiaturchese
68 large rooms, some of them with
views of the bay, separated from the
sandy beach by a road

▶ **Budget/Mid-range**
Lampedusa · Borgo Cala Creta
Contrada Cala Creta
Tel. 09 22 97 03 94, fax 09 22 97 05 90
www.calacreta.com
The villagio turistico around 1.5km/
1mi from the centre is a nice place to
stay; 23 rooms, some of them in
traditional stone houses (known as
dammusi)

WHERE TO EAT

▶ **Expensive**
Lampedusa · Gemelli
Via Cala Pisana 2
Tel. 09 22 97 06 99
Evenings only, May–Nov
Excellent gourmet restaurant

▶ **Moderate**
Linosa · Errera
Via Scala Vecchio, tel. 09 22 97 20 41
www.linosaerrera.it
Excellent cuisine with many local
products; also help with finding
private accommodation

northwest (133m/436ft). The 5000 inhabitants used to live mainly
off fishing, but now increasingly off tourism. Italy's southernmost island keeps making the headlines: as a result of the rebellions in
northern Africa in 2011 the number of immigrants in Lampedusa
has exploded. Accommodating them is a huge challenge. Even bigger
problems are caused by plans of the Italian government that aim to
turn the »initial accommodation camp« into a »deportation camp«.
Lampedusa's coastline is largely rocky with many gorges and grottoes; Cala Croce, Spiaggia dei Conigli and Guitgia are the names of
the dream beaches with white sand and deep-blue water in the
southeast. The vegetation is limited to fig and carob trees, prickly
pears and oleander bushes. A few walls from the time of ancient Lo-
padusa remain. Uninhabited until the 19th century, the waterless island only became inhabited again in 1843. The author Giuseppe
Tomasi had the titles Duke of Palma and Prince of Lampedusa, but
he did not mention the island once in his novel *The Leopard*.

The **main town of Lampedusa** on a small bay in the eastern part of the south coast has an almost African character and is dominated by the pilgrimage church Madonna di Porto Salvo (near the small airport). There are only mule tracks outside the town, so trips are best done by boat (round trip of the island in 3 hrs). This is also the way to get to the best swimming areas and underwater regions, such as around Capo Ponente in the west or on the north coast.

The island of **Lampione** (180m/200yd wide, 200m/220yd long) is 18km/11mi from Lampedusa and uninhabited.

Linosa Linosa, the smaller island of the group, lies 42km/26mi north of Lampedusa. Around 500 people live on an area of 5.43 sq km/2.1 sq mi. The island consists of basalt, lava and tufa, ash and lapilli and has five extinct volcanoes. The highest elevation at 195m/640 ft. is Montagna Rossa The vegetation is dominated by maquis (mastic, euphorbia). Figs and grapes flourish on the fields. Linosa, the island's only town, has pastel-coloured fishermen's houses and is located on the southern coast near Porto Vecchio. The people make a reasonable living from fishing and farming.

Underwater area ► As on Lampedusa there are no surfaced roads outside the town. Thanks to the crystal-clear water and the rich marine fauna (latidae, common dentex, shade-fish, swordfish etc.) the marine areas around this island are perfect for divers who are happy to stay in simple accommodation or tents (www.mare nostrumdiving.it).

✱✱ Piazza Armerina – Villa Casale

08

Province: Enna   **Altitude:** 721m/2365ft
Population: 21,000

Situated on three hills in the midst of the Monti Erei with plentiful churches and palaces, the garrison town is usually only driven through on the way to the mosaics in the nearby Villa del Casale, but it is worth a visit in its own right.

Piazza Armerina is a relatively young town, founded by the Norman Count Roger in 1080. He moved people from the Lombard region here to control the surrounding towns inhabited by Saracens. In 1161 it was razed on the orders of William I following a rebellion by

▶ VISITING PIAZZA ARMERINA

INFORMATION

Ufficio Informazione
94015 Piazza Armerina
Via S. rosalia 5
Tel. 09 35 68 30 49 65
www.piazzaarmerina.com

EVENTS

Every year on 13th–14th August, the Palio dei Normanni, a popular festival, is celebrated to commemorate liberation from Arab rule. It attracts many visitors to Piazza Armerina.

WHERE TO EAT

▶ **Moderate/Inexpensive**
La Ruota
Contrada Paratore-Casale
Tel. & fax 09 35 68 05 42
www.trattorialaruota.it. Only open at lunchtime; 800m/900yd from Villa

del Casale, traditional cuisine with nice outdoor seating area; also a pleasant bed & breakfast

WHERE TO STAY

▶ **Budget**
Mosaici da Battiato
Contrada Paratore Casale 11
Tel. 09 35 68 54 53
Fax 09 35 68 54 53
www.hotelmosaici.com
23 rooms; basic, friendly hotel with a restaurant, closest to Villa del Casale

Agroturismo Sávocca
Contrada da Polleri 13
Tel. 09 35 68 30 78
Fax 09 35 68 26 99
www.agrisavoca.com
12 pretty rooms, some of them with kitchens, in an estate on the SP 16

---

the barons. By 1296 it was sizeable enough again for Frederick III of Aragon to convene the Sicilian parliament here. The town has been an episcopal see since 1817.

What to See in and Around Piazza Armerina

The townscape is dominated by the cathedral of Santissima Assunta because of its hill-top site and conspicuous dome. It was built in 1627 to designs by Orazio Torriani. The late Gothic bell tower of 1420 survives from a previous building. The façade still features Renaissance elements that are nicely contrasted with the Baroque portal of 1719. The interior of the basilica is Neoclassical and dominated by a crossing dome. It houses a crucifix painted on both sides, depicting the Crucifixion and Resurrection (1485 by the Maestro della Croce di Piazza Armerina), as well as the baptistery by Gagini (1594). The church treasure also includes a silver altar with the jewel-encrusted Byzantine icon »Madonna delle Vittorie« that Roger I had with him during the battle against the Arabs.

Santissima Assunta

Palazzo Trigona on the cathedral square is a good example of secular Baroque architecture in Piazza Armerina. The church of Sant'Ignazio

Further attractions

(1603) also dates back to the Baroque period. The library and municipal museum are now housed in the former convent. The church of San Giovanni (frescoes by Borremans) and particularly the church of Gran Priorato di Santo Stéfano were built in the Norman style; frescoes from the Norman period were uncovered in this latter 12th-century building.

The church of Sant'Andrea, somewhat outside town, was built in 1096. A huge fresco depicts Pope Pius II (1458–64) celebrating a mass of St Gregory together with cardinals.

✷ ✷ Villa Romana del Casale

The Roman villa (around 6km/4mi to the southwest), a UNESCO World Heritage site, is a tourist magnet, attracting many visitors to the island's interior. It was not until 1929, after mosaic stones were found, that scholars were motivated to explore the area, uncovering parts of a luxurious villa buried in a landslide in the 12th century. To date the main building with its nearly 50 rooms has been uncovered and preserved, but the utility rooms and the servant quarters still wait to be explored.

⏱ Opening hours: Daily 9am – 6pm www.villaromana delcasale.it

A media mogul of the empire

A previous building from the 2nd century AD was extended into a magnificent villa in the 3rd and 4th centuries. It is unusual both in size and in the lavish interior: the surviving mosaic floors cover an area of 3500 sq m/38,000 sq ft!

Naturally the question has been asked: Who commissioned it? It has not been answered with certainty to this day. The theory that it was not Maximian (285–305), one of the emperors of the Tetrarchy, but rather a livestock wholesaler has brought fresh wind into the controversy. Valerius Proculus Populonius from north Africa, who governed Sicily between 327 and 331, put on gladiator fights and animal spectacles for Emperor Constantine. The mosaic programme with its depictions (chariot races in Circus Maximus, capturing exotic animals for the arena) provides tangible clues. But the matter still has not been settled. The villa was inhabited until the 5th century. It later became derelict, but Arabs settled in the ruins.

Mosaics

The mosaics address a wealth of subjects from everyday life and life at court, from mythology to hunting scenes; there are also motifs associated with the Roman custom of using animals in their games. Such scenes in particular make the connection with mosaics of Roman North Africa likely: it is regarded as certain that artists from Africa worked here and created one of the largest and most beautiful set of mosaics of Roman Antiquity. Today the entire complex is covered. The set of walkways has been a successful development, enabling visitors to take in the floor mosaics from above.

← *The intact old quarter of Piazza Armerina is crowned by the cathedral*

Floor plan The single-storey complex consists of five areas: the entrance area: the elaborate three-gate portal leads into a polygonal **atrium** (10). Adjoining it to the north is a **bath** (1 – 5). Through the vestibule (11) is the **peristyle** (13), a building designed to impress, which is surrounded by several rooms. To the east, i.e. along the main axis, is the area of the magnificent **Great Basilica** (40). In the south is the elliptical **xystus** (29; portico) with the adjoining triclinium (36).

Entrance From the ticket office, walk along the ancient aqueduct (supported by arches) to get to the villa.

Baths **1** The route goes past the three praefurnia (furnaces). This is where the hot air was produced which was then channelled through clay pipes in the floor (hypocausts, an early form of underfloor heating) and in the walls to the **2** caldarium (hot bath).
3 Adjoining it is the tepidarium (warm bath).
4 Walk through the small massage parlour to get to the
5 frigidarium (cold bath), once a vaulted octagonal room. There are deep niches on four sides. These were the changing rooms. On the

Villa Romana del Casale Map

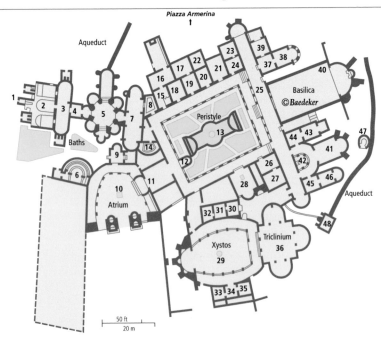

mosaic in the western niche two servants are receiving clothes from a lady. Opposite the baths are the **6** latrines.

7 Exercises to loosen up took place in the palaestra. The well-preserved floor mosaic depicts the Circus Maximus in Rome. It shows the racetracks with the spina down the centre and the two turning markers as well as the red, green, white and blue teams, the four teams of Rome, and later of Constantinople (the motif also occurs in room 45, on the scale of a children's game). The different phases of the race up until the handing over of the victory palm are also shown. Access to the baths **9** from the villa was via the small anteroom **8**. Aphrodite was worshipped in the nearly square room that culminates in an apse (fragmentary remains of cult images).

10 The **former main entrance**, a triumphal arch with three gateways, led into the courtyard (atrium), the centre of which is adorned by a fountain. It was surrounded on three sides by open colonnades.

11 The main complex of the villa, the peristyle, was accessed via the atrium, through the open vestibule. A welcome scene (adventus) is depicted on the floor. **12** Opposite the entrance is the peristyle's aedicula, a small shrine, maybe for the imperial cult.

Peristyle

13 This is now the peristyle, the rectangular, central area surrounded by 10 x 8 Corinthian columns, and a pool in the middle. The mosaics of the colonnade depict animal heads in medallions.

14 To the left of the vestibule is the access to the small latrine via a courtyard.

Rooms 15–24 now follow to the left of the portico: **15** room with furnace; **16** inner hall; **17** room for dancing; **18** geometric star mosaics; **19** room without mosaics; **20** room of the seasons; **21** room of the small hunt: five picture strips depict the sequence of a hunt: the hunters set off, sacrifice to Diana, feast, bringing back the prey. **22** depictions of Amor fishing; **23** mosaic with squares; **24** mosaic with octagons.

25 On the eastern, narrow side of the main peristyle is the corridor or colonnade of the Great Hunt, whose importance is emphasized by the double row of columns. This narrow, rectangular room, which ends in apses, is around 65m/215ft long and 5m/16ft wide. There are personifications of Egypt (in the south) and Armenia (in the north) in the apses.

Starting in the south (right), animals are captured, loaded on to the ship and brought to Italy, where their intended use is in the arena. The elegantly dressed man to be seen here is believed to be the person who commissioned the villa.

26 square mosaics.

27 girls doing gymnastics, the »**bikini girls**« (they are actually wearing underwear that women wore while doing gymnastics in the late Roman period), even made it on to the cover of *Time Magazine* (photo p. 55).

28 room of Orpheus: the wild animals gather around the musician Orpheus (fragments preserved). Parts of a Roman copy of Apollo Lyceus by Praxiteles were found in this room.

Great Basilica **40** The Great Basilica is a rectangular room ending in a semi-circle that features a marble floor. It is similar in character to a palace aula and must have had a similar function during ceremonial receptions. It is flanked by rooms with exquisite mosaics.

South of the Basilica **42** atrium with colonnade; **41** state room, whose well-preserved mosaics address the myth of the singer Arion riding on a dolphin; **43** hunting boys; **44** vestibule with Amor and Pan; **45** vestibule with small circus (compare this with the circus depiction in the palaestra, room 7); **46** musicians

Hunting scenes fascinated the former owner of Villa Romana.

29 South of the main peristyle is the elliptical xystus, a courtyard surrounded by colonnades with a foundation, a western exedra with a statue niche, as well as six smaller rooms on the northern and southern sides: **30** depictions of Amor harvesting grapes; **31** wine press; **32** wine cultivation; **33 – 35** depictions of Amor fishing. **36** There are a few steps in the east of the xystus, leading into the **triclinium**, a square room with three apses (dining room). The mosaics address the Twelve Labours of Hercules (centre), the defeated giants (eastern apse) and the apotheosis of the hero (northern apse). Xystus

Leave this solemn room and walk around the outside of the villa (eastern side) to get to rooms **37 – 39** north of the basilica. On the way there is a **47** latrine as well as the remains of the **48** aqueduct.

This area is only accessible from the outside; this is why visitors tend to go to this area last: **37** vestibule of Polyphemus, who is being given a goblet of wine by Ulysses; **38** mosaics depicting fruit; **39** well-preserved mosaics with erotic scenes, presumably the owner's bedroom. North of the Basilica

Aidone · ✷ Morgantina

The small medieval mountain town of Aidone (800m/2625 ft, in the Monti Erei, 10km/6mi north of Piazza Armeria, population 5200) was founded by the Arabs. Two noteworthy churches here are Sant'Anna (wooden crucifix by Fra Umile da Petralia) and Santa Maria La Cava (14th-century apse, Renaissance campanile). The excellent **museum** exhibits finds from Morgantina. The Ristorante Al Cordova is also worth visiting (Piazza Filippo Cordopva, tel. 0 93 58 81 12, Mon – Sat 8am – 8pm, Sun until 2pm). Aidone

◀ Sustenance in Aidone

Morgantina, located 5km/3mi to the east on the ridge Serra Orlando, is an **ancient Sicel settlement**. They were joined in the 6th century BC by Greek settlers from Katane. They settled in their own town, alongside which the Sicel town continued to exist. The town was surrounded by a wall almost 10km/6mi long, and extended to the top of Monte Citadella, on which the Greek acropolis was located. During the first half of the 5th century BC it was destroyed by the Sicel prince Ducetius; Syracuse rebuilt it. Diodorus described Morgantina in the 1st century BC as a significant, well-fortified town. The heart of the atmospheric, hardly visited excavation site is the **agora** and the buildings surrounding it (4th–3rd century BC). It is a rectangular square that was surrounded by halls on three sides. Parallel to the access route is a hall, 90m/100yd long, called the gymnasion, in which sporting events took place. There was a stoa on the eastern side, which was divided into two by a row of columns; the walls were covered in stucco and then painted. A similar stoa was probably planned for the opposite western side, but remained incomplete. The bouleuterion on the corner probably served as an assembly room. At ap-

✷ Morgantina, an ancient insider tip

⏲ Opening hours: Daily 9am–1 hr before sunset

Morgantina Map

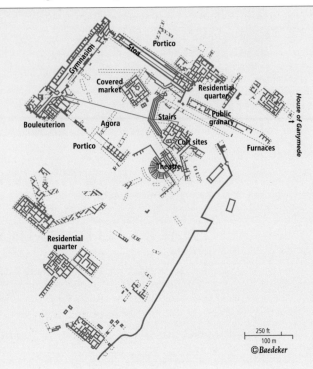

Morgantina Map

Portico
Gymnasion
Stoa
Covered market
Residential quarter
Bouleuterion
Agora
Stairs
Public granary
Portico
Cult sites
Furnaces
House of Ganymede
Theatre
Residential quarter

250 ft
100 m
©Baedeker

proximately the centre of this open space surrounded by these halls stood a square market building (macellum).

To the south of it, a peculiar **staircase** was uncovered. It does not run in a straight line. It describes two obtuse angles and had a double function. It separated the higher northern section of the agora (the market) from the southern section, which was dedicated to public functions; in addition its steps served as seating during assemblies.

Immediately to the south of the stairs are remains of cult buildings (Temple of Demeter, 4th century BC). Opening up to this building is a small theatre nestling into the western slopes (views of Mount Etna!). In the east the lower agora is bounded by a building almost 100m/110yd long. It is believed to have been a public granary. This area possessed a potter's kiln and a smelting furnace (both now covered).

To the east, above the agora, it is possible to visit a **residential quarter**. It had peristyle houses, some of which date from Hellenistic and

Roman times. One of them is the house of Ganymede, named after its partially destroyed mosaic floors that depict the Abduction of Ganymede by the eagle of Zeus (2nd century BC).

Barrafranca (population 13,000), also in the middle of the Monti Erei, 20km/12mi west of Piazza Armerina, is known for its olives, almonds and hazelnuts. The Chiesa Madre contains a *Santa Maria della Purificazione* by Filippo Paladino (1544–1614) from Tuscany, who moved to Sicily in 1601; the Chiesa dell'Itria has a painting by Mattia Preti (2nd altar to the left). **Barrafranca**

★ Ragusa

Q 11

Provincial capital
Population: 73,600

Altitude: 502m/1647ft

The provincial capital, one of Sicily's three most significant Baroque cities, runs along a rocky ridge of the Monti Iblei between the deep valleys of the Torrente San Leonardo and the Torrente Santa Domenica.

The town consists of two parts separated by a depression: in the west is the sprawling, modern upper town, Ragusa Superiore, dating from the 18th century and home to the administration, the cathedral and most of the inhabitants, while in the east is the lower Ragusa Ibla, with picturesque winding alleys and elegant Baroque buildings. Note the oil drilling rigs at the entrance to the town; agriculture is also booming here. Provolone cheese from Ragusa possesses the sought-after DOP quality seal (Di Origine Protetta). **Two faces of a Baroque gem**

The Sicel town of Hybla fell under the influence of the Sicilian Greeks in the 6th century BC. In Byzantine times the town was refounded, probably with settlers from Ragusa (modern-day Dubrovnik) on the Dalmatian coast. In 1693 the great earthquake caused such substantial damage that it was decided not just to rebuild the town in its old location but to also develop the area on the higher plateau to the west, where the new town was then built on a relatively rectangular grid pattern: a unique Baroque ensemble. **History**

Ragusa Superiore · New Town

The best place to start a tour of the upper town is Piazza del Popolo near the station (central bus station). It is situated to the south of the gorge of Torrente Santa Domenica, which is spanned by three bridges: the modern Ponte di Papa Giovanni XXIII, furthest below, Ponte dei Cappuccini (also known as Ponte Vecchio; 1st half of the **Piazza del Popolo**

⏵ VISITING RAGUSA

INFORMATION

Ufficio Informazione
Piazza San Giovanni
97100 Ragusa Ibla
Tel. 09 32 67 66 35
www.ragusaturismo.it

WHERE TO EAT

▶ **Expensive**

Marina da Ragusa ·
① *Lido Azzuro*
Lungomare Andrea Doria
Tel. 09 32 23 95 22; April–15 Oct
Situated on the wonderful sandy
beach; delicious seafood and outstanding wines. Open all year round;
equally good are Locanda Don Ser-
afino (Via Orfanotrofio 39, tel.
093 22 48 77 81, closed Tue) and the
hotel in Ragusa Ibla (Via XI Febbraio
15, tel. 09 32 24 87 78); www.locanda
donserafino.it.

North of Camarina · Sakaleo
▶p. 374

▶ **Moderate/Inexpensive**

② *U'Saracinu*
Via del Convento 9 (Ibla)
Tel. 09 32 4 69 76
closed Wed; rustic food in a former
monastery

③ *La Rusticana*
Via 25 Aprile 68 (Ibla)
Tel. 09 32 22 79 81, closed Tue;
good traditional cuisine in the attractive centre

Donnafugata · Al Castello
▶p. 375

WHERE TO STAY

▶ **Mid-range**

① *Mediterraneo Palace*
Via Roma 189,
Tel. 09 32 62 19 44
Fax 09 32 62 37 99
www.mediterraneopalace.it
92 rooms; best hotel in town

② *Il Barocco*
Via S. Maria La Nuova 1 (Ibla)
Tel. 09 32 66 31 05, fax 09 32 66 31 05
www.ilbarocco.it; 15 pretty rooms in
the renovated old building

Cómiso · Villa Orchidea
Contrada da Bosco Rotondo on the
road to Pedalino
Tel. 09 32 87 91 08, fax 09 32 87 90 34
www.villaorchidea.it – 56 rooms in a
well-tended hotel complex, approx.
20km/12mi west of Ragusa and just as
close to the coast (sandy beach)

19th century) as well as Ponte Senatore Pennavaria (also known as
Ponte Nuovo; 1936). Walk northwards from Piazza del Popolo to the
nearby Piazza della Libertà and on over the wide Ponte Senatore
Pennavaria to Via Roma, which lies in the area of the original new
town with its grid-pattern layout. At the intersection with Corso Italia, the main road running east-west, turn right to get to Piazza San
Giovanni.

Cathedral   This square forms a terrace in the sloping terrain and is dominated
by the imposing façade of the cathedral of San Giovanni (1706–60),

next to which there is a high campanile. The chapels in the interior are adorned with artistic stucco work. The town hall (municipio), the courts, the prefecture and the **Museo Archeologico Ibleo** in Palazzo Mediterraneo (Via Natalelli; daily 9am–2pm, 3.30pm–6.30pm) are all nearby. The museum exhibits prehistoric, Greek and Roman finds from Ragusa and the surrounding area.

! *Baedeker* TIP

Views

The approach to Ragusa is particularly picturesque from Módica: on the way to the upper town the road passes the lower, picturesque old town.

At its lower end Corso Italia becomes Corso Mazzini, which leads down to Ragusa Ibla in a series of hairpins. At the beginning of this road is the church of **Santa Maria delle Scale**, thus named because of the Scale, the steps to the lower town that begin here. The 18th-century church still has some late Gothic elements from the previous building (15th century), such as the campanile and the portal-like opening into a side chapel within the church.

From the square in front of the cathedral, the views of Ragusa Ibla all the way to the striking dome of San Giorgio are lovely. For those not following Corso Mazzini, this is the start of the descent (242 steps) of a stair leading to the older part of town.

✳ Views

◀ La Scala

✳ Ragusa Ibla · Old Town

The old town or lower town, which is best visited on foot because of the narrow streets and lack of parking space, is in the same place where, presumably, the original Sicel town of Hybla, the later Greek Hybla Heraia, was located. This now quieter area was also rebuilt in the Baroque style after 1693.
At the lower end of La Scala is the small Piazza della Repubblica, situated on a saddle, where a wide stair leads up to the Baroque church of Anime del Purgatorio. There are two 18th-century palazzi nearby, Palazzo Cosentini with bizarre balcony sculptures and Palazzo Bertini.

The glazed dome of San Giorgio, 1744–75, built to plans by Rosario Gagliardi, is a good landmark and a particularly nice example of Sicilian Baroque architecture. In a dominant position above a wide staircase, the façade's convex central section with the main entrance juts forward between three columns on either side. The order of the columns continues on the upper floor, on which the tower-like bell chamber, much adorned with sculptures, rises high into the sky. The high tambour dome was only built in 1820. Inside the church is an altarpiece by Vito d'Anna (1720–69), *The Glory of Saint Nicholas*.

✳ San Giorgio

Ragusa Map

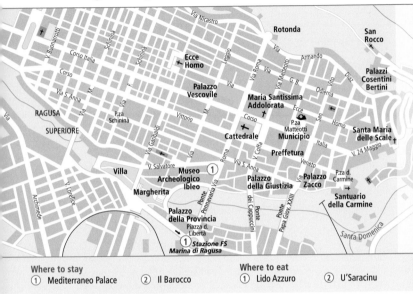

Where to stay
① Mediterraneo Palace   ② Il Barocco

Where to eat
① Lido Azzuro   ② U'Saracinu

Further Attractions

Chiesa di San Giuseppe
Somewhat to the east, on Piazza Pola, is Chiesa di San Giuseppe (R. Gagliardi). The façade is incredibly dynamic. The interior features an elliptical floor plan and rich furnishings. The silver statue of St Joseph dates back to the 16th century.

Giardino Ibleo
From here Corso 25 Aprile leads to the nearby city park of Giardino Ibleo. In the garden itself the belvedere is a good vantage point for views of the surrounding landscape; the bell tower, clad in majolica, is part of the church of San Domenico. To the right of the entrance into the city park, the Gothic portal of the church of San Giorgio Vecchio, destroyed in 1693, still survives. The **Chiesa dei Cappuccini Vecchi** with a chief work by Pietro Novelli (1603–47), *The Assumption of the Virgin*.

Via Mercato
Via Chiaramonte becomes Via Mercato, which, past the arches of a handsome market hall, leads back to the starting place at Piazza della Repubblica.

Around Ragusa

Cómiso
No nuclear weapons ▶
This small southern Sicilian farming town, 16km/10mi west of Ragusa at the foot of the Hybaean Mountains (209m/686 ft, population

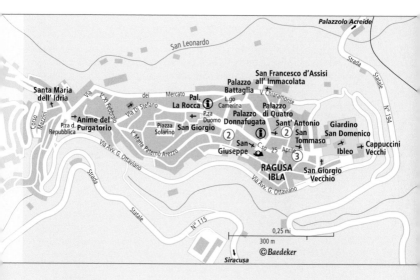

③ La Rusticana

30,000), was rebuilt after the 1693 earthquake, which gave the town a strong Baroque character. In the early 1980s the town hit the headlines because NATO had stationed nuclear weapons here (they were dismantled again after the end of the Cold War). The author Gesualdo Bufalino (1920–96), who subjected Sicily to a critical examination in his works (*Museo d'ombre*, 1982; *L'uomo invaso*, 1986), lived here. The castle of Naselli d'Aragona goes back to the 14th century (Gothic portal and octagonal tower, which surrounds a Byzantine baptistery with 14th-century frescoes) and was expanded in the 16th century. Among the town's churches are Chiesa di San Francesco (13th–14th century; in Cappella Naselli from 1517 is the tomb of Gaspare Naselli by Antonello Gagini) and the Baroque Chiesa Madre (rebuilt after 1693 with a three-storey façade) as well as Sant'Annunziata on a terrace in the upper town, a domed basilica with a powerful façade and a late Baroque interior verging on the Neoclassical (dome with columned tambour from 1877–85), which was designed by G. B. Cassione and built between 1772 and 1793. It is »proof of the longevity of Baroque in Sicily« (W. Krönig).

Vittória

Vittória, a centre of wine, oil and fruit growing (6km/4mi west of Cómiso, population 63,000), is situated on a plateau on the southern foothills of the Monti Iblei. The town was founded in 1607 by the Spanish viceroy Marcantonio Colonna, who named it after his daughter. It is built on a chequerboard pattern, at the heart of which is Piazza del Popolo, the location of the church of Madonna delle Grazie (18th century) and the Neoclassical Teatro Vittorio Emanuele by Bartolo Marelli (1869). Another Baroque church is the Chiesa Madre (San Giovanni), a cruciform basilica with a nave, two aisles and a crossing dome. The façade with its slender pilasters indicates the transition to Neoclassicism.

Camarina The ruins of the ancient town of Camarina are 16km/10mi from Vittória on the south coast on a terrace on the mouth of Fiume Ippari (ancient Hipparis). The town was founded from Syracuse in the early 6th century. Morgantina was also in its sphere of influence. In 405 BC Carthage devastated the town and the population went into exile in Leontinoi (Lentini). During the later confrontation between Carthage and Rome the town was destroyed in 258 BC and the population enslaved. During **excavations** parts of the town wall, once 7km/4.5mi long (5th–4th century BC), the remains of a Temple of Athene and residential buildings were uncovered. 167 lead tablets were found in the Temple of Athena. They probably served as personal identification. Some of the discoveries are exhibited in the Antiquarium by the temple, while others were moved to the Archaeological Museum in Ragusa (May–Sept 9am–2pm, 3.30pm–6.30pm, Oct–Apr only until 5.30pm).

! **Baedeker** TIP

Qui si magnifica il porco
In Chiaramonte Gulfi (668m/2192 ft, 20km/12mi north of Ragusa, population 8100) Ristorante Majore (Via Martiri Ungheresi 12, tel. 09 32 92 80 19, closed Mon) has been serving top-quality pork dishes since 1896.

Film set by the sea The endless **sandy beaches** north of Camarina and the fishing village of **Scoglitti** were used as the backdrop for the film *The Stolen Children* (*Il ladro di bambini*, 1992). Immediately beyond are the polytunnels for tomatoes, cucumbers and early strawberries. The large necropolis of Passo Marinaro lay to the southeast, on the other side of Cava di Randello. **Restaurant tip ▶** Ristorante Sakaleo (cat. expensive, Piazza Cavour 12, tel. 09 32 87 16 88) puts on a great show; the former footballer Pasquale Ferrara now wins every culinary home game. Fish and seafood are so fresh that they are often even served raw.

Donnafugata Donnafugata Castle (16km/10mi southwest of Ragusa) was built in the 14th century by the Chiaramonte family, but is largely a Romantic creation built by Corrado Arezzo, Barone di Donnafugata (1824–95). A crenellated building has a Gothic loggia on the main, Venetian façade. The castle became famous when it was named in Giuseppe Tomasi di Lampedusa's (1896–1975) *The Leopard*; however when Visconti made it into a film in 1962, he did not used not Donnafugata but the castle in Palma di Montechiaro that was built by Lampedusa (open: Tue–Sun 9.30am–12.30pm, 3.30pm–6.30pm in

Bird's eye view of the former residence of Barone di Donnafugata

summer). After visiting the castle, fortify yourself in Trattoria Al Castello (cat. moderate, closed Mon; Viale del Castello, tel. 09 32 61 92 60), housed in the former stables. ◄ Restaurant tip

Huge nightclubs and water parks are particularly popular with Sicilian young people, attracting them to Marina di Ragusa 24km/15mi south of Ragusa. Further bathing resorts frequented by the locals are Plaia Grande and Donnalucata (8km/5mi and 11mi/7mi east of Marina di Ragusa). **Marina di Ragusa**

Santo Stéfano di Camastra

Province: Messina
Population: 4500

Altitude: 70m/230 ft

Santo Stéfano di Camastra, attractively situated on a promontory on the north coast, is the most important centre of traditional ceramic production after ►Caltagirone.

▶ VISITING SANTO STÉFANO DI CAMASTRA

WHERE TO EAT
▶ **Moderate**
Da Giannino
Via Garibaldi 14
Tel. 09 21 33 17 48
Long-established restaurant with local dishes in an elegant family atmosphere

WHERE TO STAY
▶ **Mid-range**
La Plaia Blanca
Contrada Fiumara
Tel. 09 21 33 12 48
www.laplayablanca.it
42 rooms close to the sea (pebble beach)

Castel di Tusa · Museo Albergo
L'Atelier sul Mare
Via Cesare Battisti 4
Tel. 09 21 33 42 95

Fax 09 21 33 42 83
www.ateliersulmare.com
50 rooms, right on the sea; some of the rooms were designed by contemporary artists.

Sant'Àgata di Militello · Parimar
Via Medici 1
Tel. 09 41 70 18 88
Fax 09 41 70 14 97
48 rooms; basic hotel at the eastern end of town

Sant'Àgata di Militello · Giardino di Sicilia
Contrada Contura
Tel. & fax 09 41 70 36 72
Mobile 32 87 07 46 15
www.giardinodisicilia.com
12 rooms; bungalows in a nice garden, good food; language courses

Santo Stéfano di Camastra and Around

Santo Stéfano di Camastra
The workshops along the main road sell everything from solid workaday crockery to knick-knacks and replicas of old Sicilian motifs. The Museo della Ceramica in Palazzo Sergio displays local works. The town has a small **beach**. Further beaches are located further east near Canneto and Marina di Caronìa.

Letto Santo
Letto Santo – »Holy Bed« – is the name of the approx. 500m/1640ft **local mountain of Santo Stéfano**, on top of which stands a small 18th-century church; a side room stores countless votive gifts by believers from the Nebrodi communities; a small »museum« of piety. From up here the views of the Nébrodi Mountains are lovely, as are the views of the Lipari Islands and Sicily's northern coast.

Castel di Tusa
Castel di Tusa (8km/5mi west of Santo Stefano di Camastra) is a small seaside resort that comes under the commune of Tusa, located 10km/6mi to the south in the mountains. In 1986 Antonio Prestidas founded the Land Art open-air museum »Fiumara d'Arte« (»riverbed of art«) here. Renowned artists created sculptures for it,

Fiumara d'Arte open-air museum ▶

including Pietro Consagra, Tano Festa, Italo Lanfredini, Hidetoshi Nagasawa, Paolo Schiavocampo, Pietro Dorazio and Graziano Marini. The complex also includes the hotel Museo Albergo L'Atelier sul Mare.

On the road to Tusa, 3km/2mi from the coast, is the excavation site of the ancient town of Halaesa. Some of the ancient town wall with its square towers and the agora with the foundations of a Hellenistic temple remain.

Halaesa

Mistretta (16km/10mi to the south, population 5200) lies at an altitude of 950m/3117ft in the Nebrodi Mountains and is a good starting point for hikes in the area (Norman castle).

Mistretta

The old charcoal-burners' town of Caronìa is situated on a steep hill in the Bosco di Caronìa (304m/997ft, 12km/7mi east of Santo Stéfano, population 3400). This broad-leaf forest is the largest forest on the island. Its cork oaks were much sought-after in Antiquity. The Museo Etnoantropologico mainly focuses on burning charcoal, which was a traditional occupation here. In the valley of the Fiume di Caronìa the Romans built a bridge in the 2nd or 3rd century, of which several arches are still standing.

Caronia

The small town of Sant'Àgata di Militello (population 13,200) lies on the north coast on the floodplains of the rivers Rosmarino and Inganno, around 30km/20mi east of Santo Stéfano (sandy beach). The

Sant'Àgata di Militello

A mecca for ceramics lovers: Santo Stefano di Camastra

Museo dei Nébrodi, an ethnographic collection compiled by various mountain villages, informs visitors about the history and everyday lives of the people in the Nebrodi Mountains. Sicily's first Norman capital, **San Marco d'Alunzio** (5km/3mi to the northeast), includes the summit of Monte Rotondo. The Greek Temple of Heracles has been replaced by the church of San Marco. The church of San Teodoro dates back to Byzantine times. The Convento degli Agostiniani possesses a Gagini Madonna. On both sides of Sant'Àgata di Militello there are basic **seaside resorts**; Acquedolci, Torre di Lauro and Marina Caronía in the west, Torrenova and ►Capo d'Orlando in the east.

Monti Nébrodi

Sant'Àgata di Militello is a good starting point for an excursion to the Nebrodi Mountains, also known as the Caroníe. They consist of limestone and sandstone and are the western continuation of the Peloritani Mountains. The commune of **San Fratello** ► (675m/2215ft, 15km/9mi to the southwest, population 4500) was founded in the 11th century by Adelasia, the wife of Roger I. The horse-breeding population has held on to its old dialect. Among the old-established customs are the noisy Festa dei Giudei, the »Festival of the Jews« on Maundy Thursday and Good Friday. The domed hall church of Sant'Alfio e Cirino is of Norman origin. Continue along the SS 289 **Portella della Femmina Morta** ► to get to Portella della Femmina Morta, a watershed, after 19.5km/12mi, at an altitude of 1524m/5000ft. Shortly beforehand there is a left turn (road only surfaced at the beginning) to **Monte Soro**, the highest peak (1847m/6060ft) of the Monti Nébrodi.

Bluer than the sky: Lago di Ancipa in the Monti Nebrodi

Sciacca

G 7

Province: Agrigento
Population: 38,300

Altitude: 60m/197 ft

Sciacca is set attractively on a terrace above the sea on the south-west coast. The Romans appreciated the hot springs that have made this town the most popular spa on the island.

Founded from Selinunte, the town came under Carthaginian rule after its destruction in 409 BC. In the 3rd century BC it became Roman and was named Thermae Selinuntinae. It has been known as Sciacca since it was conquered in AD 840 by the Arabs, who in turn were forced out by the Normans in 1087. The 15th and 16th centuries were characterized by a feud between the merchant families of Luna and Peralta, the »Casi di Sciacca«. The partially extant town walls also date back to this time.

Spa and fishing port

 VISITING SCIACCA

INFORMATION

Servizio Turistico
Via Vittorio Emanuele 84
92019 Sciacca
Tel. 0 92 52 27 44, 0 92 52 11 82
Fax 0 92 58 41 21
www.sciacca.it

EVENTS

Famous Carnival

WHERE TO EAT

► Expensive
Hostaria del Vicolo
Vicolo Sammaritano 10
Tel. 0 92 52 30 71
closed Mon; fine restaurant in the town centre that combines traditional and innovative cuisine in a wonderful way

► Moderate
Al Faro
Via Al Porto 25, tel. 0 92 52 53 49
Closed Sun; inexpensive seafood dishes straight off the boats

WHERE TO STAY

► Mid-range
Grand Hotel delle Terme
Via delle Terme 1
Tel. 0 92 52 31 33, fax 0 92 58 70 02
www.grandhoteldelleterme.com
77 rooms; spa hotel right by the hot springs

Villa Palocla
Contrada Raganella
Tel. & fax 09 25 90 28 12
www.villapalocla.it
8 rooms; 3km/2mi outside town, late Baroque manor with a good restaurant

► Budget/Mid-range
Al Moro
Via Liguori 44
Tel. & fax 0 92 58 67 56, www.almoro.com, 10 rooms; sophisticated, modern B & B in an old palazzo. The padrone also runs the Hosteria del Vicolo. Generous breakfast buffet with organic produce

Fishing is still the main source of income in Sciacca.

What to See in Sciacca

Piazza Scandaliato
The town centre is Piazza Scandaliato with a nice terrace out to the sea and the town hall (a former Jesuit college) of 1613.

Casa Museo Scaglione
Somewhat to the southeast, on Corso Vittorio Emanuele, Sciacca's main boulevard, is the 18th-century Casa Scaglione with ceiling paintings, original furniture, and majolica floors (the town is known for its pottery). Today paintings, archaeological discoveries, old postcards and coins are exhibited here (Mon 9am – 1pm, Tue, Thu, Fri 9am – 1pm and 3pm – 7pm).

Cathedral
Next along is Piazza Don Minzoni with the 12th-century cathedral of Santa Maria Maddalena (16th-century façade). The interior houses a marble tabernacle with depictions of the Passion, attributed to Antonino Gagini.

Palazzo Steripinto
The imposing Palazzo Steripinto, built by Antonio Noceto in 1501 in the Catalan Gothic style, stands at the western end of Corso Vittorio Emanuele. Above a sloping pedestal the façade features lozenge-shaped rustication.

Chiesa del Carmine
Leave Palazzo Steripinto and walk down Via P. Gerardi to get to Piazza Carmine. Above a wide staircase is the Porta di San Salvatore

(city gate, 16th century). The Gothic Chiesa del Carmine on the square was altered during the Baroque period. The extant rose window was part of the original building. The main Baroque portal was never completed (column stumps). Opposite the church is the Chiesa Santa Margherita (now deconsecrated), donated by Infanta Eleonora d'Aragona in 1342, whose bust can be seen in Palazzo Abatellis in ► Palermo. The main portal of the Gothic building survives. On the northern long side is a further portal dating from 1468 with sculptures by Francesco Laurana. Since its refurbishment in 1595 the interior has been a hall church with rich stucco ornamentation.

◄ Chiesa Santa Margherita

The stairs to the upper town start at the cathedral. The upper town is the site of the Norman church of San Nicolò la Latina with its three apses. The Castello dei Luna (1380) is nearby. Only the external walls and a tower remain. The church of San Michele (16th century) stands on Piazza G. Noceto.

Upper town

Behind the well-tended Giardino Comunale in the east of town is the **spa centre** on the site of the ancient baths. It offers therapeutic hot springs, mud treatments and inhalations.

Terme Selinuntine

The limestone summit of Monte Calògero (388m/1273 ft) rises east of the town (7.5km/4.5mi of switchbacks). On the summit is the Santuario di San Calògero (Calògero statue by G. Gagini). Below the church, steam emerges from natural grottoes (Stufe vaporose di San Calògero); they have been used since prehistoric times for healing purposes.

Monte Calògero

Thousands of heads chiselled in stone, devils, paladins, deities, populate the walls and paths of an olive grove around 2km/1mi east of Sciacca along the old SS 115 (photo p. 382). They are the life's work of Filippo Bentivegna (1888–1967), who, after a failed relationship in the United States, returned to his home in Sicily, where he became a hermit and dedicated his life to sculpture (Tue – Sun 9am – 1pm, 4pm – 8pm, in winter 9am – 1pm, 3pm – 5pm).

Castello Incantato

🕐

Around 3km/2mi outside of town (first towards Agrigento, then towards Sciaccamare; signposted) there is a new thermal swimming pool (Piscine Molinelli). The beautiful beach of San Giorgio runs for around 6km/4mi east of Sciacca (some sections are free, others have to be paid for). There is also a long sandy beach to the west. It starts behind Capo San Marco and runs almost to Menfi and Porto Palo.

Thermal swimming pool

◄ Beaches

The Hinterland of Sciacca

The excavation site of Adranone is located 35km/22mi north of Sciacca on the road to Contessa Entellina, at an altitude of 900m/2953ft on the western slopes of Monte Genuardo (1179m/3868 ft). It

Adranone

is a Sicel settlement that later came under Punic, then Greek influence. One of the features uncovered is the monumental »Queen's Tomb«.

Giuliana

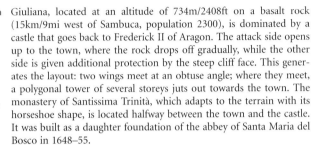

Giuliana, located at an altitude of 734m/2408ft on a basalt rock (15km/9mi west of Sambuca, population 2300), is dominated by a castle that goes back to Frederick II of Aragon. The attack side opens up to the town, where the rock drops off gradually, while the other side is given additional protection by the steep cliff face. This generates the layout: two wings meet at an obtuse angle; where they meet, a polygonal tower of several storeys juts out towards the town. The monastery of Santissima Trinità, which adapts to the terrain with its horseshoe shape, is located halfway between the town and the castle. It was built as a daughter foundation of the abbey of Santa Maria del Bosco in 1648–55.

Santa Maria del Bosco

The former Benedictine monastery of Santa Maria del Bosco (10km/6mi northwest of Giuliana) stands alone at an altitude of 831m/2726ft. The existing building were constructed on the site of an older complex in 1593. The monastery underwent development until the

Castello Incantato: heads chiselled in stone

18th century. Since the dissolution of the monasteries in 1866, the complex has been used as an agricultural business. The entire movable art treasures have disappeared. One of them was the tomb of Eleonora d'Aragona, one of the monastery's benefactors, who died in her castle in nearby Giuliana in 1405; the famous marble bust by Francesco Laurana (now in Palazzo Abatellis in ►Palermo) was saved from this tomb.

The small town 17km/11mi north of Sambuca (521m/1709 ft, population 2000) was founded by refugees from Albania in the 15th century. The inhabitants still speak an Albanian dialect. **Castello di Calatamauro** (5km/3mi to the west) is of Arab origin.

Contessa Entellina

This town (population 11,200) is situated 20km/12mi north of Contessa in the interior between the peaks of the Monti Sicani. In Arab times Qurlayum, with its two castles on the hills in the south and east, was of strategic significance. In 1237 Emperor Frederick II founded a Lombard colony here. In 1536 a rock fall destroyed part of the town. After the Second World War Corleone served as a marshalling yard for rustled livestock, hence its dubious reputation as one of Sicily's Mafia strongholds. The **anti-Mafia centre** provides information about the Mafia through files, photographs and videos as well as trial records of the Pentiti (»penitent« Mafiosi) and also operates tours of the town (Centro Internationale Documentazione sulle Mafie e sul Movimento Antimafia, Via Orfano Trofio 7, tel. 09 18 46 12 63).

Corleone

The »wood of Ficuzza« is best reached from Corleone by travelling northbound on the SS 118 to Mass. Castellaccio (18.5km/11.5mi), then turn right via Ficuzza to Bosco della Ficuzza (4.5km/3mi). This wood on the northern slopes of Rocca Busambra is considered the most beautiful in Sicily. There is a hunting lodge in Ficuzza (683m/2240 ft, now the seat of the forestry administration), which was built in 1803 by Giovanni Venanzio Marvuglia for Ferdinand IV, who had fled from the French from Naples to Sicily in 1799. This is a starting point for a hike (►suggestion p. 142) or climb up the 1613m/5292ft Rocca Busambra (panoramic views; this climb is best done with a guide).

Bosco della Ficuzza

◄ Hiking route 5, p. 142

There is a breathtaking winding road between Sciacca and Caltabellotta, which clings to a bizarrely rugged mountain (849m/2785 ft, around 20km/12mi to the northeast, population 4100) like an eyrie. In Antiquity the Sicani town of Triocala was located here. During the Second Servile War (104–99 BC) it was extended by Salvius Tryphon into a fortified castle, then later it was captured and destroyed by the Romans. The Arabs founded Qalat-al-Ballut (castle of the oaks) in its place in the 9th century. In 1090 the Normans under Roger I took the castle. In 1194 Sibylla, the widow of the last Norman king Tan-

Caltabellotta

◄ Location

cred, sought refuge from Henry VI here with her children, but to no avail. In 1302 the treaty between Anjou and Aragon was signed in Caltabellotta. Anjou relinquished Sicily, lost since the Sicilian Vespers of 1282, allowing Frederick III of Aragon to have it. In the church of San Lorenzo in the middle of town is a sculpted terracotta group of the Lamentation of Christ by Antonino Ferraro (1552). Behind the Gothic church of Sant'Agostino (Descent from the Cross by A. Ferraro) there is a path up to the ruins of the hermitage of San Pellegrino (pilgrimages on 18 August), which then leads on to the Chiesa Madre. It dates back to Norman times and houses a Madonna by Gagini. Finally there is the small Gothic church of San Salvatore. Climb up the steep steps to a crag on which stand the ruins of the Arab and Norman castle (fantastic views).

★ ★ Segesta

F 5

Province: Tràpani   **Altitude:** 304m/997ft

Remotely situated in the hills on the outskirts of a wide valley are the ruins of the ancient town (not yet excavated) with its incomplete temple and its theatre.

The cousins of Rome
Segesta (Greek: Egesta) was the third Elymian town in western Sicily along with Eryx and Entelia. It was founded by Aeneas who had fled from Troy. His son, Ascanius, is said to have founded Alba Longa, from where the legendary founders of Rome came. Segesta resisted Greek expansion and was traditionally allied with Carthage. During the first Sicilian Expedition by Athens (427–424 BC) it took its side. In 416–415 BC it again asked Athens for help in its battle against Selinunte. When the Athenians hesitated, the people of Segesta, using borrowed silverware, pretended to the Attic envoys that they were extremely wealthy, whereupon Alcibiades, as a »hawk«, was able to assert himself against Nicias in the popular assembly. Thus came about the second Sicilian Expedition, which ended disastrously for the Athenians. The following period includes a victory by Segesta over Selinunte (410 BC), growing dependence on Carthage and the devastation by Agathocles of Syracuse (307 BC). At the start of the First Punic War in 263 BC it joined forces with Rome because of their shared Trojan ancestors and in 260 it became the main Roman base in western Sicily. With modern-day Castellammare del Golfo, Segesta was given a harbour that soon outdid its mother town. The decline began in 73–71 BC when it was plundered by the Roman praetor Verres. Segesta became desolate, and the town disappeared almost completely. Just the temple and the theatre remained extant and survived the centuries. Current excavations have uncovered walls, gates and residential areas.

✷ ✷ Temple

The peripteral temple is situated outside the ancient urban area on a hill surrounded on three sides by Pispina Gorge. The Doric structure was presumably begun in 426 BC after Segesta entered a defensive alliance with Athens, and was built by an Attic architect, but it had not been completed when there were more conflicts with Selinunte in 416 BC. A stylobate measuring 23.12 x 58.35m/76 x 191ft supports six columns at the ends and 14 columns along the sides. Two of them had collapsed, but they were re-erected in the 18th century, so that all of the columns with their pediments and entablatures survive. Since the building was never completed, the columns were not fluted and the capitals were only roughly finished, while the tabs used for lifting the blocks are still present at the base. This stepped building is an example of one of the fine features of Greek architecture, its curvature: the stylobate is not exactly horizontal; along the ends it rises in a very slight arch towards the centre by 4cm/1.5in, along the sides by around 8cm/3in. For a long time it was thought that this structure was not actually a temple, but a monumental sur-

🕐
Opening hours:
Daily 9am
to 1 hr before sunset

The Elymian temple of Segesta, never completed

▶ VISITING SEGESTA

EVENTS

Estate Calatafimese: mid-July – Sept: plays and musical performances in the theatre (www.calatafimisegesta.com)

TRANSPORT

Segesta station, approx. 1.5km/1mi from the excavation site higher up

WHERE TO EAT/WHERE TO STAY

▶ **Inexpensive/Budget**

Below the temple there is a kiosk selling refreshments with tables in the shade.

Bar and Ristorante Antica Stazione Turistica di Segesta
Tel. 09 24 95 13 55 and 33 08 32 537
Closed Tue – in Segesta's station building

Agriturismo Baglio Pocoroba
Mobile 33 81 13 91 50
www.pocoroba.it
2.5km/1.5mi from Segesta, well-signposted. The food here is excellent and the rooms are also pleasant.

rounding roofless structure built around an Elymian temple. More recent excavations have revealed that a cella (naos) had at least been planned.

✷ ✷ Theatre

To the east of the temple rises the 431m/1414ft Monte Bàrbaro. The theatre, situated at 415m/1362ft (shuttle buses or on foot, approx. 30 mins) was built in the 3rd or 2nd century and redesigned by the Romans in around 100 BC. The semi-circular cavea is carved into the rock. It has twenty rows of seating in seven wedges separated by steps and a diameter of 63m/69yd. Only the foundations remain of the Roman stage building. Modern visitors, unlike those in Antiquity, are therefore presented with a magnificent view all the way to Monte Érice and Castellammare del Golfo, Segesta's former port.

Hiking trail ▶ A newly constructed path branches off halfway up the southeast side of Monte Bàrbaro and leads to an Elymian temple (6th–5th century BC).

Terme Segestane Beyond the bridge a turning from the road to Castellammare leads to the Terme Segestane (thermal pools, daily except Mon mornings and Thu, 10am – 1pm, 4.30pm – midnight). The locals have fun at a spring 300m/330yd upriver.

Calatafimi Calatafimi (355m/1165ft, 4km/2.5mi south of Segesta), founded by the Arabs (Arabic »qalat« means »castle«), became famous as a result of Giuseppe Garibaldi's first victory over the Bourbon troops (15 May 1860). An ossuary on a hill 4km/2.5mi southwest of the town on a hill, built in 1892, commemorates the battle and its victims.

✷ ✷ Selinunte

Province: Tràpani   **Altitude:** 35m/115ft

With its eight Greek temples from the 6th and 5th centuries BC and the nearby Temple of Demeter, Selinunte is one of the largest and most significant ancient sites in Sicily.

The compound declared an **archaeological park** is situated on steep terraces on Sicily's southwest coast. The acropolis on the western terrace and the (not yet excavated) town to the north are located between two small rivers, the Selinus (modern-day Modione) in the west and the Hypsas (modern-day Gorgo di Cottone) in the east. At the mouths of the rivers were harbours, which have, however, long since silted up. To the east of the Hypsas, a little further from the sea, is the eastern temple group; this is where the round tour starts. Beaches, restaurants and accommodation can be found somewhat to the east in the small resort of **Marinella**.

🕐
Opening hours:
Daily 9am–1 hr
before sunset

In 650 BC colonists from Megara Hyblaea near Syracuse founded a sister city far to the west in a hitherto uninhabited area, which they called Selinus. Selinon is the Greek word for wild celery; its leaf adorns the town's coins, often in conjunction with a picture of the horned river deity Selinos. This westernmost Greek town on Sicily was, like Himera on the north coast, an outpost against the Carthaginian western part of the island. It rapidly expanded its area of influence along the coastlines. Towards the north it soon encroached on the area of the Elymian town of Segesta. The argument about where the boundary should be was a constant issue. The 6th and 5th centuries BC were Selinunte's heyday. It was built on agriculture as well as inland and maritime trade. The people of Selinunte, estimated to

Celery town

Selinunte *Map*

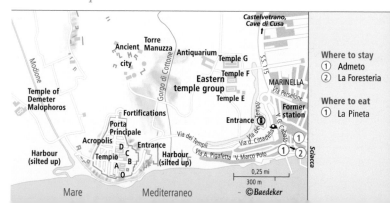

⏵ VISITING SELINUNTE

INFORMATION

At the entrance to the
Parco Archeologico
Tel. 0 92 44 62 77, www.selinunte.net

GOOD TO KNOW

Buses to Castelvetrano and Sciacca;
they stop at the former station in
Selinunte
Nice sandy beaches at the mouth of
the Belice between Marinella di Selinunte and Porto Palo

WHERE TO EAT
► **Moderate**
① *La Pineta*
Via Punta Cantone, tel. 092 44 68 20
www.ristorantelapinetaselinunte.it

Fresh fish and cocktails served right
on the beach in a nature reserve east
of Marinella.

WHERE TO STAY
► **Mid-range**
① *Admeto*
Via Palinuro 3, tel. 092 44 67 96
www.hoteladmeto.it, 56 rooms Great
quality, modern. Breakfast room on
the fourth floor with views of the sea
and temples

Menfi · ② *La Foresteria*
Contrada Passo di Gurra, Menfi
Tel. 092 512 95 54 60, www.planeta.it
►Baedeker Tip p. 118

have numbered 20,000 free citizens and 100,000 unfree individuals,
had the will and also the financial means to adorn their town with a
sizeable number of temples.

Selinunte had close trading relationships with Carthage, and in 480
BC it was the only Greek city to take Carthage's side in the battle of
Himera; but in 466 BC it helped Syracuse to topple the tyrant Thra-
sybulus. This change of sides was to have a disastrous impact. When
disagreements with Segesta triggered Athens's Sicilian Expedition in
416 BC, Carthage seized the opportunity seven years later to launch
a counter-attack. Selinunte was conquered and destroyed. According
to reports, 15,000 inhabitants were killed, while the rest were enslaved. In the 4th century BC Syracuse razed the huge bastions of the
acropolis, but later relinquished the town without a fight to Carthage, which in turn abandoned it in the face of the approaching Romans in 250 BC. Any buildings still extant were destroyed by a devastating earthquake in the 6th century AD. For a millennium Selinunte lay in oblivion and was only rediscovered in 1551 by T.
Fazello. Excavations began in 1822, initiated by the Englishmen Samuel Angell and William Harris, and in 1824 by the Jacques-Ignace
Hittorff and Ludwig von Zanth. In 1927 a row of columns belonging
to Temple C on the acropolis was re-erected, while in 1957–58 Temple E in the eastern temple group was re-erected.

Temple naming ► Scholars just named the temples with letters, because in most cases it
is not clear to what deity they were consecrated. As architectural

Temple E, a paradigm of a classic Doric temple

achievements and because of the sculptural ornamentation of their metopes (Archaeological Museum of ▶ Palermo) they are outstanding records of Greek art of the Archaic and Classical periods.

✳ ✳ Eastern Temples

The eastern group consists of three temples in a parallel arrangement. Going in chronological order, the earliest is the central one, Temple F, which was built in around 530 BC and was possibly dedicated to Athena. With a stylobate of 24.37 x 61.88m/26.65 x 67.67 yd, it has the same dimensions as Temple C, but a different number of columns, namely 6 x 14 (instead of 6 x 17). In order to achieve this for a very elongated cella, it was necessary to deviate from a basic rule of Greek temple architecture and make the distance between the column centres longer at the sides (4.60m/15 ft) than at the ends (4.47m/14ft 8 in). In addition, the inner row of columns was moved so close to the cella that the bronze gates almost touched it. The gaps between the columns were closed by stone barriers 4.50m/15ft high, so that the wide gallery between the columns and the cella was completely closed off to the outside world. The entablature on the eastern side featured sculpted metopes, of which two reliefs with gods fighting the giants were found. Inside, there was a second row of columns on the eastern side, as was the case with many Sicilian temples.

Temple F

THE GREEK TEMPLE

There are a number of unusually well-preserved temples in various stages of completion in Sicily. Thus it is possible study the construction of a temple from the quarry to the shell and the finished item.

Metope of Temple E in Selinunte: Wedding of Zeus and Hera (now in the museum in Palermo) Selinunte Temple Forms

① **Temple layout**
The **Temple of Concordia** in Agrigento shown here is one of the best-preserved temples of the Greek world. It rises above a stepped podium. It is surrounded by columns on all four sides. Its interior consists of three rooms: the pronaos, cella and the opisthodomos (photo p. 392, temple in Segesta).

② **Cella**
This slightly elevated room contained the cult image of the deity. Simple believers were denied access. Services took place outside in front of the temple.

③ **1. Opisthodomos**
This room behind the cella housed the temple treasure and the votive offerings.

④ **Entablature**
Columns support the entablature. It consists of the architrave and the metope-triglyph frieze above it.

⑤ **Construction material and method**
The temples are made of rough shell limestone. No mortar was used. The building mainly consisted of pre-fabricated parts that were assembled, covered in stucco and subsequently painted. The stone was cut close to the temple site. First trenches 50–60cm/20–25in deep were dug out. In order to separate the column section, the workers rammed wooden wedges into the stone and poured water over them until they swelled up and cracked off the stone. A chisel and mallet were used for the detailed work. Pack animals were used to transport them. Holes were drilled into the individual column sections and they were firmly fixed to each other with lead pegs. In order to lift the individual sections or other loads, the Greeks used a pulley system. They were able to lift loads weighing up to 6 tons.

Selinunte Temple forms

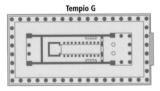
Tempio G

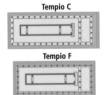
Tempio C
Tempio F

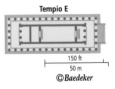
Tempio E

150 ft
50 m
©Baedeker

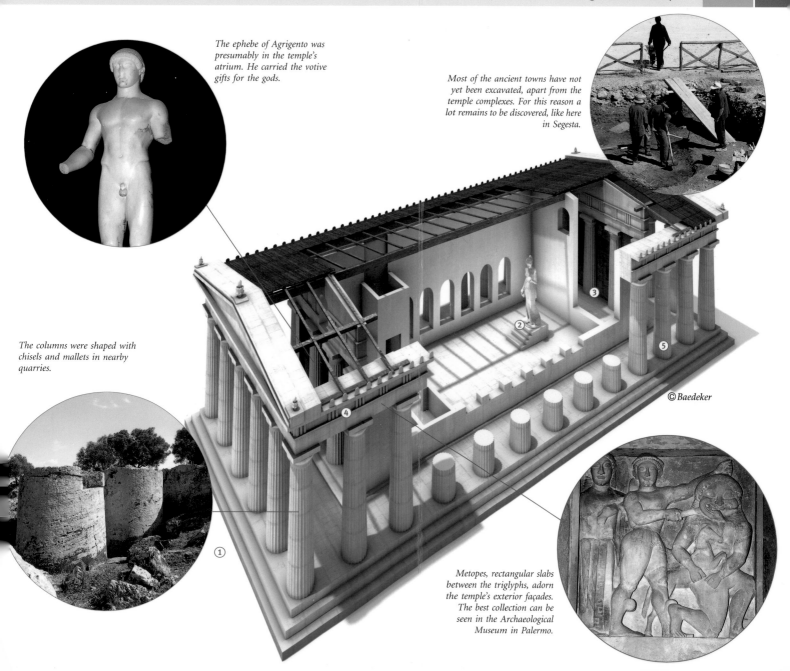

The ephebe of Agrigento was presumably in the temple's atrium. He carried the votive gifts for the gods.

Most of the ancient towns have not yet been excavated, apart from the temple complexes. For this reason a lot remains to be discovered, like here in Segesta.

The columns were shaped with chisels and mallets in nearby quarries.

© Baedeker

Metopes, rectangular slabs between the triglyphs, adorn the temple's exterior façades. The best collection can be seen in the Archaeological Museum in Palermo.

Temple G In around 520 BC, immediately after Temple F was completed, construction began on the neighbouring Temple G, which, according to an inscription, was consecrated to Apollo. Today it is completely in ruins, a veritable mountain of column sections, capitals and pieces of entablature. It is a good idea to wear shoes with a good grip if intending to venture on the impressive climb through the stony chaos. Its re-erection is shown as a computer simulation. Temple G had a stylobate that measured 50.07 x 110.12m/162ft 9 x 361ft 4 in, meaning it covered an area of more than 5500 sq m/ 6500 sq yd and had a height of around 30m/100ft. It thus had the dimensions of the huge Ionic temples (Samos, Ephesus, Didyma). It did not, however, possess their more slender Ionic forms; instead it was a Doric colossus. The floor plan specified: 8 x 17 columns surrounding halls in a pseudo-dipteral manner, which were two bays (12m/39ft) deep. A staircase led into the eastern gallery, from which visitors could access the pronaos with 6 x 2 columns and then the cella. Their roof was supported by two rows of ten monolithic columns each; it ended in a small square structure, which can clearly be made out amidst the ruins and served as the adyton for the cult image. Adjoining the cella to the west was an opisthodomos.

The construction period was naturally quite long, which meant that there were a few changes to the design and execution. The Classical style started wielding its influence from around 490 BC. As a result, the 14.70m/48ft columns on the eastern, northern and half of the southern sides, built in the 6th century BC, are slimmer, and taper strongly towards the top, where they have Archaic capitals; the remaining columns on the southern side feature transitional designs, while those on the western side have stocky shafts and feature the austere Classical capitals. Incidentally, only some of the columns are fluted, a design element that was only added after the columns were fully in place. This suggests that Temple G was not yet completed when Selinunte was destroyed by the Carthaginians.

Temple E The southernmost structure of this group is Temple E. In the early 5th century BC the people of Selinunte lost interest in the huge Temple G and built this Temple of Hera in 465–450 BC. In 1957–58 the Cassa per il Mezzogiorno paid for its reconstruction in order to stimulate tourism. All of the columns of the peristasis are standing again and with them also some of the entablature. The peripteros has a stylobate measuring 25.52 x 67.74m/83ft 9 x 222ft 3 in, meaning it was small next to the gigantic Temple of Apollo (G), but it was nevertheless around the same size as the Temple of Zeus in Olympia. It has 6 x 15 columns, all of which are 10.15m/ 33ft 4in high. They stand closely together and have a monumental presence. The corner conflict is solved by severely narrowing the corner bays, following examples in Greece. The gallery around the cella is one bay deep on the long sides and two bays deep on both of the narrow sides. As was the case with temples in Greece, the counterpart to the pronaos in the east was the opisthodomos in the west. The use of sculptured ornamentation is highly reminiscent of Olympia: as on the Temple of Zeus, the metopes of the peristasis are smooth, while there were six sculptured slabs above the pronaos and opisthodomos (Archaeological Museum of ▶Palermo). Their motifs include Heracles fighting the Amazons, the wedding of Zeus and Hera, the story of Artemis and Actaeon, and the battle between Athena and the giant Enceladus. The interior layout of the cella is in line with Sicilian traditions. The indispensable adyton was at the end of the cella. The increasing sanctity on the way to the adyton was emphasized by a sequence of steps: a staircase of ten steps led into the temple, six steps led up into the cella and three more to the adyton.

✳ ✳ Acropolis

The Via dei Templi crosses the valley of the Gorgo di Cottone in the area of the ancient eastern harbour (silted up) and leads across to the acropolis. Powerful walls protect the upper town (7th–4th century BC). It occupies an area of 17ha/ 42 acres and has a pear-shaped outline. A north-south street and an east-west street form the co-ordinates that cross at a right angle. The rest of the town was also arranged in a chequerboard pattern in line with the »Hippodamian grid«. The south-eastern quarter of the acropolis is taken up by temples that replaced smaller temples from the town's founding days. They can be found in two temene, Temples O and A in the southern one, Temples C and D in the northern one. Between A and C, shifted somewhat to the east, are the remains of the small Temple B, which was only built in Hellenistic times.

Temple C, the oldest and largest temple on the acropolis of Selinunte

Temples A and O Only the foundations survive of Temples A and O ((6 x 14 columns) built in 450 BC.

Temple B On the other side of the east-west road are the remains of Temple B. It does not have a peristasis, and there were merely columns on the entrance side (prostyle). It was built in around 280 BC, three decades before the decline of Selinunte – a modest conclusion to the town's magnificent architectural activity.

Temple C Because of its monumental row of columns (re-erected in 1927), the eyes are drawn to Temple C, the largest and oldest temple on the acropolis. Built in the highest location in around 550 BC, the stylobate measures 23.94m/78ft 7 in x 63.72m/209ft and has a peristasis of 6 x 17 columns with a height of 8.43m/27ft 8in. The first columns to be made were monolithic, while the later ones were made in sections. A typically Archaic feature is that the gaps between the columns differ by up to 23cm/9in, while the number of flutings fluctuates between 16 and 20.

Untamed vitality ▶ When this temple was built without attention to exact regularity, the expressive force was heightened further by adding rich terracotta ornamentation to the pediment and edge of the roof. The eastern pediment was dominated by a massive, brightly painted gorgon head (reconstruction in the Archaeological Museum in ▶ Palermo). This 2.75m/9ft clay relief stands as an equal next to the limestone relief of the gorgon of the Temple of Artemis from Corfu, which is four decades earlier. Also on the entrance side, the entablature below this pediment featured sculpted metopes: the quadriga of Apollo, Perseus and the gorgon, Heracles and the cercopes (Museum ▶ Palermo). Maybe there was a cult image of Heracles in the adyton, which only priests were allowed to access.

Temple D The neighbouring Temple D is estimated to have been built in around 540 BC. It already features the classical proportions of 6 x 13 columns. The interior consists of a deep pronaos, the cella and the adyton. As was the case for Temple C, Temple D does not have an opisthodomos.

Residential quarters and northern strongholds Follow the north-south road northbound, walk through the remains of the residential quarters from the period following 409 BC, to get to the main gate of the acropolis, in front of which the tyrants of Syracuse had powerful defensive structures built with trenches, bastions and towers (presumably 4th–3rd century).

✳ Temple of Demeter Malophoros A trail leads across the Modione (Selinus) to the sector of Demeter Malophoros. The first harbinger is a megaron to the left of the path. Just beyond it is the Demeter temenos, which itself stands amid a field of tombs. The temple's function is probably connected to its location on the way to the large necropolis of Manicalunga: funeral processions stopped here to perform invocations of Demeter and her daughter Persephone, who, as goddesses of fertility and decay, life and death, were Sicily's main goddesses. Here, in the district of Gaggera near Selinunte they had one of their most important cult sites, where they were worshipped as Malophoros (apple-bearer) and Pasikratea (Almighty Ruler). In addition, this district was also home to the cult of the chthonic goddess Hecate and the god of atonement Zeus Meilichius, a chthonic manifestation of Zeus.

The Demeter temenos is an irregular square on the slope above the river. It is accessed via propylaea in the east (5th century BC). The courtyard contains a small archaic altar and a large rectangular sacrificial altar. This is part of the Temple of Demeter, which replaced an older spring sanctuary in the 6th century BC. During the Hellenistic period a small cult area was erected for the goddess Hecate to the south of the propylaea.

Opposite the northeastern corner of the Demeter temenos is the sector of the Zeus Meilichius cult; it is possible to make out the remains of two altars and a small temple (300 BC) that only measured 2.97 x 5.20m/9ft 9in x 17ft. There were more than 10,000 small steles nearby, which depict the heads of Zeus Meilichius and a goddess associated with him (Archaeological Museum ▶Palermo).

Meilichius cult sector

There is a highly interesting excursion to the Cave di Cusa, the ancient quarries of Selinunte (▶Castelvetrano, around).

✷
Quarries

✷✷ Siracusa · Syracuse

Provincial capital
Population: 123,500

Altitude: 10m/33 ft

In Antiquity, Syracuse was for centuries the largest and most powerful city on the island. The many witnesses to this importance – the Greek theatre, ancient quarries, early Christian catacombs, a temple of Athena turned into a Christian cathedral and the archaeological museum – make the city one of high points of any trip to Sicily. The island of Ortygia with its romantic palazzi – the »Venice of Sicily« – retains its charming old-town atmosphere.

The germ-cell of the city is the island of Ortygia, the 40ha/100-acre »quail island«. Situated between two large natural harbours, with a plentiful supply of fresh water, separated from the mainland only by a narrow channel and yet easy to defend, it provided the ideal conditions for settlement. It was inhabited from the 10th century BC, certainly by Siculi, perhaps also by Phoenicians.

From quail island to cosmopolitan centre

Pentapolis – The
Five Towns ►

In 734 BC colonists from Corinth led by Archias drove out the Siculi and settled on Ortygia and on the mainland opposite. Just a few decades later daughter cities were founded: in 664 BC Akrai, in 644 Kasmenai, in 599 Kamarina. At the start of the 6th century Sicily's first Doric temple was built on Ortygia, while the district of Achradina spread out on the mainland, joined in the 5th century BC by the districts of Tyche and Neapolis. Syracuse was developing into the largest city in the whole Greek world. According to classical sources, in its heyday it had a population of half a million.

734 BC	Colonists from Corinth settle on Ortygia.
5th century BC	Syracuse is the largest city in the Greek world.
End of 5th century	Victory over Athens
212 BC	Romans take Syracuse.
535–878	Syracuse is part of Byzantine Empire.
878	Sicily falls to the Arabs, Palermo becomes the capital – Syracuse loses all significance.

At the start of the 5th century BC the people and their Sicel slaves rose up in revolt against the land-owning aristocracy known as the Gamori. Gelon of Gela, who already ruled large tracts of southeast Sicily, intervened. In 485 BC he conquered the city and established the first tyranny (485–478 BC). Syracuse thus became the capital of an eastern Sicilian state and enjoyed a phase of great prosperity, albeit enforced by rigorous measures such as the resettlement of inhabitants of Gela and Camarina to Syracuse. The zenith of Gelon's career came in 480 BC, when together with his father-in-law Theron of Akragas he inflicted a crushing defeat on the Carthaginians at Himera, in consequence of which he built a temple to Athena (now the cathedral) on Ortygia. He was succeeded by his brother Hieron I (478 BC 466 BC), who in 474 extended his power by defeating the Etruscan fleet off Cumae. A patron of the arts, he summoned Aeschylus, Pindar, Bacchylides and Simonides to his court. He was succeeded in his turn by his younger brother Thrasybulos, whose cruelty led to his being toppled just eleven months later. The tyranny was replaced for a while by a democracy (466 Bakchylides 405). This was celebrated annually at the Festival of Zeus Eleutherios (Zeus of Freedom). In 450 BC Syracuse and Akragas suppressed an insurrection led by Duketios, leader of the Siculi. The next few decades saw the major conflict with Athens, which sent two expeditions against Sicily in 427 and 415 BC. Syracuse was besieged, but the Athenians were crushed both on land and at sea. 7000 Athenians were herded into quarries for want of anywhere else to put them, and most died of starvation or disease. But the war also weakened Syracuse. This incited the Carthaginians to take their revenge. In 409 BC they launched a general assault, whose victims included Selinunte, Himera and Akragas.

At this point Dionysius I (405 Bakchylides 367 BC, ▶Famous People) rose to become tyrant of Syracuse; he concluded delaying treaties with Carthage and used the time to fortify Syracuse; Ortygia was given a double surrounding wall, while to the northwest of the city

Siracusa Map

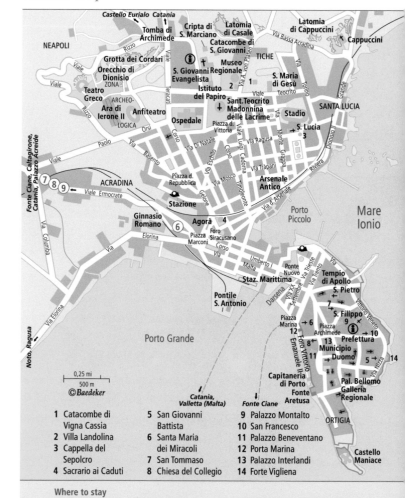

1. Catacombe di Vigna Cassia
2. Villa Landolina
3. Cappella del Sepolcro
4. Sacrario ai Caduti
5. San Giovanni Battista
6. Santa Maria dei Miracoli
7. San Tommaso
8. Chiesa del Collegio
9. Palazzo Montalto
10. San Francesco
11. Palazzo Beneventano
12. Porta Marina
13. Palazzo Interlandi
14. Forte Vigliena

Where to stay
⑥ Centrale   ⑦ Case Damma   ⑧ Limoneto   ⑨ Don Mauro

the enormous citadel of Euryalos was built. Purposefully, Dionysius extended his influence, and when he died in 367 he was seen as second only to the Persian king in terms of power. His court became the haunt of artists and philosophers, including Plato (388–387 BC), who in 367 and 361 came to Syracuse twice more to act as tutor to Dionysius's son and successor Dionysius II (367–357 and 347–345 BC). The attempt to put his philosophy into practice, however, came to nothing. Dionysius II's rule ended in conflict with Dion. Timoleon was fetched from Corinth (344–337 BC) to restore the democracy. In 317 BC Agathocles made himself master of Syracuse, and in 304 king. He was a daring upstart, son of a potter. Then rule passed to Hieron II (275–215 BC). He made alliances with Carthage (264) and Rome (263), created an exemplary financial administration, and successfully encouraged agriculture. During his long rule he revived the Syracusan Empire, which enjoyed its final heyday under him. Two years after his death the Romans attacked Syracuse, which they took in 212 BC. In the battle, the mathematician Archimedes was killed. This was the end of the city's independence, but it remained the island's capital throughout the Roman period. In his speeches »Against Verres« Cicero paints a picture of the city which we can still recognize: it »is so large, that people say it consists of four huge cities (4, 117 – 119).

Nice old palazzo in the old town by the harbour

▶ VISITING SYRACUSE

INFORMATION

Servicio Turistico
96100 Siracusa, Via Maestranza 33
Tel. 09 31 46 42 55, fax 093 16 02 04

WORTH KNOWING

A regular bus service runs along Corso Gelone between Ortygia and the Archaeological Zone/Archaeological Museum. Ortygia, the old town, can be explored on foot. With a bit of luck there is somewhere to park just on the far side of the bridge. Giuseppe (Siracusa Taxi, mobile 33 96 50 08 59, www.aretusataxi.it; c. €40 return) specializes in the taxi service to the River Ciane (papyrus!). A list of accommodation with prices for the many bed & breakfast addresses can be had from the information bureau. »Il Gusto dei Sapori«, a very good deli, can be found near the Temple of Apollo on Piazza Cesare Battista 4. One speciality of the old-town diners is »zuppa di cozze« spiced with peperoncini, while the mussels come fresh from the Porto Grande.

Chic boutiques line Corso Gelone in the new town and Corso Matteotti in Ortygia. Small traditional shops can be found hidden away in the alleys of the old town, including the elegant jeweller Izzo in Via Roma, who will put ancient coins in a setting or re-cut gemstones, and pottery shops in Via Cavour. Many workshops continue to make papyrus, a tradition revived at the end of the 18th century.

EVENTS

Colourful processions, cannon salvoes and candles in honour of Santa Lucia (1st Sun in May, 13 Dec.)
Performances in the Teatro Greco, see tip p. 414
Opera dei Pupi, Vaccaro-Mauceri, Via della Giudecca 17, in Ortygia, tel. 09 31 46 55 40, www.pupari.com (good website)

WHERE TO EAT
(▶ maps p. 397, 404)

▶ Expensive

① *Don Camillo*
Via Maestranza 96, tel. 0 93 16 71 33
www.ristorantedoncamillosiracusa.it
Closed Sun; the no. 1 address in Syracuse, in an old palazzo, first-class fish cuisine and great wine list.

② *Archimede*
Via Gemmelaro 8, tel. 0 93 16 97 01
Closed Sun; in a former wine cellar; has won numerous awards with its gourmet Sicilian cuisine

▶ Moderate

③ *Porticciolo*
Via Trento 22
Tel. 0 93 16 19 14
Closed Mon; good fish restaurant

④ *La Foglia*
Via Capodieci 29
Tel. 0 93 16 62 33
Vegetarian Mediterranean cuisine in an unusual ambience (the padrone is a sculptor)

▶ Inexpensive

⑤ *Da Mariano*
Vicolo Zuccalà 3
Tel. 0 93 16 74 44
Closed Tue; traditional cuisine of the Monti Iblei in a family atmosphere

⑥ *La Ragazza Ladra*
Via Cavour 8
Tel. 34 00 60 24 28
Closed Mon; attractive little place with an open kitchen, not many tables, regional dishes

Camillo Guarneri, head chef at Don Camillo

WHERE TO STAY
(▶ maps p. 397, 404)

▶ Luxury

① Grand Hotel Ortygia
Viale Mazzini 1
Tel. 09 31 46 46 00, fax 09 31 46 46 11
www.grandhotelsr.it
58 rooms; top hotel in Ortygia in
splendid quayside location; restaurant
on the roof terrace

② Roma
Via Roma 66
Tel. 09 31 46 56 26, fax 09 31 46 55 35
www.hotelroma.sr.it
41 rooms; elegant city hotel just off
the cathedral square; good restaurant

▶ Mid-range

③ Aurora
Via della Maestranze 111
Tel. 093 16 94 75, www.siracusahotel.
com; 23 rooms; charming establishment in a good location in Ortygia,
parking facilities, minimal breakfast

④ Gran Bretagna
Via Savoia 21
Tel. 0 93 16 87 65, fax 09 31 44 90 78
www.hotelgranbretagna.it
16 rooms; labyrinthine corridors,
pleasantly furnished

⑤ Domus Mariae
Via Vittorio Veneto 76
Tel. 9 93 12 48 58 or 54
www.sistemia.it/domusmariae/; 16
rooms; pleasant establishment run by
Ursuline nuns; some rooms with sea
view; good restaurant

⑧ Agriturismo Limoneto
Via del Platano 3, tel. 09 31 71 73 52
www.limoneto.it
10km/6mi out of town, on the road to
Palazzolo Acreide; quiet location,
child-friendly Agriturismo in 6ha/15
acres of organically managed lemon
groves

▶ Budget

⑥ Centrale
Corso Umberto 141, tel. 0 93 16 05 28,
www.hotelcentralesr.com; eleven
cheerfully redecorated rooms

⑦ Agriturismo Case Damma
Strada per Cannicatini Bagni km 9
Tel. 09 31 70 52 73 and 33 58 08 65 13
www.casedamma.it – Simple, quiet
location some 10km/6mi out of town,
on the road to Canicatti; large garden,
restaurant

Floridia · ⑨ Agriturismo Don Mauro
Contrada Cugno di Canne
Tel. 09 31 94 10 25, mobile
33 35 95 77 63, www.donmauro.com
10 rooms; agriturismo attentively run
by a German-Sicilian couple some
10km/6mi to the west of Syracuse in
the middle of orange groves. Attractive rooms, hearty breakfasts

Christianity came to Syracuse early. In 61 AD the apostle Paul spent three days here on his way to Rome (Acts 28, 12). The congregation must have grown very rapidly, if the catacombs, as large as those in Rome, are anything to go by.

When the Roman Empire was re-divided in 395, Syracuse and the rest of Sicily were allocated to the western half, whose emperor, however, was unable to provide any protection against Geiserich's Vandals (440). A new era was ushered in when the Byzantine general Belisarius took Sicily from the Ostrogoths in 535, whereupon, for almost 350 years until 878, Syracuse became part of the Byzantine Empire. Emperor Constans II even moved his residence here from 663 to 668 when Constantinople came under threat from the Arabs. In 751 Syracuse was withdrawn from the jurisdiction of the pope, and placed under the patriarch of Constantinople. The major break came in 878, when the Arabs replaced the Byzantines and made Palermo the capital of Sicily. Syracuse was no longer even the provincial capital, a function it ceded to Noto, an arrangement which remained in force until 1865! The Arab period ended for Syracuse in 1038 with the Byzantine reconquest under Georgios Maniakes (builder of Maniace Castle). In 1086 the Normans took the declining city, which was further impoverished by the earthquakes of 1693 and 1757. Not until the 20th century was there an economic turnaround, when Syracuse proved to be a suitable port for the Italian colonial empire in north Africa (from 1912). In 1921 a population of 40,000 was reached, which has since trebled. Today, Syracuse is both a tourist attraction, a reloading point for agricultural products from the hinterland, and an industrial location.

◀ Imperial residence in place of Constantinople

✳ Old Town · Ortygia

If you cross to the island of Ortygia by the Ponte Nuovo, one of three bridges, you'll find yourself on the Piazza Pancali facing the remains of the Temple of Apollo. Built c. 570 BC, it is the oldest Doric temple in Sicily. If the inscription is anything to go by, it was dedicated by Kleomenes to Apollo. In post-classical times it became in turn a Byzantine church, a mosque, a Norman church and a Spanish barracks. The foundations have been preserved, along with some columns and a cornice, and parts of the cella wall. Standing on a stylobate measuring 21.57 x 55.33m/77 x 182ft are 6 x 17 columns – a ground plan that came about because an anteroom with 6 x 2 columns was added to the 15-column sides known from contemporary temples in Greece itself. The emphasis of the eastern side, where the entrance is, was typical of Sicilian temples. The massive monolithic columns, almost 8m/25ft high, have 16 grooves instead of the usual 20, and are so close to each other that the gaps are narrower than the columns themselves. The piazza is busy in the mornings especially: it is the location of the bus station, a taxi rank, and in the mornings overspill stalls of the market in neighbouring Via Trieste.

Piazza Pancali

Highlights Siracusa

Ortygia
Old-town idyll on the island
► page 401

Duomo
Doric Temple of Victory
► page 403

Galleria Numismatico
The most beautiful Greek coins
► page 405

Fonte Aretusa
Meeting-place and fount of myths
► page 405

Basilica di Santa Lucia
Masterpiece of chiaroscuro: Caravaggio's
Burial of Santa Lucia
► page 409

Santuario Madonna delle Lacrime
»Lemon squeezer« for a plaster Virgin
► page 411

Catacombe di San Giovanni
Not only in Rome: subterranean labyrinths
for the Christian dead
► page 411

Museo Archeologico
Magna Graecia and a lot more in glass
cases
► page 412

Teatro Greco and the Latomie
Classical stage and the world's largest ear
► page 414

Castello Eurialo
Ancient fortification technology: Sicily's
»Maginot Line«
► page 416

Fiume Ciane
A stroll along the papyrus stream
► page 417

Ortigia, charming old-town atmosphere not just along the promenade

In the network of alleyways to the south of the temple are the church of San Tommaso (12th century) and the atmospheric Chiesa di San Pietro (4–5th and 15th century; concerts).

From the Temple of Apollo, Corso Matteotti leads to the Piazza Archimede with its 14th and 15th-century palaces and an Art Nouveau fountain (**Fontana di Artemide** by Giulio Moschetti): the nymph Arethusa was transformed with the help of the goddess Artemis into a spring – a motif that points to the nearby Arethusa spring (▶see p. 405).

Piazza Archimede – Salotto di Ortygia

A diversion down Via della Maestranza leads to richly decorated buildings. The Baroque church of San Francesco all'Immacolata (1769) still preserves its Gothic structures on the inside. Grotesque masks decorate the Palazzo Impellizzeri, shortly before the belvedere. To the south is the former Jewish quarter, Giudecca. The ancient urban layout can still be seen in the grid structure of the alleyways.

Between Piazza Archimede and the east coast

Returning to the Piazza Archimede, the Via Roma and Via Minerva lead to the cathedral of Santa Maria delle Colonne. The Doric columns of the exterior walls of the former Temple of Athena are conspicuous even from Via Minerva. What a contrast to this is the exuberant Baroque façade by Andrea Palma (1693) with its statues of the apostles Peter and Paul (by I. Marabitti) on the steps. This façade harmonizes nicely with the other buildings on the Piazza Duomo

★
Piazza Duomo

> ! *Baedeker* TIP
>
> ### Enoteca Solaria
>
> The best wines on Sicily and stuzzicheria (snacks on toothpicks) are at Enoteca Solaria in Via Roma 86 (Tel. 09 31 46 30 07 or 33 88 12 16 21, www.enotecasolaria.com).

(17th–18th century): the archbishop's palace (1618, by A. Vermexio and the church of Santa Lucia alla Badia (1695–1703 by L. Caracciolo), the Palazzo Beneventano del Bosco (1788, restored by L. Alì) and the city hall (municipio, built in 1633 by G. Vermexio as the Palazzo del Senato).

From the vestibule one walks straight into classical Antiquity: the nave occupies the former cella of the Temple of Athena, which was founded by Gelon and Hieron I after the victory over the Carthaginians at Himera in 480 BC. The temple was a Doric peripteros temple with a stylobate of 22 x 55m/70 x 180 ft, with 6 columns at the ends and 15 along each side. The columns are 8.70m/29ft high, have the usual 20 grooves, and are notable for their discreet convexity (entasis). The naos consisted, as was also usual in Greece itself, of a pronaos, cella and opisthodomos; the holy of holies (adyton) for the cult image, otherwise usual in Sicily, is absent.
In Antiquity the temple was particularly richly appointed. Thus for the eaves (sima) and edge tiles of the roof, marble was imported

★ ★
Cathedral of Santa Maria delle Colonne Temple of Athene

🕐
Opening hours:
7.30am – 7.30pm

Siracusa · Ortigia Map

Porto
Piccolo

Mare Ionio

Piazza
d. Posta

Lungomare

Via Trieste

Via Trento

Via di

③

⑥ ⑧
⑦ ⑨
Ponte
Nuovo

Piazza
Pancali

Largo
XXV Luglio

**Tempio
di Apollo**

Stazione
Marittima

Darsena

Viale Mazzini

**Mura
Greche**

④

Via Resalibera

Via Savoia

Via XX Settembre

Via

Corso Matteotti

Via Cavour

Via Dione

Via

Via Vittorio

Via Levante

**Palazzo
Abela**

**San
Pietro**

**Chiesa del
Carmine**

Via Mirabella

**Palazzo
Bongiovanni**

**Santa Maria
dei Miracoli**

San Tommaso

**Palazzo
Interlandi**

San Filippo Neri

**Palazzo
Montalto**

**Isole
dei Cani**

**Porta
Marina**

②
**Palazzo
della Banca
d'Italia**

Piazza
Archimede

⑥

ⓘ

Via Gargallo

⑤

Via Veneto

San Francesco

③ **Belvedere
San Giacomo**

**Chiesa del
Collegio**

Foro Italico

**Palazzo
Lanza**

Via della Maestranza

Prefettura

①

**Palazzo
Beneventano
del Bosco**

Via Landolina

Municipio

Via Giudecca

**San Giovanni
Battista**

Via Nizza

Porto
Grande

V. Emanuele

Passaggio Adorno

②
Piazza
Duomo

**Santa Maria
delle Colonne**

Piazza
Roma

**Palazzo
Arcivescovile**

S. Giuseppe

Via

**Capitaneria
di Porto**

V. Picherali

**Santa Lucia
alla Badia**

**Palazzo Bellomo
Galleria Regionale**

Via Capodieci

San Martino

**Fonte
Aretusa**

⑤

Lungomare Ortigia

Lungomare Maniace

Fonte Ciane

**Palazzo
Blanco**

Mare Ionio

Lungomare Alfeo

**Spirito
Santo**

P.za Federico
di Svevia

**Castello
Maniace**

0,1 mi
—————
200 m

©Baedeker

Where to stay

① Grand Hotel
   Ortigia
② Roma
③ Aurora
④ Gran Bretagna
⑤ Domus Mariae
⑥ Centrale
⑦ Agriturismo
   Case Damma
⑧ Agriturismo
   Limoneto
⑨ Agriturismo
   Don Mauro

Where to eat

① Don Camillo
② Archimede
③ Porticciolo
④ La Foglia
⑤ Da Mariano
⑥ La Ragazza
   Ladra

from the Cyclades. The eastern pediment was adorned by a large, golden round shield. The doors had costly gold decoration and ivory carvings. Inside there was a gallery of 27 portraits of 27 Syracusan rulers. Much of this was plundered in the 1st century BC by the Roman praetor Verres. In the 7th century this temple, dedicated to the Athena Parthenos (Virgin Athena), was converted into a church dedicated to the Virgin Mary. The spaces between the columns at the entrance were walled up, and the cella walls pierced with eight arches on each side. Thus the lateral ambulatories were turned into the aisles of a basilica. In the process, the ceiling of the nave was raised, and the whole building »turned round«: the old temple entrance at the east end was closed off to make way for the chancel; the entrance was moved to the west end between the two (still visible) opisthodomos columns.

◄ The first Christian congregation in Italy

A side chapel on the right is dedicated to Santa Lucia. Here, photographs and an inscription recall that the relics of the saint were taken to Constantinople in 1038, when the Byzantine general Georgios Maniakes drove the Arabs out of Syracuse and re-took the city for Byzantium, and then removed by the Venetians when they plundered Constantinople during the Fourth Crusade in 1204 (today in San Geremia, Venice). A marble statue by Gagini of the saint carrying a pair of eyes in a dish (she is the patron saint of the blind) stands in the north transept. Tiny Norman bronze lions support the stone font, a pre-Christian cult bowl.

Diagonally opposite the cathedral a sensational coin collection awaits anyone interested (Mon–Fri 9.30am – 1pm, Wed also 3.30pm – 5pm, tel. 09 31 48 11 11).

★
Galleria Numismatica

From the cathedral square continue southwards past the church of **Santa Lucia alla Badia** (1695–1707, L. Caràcciolo; inside is the painting *Burial of Santa Lucia* by Caravaggio, 1608) and down Via Picherali to the Arethusa Fountain (Fonte Aretusa), a pool fed by a fresh-water spring and surrounded by papyrus plants right by the

★
Fonte Aretusa

Siracusa Santa Maria delle Colonne

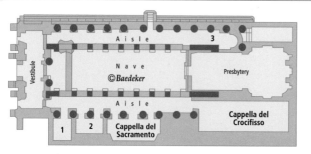

1 Baptismal font (12th century)
2 Cappella di Santa Lucia (18th century)
3 Byzantine apse

■ Temple of Athene

□ Later elements

Aisle   3
Nave
©Baedeker
Presbytery
Vestibule
Aisle
Cappella del Crocifisso
1 2 Cappella del Sacramento

The patron saints of the cities were martyrs like Lucia, who is venerated in Syracuse

AGATA, LUCIA, ROSALIA – THE GREAT SAINTS

In addition to Mary, who is the most revered of all, other female saints enjoy very high standing with the pious Sicilians. Their feasts are always major events. Here we feature three of them, who are venerated as the patron saints of Catania, Syracuse and Palermo.

Agata

Saint Agatha (Sant'Agata) lived in Catania in the 3rd century. As a Christian, she rejected the Roman prefect Quintianus, who was »of an ignoble nature, salacious, greedy and a heathen«, as Jacobus de Voragine claimed in his *Legenda Aurea*, written in around 1270. In response, during the time »when Decius was the emperor« (AD 249–251) Quintianus gave her to a brothel keeper, who, with the help of his nine daughters was supposed to seduce her into committing fornication. However, when Agatha stood firm, she was cruelly martyred. Her breasts were mutilated and cut off. In prison she saw an old man, Saint Peter, with healing salves, but she refused to be healed by medication: »If Christ wishes, he can heal me«. Peter answered: »I am your Lord's apostle, He sent me to you, so know that you were healed in His name«. Miraculously healed, Agatha was thrown on burning coals and sharp shards a few days later.

After praying in prison she died. The *Legenda Aurea* writes, »but when the Christians buried her body with fragrances and laid it in the tomb, a young man in a silk gown appeared ... he went to the body and placed a marble tablet at its head, after which he disappeared. The tablet read: »Mentem Sanctam Spontaneam Honorem Deo et Patriae Liberationem« (Holy and Lively Mind, Honour to God, and the Liberation of her Homeland).

The legend of the saint is closely associated with her home town of **Catania** through the story of how Agatha stopped the lava flow from Mount Etna, thereby »saving the land«: »Then ran the paynims to the sepulchre of S. Agatha and took the cloth that lay upon her tomb, and held it abroad against the fire, and anon on the ninth day after, which was the day of her feast, ceased the fire as soon as it came to her cloth that they brought from her tomb...« The saint was called on for help during the devastating eruption of 1669. Henry

Knight reported with a sceptical undertone in his diary of his trip to Sicily in 1777: instead of making any efforts to build dams and dig trenches in order to fend off the violence, the people of Catania brought out the cloth of Saint Agatha in accompaniment of many saints«.

The memory of the saint is kept in two places in Catania. The **prison** in which she was incarcerated before her martyrdom is shown in the church of Sant'Agata al Carcere, an 18th-century building on Piazza San Carcere not far from the main road, Via Etnea. On the site of her death, according to tradition, the cathedral Sant'Agata was built. The **Cappella di Sant'Agata** is located in the southern transept. The saint, whose feast day is 5 February, is depicted in paintings with a crown, a palm leaf, a torch or a candle; she carries her breasts on a tray and at her feet lies the tablet with her epitaph. She is considered a protector from fire.

Lucia

Saint Lucy (Santa Lucia) lived in Syracuse, around half a century after Agatha. Together with her sick mother she went on a pilgrimage to Agatha's tomb in Catania, because she hoped her mother would be cured of a haemorrhage, a hope that was fulfilled. According to the *Legenda Aurea*, after this event Lucy decided to break off her engagement and give her possessions to the poor. Her groom subsequently exposed her as a Christian to the judge Paschasius, who arrested her as his colleague had done in Agatha's case: Lucia was to be brought to a brothel. But since even a thousand men and a team of oxen were not able to move her from the spot, she was stabbed with a sword in the throat, after other tortures. Other reports claim that her eyes had been ripped out. However, she was able to proclaim before her death: »As the city of Catania has been given to my sister Agatha for protection, I belong to the city of Syracuse and am its intercessor.« Lucy's martyrdom probably took place in the year of the Christian persecution under Emperor Diocletian, in AD 304, i.e. a few years before Constantine the Great proclaimed the toleration of Christianity throughout the Roman Empire in the Edict of Milan. The *Legenda Aurea* also reports that Paschasius was arrested, even before Lucy's death, and taken to Rome, where he was decapitated for corruption.

In **Syracuse** the Santa Lucia neighbourhood is dedicated to her. It surrounds the church of the same name in the place, where according to tradition, Lucia suffered her martyrdom. Next to it is the Chiesa del Sepolcro above the traditional grave of the saint. The name Lucia is associated with the Latin word »lux« (light). She is the bearer of light, from Dante (*Inferno*, II 97) to the Swedish custom of the Christmas candle crown. Her saint's day is 13 December, which is often combined with light rituals. She is shown with a sword through her neck, a palm, a book, an oil lamp and sometimes a pair of eyes on a bowl. People pray to her when they suffer from eye problems, haemorrhage, a sore throat or dysentery.

Rosalia

Rosalia was active around Palermo during the Norman period. During the reign of William I (1154–66), the Norman barons unleashed a rebellion against the king and his grand admiral Maio of Bari. The hated Maio was killed on 10 November 1160. Among the rebels was Count Sinibaldo della Quisquina, who, as the husband of Maria Guiscarda, was related to the royal household. The rebellion was put down, the count executed and the family fortune confiscated. The count's daughter, maid of honour to Queen Margherita, had to flee from the court. She withdrew to a grotto on Palermo's local mountain. Rosalia, according to tradition, died just five years later on 4 September 1166, after leading a saintly life. Almost half a millennium later, on 15 July 1625, she appeared to two hermits who were living on the same mountain, pointing out her hermitage. According to legend, a grotto with her well-preserved body was found in that location. She had a rosary on her head and there was a stone with her name. When her remains were brought to Palermo, a plague epidemic that had ravaged the city ceased immediately. As a result Rosalia is considered the city's patron saint, and people started making pilgrimages to her grotto. Since then the mountain on which she lived has been called Monte Pellegrino, or Pilgrimage Mountain. The **Santuario di Santa Rosalia** is located 14km/9mi from the centre on this mountain at an altitude of 429m/1407ft. The grotto lies behind a Baroque façade. The saint's feast days are 13–15 July, in memory of the discovery of her body in 1625, and 4 September, the day of her death. She is depicted with a long hermit gown, with roses, a necklace and a cross. She is believed to offer protection against the plague.

sea. The nymph Arethusa was fleeing from the Greek river god Alpheios, and on the eastern coast of the Peloponnese threw herself into the sea, surfacing once more on Ortygia, according to mythology. In memory of Virgil, »who revived in Latin verses the rhythms of Theocritus of Syracuse«, the city council put up a plaque in 1981, the 2000th anniversary of the Roman poet's death, »next to the mythical waters of Arethusa«.

Via Capodieci now takes us to the Palazzo Bellomo, a Hohenstaufen building with an austere façade, whose ground floor is original (c. 1250), and three-part Catalan windows with thin columns (15th century) in the upper floor. Here the Galleria Regionale has a display of sculpture, painting and crafts (Tue – Sat 9am – 7pm, Sun to 1pm). The highlight of the paintings collection is a badly damaged *Annunciation* by Antonello da Messina (1474). A large wooden model shows Syracuse as it looked in the 18th century. On the ground floor there is an exhibition of 17th-century carriages.

Palazzo Bellomo
✷
◀ Galleria
Regionale
◔

> ## Baedeker TIP
>
> ### Ortigia as seen from the water
> A harbour tour on the *Selene* gives a completely new impression of Ortigia. The landing is at Foro Vittorio Emanuele II.

Castello Maniace on the southern tip of the island goes back to the Byzantine general Georgios Maniakes, but in 1239 it was rebuilt by Emperor Frederick II as a square building with round corner towers. Next to the marble portal two ancient bronze rams once stood (one now in the Archaeological Museum in ▶Palermo). The hall of columns in particular is worth seeing (Tue – Sun 9am – 1pm).

✷
Castello Maniace

The promenade of Foro Vittorio Emanuele II is a »**passeggiata lungo al mare**«, inviting strollers to sit on the benches beneath the fig trees. It stretches from the Arethusa Fountain to the Molo Zanagora quay, the Porta Marina (15th century; remains of the medieval city wall) and the little church of **Santa Maria dei Miracoli** (c. 1500).

Acradina

The centre of the mainland district of Acradina, smaller now than it was in Antiquity, is the Foro Siracusano with its striking war memorial in the small park (the modest remains of the classical agora with paving stones and a few columns).

Foro Siracusano

Following the Via Elorina westwards from nearby Piazza Marconi (bus station) and crossing the railway, on the right one comes to the fenced-in area of the Ginnasio Romano (1st century AD), actually a small theatre once surrounded by colonnades. The lower section of the auditorium has been preserved, as has an altar on a high base behind the stage.

Ginnasio Romano

Naval arsenal Leaving Foro Siracusano to the northeast, Via Armando Diaz and Via dell'Arsenale between the railway track and the northern side of the small harbour lead to the remains of an ancient naval arsenal. Soon the road reaches the Tyche district.

Tyche · Santa Lucia

Piazza Santa Lucia The focus of the densely populated district of Tyche (today Santa Lucia) is the large, rectangular, tree-lined green space of the Piazza Santa Lucia. Its northern short side is closed off by the church of the same name and the octagonal Chiesa del Sepolcro (17th century) with the grave of St Lucy, the city's patron saint (►Baedeker Special p. 406). The mausoleum can be visited from the church in the company of a monk. The catacombs beneath the church and piazza, however, are not accessible.

✳ Santa Lucia The church, a 12th-century basilica, replaced a previous building (6th century) on the site of the martyrdom of St Lucy. The portal and rose window at the west end are still Gothic. The original rafters are still visible on the inside, but otherwise the building was rebuilt in the Baroque style. The altarpiece *The Burial of Santa Lucia* by Caravaggio (1609) was in the museum in the Palazzo Bellomo for some years.

In the catacombs of San Giovanni

To the northwest of the Piazza Santa Lucia (Via dello Stadio – Via Gorizia – Via Sofocle) is the Piazza Vittoria with a large excavation area; this was the site of an important shrine to Demeter. The votive gifts are now in the Archaeological Museum.

Piazza Vittoria

To the north looms the 76m/240ft-high pilgrimage church of the Santuario della Madonnina delle Lacrime (»lemon squeezer«) by E. Castiglioni. The concrete structure stands where, in 1953, a plaster Madonna is said to have wept several times when a woman in difficult labour invoked the name of the Virgin.

Santuario della Madonnina delle Lacrime

On the other side of Viale Teocrito a strip of grass leads to the church of San Giovanni, which dates from the early Christian period. It has been in ruins since the earthquake of 1693. Mainly what remains is the 14th-century portal wall.
Beneath the remains of the church is the **crypt of San Marziano**, named after St Peter's disciple Marcian, who founded the first Christian congregation in Syracuse in AD 44 and according to local tradition was martyred on this spot. The crypt was doubtless originally a Roman hypogaeum; eight Ionic column bases are still preserved. It was the oldest church in Syracuse and in the 3rd or 5th century was rebuilt as a three-apse structure with the ground-plan of a Greek cross. The crossing pillars have expressive capitals with classical and Christian elements: symbols of the evangelists above shallow Ionic scrolls. In the eastern part of the crypt are an altar, where the apostle Paul preached in AD 61, and the tomb of St Marcian. The crypt is adjoined by the **catacombs of San Giovanni**, a labyrinthine subterranean necropolis dating from the 4th to the 6th century (Tue – Sun 9am – 12.30pm, 2.30pm – 5.30pm). The Adelphia sarcophagus (c. 340) was found here, today one of the chief exhibits in the early Christian department of the Archaeological Museum (▶below).

**★ ★
Basilica e Catacombe di San Giovanni**

> **? DID YOU KNOW …?**
>
> ■ About 5000 years ago the Egyptians discovered that the flesh of the papyrus plant, a kind of reed, could be turned into sheets on which one could write and paint, and store as scrolls or in book form. In addition papyrus was a cheap foodstuff, and the straw could be woven to make boats, baskets, sails, mats and nets. In the 6th century BC papyrus paper probably reached Greece, and with Greek literature, it found its way to Rome and the rest of Italy. Sicily is the only place in Europe where papyrus grows.

This museum can be reached by taking the narrow street on the left in front of the entrance to the Archaeological Museum. There are three rooms with original material and video films providing information on the ancient writing material. In 1781 Count Saverio Landolina from Syracuse became the first modern man to produce papyrus for writing according to ancient texts (Tue – Sun 9am – 1pm).

Papyrus Museum, Istituto di Papiri

✷ ✷ Museo Archeologico Regionale Paolo Orsi

On the corner of Viale Teocrito/Via Augusto von Platen is the **Villa Landolina** with the Archaeological Museum. In the garden is the Protestant cemetery with its monument to the British sailors who died in the Napoleonic wars, and to the left of this is the mural tomb of the German poet Count August von Platen. He died while visiting Count Landolina, who praised him in an epitaph as the German Horace. Opposite, friends later set up a memorial with a portrait bust of the poet.

Archaeological Museum
🕐
Opening hours:
Mon – Sat
9am – 8pm
Sun to 1pm

The collections of the museum, which opened in 1988, range from prehistory and early history to the early Christian and Byzantine periods. At the heart of the building (Franco Minnisi) is a roundel from which the individual departments lead off:

A   Geology, Pre- and Early History
B   1. Chalchid Colonies, Megara Hyblaea; 2. Syracuse
C   Hellenized Native Centres and Agrigentum and Gela.
D   On the first floor: Hellenistic and Roman Periods.

Department A ▶

Geology is graphically explained along with palaeontology, Old and New Stone Ages (cave finds from the 4th and 3rd millennia BC) and the Bronze Age. Among the exhibits are the Bronze Age tomb of Vallelungo (coloured, high handled vases with narrow tapering feet, 19th–15th century BC), items from Castelluccio (19th–15th century), and the limestone door of grave 31 with a relief (schematic depiction of the clan?), pithoi and large clay basins on tall stands, the high backs decorated with geometric scratched drawings and pictures of fish and birds – Thapsos (15th–13th century), finds from Pantálica, including a collection of bright red vessels (13th–11th century), vases and bronze weapons from the necropolis of Montagna near Caltagirone (1270–1000 BC), three burials from the necropolis of Madonna del Piano to the north of Grammichele, where since 1959 300 graves of the 11th–9th centuries BC have been found; displayed next to each other are a stone casket grave, a burial in bare earth, and another in a large clay vessel.

Department B ▶

This department uses excavations from Naxos, Katane, Leontinoi and Megara to explain Greek colonization from the 8th century BC. The most magnificent find from one of the cemeteries of the city is a large-breasted limestone goddess nursing two infants (local work, remains of paint on the plinth, c. 550 BC); she is reckoned to be a depiction of the »Earth Mother« worshipped by the pre-Greek peoples of Sicily. The **Syracuse collection** is arranged topographically by district. An interesting section shows models of temples in Syracuse.

Department C ▶

Here we find items from Heloros, Akrai, Kasmenai, Monte Casale and Canicattini, including a seated female deity from Grammichele, with a mysterious and enchanting smile (terracotta, c. 470 BC); »pi-

Siracusa Museo Archeologico Paolo Orsi

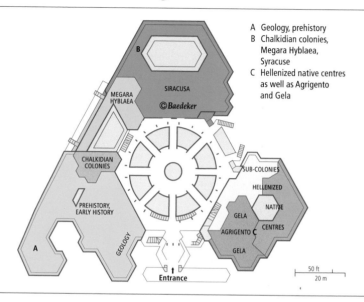

A Geology, prehistory
B Chalkidian colonies,
   Megara Hyblaea,
   Syracuse
C Hellenized native centres
   as well as Agrigento
   and Gela

nakes« (relief plaques) from Francavilla tell of the cult of Demeter: Demeter and Hades in majesty, Persephone and a girl in front of her, Hermes approaching the divine couple of the underworld etc.

The most famous exhibits in this department, dedicated to the Hellenistic and Roman periods, are the **Venus Landolina**, the Roman copy of a Hellenistic work dating from the 2nd century BC, and the Adelphia sarcophagus (4th century) with scenes from the Old and New Testaments, all found by Landolina in 1804.

◄ Department D

On the northeast edge of Tyche, not far from the coast near the stylish Grand Hotel Villa Politi, is a broad, overgrown quarry with bizarre rock formations. The luxuriant vegetation softens the memory of the fact that in 415 BC 7000 captive Athenians were confined here, where they died of disease and starvation.

Latomia dei Cappuccini

Neapoli · ✷ ✷ Parco Archeologico

The »New Town« (Neapolis) of Antiquity can be visited today as the Parco Archeologico. If you drive around the park on the Viale Rizzo, from the higher northern part of the road there is a view of the excavations, and from the junction with Viale Teracati, a panorama of the burial grounds of Grotticelli (►below) with the so-called grave of Archimedes.

Opening hours:
Daily 9am – 6pm, in
winter to 3pm

Buses, taxis etc. go as far as the Largo Anfiteatro, where, alongside the former church of San Nicolò (built in the 11th–12th century above a Roman cistern) there are countless orange presses and souvenir shops. This is the entrance to the archaeological sensations (keep your ticket, it will be inspected again inside the park).

Altar of Hieron II

The altar of Hieron II is a truly monumental affair. It was donated by Hieron II (275–215 BC) in memory of the ousting of the tyrant Thrasybulos, which was celebrated annually in Syracuse at the feast of Zeus Eleutherios. This was the occasion, as the historian Diodorus reports, of the sacrifice of 450 bulls, the meat then being consumed by the inhabitants. A base hewn from the rock has been preserved. It is more than 180m/600ft (= 1 stadion) long and 23m/75ft wide, and ramps for the sacrificial beasts can be seen at its ends. The superstructure has gone, but it will have been some 15m/50ft high, and decorated with sculptures.

**★ ★
Greek theatre**

The Greek theatre was originally built by Hieron I in 470 BC: the architect's name was Demokopos. It was here that *The Persians* by Aeschylus had its Sicilian premiere. The drama *The Women of Aetna*, written in Syracuse by Aeschylus especially for Hieron I, was also premiered here. In addition, the theatre saw productions of tragedies by Sophocles and Euripides, as well as plays by the Sicilian writer of comedies Epicharmos. The theatre owes its present appearance to a rebuilding which took place (as an inscription on the diazoma wall tells us) under King Hieron II, his son Gelon and their two consorts. As Gelon married in 238 BC and Hieron died in 215, we can pinpoint the renovation of the complex fairly exactly. 138m/450ft in diameter and with 61 rows of seats hewn from the rock, with room for 15,000 spectators, it was one of the **largest theatres** of the ancient Greek world. The auditorium (cavea) has been largely preserved. The stage and the scena building were located between two rocks carved into cubes, but they have disappeared. During the Flavian period (AD 69–96) the orchestra was altered in the Roman manner for gladiatorial contests (for which, later, the Roman amphitheatre was built). In the summer Greek plays are staged here, albeit in Italian.

> ! **Baedeker TIP**
>
> **A must-see, and not just for classicists ...**
>
> ... is the ambitious series of classical tragedies and comedies (in Italian) in the Greek Theatre (www.indafondazione.org). Note: hotels are booked out months in advance!

Nymphaeum

Above the theatre there was a colonnade on a terrace; in the cliff wall behind it, there was a nymphaeum dedicated to the muses. From one of the niches spring water still flows through channels constructed in Antiquity. Hollowed into the rock to the left is a row of graves, with funerary niches dating to Byzantine times.

Some of Aeschylus's tragedies had their premiere in the Teatro Greco.

The Latomia, ancient quarries, were exploited from the 6th century BC, and over time were hewn 20–40m/70–140ft into the limestone. They were not always open to the sky, but underground. Their ceilings were supported by pillars. Today the terrain is overgrown, and only individual bizarre supports remain.

Latomia

The largest and most famous of these quarries is the Latomia del Paradiso to the east of the Greek theatre. A gigantic tunnel (60m/200ft long, 5–11m/18–38ft broad and 23m/80ft high) is known as the »**Ear of Dionysius**« (Orecchio di Dionisio) on account of its acoustics. Tradition has it that the tyrant Dionysius could, from one end of the tunnel, eavesdrop on the softest whispers of prisoners at the other end; however the name is first recorded in 1608 with the painter Michelangelo Caravaggio.

✷ ✷
◀ Latomia del Paradiso

In the ropemakers' grotto, **Grotta dei Cordari**, the ropemakers pursued their trade for centuries. The humid climate facilitated the storage and processing of the hempen fibres.

Back on the Via Paradiso, the entrance to the amphitheatre is hidden behind shops selling trinkets. This entertainment centre dating from the 3rd century AD is partly hewn from the surrounding cliffs. The entrances were at both ends of the long axis. Beneath the front rows of seats is a passage for gladiators and wild beasts. The tradition continues with the occasional rock concert.

✷
Roman amphitheatre

To the northeast lies the Necropoli Grotticelli with its numerous graves hewn out of the limestone cliff during Greek, Roman and By-

Necropoli Grotticelli

zantine times. Below it is the so-called **Tomb of Archimedes**, recognizable by its pediment façade which can also be seen from outside, if the area is closed. The famous mathematician, who lost his life when the Romans took Syracuse in 212 BC, was not buried here, however, but outside the gate on the road to Agrigento, as Cicero noted. This structure is a Roman columbarium of the 1st century AD.

Epipolai · ✳ ✳ Castello Eurialo

Opening hours:
Daily 9am – 7.30pm

Epipolai, today virtually deserted, was the most northerly and largest district of Syracuse in Antiquity. It lies on a triangular limestone plateau with an area of some 1.5ha/3.75 acres. This plateau dominated the important road into the hinterland and was fortified by Dionysius I c. 400 BC with a 6km/4mi wall. As Diodorus reports, 60,000 workers were involved, under the personal supervision of the tyrant, and they completed the task in just 20 days. The short eastern side of the wall runs parallel to the coast, the long sides on the south-west and north join at the Castello Eurialo, which lies 8km/5mi to the northwest of the city centre. (Note: there is a shortage of parking space; bus connection route 11 from Riva della Posta; in the afternoon there is a glorious view of Ortygia and the Great Harbour).

The Castello occupies an area of 1.5ha/3.75 acres and is one of the strongest fortifications dating from Greek times. This is said to have been the site, during the Roman siege of 213–212 BC, of the concave mirror which Archimedes built to set fire to the sails of the enemy fleet. The entrance is on the west (small museum), on the most endangered side, which was accordingly well defended. Three tombs are hollowed into the cliff here, while behind stands the main bastion, reinforced by five massive towers. A later wall, maybe only dating from Byzantine times, separates the eastern part (which includes a number of drinking-water cisterns) from the rest. Underground passages in which soldiers could move unnoticed (still accessible in places) are among the cleverly thought-out defences. Particularly interesting is the pincer-gate beneath the castle to the north.

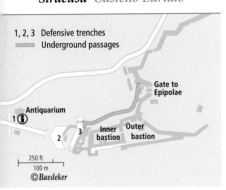

Siracusa *Castello Eurialo*

1, 2, 3 Defensive trenches
▬▬▬ Underground passages

Gate to
Epipolae

Antiquarium
1 ⓘ
2 3 Inner Outer
      bastion bastion

250 ft
100 m
© Baedeker

Outside the City

On the west side of the Great Harbour are two very different sites of classical tradition: the Cyane Spring and the Temple of Zeus.

Ancient fortification technique: Castello Eurialo

The Cyane Spring, Fonte Ciane, 7km/4.5mi southwest of the centre, is most romantically reached by boat (and then on foot) from the Foro Italico (by car towards Canicattini Bagni, then follow the signs to the left). It takes its name from the nymph Cyane, who sought to prevent the abduction of Demeter's daughter Persephone by Hades, the god of the underworld, who in revenge turned her into a spring. It was at this spring that the inhabitants of Syracuse in Antiquity held a feast in honour of Persephone and Cyane every year. The pool, surrounded by the remains of picnics and wild growths of papyrus, is the source of the 6km/4mi-long River Ciane.

The Ciane river has its source here

Temple of Zeus   Immediately to the south of the Anapo and Ciane rivers, which join shortly before reaching the sea, the approach to the Temple of Zeus branches off from the SS 115: foundations on which two columns have been re-erected (c. 560 BC). The golden cloak of the cult image has long since disappeared; in 480 BC Gelon donated the unimaginable sum of 85 talents after a victory over the Carthaginians (1 talent corresponded to c. 26 kg/65 lb of pure silver). Dionysius I appropriated it c. 400 BC and clothed the god in a woollen garment.

Magdalene peninsula   A worthwhile excursion starts from the Temple of Zeus, at first southwards along the SS 115, and then to the left to the Magdalene peninsula, known to the ancients as Cape Plemmyrion, which closes off the Great Harbour of Syracuse to the south. From the rocky coast the lighthouse provides a fine view to the north of the island of Ortygia dominated by the cathedral and Castello Maniace.

Surroundings of Syracuse

Thapsos   Thapsos is 18km/11mi to the north-west. Reach it via the SS 114 as far as Priolo Gargallo, then turn off towards the sea and get to the Magnisi peninsula past the Priolo Melilli railway station. This was the site of the pre-Greek Bronze Age settlement of Thapsos (15th–13th century BC). In about 730 BC Greek colonists led by

Lamis, arriving from Megara, made a stopover here before founding Megara Hyblaea 8km/5mi to the north-west. The remains of two harbours, streets, public buildings and private houses have been found. Rich finds of local and Mycenean pottery were discovered in a necropolis with more than 4000 rock tombs (today in the museum in ►Syracuse).

The ruins of Megara Iblea on the Gulf of Augusta, the ancient city of Megara Hyblaea (today in the industrial estate 21km/13mi to the north of Syracuse on an unsigned branch road leading off the SS 114), is one of the oldest, if not the oldest, Dorian colonies in Sicily. Settlers from Megara near Athens, led by Lamis, settled at first in Leontinoi, then in Thapsos, before at last, in 728 BC, in agreement with Hyblon, the king of the Siculi, finding a place where they could settle permanently. 100 years later Selinunte was founded from here. In addition, Megara Hyblaea is famous as the birthplace of the first comic playwright Epicharmos (c. 550–460 BC). During his lifetime the city was taken by Gelon, who resettled the aristocracy in Syracuse and sold the remaining population into slavery. Megara lay waste until 350 BC, when it was resettled. This smaller settlement came to an end when conquered by the Romans under Marcellus (214 BC). From then on there was only an anchorage and maybe a village.

★
Megara Hyblaea

◄ The birthplace of comedy

French **excavations** uncovered the Archaic city between 1872 and 1889: a perimeter wall, two Archaic temples, dock facilities and two cemeteries (daily 9am until 1 hour before sunset). More recent excavations (1949–1961) have examined the later, Hellenistic city, which existed from 350 to 214 BC; the smaller perimeter wall, the agora and a small Doric temple were found, along with large quantities of Archaic pottery. Some of the finds can be seen in the little Antiquarium by the sea, but most are in the Archaeological Museum in Syracuse; one outstanding item is the limestone figure of a seated fertility goddess nursing two infants (kurotrophos, c. 550 BC).

🕐

Augusta (pop. 34,000) lies on Sicily's east coast (10km/6mi to the north of Megara Iblea and 34 km northwest of Syracuse) on a narrow peninsula projecting south into the Golfo di Augusta, which is flanked by two natural harbours. The town formerly prospered on sea-salt production. Today Augusta is characterized by its industrial plants (cement, chemicals, refineries, petroleum docks) and an Italian naval base.

Augusta

In 1232 Emperor Frederick II founded Augusta, the »imperial« city, on the site of ancient Xiphonia. At its heart was the castle, a square, four-wing structure. The double fortification ring dates from the 16th and 17th centuries. After many alterations, the original form of this building is no longer recognizable, either inside or out. The cloister of the Chiesa di San Domenico is medieval (13th century).

★★ Taormina

T 5

Province: Messina
Population: 10,120

Altitude: 204m/673ft

Taormina lies high above the Ionian Sea on a rocky terrace with a view of the mostly snow-capped Mount Etna. This location, luxuriant vegetation and a mild climate in winter, along with a townscape in which urban sophistication and history are combined – all this made Taormina the most popular holiday destination in Sicily as long ago as the 19th century.

Sicily's best room A touch of this has been preserved here to this day, in spite of all the souvenir shops lined up above all on the Corso Umberto, the main boulevard.

 VISITING TAORMINA

INFORMATION

AAST
Palazzo Corvaja
Piazza Santa Caterina
98039 Taormina
Tel. 0 94 22 32 43
www.gate2taormina.com

EVENTS

»Festival of the Sicilian Carts« in May; music in the Teatro Greco

TRANSPORT

Catania Airport is 47km/28mi away; cruise ships put in to Naxos. Taormina's old quarter is largely closed to motor traffic; there are two multistorey car parks outside: Porta Catania to the west, and Lumbi to the northeast. There are also parking facilities at the lower end of the funicular. There are regular bus services to neighbouring towns. The Funivia (funicular) links the (upper) town with the beach estate of Mazzarò. There are also flights of steps leading to the small but enchanting bays.

WORTH KNOWING

Alongside the souvenirs, the shop windows on Corso Umberto display everything that Sicily has to offer, from Caltagirone pottery to culinary delights and the great names of high fashion.

The *La Torinese* delicatessen is the place to go for Sicilian specialities such as prickly-pear grappa or tuna caviar (Corso Umberto 59).

The moustachioed cart painter *Cesare Filistad* uses his brush to conjure up naive scenes, for example from *Cavalleria rusticana*, on thin board (Via Calapitrulli 19).

At weekends the discos, night clubs and wine bars are full to bursting.

WHERE TO EAT

▶ **Expensive**

① *Maffei's*
Via San Domenico Guzman 1
Tel. 0 94 22 40 55
Closed Tue in winter; elegant ambience, exquisite little snacks and wide choice for gourmets

⑥ *Osteria Nero d'Avola*
Vico Spuches 8
Tel. 09 42 62 88 74
Imaginative cooking and splendid
wine list near the Porta Catania.
Worth every cent

▶ Moderate
② *L'Arco dei Cappuccini*
Via Cappuccini 1
Tel. 0 94 22 48 93
Closed Wed; to the north of the Porta
Messina; deliciously prepared fish is at
the centre of (almost) everything
here. Booking essential. Long wine list
and expert advice

③ *Al Giardino*
Via Bagnoli Croci 84
Tel. 0 94 22 34 53; closed Mon – The
whole family work in Al Giardino. All
sorts of pasta and other outstanding
regional specialities

④ *Al Duomo*
Vico Ebrei 11, tel. 09 42 62 56 56
www.ristorantealduomo.it; closed
Wed in winter; on the cathedral
square, but access is to the right of the
pavement café! Very popular not only
with tourists but also with the locals,
serves classic Sicilian cuisine

▶ Inexpensive
⑤ *Vecchia Taormina*
Vico Ebrei 13, tel. 09 42 62 55 89
Good pizzas in an alley off Corso
Umberto, between Piazza Duomo and
the Porta Catania

WHERE TO STAY
▶ Luxury
① *Grand Hotel Timeo*
Via Teatro Greco 59, tel. 0 94 22 38 01
www.grandhoteltimeo.com
73 rooms; in an attractive park below
the theatre with a magnificent view
and all comforts

▶ Mid-range
② *Villa Schuler*
Piazzetta Bastione 16
Tel. 0 94 22 34 81, fax 0 94 22 35 22
www.villaschuler.it; 29 rooms and one
small holiday apartment – Lovingly
cared-for villa in park-like grounds
which provide direct access to the
town centre; there is an à la carte
breakfast on the terrace with a view of
the Bay of Naxos and Etna. Mountain
bikes and tour ideas are provided free
for guests

Villa Schuler, breakfast terrace

Giardini Naxos · ④ *Arathena Rocks*
Via Calcide Eubea 55, tel.
0 94 25 13 49, www.hotelarathena.it
49 rooms; beyond the headland on
the south side, rooms with repro-
duction antique furniture; garden
overlooking the sea, lava rock beach

▶ Budget
③ *Pensione Svizzera*
Via Luigi Pirandello 26
Tel. 0 94 22 37 90, fax 09 42 62 88 74
www.pensionesvizzera.com
16 clean rooms in a pretty villa, small
garden

Sought-after belvedere

There was a Siculi settlement near the present-day castle on Mount Tauros. In 396 BC Himilkon from Carthage founded the city of Tauromenion here and populated it with Siculi from the surrounding area. After just four years it was ceded to Syracuse as part of a peace treaty. Dionysius I expelled the Siculi and settled his own mercenaries there. But rule by Syracuse was also short-lived, for in 358 BC Andromachos brought the surviving inhabitants of Naxos, which had been destroyed by Dionysius in 403, to Tauromenion. Under this Andromachos, the father of the historian Timaeus, the city grew prosperous. In 345 BC Andromachos also brought in Timoleon, who had come from Corinth, and was on his way to Syracuse – which is why the latter, having established himself there, allowed him to stay in power as the only Sicilian tyrant. In around 315 BC the city was ruled by Agathokles of Syracuse, but after his defeat it passed to Carthage. The succeeding period too witnessed several changes of ruler: from 285 BC the tyrant Tyndarion ruled in Tauromenion. In 278 BC he allowed Pyrrhus of Epirus to land and thus made possible the latter's Sicilian campaign. Later Tauromenion changed hands again, this time to the Romans under Marcellus, whereupon Rome

Taormina Map

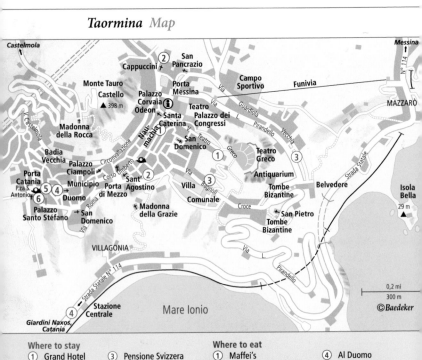

Where to stay
1. Grand Hotel Timeo
2. Villa Schuler
3. Pensione Svizzera
4. Arathena Rocks

Where to eat
1. Maffei's
2. L'Arco dei Cappuccini
3. Al Giardino
4. Al Duomo
5. Vecchia Taormina
6. Nero d'Avola

raised the city to the status of civitas foederata. In the first slave rebellion, the city was one of the slaves' main strongholds. Octavian
(the future Augustus) suffered a serious defeat here in his struggle
with Sextus Pompeius, the son of Pompey the Great, but in 30 BC
he rebuilt the city as a settlement for veterans. Under the empire the
city flourished. Taormina only fell into Arab hands in 902. It
achieved greater significance after the Normans expelled the Arabs in
1079. In 1410 the Sicilian parliament met here to elect a successor to
the late King Martin of Aragon. In the subsequent period Taormina
served as a base from which to pursue pirates. In the 19th century   ◄ Winter holiday
the town discovered a new trend: it became a health resort (on account of its good air) and a place for the central European intellec-
tuals and upper middle classes to spend a winter holiday. The English author D.H. Lawrence spent some months here in 1920–21. The
atmosphere that developed here especially before the First World
War even survived the Second, during which Taormina, as the base
of German commando positions, was subjected to Allied air-raids.
Even today this flair is palpable, in spite of the mass tourism. In recent years it has been discovered by the rich of Messina and Catania
as a weekend retreat in the mountains.

What to See in Taormina

From the coast road on Cape Taormina, Via Pirandello winds its way
up through numerous hairpin bends. Passing Byzantine rock tombs,
the belvedere, the bus park and the top end of the funicular (Funivia) on its way to Mazzarò, it finally ends in front of the Porta Messina, which together with the adjoining Piazza Vittorio Emanuele
forms the entrance to the town itself. This is the start of Corso Umberto, which leads southwest through the town, past the cathedral,
and ends at the Porta Catania – a boulevard to stroll along, do some
shopping, to see and be seen.

To the right on a busy piazza is Palazzo Corvaia, where in 1410 the   **Palazzo Corvaia**
Sicilian estates met. The building, which had only recently been
completed, and includes a tower from the Arab period (10th century), is regarded as the best-preserved palazzo in town. On the first
floor is the **Folk Museum** with naive paintings (Tue – Sun 9am – 1pm,   ☉
4pm – 8pm). Next door is the 17th-century **church of St Catharine**,
and behind are the remains of a small **Odeon** dating from Roman
times, and the marble steps of the lower portion of a Greek temple.

Opposite the Palazzo Corvaia the Via del Teatro Greco leads away   **Hotel Timeo**
from the Piazza V. Emanuele, past the Hotel Timeo, which is named
after the historian Timaeus of Tauromenion; among those who slept
here were the writers Guy de Maupassant, Anatole France and André
Gide, as well as Prince Felix Yusupov, one of the murderers of Ras-
putin, and the German Emperor Wilhelm II.

Greek theatre

⏲ Opening hours:
Daily 9am – 7pm, in winter until 4pm

The street ends, as its name suggests, at Taormina's most famous sight, the Greek theatre. This description is only accurate to the extent that the theatre was laid out in the 3rd century BC under Hieron II of Syracuse; during the Roman period (2nd century AD) it was given a thorough make-over, and thus has all the features of a typically Roman theatre: a precisely semicircular cavea (nine wedges of seating, diameter at the top 109m/330ft), a stage raised above the orchestra level – the Corinthian columns and the piece of marble cornice are reconstructions – and a richly adorned stage building, which is so high that it adjoins the top row of seats on each side, thus producing a closed space. There is a view of Etna through the broad gap in this stage wall. Un-classical, it is true, but romantically modern and hence described and painted thousands of times, and photographed millions of times. Also splendid is the view from the Antiquarium terrace to the sea, Etna, the north coast, and across to Calabria.

> ## Baedeker TIP
>
> ### Il Fascino delle Pietre
>
> The fascination of stones can be experienced in the little shop run by Michael Samperi, where marble inlays and mosaics are made. The mural pictures and table-tops are for sale: they can be dispatched to your home address if required (Via G. di Giovanni 52, tel. 09 42 62 52 66).

Naumachia

Back to Corso Umberto: through the Vicolo Naumachia down to the left we come to the Naumachia, a 122m/125yd brick wall decorated with niches. But it has nothing to do with any arena where sea battles (naumachia) were staged. It probably served as the wall of a very large imperial-age reservoir or a nymphaeum erected for display purposes.

Piazza IX Aprile

The trademarks of Piazza IX Aprile are its legendary cafés, a wonderful terrace with a view, the municipal library in a secularized church (1448) and the clock tower. This is where the older part of the town begins. To the right above a lane with steps can be seen the **Palazzo Ciampoli** (1412), with the town hall immediately adjacent.

Cathedral of San Nicola

Opposite, the street opens out to become the cathedral square. San Nicola, founded by the Hohenstaufen in the 13th century, altered several times in the 15th, 16th and 17th centuries, combines medieval and more recent elements. The unrendered exterior with its battlements dates from the earliest period, while the Baroque main portal was added in 1636 and is the counterpart of the Baroque fountain (1635) in the middle of the square. The interior is richly decorated with works of art, including on the right the *Visitation* by Antonio Giuffrè (15th century) and the *Madonna with Child and Saints* by Antonello da Saliba (1504).

Emblematic gargoyles ▶

Porta Catania

The corso ends with the Porta Catania (1400), adorned with the coat of arms of Aragon, below which is the three-storey, tower-like **Palaz-**

Ancient theatre in Taormina with Mount Etna as a natural backdrop →

Letojanni: there are lovely beaches north of Taormina.

the vicinity, mostly »stabilimenti« for which you have to pay to get access, are as a rule overcrowded in summer. In addition, the beaches of **Isola Bella** (actually a peninsula and a protected nature reserve) and **Mazzarò** are pebbly. There is more room on the beach at **Letojanni** to the north and **Capo Schisò** and **San Marco** to the south. The quickest way to get to Mazzarò is the funicular Funivia (▶p. 423); there are buses to the beaches between Capo Schisò and Letojanni. Timetables can be obtained from all the hotels and at the bus station (Via Pirandello).

5km/3mi to the south the basalt cliff of Capo Schisò projects eastwards into the sea. At the mouth of the River Alcántara there once stood the city of Naxos, the **first Greek city in Sicily**, founded in 735 BC by settlers from Chalcis (Euboea) and the island of Naxos in the Cyclades, once the site of an oracle of Apollo. In view of the unprepossessing area of rubble that was once the germ-cell of Greek life in Sicily, and is today wedged in between holiday homes and an orange grove, Dagmar Nick said: »Nowhere in Sicily can less past be discovered and at the same time more reverence be felt than here in front of the steps of a sacrificial altar that have slid into the ground or the foundations of a city gate that is older than the remains of the walls of Rome. This lava-black solitude is still a secret for all those who want to learn about Sicily's roots – and not just any old lido with a raving mad road behind.«

Naxos

Giardini

The bathing resort of Giardini is situated below Taormina on Sicily's east coast in the bay between Capo Taormina and Capo Schisò. It largely consists of two parallel streets running between the railway track, the busy through-road and the sea. Extensive sandy and pebbly beaches have made it a popular holiday resort.

Forza d'Agrò

Beneath the towering ruins of a 16th-century castle, the mountain village of Forza d'Agrò is situated some 12km/8mi northeast of Taormina, near the mouth of the River Agrò at an altitude of 420m/1378ft (approach from the seaside resort of Sant'Alessio Siculo). In 1117 Roger II made a gift of the village to the Greek Orthodox Basilian monastery of Santi Pietro e Paolo (►p. 272), which is worth a visit. In the Chiesa della Triade there is a moving picture by Antonio Giuffrè, a member of Antonello da Messina's circle (*Abraham Feeding the Three Angels*, c. 1500).

* *
Gola dell'Alcàntara
🕒
Opening hours:
8am – 7pm
in winter till 6pm

The 48km/30mi-long River Alcàntara (Arabic: the bridge), known for its gorges and waterfalls, has its source at an altitude of 1250m/4100ft in the Monti Nébrodi, flows southeast at first, then turns east near Randazzo on the northern edge of Etna, and reaches the sea to the south of Taormina. Its valley is fertile and densely populated. Lava and tuff make for interesting formations and give the river its

Impressive natural scenery and watery fun in Gola dell'Alcantara

varied appearance. A **wild romantic gorge** with fantastical basalt columns, in places 50m/240ft deep and only 5m/16ft wide, is an exciting excursion 18km/11mi west of Taormina. Most visitors access the gorge, which is worth wading along in spring and summer, with the elevator from the large car park on the road to Francavilla. Rubber dungarees and boots can be hired at the entrance. For those who do not wish to part with their money, starting some 200m/220yd from the car park there is a footpath down to the gorge (www.goleal cantara.it).

Castiglione di Sicilia, a charming little hill town with the ruin of a Norman castle, is some 20km/13mi from Taormina. Thanks to its strategic location, it has an amazing **view of Etna**. As »Città del vino«, Castiglione is in an important wine-growing region and there are many rustic trattorie to entice gourmets. Among those to be recommended is the Trattoria La Porta del Re (closed Mon, Via V. Doberdó 2, tel. 32 86 55 95 72, www.laportadelre.com). The friendly proprietor serves local mountain food.

Castiglione di Sicilia

◄ Salsiccia e vino

> ! *Baedeker* TIP
>
> **Good location**
>
> Hotel d'Orange in Francavilla di Sicilia is a good base for excursions to the Alcàntara gorge and Mt Etna; rooms with a balcony facing the road (cat. »mid-range«; 42 rooms; Via dei Mulini, tel. 09 42 98 13 74, fax 09 42 98 17 04, www.hotel-dorange.it).

Termini Imerese

K 5

Province: Palermo
Population: 28,000

Altitude: 77m/250ft

Termini Imerese is situated in the foothills of the 1326m/4350ft Monte Calògero on the north coast of Sicily. A port and spa, it also has some industry, which is not doing very well. The name Termini goes back to the thermal springs (42°C/106°F), which have been known since Antiquity.

The town is really two towns: the quiet, older upper town with most of the sights is situated on a terrace; the lower town with its narrow lanes and little piazzas is where everyday life goes on; it is also where the hot springs are. In Antiquity this was a Sicani settlement; they probably traded with nearby Greek Himera, and after the disaster of 409 BC (►p. 433) took in the few survivors from the neighbouring city. Since then, the place has been known by the double name of Thermai Himeraiai (Greek), Thermae Himerenses (Roman) and Termini Imerese (modern). The baths enjoyed a heyday in Roman times and were also popular with the Arabs and Normans.

▶ VISITING TERMINI IMERESE

INFORMATION

Ufficio Informazione
Via Cortile Maltese, 90018 Termini
Imerese, tel. 09 18 12 82 53
 www.comuneterminiimerese.it

EVENTS

The carnival procession in February is
well-known, with the traditional
masks of »U Nannu« and »La Nanna«
(grandpa and grandma), as well as
lovingly decorated floats (www.car-
nevaleterminitano.it)

WHERE TO STAY

▶ **Mid-range**
① *Grand Hotel delle Terme*
Piazza Terme 2
Tel. 09 18 11 35 57

Fax 09 18 11 31 07
www.grandhoteldelleterme.it
69 rooms; nice old spa hotel with park

② *Il Gabbiano*
Via Libertà 221
Tel. 09 18 11 33 62, fax 09 18 11 42 25
www.hotelgabbiano.it
24 rooms; new building on the edge
of town on the road to Cefalù, mostly
commercial travellers

Trabia · ③ *Tonnara di Trabia*
Largo Tonnara
Tel. 09 18 14 79 76, fax 09 18 12 48 10
www.hoteltonnaratrabia.it
114 rooms; 6km/4mi to the west,
right by the sea, in a former tuna
fishery

What to See in Termini Imerese

Cathedral of San Nicola
The centrepiece of the **upper town** is Piazza del Duomo. The campanile of San Nicola (15th–16th centuries) includes Roman spolia. The
interior has a Crucifixion by Pietro Ruzzolone (1484) as well as
sculptures dating from the Renaissance and Baroque periods.

Museo Civico
Opposite the cathedral three streets lead away from the square. On
the left is the former Fatebenefratelli hospital (14th century), today
the Museo Civico, which has an exhibition of archaeological finds,
including the lion's head gargoyles from Himera, coins, and paintings (opening times: Tue–Sat 9am–1pm, 4pm–6.30pm, Sun 8am–
12.30pm).

Santa Caterina
On the piazza of the same name is the 15th-century church of Santa
Caterina. Inside is a folksy depiction, decorated with Sicilian sayings,
of saints (by Giacomo and Nicolò Graffeo, late 15th century).

Further sights
Via Mazzini leads from the cathedral square to Piazza Umberto I; on
the latter to the right are the **Chiesa di Santa Maria della Misericor-
dia** (inside, a triptych by Gaspare da Pésaro, 1453) and to the left the
Chiesa del Monte. On Via Garibaldi, which leads away from the cathedral square to the right, is the municipal park **Villa Palmeri** with a

few remains of the Roman forum and the amphitheatre. The main spa building, the Albergo delle Terme (19th century, Damiani Almeyda) is in the lively **lower town**. Also worth seeing is the painting of *St George and the Dragon* by Nicolò da Voltri (14th–15th century) in the church of **Santa Maria del Gesù** (1472) in the south of the town (Largo Gancia).

Surroundings of Termini Imerese

Càccamo (pop. 8400), a picturesque mountain town situated at an altitude of 521m/1709ft, 10km/6mi to the south of Termini Imerese, can be reached along a winding scenic road. Standing on a rock is the imposing castle, which was built by the noble Chiaramonte family in the 12th century on the site of a complex dating back to Antiquity. Matteo Bonello withdrew here in 1161 after murdering Maione da Bari, the chancellor and admiral of the Norman king William I. Also dating from the Norman period is the Chiesa Madre, rebuilt many times since.

Càccamo

Termini Imerese Map

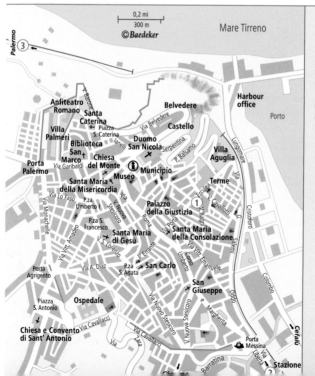

0,2 mi
300 m
©Baedeker

Mare Tirreno

Palermo

Where to stay
① Grand Hotel delle Terme
② Il Gabbiano
③ Tonnara di Trabia

Caccamo: a castle guards the mountain town.

Himera   The ancient temple site lies on the coast road 15km/9mi to the east (near the motorway exit Buonfornello). In 649–648 BC Himera was founded by colonists from Zankle (Messina) as a mixed Dorian-Ionian settlement. The pre-Greek name was understood by the newcomers as Hemera (day), which is why they chose a cockerel as the emblem on their coins: the harbinger of daybreak. It was, alongside Selinunt on the south coast, the most westerly Greek settlement and closest to Carthaginian territory. Its most significant citizen was the choral lyricist Stesichoros from southern Italy, who treated material from the heroic legends in ballad form (c. 600 BC). Himera's great hour came in 480 BC. Called upon by the tyrant Terillos to help defend him against the threat from Theron of Akragas, the Carthaginians under the command of Hamilcar landed in Himera, without doubt in consultation with the Persian king Xerxes, who attacked Greece at the same time. They

! **Baedeker** TIP

New sprouts

Cerda in the hinterland between Cefalù and Termini Imerese is the artichoke capitol of Sicily. The high season takes place every year between February and April. Apart from the »Sagra di Carciofi«, the artichoke fair, the community offers menus with at least ten different variations on the theme of artichokes. The local ristorante owners are happy to inform guests on the cultivation and recipes. After each meal at least one herbal liqueur or – as long as it lasts – an artichoke schnapps is served.

were, however, crushed by Theron of Akragas and his son-in-law Gelon of Syracuse. According to Herodotus, this happened on the same
day that the Athenians defeated the Persians at the Battle of Salamis.
In 409 BC the Carthaginians took their revenge; commanded by
Hamilcar's grandson Hannibal (not to be confused with his name-
sake, the great general), they conquered Himera and razed it to the
ground. The few surviving Greeks fled to the neighbouring Thermai,
which has since borne the double name Thermai Himeraiai/Termini
Imerese.

All that is left after the destruction in 409 BC of once-flourishing Himera are, alongside a few remains of the city, the ruin of the temple,
which was built after the victory of 480 BC and probably dedicated
to Zeus Eleutherios (Zeus of Freedom). The building was commissioned by Theron of Akragas, whose brother Gelon built the temple
of Athene in Syracuse at the same time. The temple in Himera is
built of limestone and has a four-step stylobate measuring 22.5 x
56m/70 x 180 ft. All that is left are the foundation and the lower sections of the columns and cella walls. The characterful lion's head gargoyles are in the Archaeological Museum in ▶Palermo, though some
are on display in the Museo Civico in Termini Imerese.

✱
◀ Excavations
🕐
Opening hours:
Mon – Sat
9am – 5.30pm
Sun to 12.30pm

✱ Tìndari

Province: Messina   **Altitude:** 280m/900ft
Population: 70

**Standing majestically above a steep 280m/900ft drop on the north
coast of Sicily is the pilgrimage church of the Black Madonna, visible from afar. This is Tìndari, known in classical times as Tyndaris,
one of the last Greek settlements in Sicily.**

Tyndaris was a late foundation as Greek colonization went. In 396
BC Dionysius I of Syracuse founded the town to secure the north
coast against Carthaginian attacks. He settled it with refugees from
Greece itself, in particular Messinia, Zakynthos and Naupaktos, who
had lost their homeland in the Peloponnesian War. Tyndaris was
named after King Tyndareos of Sparta, whose wife Leda had given
birth to the twins and Dioscuri (= sons of Zeus) Castor and Pollux.
Numerous coins found in Tindari therefore depict these twins, either
as busts or as the constellation of Gemini. In the First Punic War
Tyndaris was at first allied with Carthage, but transferred its allegiance to Rome in 254 BC. Later Rome counted it as one of the »17
most loyal communities in Sicily«. In Roman times the town enjoyed
a considerable prosperity, which can be seen in the number of buildings. Verres stole a golden statue of Hermes from the town, and in
836 Tyndaris was destroyed by the Arabs.

The city of the
sons of Zeus

⏵ TÌNDARI

INFORMATION

Ufficio Turistico Regionale
Via Teatro Greco 15
Tel. 09 41 36 91 84

EVENTS

In June, classical dramas are performed in the Teatro Greco.
The major festival of the Veneration of the Black Madonna takes place on 8 September.

Tradition has it that the image, a picture on the high altar of the Santuario della **Madonna Nera**, came to Sicily from Constantinople in the 8th or 9th century, as a refugee, so to speak, from the Iconoclastic movement. According to legend, the ship in which it was supposed to be brought to safety got into difficulties off Tìndari, and could only continue its voyage after the picture of the Virgin had been brought to land. A chapel was built, which was destroyed by corsairs in the 16th century. On one occasion a woman pilgrim was said to have been disappointed at the sight of the Black Madonna, and to have made disparaging remarks. A little later, the woman's baby fell over the edge of the cliff. But as a sign of her mercy and power, the Madonna had the sea retreat, while soft sandbanks cushioned the child's fall. This time the woman is supposed to have said »Nigra sum, sed formosa« (»I am black, but comely«, Song of Solomon 1:5). Ever since, Tìndari has stood majestically above the **Mare Secco**, the »dry sea«. The pastel-coloured marble church with its dome dates from the 1950s.

✳ Parco Archeologico

⏱ Opening hours: Daily 9am – 6/7pm

The excavations started in 1812 on the initiative of the British consul Robert Fagan, have uncovered parts of the ancient town. Even before you reach the town proper you can see substantial remains of the town wall and the **Porta Principale** (3rd century BC).

From Piazzale Belvedere, make your way past the shops selling devotionalia for the pilgrims on Via Teatro Greco to the entrance to the excavation area. To the right are the **residential quarters** of the ancient town, which was laid out on an orthogonal pattern. Particularly striking is the Casa Romana, a house belonging to prosperous citizens in the 1st century BC (with alterations dating from the 1st century AD). It has a peristyle courtyard and a mosaic floor. Next comes the decumanus, which leads to the **basilica** (1st century AD). It reveals an interesting stylistic mix of Greek stone blocks and Roman vaults, and was at the same time the gateway to the agora. The **theatre** is sited on a hill and overlooks the sea. It was built in the 4th century BC but altered in Roman times, when the Greek stage structure was demolished along with the some of the lower rows of seats (there were 28 in all), and the orchestra was lowered and surrounded

Greatly revered and capable of performing miracles: →
the Black Madonna of Tìndari

Tìndari Map

by a wall: all this so that spectators would not come to harm while watching the gladiatorial contests and the animal fights (reconstruction in the Antiquarium). Excavations of the classical acropolis are not possible, because it stood on the site – beyond Piazzale Belvedere, which, as its name suggests, has a splendid view right down to the coast – now occupied by the **pilgrimage church**.

At the foot of Capo Tìndari is the **Mare Secco**, a beautiful sandbank stretching far out to sea, with a number of shallow lagoons known as laghetti. It can be reached on foot (45 min) from the little, recently established bathing resort of Oliveri.

✷ Tràpani

D 4

Provincial capital
Population : 71,000

Altitude: 3m/10ft

Situated on a tongue of land stretching far into the sea in the north-west of Sicily, the lively episcopal, commercial and industrial port of Tràpani extends right to the foot of Monte Érice.

History of the town

Drepanon is Greek for sickle. That was what Tràpani was called in Antiquity on account of the shape of its peninsula, although it was never settled by Greeks. On the contrary, it was used a base by the Carthaginians, who constructed a naval port here. In 249 BC the Romans suffered a crushing defeat when, led by the consul P. Claudius Pulcher, they attempted to take the town from the sea. In 242 BC, however, C. Lutatius Catulus managed to occupy the place.

Tràpani enjoyed an upturn in the 9th century under Arab rule; in those days Arabs and Jews lived in what was called the Arab Quarter (between Via XXX Gennaio and Via Torrearsa). The 15th century, during the Aragonese period, saw the construction of the large salt pans which are still used for obtaining the now-fashionable sea-salt today. In the 19th century there were a number of revolts against Bourbon rule (1820–21, 1848). The town suffered very heavy bombing during the Second World War. As a ferry port for Tunisia, it has a large proportion of north African inhabitants.

▶ VISITING TRÀPANI

INFORMATION

Servizio Turistico
91100 Trapani
Via San Francesco d'Assisi 27
Tel. 09 23 80 69 13 (-08 or -45)
Infopoint Strada del Vino Piazza
Saturno, tel. 09 23 54 45 33
www.apt.trapani.it

TRANSPORT

Ferry connections with Tunis and
Cagliari (once a week), the Aegadian
Islands and Pantelleria (daily.)
From the airfield (13km/8mi to the
south) daily flights to Rome, Milan
and Pantelleria (Aeroporto Birgi
Nuovo, tel. 09 23 32 11 11)
The central bus station (incl. buses to
▶ Érice) is on Piazza Malta, near the
train station.
From the eastern edge of the town
there is a cable car to Èrice (▶ Èrice).

EVENTS

Procession of the »Misteri«, huge
figures of saints, on Good Friday;
festival of San Liberante (Whit
Monday)
Mattanza del Tonno (tuna fishing, end
of May; ▶ Baedeker Special p. 204)

WHERE TO EAT

▶ Moderate

① *Da Peppe*
Via Spalti 50, tel. 09 23 2 82 46
Closed Mon; good pasta and fish
dishes in Art Nouveau surroundings

② *Cantina Siciliana*
Via Giudecca 34
Tel. 0 92 32 86 73
Closed Mon; popular trattoria with
fresh fish; good regional cuisine

③ *P & G*
Via Spalti 1, tel. 09 23 54 77 01
Closed Sun; small restaurant next to
the Margherita Park; fish and couscous

WHERE TO STAY

▶ Mid-range

① *Crystal*
Via San Giovanni Bosco 17
Tel. 0 92 32 00 00
Fax 0 92 32 55 55
www.nh-hotels.com
68 rooms; best hotel in town

② *Vittoria*
Via F. Crispi 4
Tel. 09 23 87 30 44
Fax 0 92 32 98 70
www.hotelvittoriatrapani.it
65 rooms; mid-range hotel close to
sea

③ *Agriturismo Duca di Castelmonte*
Località Xitta
Via Salvatore Motisi 3
Tel. & fax 09 23 52 61 39
www.ducadicastelmonte.it
Enchanting country estate (6km/4mi
outside town on the road to Marsala);
excellent cuisine

What to See in Tràpani

The old quarter is to the west of Piazza Umberto I (station). It begins   ✱
with Via XXX Gennaio, which runs north-south, takes in the narrow   **Old quarter**
peninsula projecting to the west, and is cut in two in an east-west direction by Corso Italia and Corso Vittorio Emanuele. Immediately

beyond Via XXX Gennaio, parallel to Corso Italia, is Via Giudecca. The former ghetto is the site of the **Palazzo Giudecca** (16th century, Catalan Gothic style). Further to the west, down a side street, is the late medieval Franciscan church of **Santa Maria del Gesù** (after 1528, in the Cappella Staiti, beneath a marble canopy by Antonello Gagini is a terracotta Madonna by Andrea della Robbia) and in the next side street to the south, Via Biscottai, is the **Biblioteca Fardelliana**, whose elaborate façade of 1748 opens onto Largo San Giacomo.

Sant'Agostino   Corso Italia ends on Piazza Sant'Agostino, where the simple apse of the church of the same name catches the eye. This 14th-century Templar church was rebuilt as a concert hall after being destroyed in the Second World War. An extraordinarily fine rose window from the old building has been preserved. The west front overlooks Piazza Saturno, named after the 16th-century Saturn Fountain, which recalls Tràpani's founding myth: the fountain depicts the Greco-Roman god Cronos-Saturn, son of the Father of the Gods, Ouranos, who kept his children captive in the underworld. At the bidding of his mother, Saturn castrated his father and threw the weapon, a sickle, into the sea. Thereupon Aphrodite emerged from the foam, and the sickle-shaped peninsula on which Tràpani stands was formed.

Tràpani *Map*

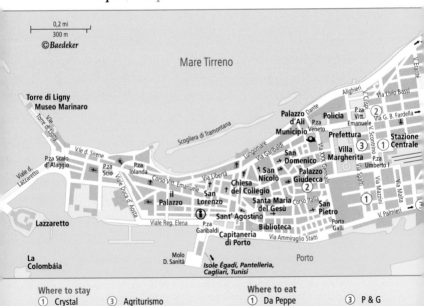

Via Torrearsa divides the labyrinthine part of old town from the western part, where the streets run in straight lines, and ends in the north at the semicircular colonnade of the market. On this street, a little to the north of Piazza Saturno, is the richly decorated façade of the **Palazzo Cavarretto** (c. 1700).

The palazzo looks on to Corso Vittorio Emanuele, the former show boulevard (now pedestrianized), where there are a number of notable buildings: first of all, the Jesuit **Chiesa del Collegio** (1606–38), by the architect Natale Masuccio, himself a member of the order. Its high altar is decorated by a relief of the Immaculata by Ignazio Marabitti (1766). The church shares its two-storey façade with the neighbouring Jesuit college (a high school).

Corso Vittorio Emanuele

There follow a Baroque palazzo (today used by the municipal administration) and the cathedral of **San Lorenzo**. Started in 1635 as an aisled basilica, it was enlarged by Giovan Biagio Amico in 1740, when the vestibule and the dome were built, the tambour of the latter flanked by four towers.

On the south side of Corso Vittorio Emanuele, corner of Via Turrette (opposite the Jesuit church) stands **Palazzo Riccio**, built in the 17th century as one of the town's first Baroque palaces; an interesting feature is the inner courtyard, surrounded on all sides by three-storey façades.

> ! **Baedeker TIP**
>
> ### Outstanding ice-cream
> Home-made ice-cream, granita or classic cakes and pastries can be had at Da Gino, Piazza Generale Dalla Chiesa 4 (near Piazza Garibaldi) and Da Gelatissimo, Via Pepoli 172 (away from the centre on the S S 113) as well as in the Pasticceria-Gelateria Ignazio Benivegna, Via Monzoni 99 (on the road to Erice).

The octagonal fortified tower at the northwest end of the peninsula dates from the 14th century; it was enlarged in around 1670 under the viceroy, the Prince de Ligny (today the Museo della Preistoria e del Mare, museum of prehistory and the sea; daily 9.30am – 12.30pm, 4.30pm – 7pm, Jan – 21 March. Mon – Fri mornings only, Sat and Sun also afternoons).

Torre di Ligny ☉

Time and again while strolling through the old town you will see, at the end of a narrow street, the blue of the sea, which surrounds the peninsula to the north and south. In the south is the harbour, with Piazza Garibaldi (ferries to the Aegadian Islands ►Égadi, Isole) and Viale Regina Elena with a view of the salt pans and the Aegadian Islands. Just outside the harbour is the **island of La Columbaia**.

Harbour

Running parallel to the north coast is Via della Libertà, which at its eastern end, as we come to the new town, opens out into a series of squares: on Piazza Vittorio Veneto stand the town hall and, facing it, the provincial administration (prefettura). It adjoins Piazza Vittorio

Piazza Vittorio Veneto

Emanuele, named after the king whose monument (1882) overlooks the neighbouring gardens of **Villa Margherita** with old trees and numerous portrait busts, among them Dante, Bellini and Piersanto Mattarella, president of the Region of Sicily, who was murdered by the Mafia in 1980; concerts are held on the piazza in summer.

★
**Santuario dell'
Annunziata**
⊙
Opening hours:
9am –noon
4pm – 7pm

In the eastern part of town is its most important building, the Marian pilgrimage church, founded in the 13th century. The façade of the present church, with its richly decorated portal and rose window, goes back to the 14th century. Otherwise the building was totally rebuilt, starting in 1742, by G. B. Amico, who created a vaulted aisleless church with an oval dome running crossways in front of the sanctuary. The interior and its chapels are rich in works of art: the late Gothic Fishermen's Chapel (Cappella dei Pescatori, 15th century) with its octagonal cupola and 16th-century frescoes, the square, domed Seafarers' Chapel (Cappella dei Marinai, 1514–40), but above all the Cappella della Madonna at the apex of the choir; it was built in 1498 to house the image of the Madonna of Tràpani, which the pilgrims come to venerate. The smiling marble statue, carved in about 1350 by Nino Pisano or someone from his school, is carried aloft in the Good Friday procession.

Religious devotion: Good Friday procession in Trapani

The Annunziata church once belonged to the Carmelite monastery (secularized in 1866), which is today the Museo Regionale Pépoli, housing the collections of the Bourbon ministers G. B. Fardella and Count Pépoli, as well as items previously owned by the monastery. On the ground floor medieval architectural fragments and sculptures are on display, including a statue of San Giacomo by Antonello Gagini (1522). A generously proportioned staircase leads to the first floor, in the 24 rooms of which the picture gallery (works by Titian, Veronese, Ribera and Serpotta), magnificent coral ornaments and the Antiquarium (finds from Lilybaion, Érice and Selinunt) are housed. Majolica floors (18th century) depict fishing scenes, including the Mattanza (Mon–Sat 9.00 am–1.30pm, Sun only to 12.30pm).

Museo Regionale Pépoli

> ! **Baedeker TIP**
>
> ### Anyone wanting to know more about salt gathering ...
>
> ... should visit the »Ettore e Infersa« salt refinery outside Mózia (Mon–Sun 9am–7pm; tel. 09 23 96 69 36, www.salineettoreinfersa.com). On Wednesdays and Saturdays (4pm–6pm) the traditional windmill is started up. In the Culcasi salt refinery (in the village of Nubia) there is a small salt museum (Museo del Sale; Mon–Sat 9.30am–1pm, 3pm–6pm) with typical tools of the trade on display. In the adjoining former warehouse it is possible to get a good meal, but only if you order in advance (tel. 09 23 86 71 42). You can also buy the locally produced salt, a good present for the folks back home.

On the coast between Tràpani and Marsala are extensive **salt pans**, glittering white or pink in the sunlight depending on their salinity. The white salt hills are covered with tiles to stop the salt blowing away, while allowing it to dry out at the same time. Since the 15th century, obtaining salt by evaporation has been the area's most important industry. With the restored windmills, it is a unique man-made landscape, and a paradise for migratory birds.

Surroundings of Tràpani

► Égadi, Isole

Aegadian Islands

In Bonagia (15km/9.5mi to the north) there is one of Sicily's few still active tonnare (tuna-processing plant). The building itself is now a four-star hotel (La Tonnara di Bonagia, cat. »mid-range/luxury«, tel. 09 23 43 11 11, www.tonnaradibonagia.it).

Bonagia

On Capo San Vito (40km/25mi to the north) is the pleasant bathing resort of San Vito lo Capo (pop. 3600) which has a sandy beach sloping gently into the sea, and a good tourist infrastructure. It only gets really busy at weekends and in the high season. The church was built in the 17th century on the site of a 16th-century fort, whose rectangular ground plan it retains. Some 10km/6mi to the east is one of the entrances to the Zingaro Nature Reserve (►Castellammare del Golfo, surroundings).

✷
San Vito lo Capo
Sandy beach

▶ VISITING SAN VITO LO CAPO

INFORMATION

AAPIT
Via Savoia 61
91010 San Vito lo Capo
Tel. 09 23 62 14 90

WHERE TO EAT

▶ Moderate/Expensive

Alfredo
Contrada Valanga 3
Tel. 09 23 97 23 66
Outside the season closed Mon; a bit
out of town, mainly fish specialities;
attractive terrace with sea view

▶ Inexpensive/Moderate

Piccolo Mondo
Via Nino Bixio 7, tel. 09 23 97 20 32
www.piccolomondohotel.net
Popular restaurant with high-class
cuisine in the hotel of the same name

WHERE TO STAY

▶ Mid-range

Capo San Vito
Via Principe Tommaso 29
Tel. 09 23 97 21 22, fax 09 23 97 25 59
www.caposanvito.it (April–15 Oct)
36 rooms; clean, pleasantly appointed
hotel right next to a sandy beach

Mira Spiaggia
Via Lungomare 6
Tel. 09 23 97 23 55, fax 09 23 97 22 63
www.miraspiaggia.it (April–Oct)
Clean beach-side hotel, also flats with
cooking facilities

Calampiso Club
Contrada Sauci Grande
Tel. 09 23 97 91 11, fax 09 23 97 40 66
www.calampiso.it
Holiday village between San Vito and
Zingaro Nature Reserve

Top address in town: hotel Capo San Vito

San Vito lo Capo boasts a family-friendly, sandy beach and crystal-clear water.

▶Érice (15km/9mi to the northeast, accessible via a steep mountain road by car or bus, or by cable-car)

Érice

▶Mózia (20 km to the south)

Mózia

★ Ùstica

Province: Palermo
Population: 1300

Altitude: 40 – 238m/130 – 780ft
Area: 8.6 sq km/3.3 sq mi

Ùstica, the divers' paradise 36 nautical miles north of Palermo, looks from a distance like a turtle in the deep blue sea. Geologically it belongs to the Aeolian Islands.

The elliptical island is surrounded by attractive bays and rocky cliffs, its landscape characterized by black lava rock and the green of the vegetation. The highest point is Monte Guardia dei Turchi (238m/ 780ft). Apart from agriculture (fruit and wine), the Usticesi still live by fishing, and more recently, from tourism. The bio-diverse underwater world is a paradise for divers. The remains of the settlement of

Landscape and history

▶ VISITING ÙSTICA

INFORMATION
www.comune.ustica.pa.it

EVENTS
Wall-painting competition in summer; international underwater sports show (June/July); Feast of the island's patron saint Bartholomew on 24 Aug.

TRANSPORT
Car ferry and fast ferry connections with Palermo

WHERE TO EAT

▶ Moderate
Da Umberto
Piazza della Vittoria 7 Tel. 09 18 44 95 42; open daily; closed Oct–Easter
Only what's been landed from the boat the same morning gets on the table for lunch and dinner in the cosy dining room or on the terrace.

▶ Budget
Schiticchio
Via Tre Mulini, tel. 09 18 44 96 62
Restaurant and pizzeria at the edge of town on the road to Spalmatore, rustic in style

WHERE TO STAY

▶ Budget/Mid-range
Clelia
Via Sindaco 1° 29, tel. 09 18 44 90 39
www.hotelclelia.it
14 comfortable rooms in the middle of town, with family restaurant

Hotel Diana
Contrada San Palo Tel. & fax 09 18 44 91 09
www.hoteldiana-ustica.com; 27 rooms
Modern building 1km/0.5mi outside town, on the cliff-top. Access to sea, attached diving school

▶ Holiday houses and flats
La Cernia Bruna di Alessandri
Via Petriera, tel. 09 18 44 90 60
www.www.lacerniabruna.it

Ustica Tour
Piazza Vittoria 7, tel. 09 18 44 95 42
www.usticatour.it

Colombaia date from prehistoric times; the tombs of Falconiera on the east coast were carved from the tuff by the Phoenicians. However, very little archaeological exploration has been carried out. For a long time Ùstica was a dreaded pirates' lair, until it was settled by migrants from the Aeolian Islands in the 18th century. Later the island was used for a long time as a place of banishment.

Ùstica Most of the inhabitants live in the chief town, Ùstica (54m/170ft) next to the 157m/515ft Cape Falconiera, where old fortification walls can still be seen. There are two quays, Cala Santa Maria and Cala Giaconi. The centre of activity is the main square. Many houses have colourful façades, the result of the annual **wall-painting competition**. A further event is the international **underwater-sports show** (Rassegna Internazionale delle Attivitá Subacquee), held every year in June/July.

Rocky coastline, lava rocks and the green vegetation characterize the scenery around Ustica.

Ùstica is connected with the western tip of the island near Cape Spalmatore by a 3km/2mi road. It was here that Italy's first marine nature reserve (Riserva Naturale Marina) was established. Fishing, boating and mineral collection are prohibited within its bounds.

Marine Nature Reserve

There are plenty of places to go swimming in the little bays and at the Faraglione beach facilities. In addition the island is a mecca for divers (there are a number of diving stations), water-skiers and sailors. Boat trips to the »green«, »golden« and »blue« grottoes (Grotta Verde, Grotta dell'Ora, Grotta Azzurra) are highly recommendable. In Caletta Sidoli, on the west coast, the bay is particularly rich in fish. Also there are walks to be had all over the island, for example to the Falconiera hill (view) or to Mt. Guardia dei Turchi, from where there is a view of the whole island and all the way to Sicily.

Leisure pursuits on Ùstica

GLOSSARY: ART AND ARCHITECTURE

Abacus square slab above the echinus, with which it forms the capital of Doric columns (diagram p. 449)

Abaton, adyton the part of a temple that only priests were allowed to access

Agora marketplace, centre of public life in a town

Acanthus known as bear's breeches, its spiny leaves were used as ornamentation on Corinthian and Byzantine (Justinian) capitals

Acropolis upper town, generally an elevated temple district

Acroterion a figurative or ornamental crest on a ridge or at the corner of a pediment (diagram p. 449)

Amphiprostyle a temple with a portico at both the front and the rear (▶ p. 51)

Ante pillar-like projecting head of a temple's cella wall (diagram p. 51)

Antetemple temple with columns between the ante-walls at the front end (diagram p. 51)

Apotheosis raising a human being to divine status

Apse usually a semicircular room at the end of a church

Architrave a horizontal stone resting on top of columns

Arena an elliptical fighting area in an amphitheatre

Arcade a sequence of arches supported by columns or pillars

Atrium 1. main room of a Roman villa
2. forecourt of an early Christian basilica

Basileus monarch

Basilian term for Orthodox monks, since their canon goes back to Saint Basil the Great (around 330–379)

Basilica 1. tribunal chamber of a king (stoa basilike), place of commerce or legal matters
2. in the 4th century AD the floor plan of Christian churches, either a nave and two aisles or a nave and four aisles
3. An honorary title bestowed on a church by the pope, regardless of its architecture

Baths baths in ancient Rome, consisting of a changing room (apodyterium), a cold-water pool (frigidarium), a warm-water pool (tepidarium) and a hot-water pool (caldarium), underfloor heating (hypocaust) as well as a few other rooms

Bay unit of space defined by two pillars of an arcade

Bema 1. raised platform for orators
2. chancel in a Christian church

Blind arcade, blind arch arches placed on a wall for aesthetic reasons

Bouleuterion seat of the council (boule)

Campanile free-standing bell tower in Italian churches

Capital Head of a column or pillar (diagram p. 449)

Cardo north-south axis of a Roman town, runs perpendicular to the decumanus

Caryatid female figure supporting an entablature in place of a column

Catalonian Gothic specific late-Gothic that flourished in Sicily in the 15th and 16th century as a result of Spanish influence, delaying the establishment of Italian Renaissance architecture

Cathedra bishop's throne

Cathedral church with a bishop's throne, bishop's church

Cavea shell-shaped area in the tiers of a theatre (see koilon)

Cella interior of a temple (diagram p. 51)

Cherubim spiritual beings, heavenly guardian with four or sometimes six wings

Chiesa Madre, Chiesa Matrice »mother« or main church

Choir room between the nave or transepts and the East end of a church

Choir arch arch that separates the nave or transept from the choir

Chthonic belonging to the earth, underground, term for deities such as Persephone

Classical order of columns in the **Doric order**, the shaft of the column narrows towards the top and has between 16 and 20 flutings; it stands immediately on the stylobate above a base featuring three steps. The entasis (swelling) of the columns is characteristic; this and the curvature of the base, a frequent feature, makes the building look less austere. The Doric capital made of the bulging ring (echinus) and the square slab (abacus) supports the architrave lintel and above it the frieze made of notched triglyphs and smooth or sculpted metopes. The tympanum is framed by a horizontal cornice and a diagonal geison and usually includes the composition of the pediment figures. Ornamentation in the form of reliefs can be found on the metopes and on the pediment. In the places where limestone was used instead of marble, it was covered in a smoothing layer and then the building was painted, blue and red being the two dominant colours besides white.

The **Ionic order** prefers slimmer, softer forms than the Doric. This is expressed in the columns in part by the fact that they stand on a base and that narrow ligaments between the fluting emphasize the vertical character. The characteristic element of the Ionic columns are the two curled volutes or scrolls. Above the three-part architrave the frieze runs around the building without triglyphs.

The **Corinthian order** is the same as the Ionic order except for the capital. The sculptural ornamentation of the Corinthian capital is made up of large, toothed acanthus leaves which surround the round body of the capital. Tendrils wind their way up to the corners of the concave top panel. The Corinthian order became particularly widespread during the Roman imperial period; it was also during this time that the composite order, made up of the Ionic and Corinthian orders, was developed and that ever richer decoration systems were created.

Composite capital see classical order of columns

Corner contraction moving the corner columns of a Doric temple closer together to solve the corner conflict the axis of the corner triglyphs is no longer in line with axis of the columns

Crepidoma platform made up of three levels on which a temple stands (krepis = »shoe«; diagram p. 449)

Crossing square area that is formed where the nave and the transepts intersect in a church

Cross-in-square church Byzantine church style with a central dome above the intersection of the nave, choir and transepts, where all arms were the same length

Crypt vault below the church

Decumanus east-west axis of a Roman castrum and a Roman town, runs perpendicular to the cardo

Dipteros a temple with a double ring of columns (diagram p. 51)

Double antetemple temple with columns between the antes of the two ends (diagram p. 51)

Echinus a convex moulding; together with the abacus above it, it forms the Doric capital (diagram p. 449)

Entasis swelling of the column in the lower third (diagram p. 449)

Epiphany appearance of a deity

Epistyle lintel lying on columns in a temple with a frieze at the top on the exterior side (diagram p. 449)

Exedra usually a semicircular room with seating

Fluting vertical grooves on the shaft of a column (diagram p. 449)

Forum main square and political centre in Roman towns

Frieze decorative area above the architrave in a temple; in the Doric order it consists of metopes and triglyphs, in the Ionian order it is smooth or sculpted throughout (diagram p. 449)

Geison cornice of a temple roof. In the pediment field the figures on the horizontal geison stand under the diagonal geison, following the roof gradient (diagram p. 449)

Giant order columns or pilasters that span several floors

Gigantomachy the battle between the gods and the giants

Greek cross all arms are of the same length

Gymnasium place for sports and education in general (from the Greek: »gymnos« = naked)

Heraion temple dedicated to the goddess Hera

Heroon cult site or grave of a hero

Hieron temple

Hippodamian grid principle of town planning based on straight roads that intersect at right angles, named after Hippodamus of Miletus (5th century BC)

Hippodrome race track for horses and chariots, consisting of two tracks running in opposite directions and separated by the spina

Hypocaust underfloor heating system used for baths and residential rooms located under the floor

Hypogaeum underground room, cult room

Iconostasis wall of icons in a Byzantine church, which separates the nave from the sanctuary

Impost die-shaped link between the capital and the arch

Incrustation covering a wall with precious materials, especially marble

In situ where it was found, on location

Intercolumniation the spacing between columns

Klinai couch

Koilon shell-shaped area in the tiers of a theatre (cavea)

Kore girl, statue of a girl; also a name for Persephone

Latin cross cross with one longer and three short arms

Lesene low-relief pillar to structure the wall

Column orders

Doric order

Painted Doric capital

Doric cymatium

Ionic order

Sima
Geison
Tympanum
Frieze
(Zophoros)
Architrave
(epistyle; three parts)
Capital
(with volutes)

g Column shaft
(with 24 flutings
separated
by wide bars)
h Attic base
(with torus and
trochilus)
i Stylobate
k Crepidoma

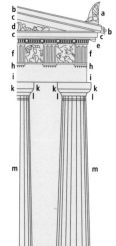

©Baedeker

a Corner acroterion
b Sima (with a lion's head spouting water)
c Geison
d Tympanum
e Guttae
f Triglyphs
g Metopes
h Regulae
i Architrave (epistyle; one piece)
k Abacus
l Echinus (moulding)
m Column shaft (with sharp-edged fluting)
n Stylobate
o Crepidoma

Structure of the
Doric entablature

Coffered vault

Lesbian cymatium

Corinthian order

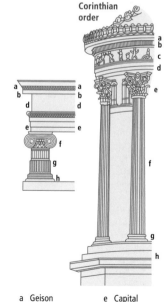

a Geison
b Dentil
c Frieze
d Architrave

e Capital
f Column shaft
g Base
h Crepidoma

Lunette half moon-shaped area above windows and doors

Meander ribbon ornament named after the Maiandros River in Asia Minor (now Büyük Menderes in Turkey)

Megaron main hall in Mycenaean palaces; also considered the primitive form of Greek temples

Metope rectangular slab between the triglyph on the freeze of a Doric temples; smooth or decorated with reliefs (diagram p. 449)

Monopteros round temple without a naos (cella; diagram p. 51)

Narthex entrance area of a Byzantine church

Necropolis cemetery, burial site

Nymphaeum monument consecrated to nymphs; a richly ornamented fountain complex

Odeon covered building for musical performances

Olympieion sacred sector dedicated to the Olympian Zeus

Opisthodomos a room corresponding to the pronaos (portico) at the back of the building behind the naos (cella) in a temple (diagram p. 51)

Orchestra place where the chorus dances; round or semicircular area between the stage and the auditorium in a theatre

Palaestra building for athletic pursuits such as wrestling

Pantocrator Christ as »ruler of all«

Peripteros temple surrounded by columns on all sides (diagram p. 51)

Peristasis hall of columns surrounding a temple

Peristyle Columned porch, colonnade, columns surrounding a courtyard (diagram p. 51)

Pilaster pillar, not free-standing, set in front of a wall

Polychromy the use of many colours on ancient sculptures and temples

Polyptych altarpiece with more than two panels

Portico columned porch

Pronaos entrance area to a Greek temple (diagram p. 51)

Prostylos temple where the entire facade features columns

Sima guttering on temples with lions' heads as gargoyles

Soffit slab on the underside of the geison on a Doric temple (diagram p. 449)

Spolia fragments from older buildings, re-used in a new one

Stadion / stadium 1. measure of length 600 ft = approx. 185 m
2. running track of the same length
3. running track and walls or seating for spectators

Stalactite ceiling Islamic ceiling with decoration hanging down like drops

Stele free-standing pillar, usually with an inscription and often with a relief

Stoa covered walkway supported by columns

Stylobate top step of the crepidoma on which the columns stand

Temenos sacred precinct

Theatre 1. the Greek theatre consists of the background building (skene), the stage (proskenion) adn the round or semicircular orchestra, around which lies the curving cavea with the seats, nestling into a natural depression
2. The Roman theatre has a similar basic layout, but the stage wall (scenae frons) was as high as the top end of the spectator area, which, covering the chorus entrances at the sides, was brought all the way to the stage

wall; this creates a closed room without a roof. The orchestra is semicircular, the stage was later elevated and located on a platform. The spectator area was generally supported by substructures in which the entrances were located

Thesauros treasure, treasure store

Tholos circular building (diagram p. 51)

Tracery geometric decorations during the Gothic period to adorn windows and balustrades

Triclinium dining room in a Roman villa

Triglyph stone slab with two grooves; separates the metopes of the Doric order (diagram p. 449)

Triumphal arch 1. a monumental gate with one or more archways in Roman Antiquity

2. choir arch in a Christian basilica

Tympanum 1. flat triangular pediment on a Greek temple (diagram p. 449)

2. curved area above a church portal

Volute spiral scroll-like element of the Ionic capital

INDEX

LIST OF MAPS AND ILLUSTRATIONS

PHOTO CREDITS

PUBLISHER'S INFORMATION

Illustrations etc: 200 illustrations, 69 maps and diagrams, one large map
Text: Dr. Otto Gärtner, with contributions by Anja Schliebitz, Peter Amann, Peter Peter, Achim Bourmer and Ralf Schick
Revision: Daniela Schetar, Friedrich Köthe
Editing: Baedeker editorial team (John Sykes)
Translation: Michael Scuffil
Cartography: Christoph Gallus, Hohberg; MAIRDUMONT/Falk Verlag, Ostfildern/GEO*next* – Istituto Geografico De Agostini, Novara
3D illustrations: jangled nerves, Stuttgart
Design: independent Medien-Design, Munich; Kathrin Schemel

Editor-in-chief: Rainer Eisenschmid, Baedeker Ostfildern

1st edition 2012
Based on Baedeker Allianz Reiseführer »Sizilien« 11. Auflage 2011

Copyright: Karl Baedeker Verlag, Ostfildern
Publication rights: MAIRDUMONT GmbH & Co; Ostfildern

Printed in China